LAW AND LIBERALISM IN THE 1980s

THE SAMUEL RUBIN PROGRAM FOR LIBERTY AND EQUALITY THROUGH LAW

The Samuel Rubin Program for Liberty and Equality Through Law was established at Columbia Law School in 1982. The program was made possible by a gift from the Reed Foundation of New York City. The program is named in honor of the late Samuel Rubin, a noted philanthropist and advocate of political tolerance and international understanding. Mr. Rubin was well known during his lifetime for his courageous opposition to Senator Joseph McCarthy and his generous gifts in support of medical services in poor communities, medical and legal education for members of minority groups, music education in Israel, and scholarships for Arab students in Israel. He endowed a chair in anthropology at Brandeis University and supported a variety of programs at the law schools of New York University and Columbia University.

LAW AND LIBERALISM IN THE 1980s

THE RUBIN LECTURES AT COLUMBIA UNIVERSITY

Edited by Vincent Blasi

Columbia University Press
New York

A gift from Corliss Lamont, friend of Columbia University Press, has helped in the publication of this book.

Columbia University Press
New York Oxford

Library of Congress Cataloging-in-Publication Data
Law and liberalism in the 1980s : the Rubin lectures at Columbia University/edited by Vincent Blasi.
p. cm.
Includes bibliographical references.
ISBN 0-231-07198-1
1. Law—United States—Philosophy. 2. United States—Constitutional law—Interpretation and construction.
3. Liberalism—United States. 4. Law and politics—United States.
I. Blasi, Vincent, 1943– .
KF379.L355 1990
342.73'085—dc20
[347.30285] 90-35699
CIP

Casebound editions of Columbia University Press books are Smyth-sewn and printed on permanent and durable acid-free paper
∞
Printed in the United States of America
c 10 9 8 7 6 5 4 3 2 1

CONTENTS

CONTRIBUTORS

Charles L. Black, Jr., is Adjunct Professor of Law, Columbia University and Sterling Professor of Law Emeritus, Yale University. He received his B.A. and M.A. degrees from the University of Texas and his LL.B. from Yale.

Abram Chayes is Felix Frankfurter Professor of Law at the Harvard Law School. He received his A.B. from Harvard in 1943 and his LL.B from Harvard in 1949. He served as Advocate and Counsel for Nicaragua in its litigation against the United States before the International Court of Justice.

Sanford Kadish is the Morrison Professor of Law at the University of California, Berkeley, where he served as Dean from 1975 to 1982. He received his B.S.S. degree from the City College of New York in 1942 and his law degree from Columbia in 1948.

Anthony Lester is Queen's Counsel of Lincoln's Inn, London. He is an Honorary Professor of Public Law, University College, London. He received his B.A. from Trinity College, Cambridge and his LL.M. from Harvard Law School.

Anthony Lewis is a columnist with the *New York Times.* He teaches courses on the First Amendment at Harvard Law School and Columbia Journalism School. He received his A.B. from Harvard in 1948.

Hon. J. Skelly Wright, now deceased, was Judge of the United States Court of Appeals for the District of Columbia Circuit. He received both his undergraduate and his law degree from Loyala University in New Orleans.

Cass R. Sunstein is the Karl N. Llewellyn Professor of Jurisprudence at the University of Chicago. He received his A.B. from Harvard University in 1975 and his J.D. from Harvard in 1978.

INTRODUCTION

Liberalism. Mere mention of the word seems to stimulate controversy—among voters, among philosophers, among proponents of clarity and precision in the use of the English language. Adam Smith was said to be a liberal. So were Thomas Jefferson, John Stuart Mill, William Gladstone, Oliver Wendell Holmes, Franklin D. Roosevelt, Huey Long, Felix Frankfurter, and William O. Douglas. Individualists and collectivists, traditionalists and revolutionaries, idealists, pragmatists, and fatalists—all have marched under the liberal banner at some time or another. For years the term "liberal" was problematic because almost everyone claimed to be one. Recently, the political cash value, and even the intellectual cachet, of the label "liberal" has plummeted. But through the vicissitudes and across a variety of settings, the concept of liberalism has figured prominently in the shaping of our political and legal cultures.

In the context of American law, the term "liberal" is most often associated with the high regard for individual rights displayed by the Warren Court, particularly individual rights that benefit the dispossessed and serve to check the depredations of the powerful. In addition, the legal structures introduced during the New Deal, such as welfare entitlements and regulatory agencies with expertise, real power, and political independence, are usually considered integral to the liberal vision of law. Theorists sometimes assert that this set of commitments is neither coherent nor stable, that rights work at cross purposes with egalitarian ideals, that expansive government never expands the freedom of its subjects, that one simply must choose between liberty and equality.

These difficulties, if such they be, were minimized during the years when the vigorous idealism of the Warren Court set the tone for the American legal culture. During the 1980s, however, the liberal view of law was the subject of unremitting challenge. Two schools of thought emerged as dominant influences during this period, and both in different ways rejected many of the premises of liberalism. One school, critical legal studies, attacked liberalism from the left. Adherents to this school strongly reject the liberal claim that certain fundamental principles of fairness and humanity can be identified and enforced by the legal system. Critical legal scholars also believe that it is self-deception to view law as a promising instrument of social reform. These critics argue that the dominant mission of legal scholarship should be to expose the inherent class bias of law and to undercut the efforts of both liberals and conservatives to make law serve as a source of legitimation for existing political structures.

Liberalism as a legal idea was also challenged from the right by the law and economics movement. Although there are liberal lawyer-economists and there is nothing inherently conservative or reactionary in the use of economics in legal analysis, the fact is that conservative economists have exerted disproportionate influence in legal scholarship. The essential message of this group is that all legal doctrines should be viewed from the perspective of market efficiency, and should be interpreted wherever possible in a manner that serves the goals of efficiency and wealth maximization. What makes the right wing or "Chicago School" economists critical of liberalism is their conviction that there exist no consensual or transcendent values such as equality or fairness that cannot be subsumed under the individual preferences that persons assert in their market behavior. Any effort by judges or legislators to promote such values in opposition to market outcomes is, in the opinion of these economists, both shortsighted and unfair.

The critical legal studies movement and the law and economics movement won over numerous adherents among lawyers during the 1980s. There is a sense of intellectual excitement and vitality about both movements. In contrast, during the last decade liberals were placed on the defensive in legal debate. It is a common perception that legal liberalism is in decline, and that no new important ideas have enriched the liberal perspective on law in recent years.

This book is intended to serve as a partial response to that perception. Drawing from the Samuel Rubin Lecture Series at Columbia Law School, the book brings together essays by seven important liberal thinkers of the transatlantic legal community. The first five essays address particular issues of law that have been at the center of the debate between liberalism and its critics. The issues considered embrace the fields of election law, freedom of the press, international law, poverty law, and criminal law. The last two essays address more general themes. One deals with the question of the proper baseline assumptions of the Supreme Court in interpreting the Constitution. The other deals with the question whether constitutional doctrines in the United States can serve as a model for other countries. The book is designed to illustrate the range and vigor of the liberal perspective on law.

No orthodoxy of liberal thought can be gleaned from these pages. The authors are too concerned about the problems and issues they address to permit their major premises to dwarf the analysis. But if no orthodoxy is discernible, certain common themes are. The essays in this book tie together in some interesting ways. A brief look at those connections may help readers to answer the oft-discussed question: What happened to the liberal view of law during the 1980s?

One belief that is shared by all the authors is that law has an important moral dimension, that legal claims cannot be resolved exclusively on the basis of linguistic analysis of authoritative texts or deference to existing political preferences and power relationships. Thus, Judge J. Skelly Wright criticizes the Supreme Court for its mechanical reading of the First Amendment in striking down limits on campaign expenditures. He argues that the gross disparities in wealth that differentiate political candidacies and ballot proposition campaigns should not be taken as simply given or natural in deciding the constitutional fate of electoral spending restrictions. Rather, the concept of representative democracy furnishes an ideal of fairness and balance in the conduct of elections, and that ideal can be incorporated in First Amendment analysis, he asserts.

Anthony Lewis also draws on the ideal of representative government in his trenchant critique of modern developments in the law of libel. He reads the Supreme Court's magisterial decision in *New York Times v. Sullivan* to embody the proposition that effective and vigorous criticism of government is the linchpin of representative democracy, so important that the protection and encouragement of such criticism must be considered one of the foremost priorities of the constitutional regime. Mr. Lewis claims that the practical dynamics of libel litigation pose a serious challenge to the *Sullivan* ideal. He recommends, accordingly, that the immunity against libel actions accorded critics of government be strengthened, even beyond the seemingly protective principles of the *Sullivan* decision itself.

Abram Chayes disputes the contention that international law, and particularly adjudication in the International Court of Justice, can play no role in the resolution of the conflict between the United States and Nicaragua. He believes there are principles of law, judicially discoverable and manageable, that govern the situation in which a foreign nation participates in efforts to undermine a domestic regime. Chayes sees in the rule of international law an egalitarian ideal: "[I]t is only in the Hague that Nicaragua can face the United States on equal terms. It is the only forum where the outcome is not preordained by the disparities of military and economic power between the parties."

In a similar spirit, Charles Black disputes the contention that constitutional law can play no role in alleviating the crushing burden of extreme poverty. He demonstrates that the Constitution is not silent on the subject of minimum standards of livelihood, and that there exists a rich tradition of judicial reasoning of the sort required to justify the recognition of a constitutional right to livelihood. Like the other authors in this book, Black objects to the view that law must defer to existing distributions of wealth and power: "The way I want to see thought reformed is by our ceasing to view the elimination of poverty as a sentimental matter, as a matter of compassion, and our starting to look on it as a matter of justice, of constitutional right."

Sanford Kadish emphasizes the moral underpinnings of the criminal law in examining the law of excuses, an area often said to be dominated by practical concerns regarding deterrence and the feasibility of proof. He finds a unifying moral principle that explains the criminal law's treatment of such factors as duress, ignorance of facts or law, addiction, and insanity. That principle, which derives from the liberal conception of moral agency, is that a person should not be held criminally responsible for an act that cannot be considered morally blameworthy in light of the capacities of the actor and the circumstances surrounding the act.

Cass Sunstein criticizes the Supreme Court for missing the moral point of the constitutional culture's emphatic rejection of the case of *Lochner v. New York.* That case, which held maximum hour legislation unconstitutional, has been considered for over fifty years the model of an improper interpretation of the Constitution. Sunstein claims that what makes *Lochner* wrong is not that the Court invalidated state legislation that served a rational purpose and violated no explicit constitutional guarantee, but rather that the Justices treated the existing distribution of bargaining power between employers and employees as presumptively ordained by the Constitution. He detects in some recent Supreme Court decisions a similar tendency to use as a baseline for constitutional interpretation the existing distribution of wealth and power as recognized, and in some respects created, by the common law. He argues that moral principles should have a larger role to play in constitutional analysis than common law doctrines and market outcomes. Like other authors in this collection, Sunstein believes that the existing distribution of wealth and power should not merely be reflected in legal doctrine, but rather should be subject to moral evaluation through the process of law.

Anthony Lester, an English barrister who has championed the cause of human rights in Europe, comments upon the moral force exerted abroad by the American Bill of Rights. He thinks that Americans underestimate the impact in other nations of the pathbreaking work of the United States Supreme Court in recognizing individual rights. He also thinks American courts have missed some opportunities to learn from the rights jurisprudence of foreign courts, as in the case of the European Court of Human Rights, which in 1981 recognized the right of homosexual adults to engage in consensual sexual activity. Lester stresses the moral foundations of rights, a key to their exportability, and expresses the "hope that the United States judiciary will not retreat from the strong interpretation of the Bill of Rights into literalism, positivism, and historicism."

The belief, shared by the contributors to this book, that law must be informed by moral principles generates derivative themes that appear repeatedly in these pages. One is the notion of positive freedom, the idea that government has affirmative duties to its citizens to facilitate the meaningful exercise of freedom. Closely related to the idea of positive freedom is the view that law should play a role in shaping some of the basic structures of the society. Liberals are reluctant to view structural injustices as "given," or too basic to be amenable to legal redress. In their willingness to address fundamental questions, in their unwillingness to treat law as a problematic and very limited force for social ordering, these authors share a perspective that was not in the ascendancy during the 1980s.

Historically, liberalism seems to gain adherents in periods of optimism, when ideals are treated as worthy objects of aspiration rather than unrealistic, and therefore false, promises. In the Western world, the 1980s was not a decade of idealism. The rich grew more materialistic and less public spirited. The poor grew more impoverished, more dependent on drugs, and more prone to commit (and be victimized by) crime. At all levels of the socioeconomic scale, racial hostility became more intense and overt; expressions of racial prejudice that would have been utterly unacceptable a few years earlier became the standard fare of public debate and private conversation. The 1980s was a decade that invited cynicism, resignation, and despair.

A striking feature of the essays in this book is the refusal of the authors to be swept up in the pessimism, escapism, and passivity of their times. These authors are realists and pragmatists. They examine the reality of injustice and the practicality of legal reform. They offer no doctrinaire solutions. Nevertheless, what most unites the essays in this collection is the way the authors take ideals seriously. Each essay, in its own way, proceeds from the premise that it is the mission of law, and of legal scholarship, to give voice to principles of justice even when the environment is unfavorable. Charles Black captures the resilient spirit that each of these authors displays. Explaining the importance of developing the liberal perspective on law in an age dominated by illiberal attitudes, Black observes: "A period of no power is a period for the reformation of thought, to the end that when power returns it may be more skillfully, more fittingly, used."

Legal liberalism is not dead; it is in exile, hard at work and growing.

LAW AND LIBERALISM IN THE 1980s

1

MONEY AND THE POLLUTION OF POLITICS: IS THE FIRST AMENDMENT AN OBSTACLE TO POLITICAL EQUALITY?

J. Skelly Wright

In the name of the very first amendment in our Bill of Rights, the present Supreme Court has put serious obstacles in the path of our society's advancement toward political equality through law. In two vitally important and, in my judgment, tragically misguided first amendment decisions, *Buckley v. Valeo*[1] and *First National Bank of Boston v. Bellotti*,[2] the Court has given protection to the polluting effect of money in election campaigns. As a result, our political system may not use some of its most powerful defenses against electoral inequalities. Concentrated wealth, often channeled through political action committees, threatens to distort political campaigns and referenda. The voices of individual citizens are being drowned out in election campaigns—the forum for the political deliberations of our people. If the ideal of equality is trampled there, the principle of "one person, one vote," the cornerstone of our democracy, becomes a hollow mockery.

Buckley and *Bellotti* create an artificial opposition between liberty and equality. The first amendment tradition of leading cases and scholarly writings shows that the ideals of political equality and individual participation are essential to a proper understanding of the first amendment. Campaign spending reform is imperative to serve the purposes of freedom of expression. Within the confines of *Buckley* and *Bellotti*, only limited reforms are permissible. More effective measures will be possible only if the Court reconsiders these unfortunate precedents.

MONEY AND THE POLLUTION OF POLITICS

The corrosive effect of money on the political process is not new to this country or to the modern era,[3] but the problem of money in politics has taken on a new urgency in the American politics of the 1980s. The development of communications technology and campaign techniques has made the political impact of money even more potent and the political consequences of meager financial resources even more devastating. Financial inequalities pose a pervasive and growing threat to the principle of "one person, one vote," and undermine the political proposition to which this nation is dedicated—that all men are created equal.

The Legal Framework

In the early 1970s, the Watergate scandals gave impetus to popular demand for strong measures to purify the political process,[4] culminating in 1974 with the passage of the Federal Election Campaign Act.[5] The legislation adopted contribution limits,[6] comprehensive spending limits,[7] and public financing of presidential campaigns.[8] It created a new federal agency[9] to enforce these laws and to supervise campaign finance reporting and disclosure.[10] It did not, however, establish a system of public funding for House and Senate elections,[11] missing a golden opportunity, not since recaptured, to diminish the influence of money in congressional politics.

Because it did not reach congressional campaign financing, the 1974 act did not go far enough. But in the 1976 decision of *Buckley v. Valeo,*[12] upholding parts of the 1974 act but striking down other basic provisions, the Supreme Court decided that the legislation had gone too far. The Court accepted public financing of presidential elections[13] and held that Congress could constitutionally attach conditions—including spending limits—to the acceptance of those funds.[14] It also approved the reporting and disclosure requirements for all federal candidates and committees[15] and agreed that ceilings on campaign contributions were justified by the need to prevent corruption and the appearance of corruption.[16] The *Buckley* decision gutted vital portions of the legislation, however. Equating spending with speech,[17] the Court treated the first amendment as a near-absolute in the sphere of political debate.[18] It unequivocally struck down the act's limits on overall campaign spending by a candidate who does not receive public financing restrictions on independent expenditures in support of or against a candidate, and ceilings on candidate spending from personal or family funds.[19] The Court in *Buckley* insisted that "the concept that government may restrict the speech [i.e., spending] of some elements of our society in order to enhance the relative voices of others is wholly foreign to the First Amendment."[20]

Justice White, who had practical experience in nationwide campaigning in 1960 as coordinator of John Kennedy's preconvention campaign in Colorado and then as head of National Citizens for Kennedy, was the sole member of the Court to disagree with the Court's holding that expenditure limits violate the first amendment.[21] He rejected the Court's contention that money is speech. Writing with an apparent touch of sarcasm, he observed: "[A]s it should be unnecessary to point out, money is not always equivalent to or used for speech, even in the context of political campaigns."[22] In his view, expenditure ceilings reinforced the contribution limits and helped "eradicate the hazard of corruption."[23] He took judicial notice that

> [t]here are many illegal ways of spending money to influence elections. One would be blind to history to deny that unlimited money tempts people to spend it on *whatever* money can buy to influence an election. On the assumption that financing illegal activities is low on the campaign organization's priority list, the expenditure limits could play a substantial role in preventing unethical practices. There just would not be enough of "that kind of money" to go around.[24]

Like the congressmen and senators—who were presumably more knowledgeable than most about corruption in politics—who passed the 1974 act, and unlike the other Justices, Justice White recognized and understood the realities of political campaigns.

Two years after *Buckley,* the Court again repudiated the goal of political equality in *First National Bank of Boston v. Bellotti.*[25] Trying to prevent one-sided corporate messages from swamping referendum campaigns, Massachusetts had enacted a statute prohibiting corporate expenditures on statewide referendum issues not directly related to a corporation's business interests. The Supreme Court, however, struck down the statute, relying on *Buckley's* facile equation of spending and speech, and insisting that there was no possibility of corruption in a referendum campaign.[26] The Court thereby effectively declared open season for the influence of concentrated wealth upon initiative and referendum campaigns.[27]

In my view, these two decisions—though they quote the landmarks of our first amendment heritage—enunciated principles that are, to borrow the words of the *Buckley* Court, "wholly foreign to the First Amendment."[28] The two decisions have also had a direct, significant, and pernicious impact on political campaigning in America.[29]

The federal campaign reform provisions that survived *Buckley v. Valeo* have worked well. The disclosure and reporting requirements allow citizens and the press to discover the sources of a candidate's financial backing.[30] Public financing of presidential campaigns has relieved candidates of much of the draining, demeaning, and obligation-creating task of begging for funds from large contributors. At the same time, the limits on spending by candidates who accept financing are sufficiently high to allow ample discussion of the issues.[31]

A similar program for congressional campaigns would also pass judicial muster, but so far, despite strenuous efforts by reformers, Congress has been unwilling to extend public financing to House and Senate campaigns.[32] Money continues to infect House and Senate races, campaigns for state and local offices, and referendum and initiative voting. In these political contests, democracy is often shadowed by lopsided inequalities in campaign resources. The predominance of money comes at the expense of the ideals of liberty and equality that underlie our political system.

Political Action Committees

Political action committees (PACs), perhaps the fastest growing phenomenon in modern American politics, epitomize the contemporary threat to electoral integrity. The stark reality of PACs is that they bring the power of concentrated wealth to bear on officeholders and candidates—national, state, and local—on behalf of special interests. Although only a small fraction of these groups promotes particular ideologies or advocates single issues,[33] PACs generally represent the interests of organizations, such as corporations, labor unions, and trade associations, that are forbidden by law to contribute or spend directly in federal campaigns.[34]

In recent years, PACs—especially those connected with corporations and trade associations—have grown explosively in numbers and influence. Provisions in the 1974 act facilitated their formation and operation.[35] In 1974 there were 89 corporate PACs; now there are 1,327.[36] Between 1976 and 1980, PACs more than doubled the amounts of money they poured into House and Senate campaigns—$22.6 million in 1976, $35.2 million in 1978, and $55.3 million in 1980.[37] And PACs are taking on growing importance in the strategies of candidates and their fund raisers.[38] They are rapidly becoming the dominant force among categories of contributors. The PAC component of House candidates' campaign funds has risen steadily from 17 percent in 1974 to 26.4 percent in 1980.[39] And PACs have far outdistanced the federal campaign funding contributions of all national, state, and local political parties combined.[40]

While the overall figures are impressive, the patterns of PAC spending make them an even more formidable influence in congressional politics. PACs concentrate their giving upon strategic categories of candidates—those who are more likely to win and to have useful influence in Congress. PACs rarely contribute to candidates who lose in the primary,[41] and they donate much more heavily to incumbents than to challengers.[42] In addition, some PACs, especially those with ideological or single-issue orientations, spend large sums of money on highly effective campaigns against "hit-listed" candidates. Collectively, PACs devoted more than $14 million in 1980 to independent campaign activities for or against particular candidates.[43] Because *Buckley v. Valeo* constitutionally invalidated ceilings on "independent" expenditures,[44] this type of spending may theoretically be unlimited.

When wealth of this magnitude is injected into the political bloodstream,[45] the legislative process itself is affected. PAC contributions are given with a legislative purpose and it is a telling fact that they are most numerous in the more highly regulated industries, such as oil, transportation, utilities, drugs, health care, and government contracting.[46] High-level corporate employees are solicited to give to the company's PAC precisely because it will advance the business interests of the firm.[47] One PAC formed by a major corporation explained to its employees, "Our aim is to gain for [our] managers the same rapt attention from their Congressmen and Senators which labor leaders now command."[48] Another PAC reported progress in achieving the corporation's goals: "We *have* strengthened our relationships with our 'constituent' Senators and Congressmen. . . . One or more of us on the PAC Steering Committee has developed a personal relationship with each incumbent to whom we give campaign contributions."[49]

The political generosity of the PACs is directed to legislators who are in a position to help, especially members of committees with jurisdiction over legislation affecting the sponsors. For example, from the beginning of 1975 through mid-1978, dairy PACs gave $380,000 to members of the House Agriculture Committee, and labor groups donated almost $600,000 to members of the House Education and Labor Committee.[50] In 1978 PACs provided 56% of the campaign money spent by twenty-two House committee chairmen,[51] compared with 25 percent for House candidates as a whole.[52] The chairman of the House Ways and Means Committee, the committee in which all tax legislation begins, received $157,425 from corporate PACs to finance his 1980 reelection campaign. He won with 84 percent of the vote.[53]

Carefully targeted PAC giving has two parallel effects on Congress. First, PAC money, like money from any source, allows a candidate to spend more on his campaign and statistically enhances his chances of winning.[54] Second, once a candidate has been elected, he knows that if he wants to be reelected it is important to give attention and deference to the views of those who helped him financially.[55] One chairman of a large corporation has said that dialogue with politicians "is a fine thing, but with a little money they hear you better."[56] PAC defenders and critics disagree on which effect is more important for PAC contributors and recipients. PAC champions insist that they simply reward their friends and withhold favors from their adversaries.[57] PAC critics charge that lavish contributions to members of key committees are not rewards for past support but down payments for future influence.[58] It is not important to my analysis to choose between these conflicting positions. In one case PACs exercise a form of "multiple voting,"[59] and in the other they engage in a form of legalized bribery.

Whatever the cause-and-effect relationship, studies of issue after issue demonstrate that a much higher percentage of legislators who voted with a PAC's position received money from that PAC in the previous campaign than those who voted the other way, and among the beneficiaries of PAC money those supporting the PAC position had received a substantially higher average contribution. Whether the issue on the floor is the windfall profits tax on oil companies,[60] hospital cost containment,[61] efforts to create a superfund for victims of toxic chemicals,[62] or any other legislation that affects powerful, organized interests,[63] PAC money augments interest group lobbying.

A graphic example of the manner in which interest groups seek political return on their PAC contributions is provided by the lobbying efforts of used car dealers. Their National Automobile Dealers Association was the fourth largest PAC contributor in the country in the 1980 elections, giving slightly more than $1 million to congressional candidates. Used car dealers successfully lobbied for a congressional veto of proposed FTC regulations requiring them to disclose known defects in used cars they offer for sale.[64] At the Association's convention in 1981 in Washington, D.C., the Association's government relations chairman gave the delegates a pep talk, urging them to go see their Congressman and adding that PAC contributions had opened the door. By the end of the convention, more than ninety House members and more than twenty senators had signed on as co-sponsors of the veto resolution. In another few weeks, thirty-three more representatives and one more senator had joined. About 80 percent of the legislators on the bandwagon had received PAC contributions in 1980.[65]

Not only do PACs buy legislative clout by investing in congressional candidates, they also squeeze out the individual voice in congressional politics. PACs tend to be bureaucratically organized and centralized, often at the national level. The voice of a PAC is not that of its small givers, whose participation is extolled by PAC publicists,[66] but that of its leadership, who decide where to bestow the money.[67] National PACs compete with local constituents for the attention of congressmen,[68] and as the PAC share of candidate funding increases, local voices and constituent concerns are bound to carry less weight.

Spiraling Campaign Costs and Monied Influence

PACs have become increasingly influential in congressional campaigns and legislative lobbying because of the dramatic escalation of campaign expenses.[69] The cost of goods and services used in campaigns has been rising faster than the consumer price index.[70] In 1972 the total cost of House and Senate campaigns nationwide was $98 million;[71] in 1980 it was $242 million.[72] Media time and production costs, which often comprise 30 to 40 percent of the amounts spent by candidates,[73] are becoming more and more expensive. For example, a thirty-second evening prime-time spot on a Portland, Oregon, television station cost $55 in 1974; today it costs $3,000. In the same period, the price of thirty prime-time seconds on TV in San Diego has jumped from $509 to $3,000.[74] Direct mailing, too, is expensive. The cost of postage continues to escalate, and the direct mail consultants charge hefty fees for their computerized mailing lists and sophisticated techniques.[75]

The fixation of American politicians upon expensive, media-dominated, highly professional campaigns has made the political process much more vulnerable to the corrosive influence of money. That is the root of my concern. I am not calling for reform on the ground that the new campaign techniques in themselves are prone to confuse or mislead American voters. I do not believe in content regulation or censorship, and all things being equal, I have faith in the common sense of the American electorate.[76] But I am worried by the side effects of the new style of campaigning.

One side effect is that political candidates, caught in a spiraling spending race, turn more readily to PACs, which can mobilize money and may legally give five times as much as individuals to favored candidates.[77] Another side effect is that able, dedicated individuals, whose ideas and personal qualifications might attract many voters, are deterred from even entering the race for political office because of the immense sums of money required to run a media-based campaign. Unless the potential candidate is personally wealthy or is willing to become beholden to special interests and wealthy donors, he or she may consider the effort hopeless.[78] Such people are the silent casualties of the political process; we do not hear about them, because they are defeated before they start. The nation is often the loser.

The growing technologic sophistication and rising costs of election campaigns are also closely related to massive inequalities in campaign spending. For a candidate or an issue position with ample supplies of money, the sky is the limit; there are always more ways to spend money if it is available. The result is sometimes grossly unequal spending totals in both candidate and referendum campaigns. Lopsided media spending, in turn, may, in the words of Dean Rosenthal, "overwhelmingly and effectively blo[t] out the messages of [a candidate's] opponents."[79]

The Federal Election Commission's spending data for House and Senate races in 1978 graphically show the extent of inequalities in spending and their correlation with winning and losing.[80] There were 307 contested House races. The winner outspent the loser in 78.8 percent of those races. Where the spending margin was more than two to one, as it was in 159 races, the bigger spender won 93 percent of the time. Where one side outspent the other by more than five to one, as occurred in fifty-eight House campaigns, the bigger spender won 100 percent of the time. The same story is repeated on the Senate side, where the bigger spender won in thirty-one of thirty-five races—88.6 percent—in 1978.[81] In open-seat Senate races, which eliminated the incumbency advantage, the winner outspent the loser thirteen out of fourteen times—92.8 percent of the campaigns. The correlation between success and money is not a statistical artifact. It is a product of the expensive goods and services—television and radio time, media consultants, sophisticated polls, computerized direct mailing operations, political strategists—that money can buy.[82]

Referenda and Initiatives

The unholy alliance of big spending, special interests, and election victory is found, perhaps in its most dramatic form, in referendum contests. Referenda and initiatives are vehicles of direct popular democracy in twenty-two states and the District of Columbia.[83] Created by the progressive reform movement in the early part of this century, these processes allow the voters to express their views on major public issues directly rather than through elected representatives. They were designed to lessen the influence of special interests and corrupt maneuvering upon major public decisions.[84] Ironically, the advent of media campaigning has made it possible for concentrated wealth to have a powerful impact on referendum campaigns as well. Drastically unequal spending for the tools of persuasion shapes and limits the people's awareness of the issues. And the Supreme Court's decision in *Bellotti* appears to leave the political system powerless to defend itself.[85]

A number of studies show that, in state after state, in election after election, massive spending and sophisticated media campaigns by special-interest groups have swamped referenda that were initially favored by a majority of the voters.[86] One study of referendum and initiative campaigns across the country in 1978 found that the side spending the most won in eleven of fifteen contested campaigns. The side with corporate support outspent its opponents in twelve cases—in eight of these by margins of ten to one or more—and won in two-thirds of these contests. When the corporate side was outspent, it lost every time.[87]

The antismoking initiative on the California ballot in 1978 gives one vivid example of the lopsidedness introduced into the political process by unlimited spending.[88] The initiative proposed to prohibit smoking in enclosed public places, places of employment, and educational and health facilities. At the beginning of September, two months before the election, polls showed 58 percent of the voters in favor of the measure and only 38 percent opposed. Then tobacco interests spent $6.4 million in the opposition campaign, almost ten times as much as the proponents of the measure. Philip Morris,

Inc. contributed $1.7 million; the R. J. Reynolds Tobacco Company gave $1.7 million. Two other tobacco companies gave $882,000 and $638,000 respectively. The combined expenditures of these four companies alone exceeded the cost of the entire general election campaign for the governorship of California. Buying extensive television spot coverage under the label "Californians for Common Sense," the tobacco industry carried the day. Support for the initiative gradually eroded in the polls, and on election day the vote was 45 percent for and 55 percent against.

A similar experience occurred in Colorado in a 1976 referendum ballot on container deposits.[89] Again, the polls showed that in late September the public was strongly in favor of the measure—57 percent in favor and 27 percent against. Again, opponents—from the soft drink industry, can manufacturing, iron, steel, and other directly affected interests—poured large amounts of money into the campaign. The opposition war chest totaled $587,000,[90] with more than half a dozen single contributors each outspending the entire campaign in favor of the measure. The industry message dominated television, radio, and newspaper advertising.[91] In prime time, opposition television spots outnumbered favorable spots by seventy-two to twelve, and in nonprime time by one hundred thirteen to twenty-eight. Perhaps it comes as little surprise that there was a significant shift in voter opinion during October and that the initiative was defeated by a vote of nearly two to one, virtually reversing the initial polling results.[92]

Not only are the two sides in referendum contests often devastatingly unequal in the amounts of money they spend, but their sources of money are also dramatically different. Large corporate and trade association contributions made up the bulk of the funds against the two ballot measures I have described, and the same was true in other initiative campaigns that have threatened special interests. In contrast, proponents have relied very heavily on small contributions.[93] To give just one more example, in 1978 the citizens of Long Beach, California voted on a referendum to reject a proposed lease between the city and Standard Oil for construction of an oil storage terminal. Community opponents of the lease raised $17,721, all of it in contributions of less than $1,000. Standard Oil and related companies pumped in $864,568; the smallest contribution was more than $16,000.[94]

The big-spending media campaigns do not always win,[95] but they win much more than they lose, distorting the expressed will of the people by the sheer inequality of financial resources and the avalanche of campaign messages. Regardless of their message, they simply drown out their opponents when they have the wherewithal to outspend them by margins of up to fifty to one.[96] In America money controls access to the communications media. In some other presumably civilized countries, those interests monopolizing access to the means of communication have used the big lie, the half-truth, and the sly innuendo, amplified and repeated over and over again, to pervert the minds of the people. We, in this country, should be too sophisticated to succumb to such crass approaches, but the election returns that I have discussed seem to indicate that our political hucksters must be pretty sophisticated people too.

As individuals are squeezed out, as the behemoths of concentrated wealth dwarf the individual and bid fair to dominate the political field, the very purpose of direct democracy is defeated, and voters are bound to become disillusioned and apathetic.[97] This picture might not trouble a convinced pluralist who sees democratic government as nothing more than the result of the pull and tug of aggregated interests in a field of political vectors and partisan forces of greater or lesser intensity.[98] But I believe in the role of equal individuals in the process of American self-government, and I am convinced that this role cannot be snuffed out without at the same time destroying the integrity of our electoral process and the essence of our political faith.

THE IDEAL OF POLITICAL EQUALITY

Political equality is the cornerstone of American democracy. Today's electoral processes, tainted by huge inequalities in funds and special access for special interests, fall far short of that ideal and are moving farther away every year. But rather than give up faith and drift with the tide, we must reexamine and renew our commitment to realizing America's fundamental political ideals.

The concepts of political equality and self-government stand or fall together. If persons are equal, then none has an inherent right to dominate or impose his will on others. Government can be legitimate only if it is based on the informed consent of all citizens.[99] Rational self-interest dictates, therefore, that each assure his or her own liberty by agreeing to equal liberties for all, including the right to equal political participation.[100] In explaining the essence of the social contract, Rousseau declared that "each giving himself to all, gives himself to nobody; and as there is not one associate over whom we do not acquire the same rights which we concede to him over ourselves, we gain the equivalent of all that we lose, and more power to preserve what we have."[101] These principles of mutual tolerance, respect, and equality are enshrined as well in our own Declaration of Independence.[102]

Throughout American history the ideal of political equality has found eloquent expression, and gradual steps have been taken toward its realization. Nearly two hundred years after the framing of the Constitution, James Madison's words in *Federalist No. 57* challenge us to fulfill their promise.

> Who are to be the electors of the Federal Representatives? Not the rich, more than the poor; not the learned, more than the ignorant; not the haughty heirs of distinguished names, more than the humble sons of obscurity and unpropitious fortune. The electors are to be the great body of the people of the Unites States. . . .
>
> Who are to be the objects of popular choice? Every citizen whose merit may recommend him to the esteem and confidence of his country. No qualification of wealth, of birth, of religious faith, or of civil profession is permitted to fetter the judgment or disappoint the inclination of the people.[103]

In the 1830s Alexis de Tocqueville captured the spirit of Jacksonian democracy when he traveled through America. "[T]he principle of the sovereignty of the people hovers over the whole political system of the Anglo-Americans," Tocqueville wrote. "[E]ach individual forms an equal part of that sovereignty and shares equally the government of the state."[104] With great interest, Tocqueville described the civic spirit, energy, and individual self-respect that pervaded American life, which he attributed to the widespread exercise of political rights and responsibilities in a spirit of equality.[105] He also engaged in more theoretical speculations about the philosophical nature of equality and, like Rousseau, postulated a point at which freedom and equality would meet and blend:

> Let us suppose that all the citizens take a part in the government and that each of them has an equal right to do so. Then, no man is different from his fellows, and nobody can wield tyrannical power; men will be perfectly free because they are entirely equal, and they will be perfectly equal because they are entirely free. Democratic peoples are tending toward that ideal. That is the completest possible form for liberty on this earth.[106]

Complete equality and complete freedom were not found in America in Madison's time,[107] or in Tocqueville's. But the Jacksonian period did see major expansions of the suffrage—elimination of property qualifications for voting in state after state.[108] At the federal level, several constitutional amendments have since extended the vote to new categories of citizens.[109]

The Supreme Court, in the twentieth century, has played a major role in eliminating artificial barriers to equal electoral participation: the white primary,[110] the poll tax,[111] and voter qualifications based on property.[112] Most importantly, in the one person, one vote cases the Court emphasized in the strongest and most eloquent manner the centrality of equal voting rights in the American democratic system.[113] In *Reynolds v. Sims*[114] Chief Justice Warren wrote, "[R]epresentative government is in essence self-government through the medium of elected representatives of the people, and each and every citizen has an inalienable right to full and effective participation in the political processes of his State's legislative bodies."[115]

In the reapportionment cases, the Court moved toward a functional view of equal political participation. Previous cases had established the right to cast a primary or general election ballot and to have the vote counted.[116] In *Wesberry v. Sanders*[117] and *Reynolds v. Sims*[118] the Court added another building block—the vote that is cast and counted must have a proportionately equal opportunity to influence the outcome of the election. Chief Justice Warren recognized that "the right of suffrage can be denied by a debasement or dilution of the weight of a citizen's vote just as effectively as by wholly prohibiting the free exercise of the franchise."[118]

In *Bullock v. Carter,*[120] the Court took a different step toward a functional view of equality. The Texas system of requiring candidates to pay high filing fees was unconstitutional, the Court held, because it tended to exclude potential candidates who lacked both personal wealth and affluent backers, "no matter how qualified they might be, and no matter how broad or enthusiastic their popular support."[121] Not only did the system deny some voters—especially the less affluent—the opportunity to vote for a candidate of their choosing;[122] it also gave the wealthy the power to place names on the ballot.[123] In other ballot access cases the Court protected the right of voters to vote effectively by invalidating state requirements that discriminated unjustifiably against minor party and independent candidates.[124]

When barriers to equality are imposed, not by state action, but by circumstances or economic resources or private persons, the equal protection clause may no longer provide protection.[125] Nevertheless, the bounds imposed by the state action requirement do not limit the fundamental ideal of political equality that underpins our democratic system of government. That ideal must inspire all of us as citizens. In the words of Dean Rosenthal,

> The goal of enriching the electoral system, through broadening the base of citizen influence and reducing inequities in the opportunities of candidates and their supporters to persuade the electorate, is a worthy one; it is not only consistent with but indispensable to the attainment of the most fundamental purposes of the Constitution.[126]

Political inequalities stemming from disparities in wealth have historically made Americans uneasy. As my late colleague Harold Leventhal observed, many Americans have long perceived a need for a "larger purpose of democratic government, the need of a self-governing people to trammel the exploding capabilities of what were called the vested interests."[127] He referred to, among others, Theodore Roosevelt, who in 1910 theorized that "if our political institutions were perfect, they would absolutely prevent the political domination of money in any part of our affairs." Recognizing, however, the reality of American politics in his time, Roosevelt called for a corrupt practices act "to prevent the advantage of the man willing recklessly and unscrupulously to spend money over his more honest competitor."[128]

Political philosopher John Rawls has recognized that the dominance of wealth in the political process is inconsistent with both the philosophical meaning and the practical exercise of political equality. Rawls maintained that the "worth of liberty" was not the same for everyone, because of "the inability to take advantage of one's right and opportunities as a result of poverty and ignorance, and a lack of means generally."[129] He added:

> The liberties protected by the principle of participation lose much of their value whenever those who have greater private means are permitted to use their advantages to control the course of public debate. For eventually these inequalities will enable those better situated to exercise a larger influence over the development of legislation.[130]

More recently Chief Justice Burger seized upon this theme to justify allowing the television networks to close their airwaves to paid political announcements.[131] Although I do not agree with the conclusion in that case,[132] the Court's discussion of the potential impact of wealth upon politics is worth noting. The public interest in providing access to the marketplace of ideas and experiences, the Chief Justice wrote, "would scarcely be served" by compelling broadcasters to accept paid political ads, because this system would be "so heavily weighted in favor of the financially affluent, or those with access to wealth." Even under a first-come, first-served system, the Chief Justice continued, "the views of the affluent could well prevail over those of the others, since they would have it within their power to purchase time more frequently,"[133] and they might monopolize the available time. Requiring broadcasters, under the Fairness Doctrine, to provide free time for opposing views would not redress the imbalance, because "the affluent could still determine in large part the issues to be discussed."[134] The right of access, the Chief Justice concluded, "would have little meaning to those who could not afford to purchase time in the first instance."[135] The unstated but inescapable premise of this discussion is that the political arena is less healthy, and less likely to serve the public interest and democratic ideals, if the agenda and the discussion are dominated by those with ample financial resources. Apparently the Chief Justice and the Court did not have these concerns in mind when *Buckley* and *Bellotti* were under consideration.

The broader purposes of our political system are ill served by allowing the power of money to drown out the voices of the relatively moneyless or by allowing too many contests to turn on the differences in the amounts of money that candidates have to spend. We cannot rest content with our past achievements, proud as they are, in advancing toward legal equality in the political process. The trenchant social critic Anatole France wrote, in the late nineteenth century, "The law, in its majestic equality, forbids the rich as well as the poor to sleep under bridges, to beg in the streets, and to steal bread."[136] A latter-day Anatole France might well write, after observing American election campaigns, "The law, in its majestic equality, allows the poor as well as the rich to form political action committees, to purchase the most sophisticated polling, media, and direct mail techniques, and to drown out each other's voices by overwhelming expenditures in political campaigns." And the law, in its majestic equality, has imported the decision criteria of the commercial marketplace into the sanctum of political decisionmaking.[137] When money becomes more important than people, when media mastery weighs more heavily than appeals to judgment, when opportunities to communicate with voters are extremely unequal, the result is a cynical distortion of the electoral process. The people's choices are not based on their informed preferences among ideas and candidates, and government of the people, by the people, and for the people becomes an empty shibboleth.

IS THE FIRST AMENDMENT THE OBSTACLE TO POLITICAL EQUALITY THE SUPREME COURT SAYS IT IS?

As I have indicated, Congress, in the aftermath of Watergate, tried to turn the tide of moneyed influence and to enhance political equality by statutory restrictions on campaign spending. In significant part, these efforts were repudiated by the Supreme Court in *Buckley* and *Bellotti,* under the guise of first amendment protection for political speech.[138] Paradoxically, by equating political spending with political speech and according both the same constitutional protection, the Court placed the first amendment squarely in opposition to the democratic ideal of political equality. This perverse result derives from a narrow view of freedom of expression, divorced from the broader ideals of our political system.

In *Buckley* and *Bellotti* the Court donned the mantle of the first amendment heritage. The Court's opinions in those two cases cited earlier decisions touching on virtually all of the major areas of sustained first amendment controversy in this century—political libel, seditious speech, freedom of the press, contempt of court, labor picketing, obscenity, commercial speech, civil rights activity, and the right to petition.[139] From Justice Holmes's dissent in *Abrams v. United States* and Justice Brandeis's concurrence in *Whitney v. California* to the opinions for the Court in *Thornhill v. Alabama, NAACP v. Alabama,* and *New York Times Co. v. Sullivan,* the authorities relied on in the two recent election law cases are virtually an honor roll of great first amendment cases.

Bellotti also cited an article by one of the leading theoreticians of the first amendment, Alexander Meiklejohn's "The First Amendment Is an Absolute."[140] Facile absolutism indeed marks the tone of the Court's discussion of expenditure limits in both *Buckley* and *Bellotti.*[141] In an earlier discussion I examined the fallacies in the reasoning in *Buckley* that led the Court to conclude that Congress may not constitutionally attempt to equalize speech opportunities by placing a ceiling on expenditures by candidates and committees.[142] Here I will attempt a broader task—showing that the Court in *Buckley* and *Bellotti* misappropriated the talismans of our first amendment past. By ritual incantation of the notion of absolute protection, by applying it to the quantity as well as the content of political expression, and by making the unexamined and unprecedented assertion that money is speech, the Court elevated dry formalism over substantive constitutional reasoning. Political discussion is indeed at the core of the first amendment's guarantees,[143] but the very centrality of political speech calls for a thorough rather than a conclusory analysis.

In order to understand the missteps taken by the Supreme Court, we must return to the first amendment heritage—the principles developed during this century to protect first amendment liberties.[144] The landmark cases invoked by the Court in *Buckley* and *Bellotti* quite properly carried the message that particular opinions and beliefs may not be suppressed by the government even if their content is unpopular with the majority,[145] threatening to dominant economic or social groups,[146] or critical of the structure or personnel of government.[147] It is not enough, however, to look at selected references from these cases. To appreciate their contribution to the development of first amendment principles, we must examine their historical context and the intellectual influences that they reflect.

Abrams and *Whitney,*[148] landmark opinions by Justice Holmes and Brandeis in the decade after the First World War, grew out of the postwar obsession with subversives and seditious groups. *Abrams* was an appeal from the conviction of a small handful of radicals who had published two pamphlets seeking to arouse workers to international unity and had flung some copies out of a Manhattan window. *Whitney* sought to overturn the conviction of an official of the California branch of the Communist Labor Party under the state's criminal syndicalism statute. Holmes and Brandeis disapproved of both convictions but failed to convince the majority of the Court.[149] Both Justices were significantly influenced by the seminal theoretical writings of Zechariah Chafee, Jr.,[150] who had begun to write about the first amendment because he was deeply troubled by the wholesale trials and convictions of radicals and pacifists under the World War I Espionage Act.[151]

A similar concern with suppression of unpopular messages is found in the context and intellectual roots of *New York Times Co. v. Sullivan.*[152] The newspaper had been subjected to a libel judgment of $500,000 by an

Alabama jury for publishing a political advertisement by a civil rights group that contained partially inaccurate statements about the actions of Alabama officials.[153] In fashioning a constitutional libel standard protecting negligently inaccurate criticism of public officials, the Court emphasized our "profound national commitment to the principle that debate on public issues should be uninhibited, robust, and wide open."[154] Underlying this commitment was the conception that the very idea of self-government bestows upon the public the privilege, the right, and the duty of criticizing government and government officials.[155] The "central meaning of the First Amendment," the Court declared, "is to secure 'the widest possible dissemination of information from diverse and antagonistic sources,' " and "to assure unfettered interchange of ideas for the bringing about of political and social changes desired by the people."[156] As Justice Brennan, the author of *New York Times Co. v. Sullivan,* has observed,[157] these ideas reflect the views of Alexander Meiklejohn, who, like Chafee, first forayed into the first amendment arena at a time of governmental suppression of ideas. Meiklejohn's *Free Speech and Its Relation to Self-Government*[158] was published in the shadow of the McCarthy era. The book decried legislative investigations and administrative programs that sought to protect the minds of critizens "from the influence of assertions, of doubts, of questions, of plans, of principles which the government judges to be too 'dangerous' for us to hear."[159]

The terrain of first amendment work on political expression up to the 1970s is thus a landscape dominated by content regulation questions.[160] The theory of the first amendment expressed in *Abrams* and *Whitney* differs in some important ways from the theory underlying the *Sullivan* case,[161] and Chafee's views are by no means the same as Meiklejohn's,[162] but these very divergences emphasize the context they have in common. That context is the need to defend political expression, no matter how unorthodox its ideas, from the majority's tendency to suppress dissident voices and from efforts by those in power to muzzle their political opponents.

I favor a reading of the first amendment that is powerful and expansive, one that accords with the view of Justice Hugo Black that the first amendment rightfully takes first place in the Bill of Rights.[163] Like constitutional law generally, first amendment thinking must necessarily adapt to the changing needs and evolving perceptions of society.[164] But while theoretical formulation and emphasis may change, the core notion of the first amendment remains the protection of diverse, antagonistic, and unpopular speech from restriction based on substance. To invoke the first amendment, not to protect diversity, but to prevent society from defending itself against the stifling influence of money in politics is to betray the historical development and philosophical underpinnings of the first amendment.

None of the rationales for strong protection of free expression—truth, autonomy and self-fulfillment, social stability, or self-government—justifies the continuing and unchecked abuses that excessive spending has brought to the electoral process. Chafee's thought, elaborated in a series of articles and books, was based on a single core idea—that freedom of expression is essential to the search for truth.[165] Holmes stated the same view with unmatched eloquence in *Abrams*:

> [W]hen men have realized that time has upset many fighting faiths, they may come to believe even more than they believe the very foundations of their own conduct that the ultimate good desired is better reached by free trade in ideas—that the best test of truth is the power of the thought to get itself accepted in the competition of the market, and that truth is the only ground upon which their wishes safely can be carried out. That at any rate is the theory of our Constitution.[166]

But the truth-producing capacity of the marketplace of ideas is not enhanced if some are allowed to monopolize the marketplace by wielding excessive financial resources. Just as proponents of the free market system generally recognize the need for government policing of the competitive economic process by enforcement of antitrust laws,[167] proponents of freedom of expression must recognize the need for government policing of the competitive electoral process by campaign finance laws.[168]

The first amendment absolutism of Justice Hugo Black[169] and Thomas Emerson[170] is consistent with financial reform of the electoral process. Emerson stressed the dynamics of freedom of expression, pointing out that intense pressures for conformity exist at all times and in all places and require the utmost vigilance to protect free speech against abridgment.[171] Both Black and Emerson also emphasized the need for self-expression as an element of personal autonomy and self-fulfillment and warned that suppression of a person's beliefs subjects his mind to the dehumanizing control of others.[172] Campaign finance reforms promote the same values that these thinkers found in the first amendment. Unchecked political expenditures, no less than crass regulation of ideas, may drown opposing beliefs, vitiate the principle of political equality, and place some citizens under the damaging and arbitrary control of others.[173] Limiting the amount that wealthy interests may spend to publicize their views enhances the self-expression of individual citizens who lack wealth, furthering the values of freedom of speech.

The safety-valve function of the first amendment, expounded by Justice Brandeis in *Whitney v. California*,[174] also harmonizes with the goals of campaign finance reform. Brandeis was concerned with the views of the downtrodden and discontented. The Founders knew, he wrote,

> that it is hazardous to discourage thought, hope, and imagination; that fear breeds repression; that repression breeds hate; that hate menaces stable government; that the path of safety lies in the opportunity to discuss freely supposed grievances and proposed remedies; and that the fitting remedy for evil counsels is good ones.[175]

But the argument of stability and order does not support unlimited political expenditures by the wealthy, nor does it immunize the lengthening shadow of PACs in congressional elections.[176] Indeed, if Brandeis, who fought vigorously against big oppressive organizations and against concentrated wealth,[177] had witnessed the contemporary electoral scene, he might have written that it is hazardous to discourage civic spirit, hope, and participation; that disillusionment breeds alienation; that alienation breeds apathy; that apathy menaces the democratic idea; and finally that the path of safety lies in allowing individuals an opportunity to persuade the public by participating freely and equally in the electoral process.

Although all of the leading first amendment rationales may be comfortably reconciled with campaign spending reforms, the theory of Alexander Meiklejohn more than any other permits—perhaps even demands—restrictions on inequalities of financial resources.[178] Meiklejohn saw self-government as the fundamental principle of the first amendment.[179] Freedom of expression, he wrote, was the indispensable prerequisite for informed, rational decisionmaking; it was therefore essential to a self-governing populace of political equals bound by voluntary compact. In earlier controversies self-government was best served by removing government restrictions on political expression. In today's political forum that ideal is also served by permitting government regulation of the influence of money in politics, so that the wealthiest voices may not dominate the debate by the strength of their dollars rather than their ideas.

Meiklejohn made a perceptive distinction between abridging speech—which is sometimes permissible—and abridging the freedom of speech—which is almost always forbidden.[180] His analogy was the town meeting, the paradigm of the direct democratic ideal.[181] There, he noted, regulating and abridging communication is necessary for orderly presentation and intelligent deliberation. "It is not a dialectical free-for-all," he reminded his readers. "It is self-government."[182] In Meiklejohn's view, the first amendment protects, not the individual's desire for self-fulfillment, but the collective thought processes of the community.[183]

It is to prevent mutilation of these communal thought processes that campaign finance reforms are so essential. An election campaign is finite in time and focuses on specific ballot decisions regarding specific alternatives.[184] Expenditure limits and other curbs on campaign finance practices are analogous to rules of order at a town meeting, enforced so that the deliberative process is not distorted. The first amendment does not permit curbs on general discussion of political, economic, or social controversies. But, like the loud mouth and long talker at the town meeting, untrammeled spending during an election campaign does not serve the values of self-government, nor can it lay claim to first amendment protection.

In two categories of cases the Supreme Court has recognized that speech may be abridged without abridging the freedom of speech guaranteed by the first amendment—those that involve time, place, and manner restrictions, and those that involve allocation schemes. Time, place, and manner restrictions limit the untrammeled freedom of would-be speakers in the interests of would-be nonlisteners. These restrictions serve interests in peace and quiet unrelated to suppressing communication. Thus, a nondiscriminatory ordinance may prohibit unreasonably loud, raucous operations by sound trucks on the streets of a community. As the Court recognized in *Kovacs v. Cooper,*[185] the Constitution does not require a community to suffer the nuisance of unregulated broadcasts that impose uninvited messages upon a captive audience.[186]

In contrast to time, place, and manner restrictions, allocation schemes limit the freedom of would-be speakers in the interest of would-be listeners. These schemes protect the integrity of the system of communications itself. When the forum is limited by physical, technologic, or economic factors, the messages of some speakers must be limited if all points of view are to be heard, so that the audience may enjoy a full range of uninhibited debate. Allocation of limited opportunities for speech prevents mutual interference or distortion and thus enhances the flow of information to listeners. Thus, in the broadcasting industry, in which the number of usable frequencies is technologically limited, the Court has been compelled to recognize the existence of clashing first amendment interests: the claimed exclusive rights of the broadcasting licensees and the rights of others who seek access to the media to express their views. To cushion the clash between the two groups the Court has focused instead on the listeners and has recognized that their first amendment rights are better served by diversity than by monopoly. As Justice White wrote for the Court in *Red Lion Broadcasting Co. v. FCC,*[187] it is "the right of the viewers and listeners, not the right of the broadcasters, which is paramount."[188]

Regulating campaign finance to prevent the polluting effects of financial inequalities involves a hybrid of both categories of permissible limitations on speech—time, place, and manner regulation and allocation schemes. Like time, place, and manner regulations, it serves social interests unrelated to suppressing communication, such as the fundamental interest in preserving political equality, and the more specific goals of removing financial barriers to candidacy, encouraging citizen involvement in the political process, and avoiding the danger that the wealthy can hold elected officials in political captivity.[189] Also, like the allocation of broadcasting licenses and the Fairness Doctrine, campaign finance restrictions protect the system of communications itself in the interest of speakers and voter-listeners. Excessive and unequal spending by one side interferes with the other's communication and, if the inequality is great enough, can effectively and completely drown out the other's message to the voters.[190] Even though the forum for electoral communications is not limited in the same technical sense that the broadcasting spectrum is, it is limited in time and subject matter, so that the first amendment interests of candidates and voters require safeguards against the potential for distortion and monopoly created by unlimited spending.

The financial structuring of political contests, like the allocation of access to the broadcast media, undeniably produces a tension between competing first amendment values. Those with unlimited resources have a colorable first amendment claim to be free to decide how, where, and when to spend their money to advertise their candidates and political viewpoints. But the first amendment analysis does not end with the identification of a single first amendment interest. In resolving the first amendment conflict, the *Red Lion* principle supplies the appropriate rule of decision. The interests of the listeners in hearing a broad range of ideas are paramount. In *Buckley* and *Bellotti*, however, the Court paid only lip service to the rights of listeners[191] and limited the *Red Lion* principle to the regulation of the media.[192] Its primary solicitude was given to the privileged few who can spend unlimited amounts of money to purchase political effectiveness, rather than to the listeners—the citizens who, by their vote, perform the most important of public duties.[193]

The Court's one-sided reconciliation of competing first amendment values is particularly skewed—if not perverse—in *Bellotti*. In giving strong first amendment protection to corporations, it ignored Justice White's sound reminder that

> [c]orporations are artificial entities created by law for the purpose of furthering certain economic goals. . . . It has long been recognized . . . that the special status of corporations has placed them in a position to control vast amounts of economic power which may, if not regulated, dominate not only the economy but also the very heart of our democracy, the electoral process.[194]

The inevitable result of the growth of corporate political power and influence, and its effective sanction by the Court, was recently analyzed by Archibald Cox.

> If liberty means the opportunity of the individual man or woman to express himself or herself in a society in which ideas are judged principally by their merit, increasing the relative influence of organizations with large financial resources and shrinking the attention paid to truly individual voices means a net loss of human freedom.[195]

Such an outcome is fundamentally inconsistent with the underlying principles of the first amendment.

To return to the question: Is the first amendment an obstacle to democratic equality? The answer to me is clear. Liberty and equality must complement each other as equally indispensable linchpins of an open, democratic society. As Kenneth Karst has written,[196] and as the foregoing discussion of first amendment theory implies, equality is part of the central meaning of the first amendment and underlies each of its most important purposes.[197]

Indeed, instead of asking the defeatist question, "Is the first amendment an *obstacle* to democratic equality?", we should be asking, "How must we interpret and implement the first amendment in order to *enhance* equality?" In a world of advancing technology, scarce resources, and practical barriers to full freedom of discussion, we must not look at the first amendment solely as a negative prohibition. Although freedom of speech has generally been perceived as a limitation on government, I agree with Professor Emerson that the frontier of the first amendment today is the need for affirmative measures by government to protect, preserve, and enhance freedom of expression.[198]

REMEDIES

Recognizing that fundamental principles of political equality are inseparable from first amendment values, the American people, the Congress, and the courts must make a concerted and timely effort to cleanse our body politic. Without providing detailed prescriptions, I would like to point to avenues of reform that respond to the grievous problems described earlier in this article.

First, there is the alarming influence of political action committees sponsored by special interests. PACs have taken a dominant position in the process of electing senators and congressmen and are increasingly active at the state level. It is vital to reduce their undue influence on candidates and, through candidates, on legislation. Congress should reduce the legal ceiling on the amount that each PAC may give to any candidate, and the amount that any candidate may receive from all PACs taken together.[199] We should recognize that PAC contributions and expenditures inflict the same evils on the body politic as direct contributions and expenditures by corporations and labor unions, which have been banned by federal law for decades.[200]

Second, there is the growing cost of political campaigns, which tends to foster inequalities in spending, and thus to distort the political debate, and to exclude all but the wealthy or the well financed from running for office. The best and most comprehensive remedy would be public financing of political campaigns for the House and Senate.[201] Public financing may constitutionally be accompanied by limits on spending and contributions.[202] With one stroke public financing legislation could do much to remove the poison of money from the political bloodstream—even within the confines of the narrow constitutional limitations the present Supreme Court imposes on us.

If public financing is not enacted, less comprehensive stopgap measures should be considered. Given the prominent share of media spending in campaign budgets, reducing the cost of access to the media would do much to alleviate the blight of rising campaign costs and the resulting inequalities. Government control over the broadcast media is pervasive; reductions in the cost of political campaign advertising would be well within the power of Congress and well within the first amendment.[203] Congress should also consider requiring broadcasters to provide specified amounts of free television and radio time to recognized candidates.[204] The Fairness Doctrine should be preserved and strengthened, so that the networks and licensees bear responsibility for assuring reasonably balanced presentations in candidate and issue campaigns.[205]

All of these measures are probably within the Supreme Court's cramped version of the Constitution. But the Court's warped interpretation of the first amendment proscribes some of society's most powerful defenses against the polluting influence of money. *Buckley* unconditionally condemns limitations on overall candidate spending, spending from personal and family resources, and independent spending activity for or against specified candidates.[206] *Bellotti* gives corporations the right to spend money in political-issue referendum campaigns, even those totally unrelated to corporate business.[207] Yet spending limits are an essential weapon against gross inequalities in campaign communications. Although public funding is a workable remedy for candidate contests, in referendum and initiative campaigns it might well be impracticable as a comprehensive solution. In these political contests, the only way to prevent distorting inequalities in campaign spending may be the imposition of spending limits at a level high enough to assure adequate debate but low enought to permit all views to find clear, unstifled expression. Clinging to its tragic misconception of money as speech, however, the Court condemns the American electorate to distorted political perceptions arising from one-sided political campaigns. I fervently hope that, as the evidence mounts that the political process is in trouble, the Supreme Court will be moved to alter its position.

CONCLUSION

The Supreme Court, of course, says what the law is. But on a number of occasions in the past when the Court's doctrine has been both wrong and harmful, the pressure of sharply-etched needs has made it clear, first to observers and then to the Court itself, that the doctrine must be changed. Such was the case in the late 1930s when the Court began to uphold New Deal legislation,[208] and such was the case in 1954 when the Court overruled *Plessy v. Ferguson.*[209]

The growing impact of concentrated wealth on the political process and the glaring inequalities in political campaign resources threaten the very essence of political equality. The warning signs are plain for all to see. Today's threat to democracy is not the impending collapse of the structure of democratic institutions but their continuing erosion from within. If this erosion is not checked, the principle of one person, one vote could become nothing more than a pious fraud. Ironically, the underpinnings of our democratic system are being menaced by decisions made by the Supreme Court in the name of the liberties of the first amendment.

The words I wrote in 1975 to close our Court of Appeals decision in *Buckley* did not then move the majority of the Supreme Court. Their message has, however, gained new urgency with the accumulated political experience of the intervening years:

> Our democracy has moved a long way from the town hall, one man, one vote conception of the Framers. Politics has become a growth industry and a way of life for millions of Americans. The corrosive influence of money blights our democratic processes. We have not been sufficiently vigilant; we have failed to remind ourselves, as we moved from town halls to today's quadrennial Romanesque political extravagances, that politics is neither an end in itself nor a means for subverting the will of the people.[210]

ENDNOTES

1. 424 U.S. 1 (1976).
2. 435 U.S. 765 (1978).
3. See L. Berg, H. Hahn, and J. Schmidhauser, *Corruption in the American Political System* (1976), 14–21 (background of corruption in America); Leventhal, Courts and Political Thickets, Colum. L. Rev. (1977), 77:345, 362–65 (history of corrupt practices legislation).
4. The Federal Election Campaign Act of 1971, Pub. L. No. 92–225, 86 Stat. 3 (1972) (codified as amended at 2 U.S.C. §§ 431–455) (1976 and Supp. IV 1980) had required

comprehensive disclosure of contributions to and expenditures by federal candidates. Id. §§ 301–311, 86 Stat. at 11–19. It also had imposed per-voter limits on media expenditures by candidates. Id. § 104, 86 Stat. at 5–7. These partial reform measures had failed to avert the Watergate abuses.

The Ervin committee was formed to investigate campaign finance practices and to propose reform measures. See *Final Report of the Senate Select Committee on Presidential Campaign Activities of the United States Senate* (1974), S. Rep. No. 981, 93d Cong., 2d Sess. Extensive hearings were held in 1972 by three congressional committees. See Federal Election Reform: *Hearings Before the Subcomm. on Elections of the House Comm. on House Administration* (1973, 93d Cong., 1st Sess.; Federal Election Reform, 1973: *Hearings Before the Subcomm. on Privileges and Elections of the Senate Comm. on Rules and Administration* (1973), 93d Cong., 1st Sess.; Federal Election Campaign Act of 1973: *Hearings on S. 372 Before the Subcomm. on Communications of the Senate Comm. on Commerce* (1973), 93d Cong., 1st Sess.

5. Federal Election Campaign Act Amendments of 1974, Pub. L. No. 93–443, 88 Stat. 1263 (1974) (codified as amended at 2 U.S.C. §§431–455 (1976 and Supp. IV 1980). The House committee report on the Act declared: "The unchecked rise in campaign expenditures, coupled with the absence of limitations on contributions and expenditures, has increased the dependence of candidates on special interest groups and large contributors. Under the present law the impression persists that a candidate can buy an election by simply spending large sums in a campaign." H.R. Rep. No. 1239, 93 Cong., 2d Sess. 3 (1974).

6. Congress placed limits on the annual amounts that any individual or committee could contribute to any candidate, in order to reduce the opportunity for corruption and undue influence and the appearance of corruption inherent in massive private campaign contributions. 18 U.S.C. §§ 608 (b) (1)–(3) (Supp. IV 1974) (current version at 2 U.S.C. §§ 441a (a) (1)–(3) (1976).

7. The act limited the overall amount of campaign expenditures by each candidate, with differing ceilings for House, Senate, and presidential candidates. 18 U.S.C. § 608 (c) (Supp. IV 1974) (repealed 1976). It also imposed a separate limit on the amount that a candidate could legally spend from personal or family resources. Id. § (608 (a) (repealed 1976). To enforce the contribution and expenditure limits, the law placed a ceiling on the amount of independent expenditures that could be made by any person or committee on behalf of or against a specifically identified candidate for federal office. Id. § 608 (e) (repealed 1976).

8. Congress adopted a system of partial public financing for primaries and conventions and complete public financing for the general election campaign. Id. §§ 403–408 (current version at 26 U.S.C. §§ 9001–9042 (1976).

9. 2 U.S.C. § 437c (1976 and Supp. IV 1980) (powers of Federal Election Commission).

10. The 1971 act had established extensive reporting and disclosure requirements for candidates and committees, including periodic reports of the sources and amounts of contributions and expenditures. 86 Stat. 3, 11–19 (1972) (current version at 2 U.S.C. § 434 (Supp. IV 1980)).

11. On April 11, 1974, the Senate passed a bill providing for public financing of congressional election campaigns by a vote of fifty-three to thirty-two, *Cong. Rec.* (1974),120:10,952; see S. Rep. No. 689, 93d Cong., 2d Sess. 4–15, reprinted in *U.S. Code Cong. and Ad. News* (1974), 5587, 5590–96 ("it is clear to us that contribution and expenditure limits which would check excessive influence of great wealth cannot be effectively and fairly implemented without a comprehensive system of public campaign financing").

The House, however, defeated a public financing proposal for congressional campaigns by a vote of 228–187. *Cong. Rec.* (1974), 120:27, 495–96. In conference, the measure was deleted from the Federal Election Campaign Act of 1974. H.R. Rep. No. 1438, 93d Cong., 2d Sess. 109–10, reprinted in *U.S. Code Cong. and Ad. News* (1974), 5618, 5685–86 (conference report).

12. 424 U.S. 1 (1976).

13. Id. at 85–109. The Court cited Congress's goals of reducing the deleterious influence of large contributions, facilitating communication by candidates with the electorate, and freeing candidates from the rigors of fund raising. Id. at 95–96. Six of the eight participating Justices fully joined in this holding. Justices Burger and Rehnquist dissented from this holding in whole or in part. Id. at 235 (Burger, C. J., concurring and dissenting in part), 290 (Rehnquist, J., concurring and dissenting in part).

14. Id. at 108–09.

15. Id. at 60–84.

16. Id. at 23–38. Six Justices agreed; Justices Burger and Blackmun dissented. Id. at 235 (Burger, C. J., concurring and dissenting in part), 290 (Blackmun, J., concurring and dissenting in part).

17. In a previous article, I examined the flaws in the Court's conclusion that money is speech. See Wright, Politics and the Constitution: Is Money Speech? *Yale L.J.* (1976), 85:1001.

18. My late colleague Harold Leventhal has pointed out the striking difference in approach between the Court's "pragmatic tone, experimental outlook, and fact-and-record oriented discussion" in the sections upholding Federal Election Campaign Act provisions and the absolutist perspective of the Court's discussion of the unconstitutionality of expenditure limits. Leventhal, supra note 3, at 358; see id. at 373 ("This sweeping pronouncement begs the question by a pejorative statement of the equality principle.")

19. 424 U.S. at 39–59.

20. Id. at 48–49. This passage has been quoted by the Court in several subsequent cases. See infra note 138.

21. Id. at 257–66. Justice White would have accepted Congress's judgment that limitations on independent expenditures and overall candidate spending are necessary to "counter the corrosive effects of money in federal election campaigns," observing that Congress "undeniably included many seasoned professionals who have been deeply involved in elective processes and who have viewed them at close range over many years." Id. at 260–61.

22. Id. at 263.

23. Id. at 264.

24. Id. at 265.

25. 435 U.S. 765 (1978).

26. Id. at 784–92.

27. The Court reversed a decision by the Supreme Court of California that had upheld a Berkeley city ordinance forbidding more than $250 in contributions by any individual to a committee formed to support or oppose a ballot measure. *Citizens Against Rent Control v. City of Berkeley,* 454 U.S. 290 (1981), rev'd 27 Cal. 3d 819, 614 P. 2d 742, *Cal. Rptr.* (1980), 167:84. The decision by the United States Supreme Court relied on *Bellotti's* premise that the problem of corruption cannot possibly arise in a popular vote on a public issue and on Buckley's insistence that government may not restrict the speech of some elements of our society in order to enhance the relative voices of others.

28. 424 U.S. at 48–49. See infra text accompanying notes 138–98 for a discussion of these cases from the perspective of first amendment theory and precedent.

29. That impact was recently reinforced in *Common Cause v. Schmitt*, 455 U.S. 129 (1982). The Supreme Court, by a four-four vote, let stand a three-judge district court decision holding that the first amendment prohibits limits on independent expenditures for the benefit of any presidential candidate, even if he accepts federal funding. The 1974 act still precludes a general election candidate who receives federal funding from accepting private contributions. 26 U.S.C. § 9003 (b) (1976). But by allowing candidates to benefit from unlimited "independent" spending, the district court's decision, affirmed by the Supreme Court, thwarts Congress's attempt to assure major party presidential candidates equal financial resources in the general election. See Claude & Kirchhoff, The "Free Market" of Ideas, Independent Expenditures, and Influence, *N.D.L. Rev.* (1981), 57:337, 364–65 (multimillion dollar war chests raised and spent by independent committees subvert intent of Congress and have potential for creating implicit obligations).

30. Arterton, The Federal Election Commission, *in* Campaign Finance Study Group, Institute of Politics, John F. Kennedy School of Government, Harvard University, *An Analysis of the Impact of the Federal Election Campaign Act, 1972–78*, (1979) at 1–24 to 1–25, 6–5 to 6–8 [hereinafter cited as Harvard Campaign Finance Study].

31. F. Wertheimer and R. Huwa, Campaign Finance Reforms: Past Accomplishments, Future Challenges 5 (unpublished paper presented at Colloquium on Election Law in the 1980s, sponsored by New York University Review of Law and Social Policy, New York, Nov. 15, 1980).

32. In 1977 proposed legislation to establish a voluntary system of matching federal grants to House and Senate candidates was blocked by a filibuster in the Senate and by opposition in the House Administration Committee. In 1978, despite two attempts to attach the measure to related election law legislation, supporters of public financing of congressional campaigns were unable to obtain consideration of the bill on the floor of the House. Again in 1979, the legislation was blocked in the House when a bill covering House elections was rejected by the House Administration Committee by a vote of eight to seventeen. See *Congressional Quarterly, Congress and the Nation, 1977–1980*, at (1981), 5:943–47.

33. Only 11.2 percent of the PACs that reported making contributions to federal candidates in the 1980 elections were unconnected with another organization; they contributed only 8.4 percent of the total dollar amount. Federal Election Commission press release (Aug. 4, 1981).

34. Since 1907, federal law has prohibited the use of corporate treasury money in federal election campaigns. Act of January 26, 1907, ch. 420, 34 Stat. 864 (current version at 2 U.S.C. § 441b (1976 & Supp. IV 1980)). The same prohibition has applied to labor unions continuously since 1947. Labor Management Relations Act, ch. 120, tit. III, 61 Stat. 159 (1947) (current version at 2 U.S.C. § 441b (1976 and Supp. IV 1980)). The law did not prevent unions or corporations from persuading their members or stockholders to contribute to separate political funds segregated from the treasury. Labor unions established, therefore, and elaborate network of separate funds. See *Pipefitters Local Union No. 562 v. United States*, 407 U.S. 385, 402–09 (1972) (discussing history of the ban on union contributions and expenditures and establishment of CIO Political Action Committee).

35. In the past, corporations were less active than unions in operating separate political funds, but one major obstacle—a ban on political activity by government contractors—was repealed in 1974. 2 U.S.C. § 441c(b) (1976) (authorizing government contractors to establish separate segregated funds), repealing Pub. L. No. 76–753, § 5 (a), 54 Stat. 772 (1940); see 5 *Congressional Quarterly*, supra note 32, at 948. The 1974 legislation also clarified the limits on solicitation by corporate PACs. See Mayton, Politics, Money, Coer-

cion, and the Problem with Corporate PAC's, *Emory L.J.* (1980), 29:375. At the same time, the limits placed on individual and party contributions by the 1974 legislation generated exploration for new sources of campaign funds. Bolton, Constitutional Limitations on Restricting Corporate and Union Political Speech, *Ariz. L. Rev.* (1980), 22:373, 405–06; Epstein, the PAC Phenomenon: An Overview, *Ariz. L. Rev.* (1980), 22:355, 360. The PAC boom had begun.

Corporate and trade association PACs now surpass labor PACs in financial activity by a large margin. In the 1979–80 election cycle, labor union PACs spent $26.4 million, including $14.1 million in direct contributions to candidates. Corporate PACs spent $31.8 million, including $21.7 million to candidates, while trade, membership, and health organizations spent an additional $33.6 million, including $17.2 million in candidate contributions. Federal Election Commission press release (August 4, 1981). Experts estimate that approximately half of the PACs in the latter category are business related. See Wertheimer, The PAC Phenomenon in American Politics, *Ariz. L. Rev.* (1980), 22:603, 606 n.19.

36. Federal Election Commission press release (January 17, 1982); *Wash. Post,* Jan. 19, 1982, at A7, col. 1. While corporate PACs have grown rapidly in number, labor union PACs have remained relatively stable. In 1975 there were 226 labor union PACs. Brief for Plaintiffs at 14, *International Ass'n of Machinists & Aerospace Workers v. FEC,* No. 81–1664 (D.C. Cir. April 6, 1982). By December 1982, the number had grown to only 318. *Political Finance/Lobby Reporter,* Jan. 20, 1982, at 11. Total union PAC funds grew from $18.5 million in 1976 to $26 million in 1979–80, slower than the increase in the cost of living. Brief for Plaintiffs, supra, at 14.

Despite the recent growth in the number of corporate PACs, the potential for future growth is immense. A significant number of leading corporations have not yet established their own PACs, Adamany, PAC's and the Democratic Financing of Politics, *Ariz. L. Rev.* (1980), 22:569, 589 (in 1978 only 40 percent of firms in top 500 had PACs); Wertheimer, supra note 35, at 607 (only 17 percent of firms with $100 million or more in assets had formed PACs by May 1978).

37. Epstein, supra note 35, at 356; Federal Election Commission press release (August 10, 1981).

38. The number of House candidates receiving more than $50,000 in PAC money more than tripled from 57 in 1976 to 176 in 1978. Those who received more than $100,000 increased from 3 in 1976 to 21 in 1978. Kenski, Running with and from the PAC, *Ariz. L. Rev.* (1980), 22:627, 640n. 71. In the 1974 campaign, 78 members of the House received 40 percent or more of their total contributions from PACs; in 1978 the number was 136. Wertheimer, supra note 35, at 607.

39. Kenski, supra note 38, at 641–42; Federal Election Commission press release (August 10, 1981).

In Senate campaigns in 1976, PACs gate 15 percent of the funds received by candidates—winners and losers, incumbents and challengers together. In 1978 the figure was 13 percent and in 1980 it was 16 percent. Kenski, supra note 38, at 641; Federal Election Commission press release, supra.

40. In the 1977–78 election cycle, the two major parties directly contributed a total of $6.4 million to federal candidates and spent an additional $4.8 million on their behalf. In contrast, during the same election cycle, PACs gave $35.2 million to federal candidates. Epstein, supra note 35, at 361. A significant shift took place during the 1970s. In 1972, political parties supplied 17.3 percent of the funds obtained by House candidates, while nonparty committees provided 14.0 percent. In 1978 parties gave only 4.5 percent of the funds, nonparty committees 25.3 percent. Jacobson, The Pattern of Campaign Contri-

butions to Candidates for the U.S. House of Representatives, 1972–1978, in Harvard Campaign Finance Study, supra note 30, at 2–2 to 2–3.

Some commentators assert that PACs have been a major factor in the decline of parties. See, e.g., Epstein, supra note 35, at 360–61; Wertheimer, supra note 35, at 616. Others believe that PACs have simply benefited from trends that have at the same time reduced party influence on elections. See, e.g., Adamany, supra note 36, at 593–94; Sorauf, Political Parties and Political Action Committees: Two Life Cycles, *Ariz. L. Rev.* (1980), 22:445, 454.

41. In the 1980 election campaign, 93.4 percent of total PAC contributions went to candidates who contested the general election—$51.7 million out of $55.3 million. Federal Election Commission press release (August 10, 1981).

42. In 1980 PACs gave $33.8 million to incumbents, many of them holding safe seats, and only $14.3 million to challengers. Id. In 1978 the largest donor, the American Medical Association, gave $823,542 to House incumbents, compared with $301,900 to challengers. Common Cause press release (Dec. 18, 1979). PAC money represented 32 percent of the total receipts of incumbents in 1978, Wertheimer, supra note 35, at 611, and 33.8 percent in 1980, Federal Election Commission press release (August 10, 1981).

43. Federal Election Commission Record, March 1982, at 7. This figure represented approximately 10.5 percent of total PAC spending. Id. For discussions of independent expenditures in United States Senate campaigns, see *N.Y. Times,* Nov. 30, 1980, § 1, at 39, col. 1; *Wash. Post,* Nov. 12, 1980, at A10, col. 1.

The Supreme Court, by a four-four vote, recently affirmed a three-judge district court's decision that Congress may not limit the amount of independent expenditures that may be made by persons or committees to support or oppose presidential candidates in the general election. See supra note 29.

44. 424 U.S. at 39–51.

45. PACs are also a growing force in state politics. See Adamany, supra note 36, at 588; Epstein, supra note 35, at 362–63.

46. Budde, The Practical Role of Corporate PAC's in the Political Process, *Ariz. L. Rev.* (1980), 22:555, 560. Coal, oil, and gas interests had twelve registered PACs in 1974 and one-hundred-ten in 1978. Utilities had no PACs in 1974 and sixty-four in 1978. Banking interests had thirty-six PACs in 1974 and one-hundred-one in 1978. Wertheimer, supra note 35, at 606; see G. Adams, *The Iron Triangle* (1981), 110–24 (activities of PACs formed by defense contractors).

47. See Findings of Fact and Constitutional Questions for Certification Under 2 U.S.C. § 437 (h), findings 4–27, at 8–16, *International Ass'n of Machinists and Aerospace Workers v. FEC,* No. 80-0354 (D.D.C. filed June 3, 1981).

48. Id., finding 11, at 11.

49. Id., finding 19, at 14.

50. Wertheimer, supra note 35, at 608. In addition, during that period, health groups contributed more than $200,000 to members of the House Commerce Committee, which handles health matters. In 1977 and 1978 alone, banking PACs gave nearly $225,000 to the members of the House Committee on Banking, Housing, and Urban Affairs. Id. at 608. During the 1980 election cycle, members of the House Ways and Means Committee received $1.73 million from corporate PACs, including large sums from the steel, auto, airline, and railroad industries, which were seeking special tax breaks. Public Citizen, Congress Watch, Supply-Side Economics: Campaign Contributions to the House Ways and Means Committee, 1979–80, at 6–10 (July 1981); see also Common Cause, Dirty Money . . . Dirty Air? (May 1981) (study of PAC contributions to congressional committees reviewing the Clean Air Act); G. Adams, supra note 46, at 116–18 (patterns of giving by defense contractor PACs).

51. Wertheimer, supra note 35, at 608. Senate Finance Committee Chairman Russell Long received $518,000 in PAC money, including $409,000 from corporate and business-related trade association PACs; Robert Dole, ranking Republican on the same committee, received $328,055 from PACs, including $255,000 from business or business-related PACs. PACs in these categories gave $170,000 to Senator Strom Thurmond, ranking Republican on the Senate Judiciary Committee, and $192,000 to Senator Jake Garn, then ranking Republican on the Senate Banking Committee. Common Cause Guide to Money, Power and Politics in the 97th Congress (1981).

52. Kenski, supra note 38, at 641–42.

53. Public Citizen, supra note 50, at 4. Sometimes the legislative purpose of campaign contributions is particularly transparent. In the first six months of 1981, one House election was just over and the next was a full cycle away, but Congress was considering legislation to lower corporate income taxes. Corporate PACs poured more than $280,000 into the campaign coffers of 24 of the 35 members of the House Ways and Means Committee, most of whom represent safe districts. Five of the six largest recipients had essentially no primary opposition and had received more than two-thirds of the vote in the general election. *Public Citizen, Congress Watch,* Dealing from a PAC'd Deck: Corporate Campaign Contributions to the House Ways and Means Committee During the First Half of 1981 (Oct. 1981).

54. By definition, only 50 percent of major party general election candidates win in contested elections. But almost 80 percent of the 176 candidates who received at least $50,000 in PAC contributions in the 1978 campaign were winners. Although only 5 percent of all challengers won nationally, 52 percent of those who received more than $50,000 in PAC money won the election. Kenski, supra note 38, at 646–48.

55. See generally G. Adams, supra note 46, at 112; Chevigny, Review Essay: The Paradox of Campaign Finance, *N.Y.U. L. Rev.* (1981), 56:206, 214. The *Washington Post* reported that Representative Phil Gramm, who received $6,200 in contributions from the used car dealers' PAC in 1980, addressed their 1981 annual convention and told them, "Your political action committee was a substantial contributor to my campaign. I can say that without your political action contribution, I would have lost. And without your contribution, I would not have been able to come up with the Gramm-Latta budget." *Wash. Post,* Nov. 22, 1981, at C2, col. 3. In fact, Gramm was engaging in hyperbole; he won the 1980 election by a margin of 70 percent to 30 percent. *Cong. Q. Weekly Reports* (1980), 38:3344.

56. Quoted in Ulman, Companies Organize Employees and Holders into a Political Force, *Wall St. J.*, Aug. 15, 1978, 1, col. 6.

57. See Budde, supra note 46, at 558; Malbin, Of Mountains and Molehills: PAC's, Campaigns, and Public Policy, in M. Malbin, ed., *Parties, Interest Groups, and Campaign Finance Laws* (1980), 152, 176.

58. See, e.g., Wertheimer, supra note 35, at 614–15. PAC critics assert that the voting patterns of freshman congressmen often conform with the positions of the PACs that helped to finance their campaigns, and they contend that the PAC money could not possibly have served as a reward for past support. In 1979, the National Association of Realtors (NAR) strongly supported a proposal to eliminate HUD enforcement powers against fraudulent real estate developers. In the previous campaign, the NAR had contributed to 51 of the 71 House freshmen; 43 of those 51 sided with the realtors. Of the 20 who opposed the NAR proposal, 13 had received no NAR contributions. Id. at 615.

In 1979 the AMA lobbied strongly against President Carter's hospital cost containment bill, which was defeated. Thirty-seven of 49 freshmen who received AMA contributions in the 1978 campaign voted with the AMA; they had received average contributions of $9,454. Those who received AMA money but voted against the AMA had received an average of less than half that figure, $4,717 per member. Thirteen of the 25 freshmen who opposed the AMA had received no AMA PAC contributions. AMA Campaign Contributions Helped Kill Hospital Cost Containment Bill, According to Common Cause Study, Common Cause press release (December 18, 1979).

59. See L. Berg, H. Hahn, and J. Schmidhauser, supra note 3, at 43–46 (discussing concept of "weighted voting," which recognizes that some persons not only cast their own ballots but also exercise a multiplier effect by contributing their money to influence the votes of others); Adamany, supra note 36, at 571 ("Money's extreme potential for multiple voting points to an important issue of political finance policy in a democracy: preventing gross inequalities in the meaning of the vote." (footnotes omitted)); id. at 570–71 (noting that ability and inclination to give large sums to political candidates "has greater potential than any other form of political activity for differential participation by presumably equal citizens"); cf. Freund, Commentary, in A. Rosenthal, *Federal Regulation of Campaign Finance: Some Constitutional Questions* (1971), 74 (Citizens' Research Foundation Study No. 18) (large contributors "are operating vicariously through the power of their purse, rather than through the power of their ideas, and . . . I would scale that relatively lower in the hierarchy of First Amendment values").

60. Nader Study Links Oil Contributions to Pro-Oil House Vote, Public Citizen, Congress Watch press release (July 23, 1979) (95 percent of House members who received more than $2,500 from oil industry PACs voted to reduce windfall profits tax; three-quarters of the 267 House members who received oil PAC money voted for the measure; 83 percent of the 236 Congressmen who supported the measure, and only 39 percent of its opponents, had received oil PAC contributions).

61. AMA Campaign Contributions Helped Kill Hospital Cost Containment Bill, According to Common Cause Study, supra note 58 (202 of 234 House members who voted against Carter administration's hospital cost containment legislation received funds from AMA PACs; bill's opponents received average AMA PAC contributions four times as great as bill's supporters).

62. Nader Group Links Chemical Contributions to Pro-Industry Efforts, *Public Citizen, Congress Watch* press release (August 25, 1980) (among top recipients of chemical industry PAC money were several Senators and Representatives leading opposition to superfund bill).

63. *Public Citizen,* supra note 50, at 6–10. In a vote on a refundable investment credit for steel, auto, airline, and railroad companies in June 1981, those who voted yes had received an average of $12,420 from corporation and labor PACs in the affected industries; those who voted present or did not vote received an average of $8,296; and those who voted no received only $3,585. Id. at 10.

64. The FTC regulations were submitted to Congress for review on September 9, 1981. Veto resolutions were introduced in both the House (H. Con. Res. 178) and the Senate (S. Con. Res. 33). The Senate committee held a hearing on October 30; the House committee held a hearing on December 8. On December 16, 1981, the House committee favorably reported the veto resolution to the floor. Congress adjourned, however, before the completion of action on the proposed veto. Under the terms of the FTC Improvements Act of 1980, the agency was required to resubmit the rule for review at the beginning of the 1982 session. See 15 U.S.C. § 57a-1(a)(2) (Supp. IV 1980). On May 18, 1982, the Senate voted sixty-nine to twenty-seven to disapprove the FTC regulation. *Cong. Rec.* 128:§5380–5402 (daily ed. May 18, 1982). On May 26, 1982, the House voted by a margin of 286 to 133 to veto the rule. *Cong. Rec.* 128: H2856–2883 (daily ed. May 26, 1982).

65. Can the Used Car Lobby Sell Congress? *Wash. Post,* Nov. 22, 1981, at C2, col. 3.

66. See, e.g., Budde, supra note 46, at 556–57; Rhodes, In Response to Obey-Railsback, *Ariz. L. Rev.* (1980), 22:670, 670–71.

67. Mayton, supra note 35, at 391.

68. Adamany, supra note 36, at 596; Campaign Finance Study Group, Summary of Findings and Major Recommendations, in Harvard Campaign Finance Study, supra note 30, at 1–8; Kenski, supra note 38, at 619; Mayton, supra note 35, at 386–87. As the Harvard study warned, "Candidates now rely more heavily on money from outside their districts or states. As Washington, D.C. has become the best place to raise campaign funds, a concomitant concern is the increasing detachment of candidates from their constituencies." Campaign Finance Study Group, supra, at 1–8.

Not all observers agree that PACs are overly influential. See Elliott, Political Action Committees—Precincts of the '80's, *Ariz. L. Rev.* (1980), 22:539, 549–50 (written by former executive director of AMA PAC) ("Those who would argue that PAC's are dominating or taking over the political process are overstating both the role and the impact of PAC's since only 17.5% of all funds spent by federal candidates in 1978 came from PAC's."); Epstein, supra note 35, at 371–72 ("Whenever PAC contributions, as a percentage of total contributions to candidates, exceeds the current level of approximately twenty-five percent, the time will have come for Congress to consider limiting PAC activities.").

69. See Adamany, supra note 36, at 570 ("The rapid shift from traditional political methods to high-technology campaigning makes money more important precisely because it is readily converted into polling, computerized appeals, professional staff, and media messages.").

70. See Brief for Appellees Center for Public Financing of Elections, Common Cause, League of Women Voters, et al. at 67–69, *Buckley v. Valeo,* 424 U.S. 1 (1976) (from 1952 to 1972, consumer price index rose 57.6 percent; federal campaign spending increased almost 300 percent; Brief of Senators Hugh Scott and Edward M. Kennedy, Amici Curiae, at 35 n. 14, *Buckley v. Valeo,* 424 U.S. 1 (1976) (separate charts for congressional and presidential campaign expenditures); F. Wertheimer and R. Huwa, supra note 31, at 18.

71. F. Wertheimer and R. Huwa, Has the Tree Really Fallen? The Role of Television in American Politics 27 (unpublished paper prepared for presentation at annual meeting of Association for Public Policy Analysis and Management, Boston, Mass., Oct. 24, 1980).

72. Federal Election Commission press release (August 10, 1981).

73. D. Graber, *Mass Media and American Politics (1980),* 161. *Time* Magazine reported an even higher estimate, 60 to 70 percent of campaign funds. *Time,* Nov. 20, 1978, at 35. A study of eighty-six House campaigns in 1978 found that "the single most expensive activity on the average . . . was broadcasting." F. Wertheimer and R. Huwa, supra note 71, at 26–27.

74. F. Wertheimer and R. Huwa, supra note 71, at 27. From 1974 to 1980, the price of thirty prime-time seconds on TV in Baltimore increased from $1,100 to $3,000; from 1978 to 1980, the cost of five minutes of TV time in rural Wisconsin escalated from $250 to $950. One political consultant in Washington, D.C., estimated that spot advertising costs generally increased 40 percent from 1979 to late 1980. Id.

75. L. Sabato, *The Rise of Political Consultants: New Ways of Winning Elections* (1981), 228–30, 250–53 (costs of direct mailing).

76. See *Business Executives' Move for Vietnam Peace v. FCC,* 450 F.2d 642, 658 (D.C. Cir. 1971) (Wright, J.), rev'd sub nom. *CBS v. Democratic Nat'l Comm.,* 412 U.S. 94 (1973). In the court of appeals decision, I rejected the contention that "spot" editorial advertisements are unworthy of protection because they may be cursory and uninfor-

mative. "We must . . . be very, very slow to judge any sort of speech on public issues worthless. The marketplace of ideas protected by the First Amendment, after all, is not governed by the tastes and intellectual standards of the universities or the broadcast newsroom—or even of judicial chambers." 450 F.2d at 658.

77. See F. Wertheimer and R. Huwa, supra note 71, at 28. PACs may legally give $5000 to a candidate in a primary or general election campaign; an individual is limited to a $1000 contribution. 2 U.S.C. § 441a(a) (1) (A) (1976).

78. See L. Berg, H. Hahn, and J. Schmidhauser, supra note 3, at 80; D. Graber, supra note 73, at 161–62; Leventhal, supra note 3, at 375; Nicholson, Campaign Financing and Equal Protection, *Stan. L. Rev.* (1974), 26:815, 816. The specter of heavy personal campaign debts may also serve as a deterrent to candidacy. One former congressional candidate has vividly described the pressures placed on him during the campaign to incur person liability in order to provide funds for his campaign, because the candidate is the only "contributor" not limited by statute. Firmage and Christensen, Speech and Campaign Reform: Congress, the Courts and Community, *Ga. L. Rev.* (1980), 14:195, 210–12. On the average, the proportion of campaign receipts coming from a candidate's own funds increased from 5.6 percent in 1974 to 8.9 percent in 1976 and 9.2 percent in 1978. The average personal contribution of a House candidate rose from $3,500 in 1974 to $10,200 in 1978. F. Wertheimer and R. Huwa, supra note 31, at 10.

On the other hand, wealthy candidates have figured prominently in recent campaigns. See Firmage and Christensen, supra, at 210; Leventhal, supra note 3, at 382–83. In 1976 nine House candidates spent more than $100,000 of their own funds in their campaigns, and three Senate candidates each spent more than $500,000. F. Wertheimer and R. Huwa, supra note 31, at 10.

79. A. Rosenthal, supra note 59, at 40.

80. Tabulations are based on Federal Election Commission, FEC Reports on Financial Activity 1977–1978, Interim Report No. 5, U.S. Senate and House Campaigns 121–340 (June 1979) (charts of financial activity in individual Senate and House campaigns arranged by state).

81. In the bulk of the Senate races, the spending was not even close. In twenty-three of the thirty-five races, the winner outspent the loser by 50 percent or more; in fifteen of the thirty-five races, the margin was two to one or more. In dollar terms, the winner outspent the loser by more than $100,000 in twenty-six races, by more than $200,000 in twenty-three races, and by more than $500,000 in eleven races.

82. L. Sabato, supra note 75, at 49–53 (fees, expenses, and commissions charged by political consultants); id. at 79–81 (costs of in-person polls and telephone polls); id. at 179–82 (costs of media advertising); id. at 250–53 (direct mailing expenses and fees).

83. Statement of Professor Larry L. Berg, in Voter Initiative Constitutional Amendment, *Hearings Before the Subcomm. on the Constitution of the Senate Comm. on the Judiciary on S.J. Res. 67*, 95th Cong., 1st Sess. 50, 51 (1977) [hereinafter cited as Voter Initiative Constitutional Amendment].

84. See Shockley, The Initiative, Democracy, and Money: The Case of Colorado, 1976 in Voter Initiative Constitutional Amendment, supra note 83, at 172. See generally Voter Initiative Constitutional Amendment, supra note 83.

85. Before 1978, eighteen states and a number of municipalities had laws that limited or prohibited corporate contributions or expenditures in ballot question campaigns. S. Lyndenberg, *Bankrolling Ballots: The Role of Business in Financing State Ballot Question Campaigns* (1979), 13. However, taken together, *Buckley v. Valeo*, 424 U.S. 1 (1976), and *First Nat'l Bank v. Bellotti*, 435 U.S. 765 (1978), protect the right of any person, group, or corporation to make unlimited direct expenditures for or against a ballot prop-

osition. The Supreme Court recently struck down a municipal ordinance limiting contributions by any person to committees favoring or opposing referenda or initiatives. *Citizens Against Rent Control v. City of Berkeley,* 454 U.S. 290, (1981); see supra note 27.

86. S. Lydenberg, supra note 85; Mastro, Costlow, and Sanchez, Taking the Initiative: Corporate Control of the Referendum Process Thorugh Media Spending and What To Do About It, *Fed. Com. L.J.* (1980), 32:315; Shockley, supra note 84, at 177–80; Brief in Support of Appellees by Amicus Curiae City and County of San Francisco at 21–25, *Citizens Against Rent Control v. City of Berkeley,* 454 U.S. 290 (1981) [hereinafter cited as San Francisco Amicus Brief].

87. S. Lydenberg, supra note 85, at 22–23 (ratios of spending in these twelve cases were 197:1, 96:1, 48:1, 26:1, 25:1, 24:1, 13:1, 10:1, 4.5:1, 4:1, 1.7:1, and unknown). The same author studied nineteen ballot issue campaigns in the 1980 election; the side with corporate backing outspent opponents by better than two to one in fifteen campaigns and won in twelve of them. See *Citizens Against Rent Control v. City of Berkeley,* 454 U.S. 290, 308 n. 4 (1981) (White, J., dissenting).

88. S. Lydenberg, supra note 85, at 30–34.

89. Mastro, Costlow, and Sanchez, supra note 86, at 320–27, 330–33, 360–69.

90. Corporate donations of $500 or more accounted for 91 percent of the opposition's campaign fund. Id. at 321.

91. Opponents spent $69,415 on television advertising; under the Fairness Doctrine supporters obtained free time valued at $13,850. On radio, container deposit opponents spent $35,076; proponents had $1,688 worth of free radio time. In the local newspapers, opponents outspent supporters by more than three to one. Id. at 325–26.

92. The authors found the same phenomena—heavy media spending by the corporate side, an overwhelming imbalance in finances and publicity, and defeat of a grassroots initiative despite strong support in early polls—in two other 1976 Colorado ballot initiatives, one on nuclear safety and one on reform of public utilities regulation. Id. at 320–27, 330–33, 360–69; see Shockley, supra note 84, at 177–89 (case studies of 1976 Colorado initiatives on nuclear safety, bottle deposits, and tax reform, arriving at substantially similar conclusions and discussing shifts in public opinion over the course of each campaign.

93. S. Lydenberg, supra note 85, at 26–27 (1978 Alaska bottle bill initiative); id. at 33–34 (1978 California antismoking initiative); id. at 37 (1978 Long Beach, California, initiative against oil storage terminal); id. at 39–40 (1978 Nebraska bottle deposit initiative); id. at 47–48 (1978 Oregon people's utility district initiative); id. at 54–56 (1978 Montana antinuclear initiative); id. at 59 (1978 Oregon utilities rates initiative); Mastro, Costlow, and Sanchez, supra note 86, at 321–23 (1976 Colorado initiatives on nuclear safety, container deposits, and public utilities regulation reform); San Francisco Amicus Brief, supra note 86, at 22–24 (1980 California initiatives on smoking limitations, oil profits tax, and repeal of rent control ordinances).

94. S. Lydenberg, supra note 85, at 37, cited in part in *Citizens Against Rent Control v. City of Berkeley,* 454 U.S. 290, 308 n. 4 (1981) (White, J., dissenting).

95. Studies in California have found that massive spending is more likely to defeat a referendum opposed by special interests than to pass a measure they favor. See Statement of Professor Larry L. Berg, supra note 83, at 54; Appellee's Brief at 11, *Citizens Against Rent Control v. City of Berkeley,* 454 U.S. 290 (1981) (quotes systematic study of California statewide ballot measures between 1968 and 1980, which concludes that "one-sided spending is ineffective when it supports the proposition but is dominant when it opposes the measure"); Brief of Amicus Curiae New England Legal Foundation in Support of Appellants, *Citizens Against Rent Control v. City of Berkeley,* 454 U.S. 290 (1981).

Money is not the only factor determining the results of a referendum campaign. Initial public attitudes, the strength or weakness of the specific measure, events during the campaign, endorsements or opposition by prominent political figures, and other factors play an important part. However, the greater the lopsidedness in spending, the greater the impact that money differentials will have on the outcome of an election.

96. See supra note 87. One media specialist who worked for two initiative campaigns during the 1976 Colorado elections stated, "I'm afraid money can buy an election. But it's not money alone. It's money cleverly spent." Shockley, supra note 84, at 178.

97. After three initially popular initiatives were opposed by high-spending media campaigns and defeated at the polls in Colorado in 1976, the *Colorado Daily* editorialized: "What was lost on Tuesday was more than . . . good amendments. The big money boys have undoubtedly put a chill on the efforts of citizen groups to put issues on the ballot. Obtaining the needed signatures for an initiative is hard work, and nobody wants to waste his or her time if all is to be stomped under the bankrolls of those with power." Shockley, supra note 84, at 188; see L. Berg, H. Hahn, and J. Schmidhauser, supra note 3, at 49–51 (discussion of voter alienation). Political apathy by the populace runs counter to the purposes and ideals of the democratic system. As Justice Brandeis wrote in *Whitney v. California,* 274 U.S. 357, 375 (1927) (Brandeis, J., concurring), "the greatest menace to freedom is an inert people."

98. See Wright, supra note 17, at 1013–21 (criticizing pluralists' vision of politics).

99. See J. Locke, *Two Treatises of Government* 2:ii, 4; viii, 95, reprinted in F. W. Coker ed., *Readings on Political Philosophy* (1938) 530, [hereinafter cited as *Readings*].

100. J. Rawls, *A Theory of Justice* (1971), 11–19, 205–07, 221–28; see also Scanlon, A Theory of Freedom of Expression, *Phil. and Pub. Aff.* (1972), 1:204, 214 (For a government to be legitimate, citizens must be able to recognize its authority "while still regarding themselves as equal, autonomous, rational agents."

101. J. Rousseau, *The Social Contract,* 1, vi, reprinted in *Readings,* supra note 99, at 639; see id. at 2, iv, reprinted in *Readings,* supra note 99, at 646–47 ("[t]he social compact establishes among the citizens such an equality that they all pledge themselves under the same conditions and ought all to enjoy the same rights.").

102. In the words of Alexander Meiklejohn, "[i]f the Declaration of Independence means what it says, if we mean what it says, then no man is called upon to obey a law unless he himself, equally with his fellows, has shared in making it." A. Meiklejohn, *Free Speech and Its Relation to Self-Government* (1948), 10–11. The people are both the governors and the governed. Under the Constitution, we are agreed that, in Meiklejohn's words, "as free men, politically equal, we alone will make the laws and that, as loyal citizens, equal before thje laws, we will obey them." Id. at 105; see id. at 3–11, 22–23.

Meiklejohn subsequently wrote that "the adoption of the principle of self-government by 'The People' of this nation set loose upon us and upon the world at large an idea which is still transforming men's conceptions of what they are and how they may best be governed." Meiklejohn, The First Amendment Is an Absolute, *Sup. Ct. Rev.* (1961), 245, 264.

103. *Federalist No. 57,* at 305 (J. Madison) (J. Cooke, ed. 1961).

104. A. de Tocqueville, *Democracy in America,* J. P. Mayer and M. Lerner eds., G. Lawrence trans. (1966) 59; see id. at 474.

105. Id. at 217–25.

106. Id. at 473.

107. Tuttle, Equality and the Vote, *N.Y.U. L. Rev.* (1966), 41:245, 246.

108. See Kirby, The Right to Vote, N. Dorsen ed., *The Rights of Americans: What They Are—What They Should Be,* (1970) 175, 179–80. Describing the Massachusetts

debate in which universal male suffrage was adopted, one historian observed, "The most impressive thing about this entire movement toward broader suffrage is that men came to be filled with a fixed determination that as this country was a democracy all men should have a hand in running it . . . " Id. at 180 (quoting K. Porter, *A History of Suffrage in the United States* (1969), 70–72.

109. U.S. Const. amend. XIX (admitting women to suffrage); amend. XXIII (enfranchising citizens of District of Columbia in presidential elections); amend. XXIV (abolition of poll tax as precondition for voting); amend. XXVI (admitting 18-to-21-year-olds to vote); see also amend. XVII (direct popular election of senators).

110. *Terry v. Adams,* 345 U.S. 461 (1953); *Smith v. Allwright,* 321 U.S. 649 (1944).

111. *Harper v. Virginia Bd. of Elections,* 383 U.S. 663 (1966). The Court declared unequivocally, "Wealth, like race, creed, or color, is not germane to one's ability to participate intelligently in the electoral process." Id. at 668.

112. *Hill v. Stone,* 421 U.S. 289 (1975); *City of Phoenix v. Kolodziejski,* 399 U.S. 204 (1970); *Cipriano v. City of Houma,* 395 U.S. 701 (1969); *Kramer v. Union Free School Dist. No. 15,* 395 U.S. 621 (1969). But see *Salyer Land Co. v. Tulare Lake Basin Water Storage Dist.,* 410 U.S. 719 (1973). The Court has also struck down unreasonably long residency requirements for voting. *Dunn v. Blumstein,* 405 U.S. 330 (1972).

113. *Hadley v. Junior College Dist.,* 397 U.S. 50 (1970) (apportionment for school district trustees election); *Avery v. Midland County,* 390 U.S. 474 (1968) (county legislature); *Reynolds v. Sims,* 377 U.S. 533 (1964) (state legislative apportionment); *Wesberry v. Sanders,* 376 U.S. 1 (1964) (apportionment for congressional seats).

114. 377 U.S. 533 (1964).

115. Id. at 565. The Chief Justice also declared, "No right is more precious in a free country than that of having a voice in the election of those who make the laws under which, as good citizens, we must live." Id. at 560 (quoting *Wesberry v. Sanders,* 376 U.S. 1, 17 (1964)).

116. *United States v. Saylor,* 322 U.S. 385 (1944) (right to vote protected against ballot box stuffing); *United States v. Classic,* 313 U.S. 299 (1941) (right to have vote counted as cast in primary election); *Guinn v. United States,* 238 U.S. 347 (1915) (right to cast general election ballot); Ex parte Yarbrough, 110 U.S. 651 (1884) (same); see Bixby, The Roosevelt Court, Democratic Ideology and Minority Rights: Another Look at *United States v. Classic, Yale L.J.* (1981), 90:741, 786–812.

117. 376 U.S. 1, 14–17 (1964).

118. 377 U.S. 533 (1964); see Auerbach, The Reapportionment Cases: One Person, One Vote—One Vote, One Value, *Sup. Ct. Rev.* (1964) 1.

119. 377 U.S. at 555 (footnote omitted). Nearly three centuries earlier, John Locke had recognized that malapportionment and rotten boroughs were inconsistent with his theory of the social contract. See J. Locke, supra note 99, xiii, 158, reprinted in *Readings,* at 572–73.

120. 405. U.S. 134 (1972).

121. Id. at 143.

122. "[T]he rights of voters and the rights of candidates," the Court wrote, "do not lend themselves to neat separation; laws that affect candidates always have at least some theoretical, correlative effect on voters." Id.

123. Id. at 143–44. Subsequently, in *Lubin v. Panish,* 415 U.S. 709 (1974), the Court struck down another filing fee requirement, stressing that "voters can assert their preferences only through candidates or parties or both and it is this broad interest that must be weighed in the balance." Id. at 716. Chief Justice Burger wrote, "[O]ur tradition has been one of hospitality toward all candidates without regard to their economic status."

Id. at 717–18. The court has also invalidated a requirement that candidates be property owners. *Turner v. Fouche,* 396 U.S. 346, 363–64 (1970).

124. *Storer v. Brown,* 415 U.S. 724, 738–40 (1974); *Williams v. Rhodes,* 393 U.S. 23 (1968). But see *American Party of Texas v. White,* 415 U.S. 767 (1974); *Jenness v. Fortson,* 403 U.S. 431 (1971).

125. See *Buckley v. Valeo,* 424 U.S. 1, 49 n.55 (1976). But see A. Pekelis, Private Governments and the Federal Constitution, in *Law and Social Action* (1970), 91, 113–14 (proposing new view of state action based on sociological test of "actual influence"; illegitimate economic pressures may be unconstitutional if they "do control in fact the political processes of a given society"); Nicholson, supra note 78, at 830 (suggesting "state action" as basis for requiring campaign finance restrictions under equal protection clause).

126. Rosenthal, Campaign Financing and the Constitution, *Harv. J. Legis.* (1972), 9:359, 360.

127. Leventhal, supra note 3, at 370.

128. Quoted in id. at 363.

129. J. Rawls, supra note 100, at 204. This distinction between rights and the power to secure these rights is also made by philosopher Bernard Williams. He writes: "It may be said that in a certain society, men have equal rights to a fair trial, to seek redress from the law for wrongs committed against them, etc. But if a fair trial or redress from the law can be secured in that society only by moneyed and educated persons, to insist that everyone *has* this right, though only these particular persons can *secure* it, rings hollow to the point of cynicism; we are concerned not with the abstract existence of rights, but with the extent to which those rights govern what actually happens." Williams, The Idea of Equality, in *Philosophy, Politics and Society* (1962), ser. II, at 110–31, reprinted in H. Bedau, ed., *Justice and Equality* (1971), 116, 128–29 (emphasis in original).

130. J. Rawls, supra note 100, at 225. Rawls suggests, therefore, public funding of campaigns, "for when parties and elections are financed not by public funds but by private contributions, the political forum is so constrained by the wishes of the dominant interests that the basic measures needed to establish just constitutional rule are seldom properly presented." Id. at 226.

These insights should carry over into constitutional analysis. As Dean Rosenthal has written, "[I]f the Constitution requires that each man's vote count equally, may not that fact be deemed pertinent in consideration of the validity of measures intended to reduce inequalities in men's opportunities to affect the vote?" Rosenthal, supra note 126, at 377.

131. *CBS v. Democratic Nat'l Comm.,* 412 U.S. 94, 123 (1973).

132. *See Business Executives' Move for Vietnam Peace v. FCC,* 450 F.2d 642 (D.C. Cir. 1971), rev'd sub nom. *CBS v. Democratic Nat'l Comm.,* 412 U.S. 94 (1973).

133. 412 U.S. at 123.

134. Id.

135. Id.

136. A. France, *The Red Lily* (W. Stephens trans. 1894), 91. This passage was quoted by Justice Frankfurter in *Griffin v. Illinois,* 351 U.S. 12, 23 (1956) (Frankfurter, J., concurring), and by Justice Brennan in *Maher v. Roe,* 432 U.S. 464, 483 (1977) (Brennan, J., dissenting).

137. See L. Berg, H. Hahn, and J. Schmidhauser, supra note 3, at 41–46 (explaining differences between principles underlying economic market and one-person, one-vote in the political arena). Financial participation in politics is far more expandable than other political activities and hence creates much greater potential for unequal influence. Adamany, supra note 36, at 570–71; see also Note, The Corporation and the Constitution: Economic Due Process and Corporate Speech, *Yale L.J. (1981), 90:1833, 1855 (criticizing*

Bellotti decision because it "allows access to political audiences to be allocated in ways that more closely reflect the dominance of corporate wealth in the economy").

138. The Court asserted that "the concept that government may restrict the speech [i.e., spending] of some elements of our society in order to enhance the relative voices of others is wholly foreign to the First Amendment." *Buckley v. Valeo,* 424 U.S. 1, 48–49 (1976); *First Nat'l Bank of Boston v. Bellotti,* 435 U.S. 765, 790–91 (1978); *Citizens Against Rent Control v. City of Berkeley,* 102 S. Ct. 434, 437 (1981).

139. *Virginia State Bd. of Pharmacy v. Virginia Citizens Consumer Council,* 425 U.S. 748 (1976) (commercial speech) (cited in *Bellotti,* 435 U.S. at 783, 784 n.20); *Miami Herald Pub. Co. v. Tornillo,* 418 U.S. 241, 250 (1974) (freedom of the press) (cited in *Buckley,* 424 U.S. at 50–51, and in *Bellotti* 435 U.S. at 791 n.30); *Mills v. Alabama,* 384 U.S. 214, 218, 220 (1966) (freedom of the press) cited in *Buckley,* 424 U.S. at 45, 50, and in *Bellotti,* 435 U.S. at 776–77, 781; *New York Times Co. v. Sullivan,* 376 U.S. 254 (1964) (political libel) (cited in *Buckley,* 424 U.S. at 48, 49, and in *Bellotti,* 435 U.S. at 783, 785 n.21, 786 n.23); *NAACP v. Button,* 371 U.S. 415 (1963) (civil rights activity) (cited in *Buckley,* 424 U.S. at 22–23, 41, 48); *Wood v. Georgia,* 370 U.S. 375, 388 (1962) (contempt of court) (cited in *Bellotti,* 435 U.S. at 790, 792); *Eastern R. Presidents Conf. v. Noerr Motor Freight, Inc.,* 365 U.S. 127 (1961) (right to petition) (cited in *Buckley,* 424 U.S. at 49); *Kingsley Int'l Pictures Corp. v. Regents,* 360 U.S. 684 (1959) (obscenity; prior restraint) (cited in *Bellotti* at 435 U.S. at 790); *NAACP v. Alabama ex rel. Patterson,* 357 U.S. 449 (1958) (civil rights activity) (cited in *Buckley,* 424 U.S. at 22, and in *Bellotti,* 435 U.S. at 780, 786); *Roth v. United States,* 354 U.S. 476 (1957) (obscenity) (cited in *Buckley,* 424 U.S. at 49); *Associated Press v. United States,* 326 U.S. 1, 20 (1945) (freedom of the press) (cited in *Buckley,* 424 U.S. at 49, and in *Bellotti,* 435 U.S. 777 n.12); *Bridges v. California,* 314 U.S. 252, 270 (1941) (contempt of court) (cited in *Buckley,* 424 at 48); *Thornhill v. Alabama,* 310 U.S. 88 (1940) (labor picketing) (cited in *Bellotti,* 435 U.S. at 776, 791 n.31); *Whitney v. California,* 274 U.S. 357, 377 (1927) (Brandeis, J., concurring) (seditious speech) (cited in *Buckley,* 424 U.S. at 53, and in *Bellotti,* 435 U.S. at 791–92 n.31); *Abrams v. United States,* 250 U.S. 616, 634 (1919) (Holmes, J., dissenting) (seditious speech) (cited in *Bellotti,* 435 U.S. at 791–92 n.31).

140. Meiklejohn, supra note 102, cited in *Bellotti,* 435 U.S. at 791 n.31. The Court referred to Meiklejohn in support of the proposition that "[g]overnment is forbidden to assume the task of ultimate judgment, lest the people lose their ability to govern themselves." Id. The *Bellotti* opinion also cited Meiklejohn's book, *Free Speech and Its Relation to Self-Government* (1948), and a book by Thomas Emerson, *Toward a General Theory of the First Amendment* (1966), 435 U.S. at 777 n.11.

141. See Leventhal, supra note 3, at 358–59, 373; Nicholson, *Buckley v. Valeo: The Constitutionality of the Federal Election Campaign Act Amendments of 1974, Wisc. L. Rev.* (1977), 323, 372; Comment, Cases That Shock the Conscience: Reflections on Criticism of the Burger Court, *Harv. C.R.-C.L.L. Rev. (1980), 15:713, 736–37 (criticizing Buckley* and *Bellotti* for "detach[ing] the auxiliary rules from their original purpose on the basis of the right's all-encompassing, indiscriminate character").

142. Wright, supra note 17; see Leventhal, supra note 3, at 358–67, 369 (discussing weaknesses in Court's analysis in *Buckley* opinion). Judge Leventhal observed pointedly, "[W]hat is missing from the Supreme Court's opinion is any sense of the history of campaign reform legislation, of the grievous abuses that prompted it, the frustration that accompanied it, the evasion and political pressures that have undermined all less-than-comprehensive measures of reform." Id. at 362.

143. *First Nat'l Bank of Boston v. Bellotti,* 435 U.S. 765, 776 (1978) ("the heart of the First Amendment's protection"); *Buckley v. Valeo,* 424 U.S. 1, 14 (1976) ("area of

the most fundamental First Amendment activities"); *Monitor Patriot Co. v. Roy,* 401 U.S. 265, 272 (1971) ("it can hardly be doubted that the constitutional guarantee has its fullest and most urgent application precisely to the conduct of campaigns for political office").

144. The Court has never developed a comprehensive theory of the meaning of the first amendment; it has used a hodge-podge of different doctrines at various times and in various contexts. See N. Dorsen, P. Bender, and B. Neuborne, *Emerson, Haber, and Dorsen's Political and Civil Rights in the United States* (4th ed. 1976), 1:57–59;
T. Emerson, *The System of Freedom of Expression* (1970), 15–16; Bork, Neutral Principles and Some First Amendment Problems, *Ind. L.J.* (1971), 47:1, 20; Van Alstyne, A Graphic Review of the Free Speech Clause, *Calif. L. Rev.* (1982), 70:107. But some principles have stood the test of time.

145. See, e.g., *New York Times Co. v. Sullivan,* 376 U.S. 254 (1964) (Alabama libel judgment against newspaper for publication of civil rights group advertisement).

146. See, e.g., *Kingsley Int'l Pictures Corp. v. Regents,* 360 U.S. 684 (1959) (censorship based on film's presentation of adultery in a favorable light); *Thornhill v. Alabama,* 310 U.S. 88 (1940) (ban on labor picketing).

147. See, e.g., *Wood v. Georgia,* 370 U.S. 375 (1962) (contempt conviction of sheriff who had criticized county judge); *Grosjean v. American Press Co.,* 297 U.S. 233 (1936) (discriminatory tax imposed by Huey Long regime on selected group of newspapers).

148. *Abrams v. United States,* 250 U.S. 616 (1919); see id. at 624 (Holmes, J., dissenting). *Whitney v. California,* 274 U.S. 357 (1927); see id. at 372 (Brandeis, J., concurring).

149. Holmes dissented in *Abrams* and was joined by Brandeis, 250 U.S. at 624. In *Whitney,* Brandeis, joined by Holmes, concurred in the Court's opinion upholding the syndication conviction, but his approach differed fundamentally from that of the majority. The majority, citing *Gitlow v. New York,* 268 U.S. 652, 666–68 (1925), held that the state legislature's decision to make criminal any association with a group that advocated violence or terrorism as a means of accomplishing political change was a legitimate exercise of police power to prohibit "utterances inimical to the public welfare, tending to incite to crime, disturb the public peace or endanger the foundations of organized government and threaten its overthrow by unlawful means." 274 U.S. at 371. Brandeis took issue with this approach. Finding the statute to aim "not at . . . criminal syndicalism . . . but at association with those who propose to preach it," id. at 373, Brandeis argued that a legislature could not curtail such speech unless it presented a clear and present danger of an immediate and a serious harm. Id. at 374–77. The mere legislative act of proscribing the speech was insufficient to support a finding of clear and present danger, he contended. Despite arguing for the significantly higher threshold, Brandeis concurred in the Court's judgment because the defendant had failed to raise the absence of clear and present danger as a defense at trial, and Brandeis felt constrained from inquiring into the issue on review of a state court judgment. Id. at 379–80. Nonetheless, the concurrence registered a fundamental disapproval of the majority approach. See Bork, supra note 144, at 23.

150. Rabban, The First Amendment in Its Forgotten Years, *Yale L.J.* (1981), 90:514, 591–94.

151. Id. at 586–91; Chafee, Thirty-Five Years with Freedom of Speech, *U. Kan. L. Rev.* (1952), 1:1, 1–2. Chafee's basic theoretical insights were set forth in a *Harvard Law Review* article published in June 1919. Chafee, Freedom of Speech in War Time, *Harv. L. Rev.* (1919), 32:932. Chafee repeated his message in several of his subsequent works. See, e.g., Z. Chafee, *Freedom of Speech* (1920); Z. Chafee, *Free Speech in the United States* (1941), 1–35.

152. 376 U.S. 254 (1964).

153. The Court found, however, that the evidence did not support a finding that the allegedly libelous statements were made "of and concerning" the particular public official who was plaintiff in the case. Id. at 288–92.

154. Id. at 270.

155. Id. at 269–72; see Kalven, The *New York Times* Case: A Note on "The Central Meaning of the First Amendment," *Sup. Ct. Rev.* (1964), 191, 209.

156. 376 U.S. at 273, 266, 269 (quoting *Associated Press v. United States,* 326 U.S. 1, 20 (1945), and *Roth v. United States,* 354 U.S. 476, 484 (1957)). These words were the centerpiece of the Court's decision to protect unlimited political spending in *Buckley v. Valeo*—but they originated in judicial protection of a newspaper that had served as a vehicle for criticism of public officials on the inflammatory issue of civil rights. See Kalven, supra note 155, at 192 (noting that the case is a major instance of the important constitutional consequences of the civil rights movement).

157. Brennan, The Supreme Court and the Meiklejohn Interpretation of the First Amendment, *Harv. L. Rev.* (1965), 79:1, 10, 14–15, 18; see Kalven, supra note 155, at 209, 221.

158. A. Meiklejohn, supra note 102.

159. Id. at xiii; see id. at x–xi, 46, 93.

160. In *Police Department v. Mosley,* 408 U.S. 92, 95–96 (1972), the Court stressed, "above all else, the First Amendment means that government has no power to restrict expression because of its message, its ideas, its subject matter, or its content . . . The essence of this forbidden censorship is content control."

161. See Brennan, supra note 157, at 9–10.

162. See A. Meiklejohn, supra note 102, at 61–70 (criticizing Chafee's first amendment theories).

163. See E. Cahn, The Firstness of the First Amendment, *in Confronting Injustice* (1962), 86.

164. See Wright, Professor Bickel, The Scholarly Tradition, and the Supreme Court, *Harv. L. Rev.* (1971), 84:769, 786 ("[P]articular fact situations influence the course of the law. If an unanticipated fact situation forces a modification of previously articulated goals and rules, then so be it. But the general thrust of constitutional adjudication should remain firmly grounded in the ideals of the constitutional text."). Cf. Brest, The Misconceived Quest for the Original Understanding, *B.U.L. Rev.* (1980), 60:204, 228–29 (constitutional decisionmaking must respond to changes in social needs and values); Reich, Mr. Justice Black and the Living Constitution, *Harv. L. Rev.* (1963), 76:673, 736 ("A constitutional provision can maintain its integrity only by moving in the same direction and at the same rate as the rest of society. In constitutions, constancy requires change.").

165. Z. Chafee, *Free Speech in the United States,* supra note 151, at 31, 137–38; Chafee, Freedom of Speech in War time, supra note 151, at 956.

166. *Abrams v. United States,* 250 U.S. 616, 630 (1919) (Holmes, J., dissenting).

167. See, e.g., R. Posner, *Antitrust Law: An Economic Perspective* (1976), 8–18 (economic inefficiency of monopoly supports effective antitrust policy).

168. See Leventhal, supra note 3, at 373–74. Similarly, structural obstacles to free competition in the marketplace of ideas create the need for government-mandated rights of access to the broadcast media. As Jerome Barron has contended, the assumption that there is a self-sustaining free-market mechanism for ideas stems from "an essentially romantic view of the first amendment." Changes in the communications industry, Barron recognizes, have destroyed the equilibrium in the marketplace of ideas, making laissez-faire irrelevant and requiring active government intervention to assure access to the media

by speakers with varying viewpoints. Barron, Access to the Press—A New First Amendment Right, *Harv. L. Rev.* (1967), 80:1641, 1647–48, 1653–56.

169. Black, The Bill of Rights, N.Y.U.L. Rev. (1960), 35:865, 881 ("Our First Amendment was a bold effort . . . to establish a country with no legal restrictions of any kind upon the subjects people could investigate, discuss, and deny."); cf. id. at 880 (other provisions of Bill of Rights buttress first amendment by protecting "the weak and the oppressed from punishment by the strong and the powerful who wanted to stifle the voices of discontent raised in protest against oppression and injustice in public affairs"). Black also relied on a slippery-slope analysis that resembled Emerson's. See Cahn, Justice Black and First Amendment "Absolutes": A Public Interview, *N.Y.U.L. Rev.* (1962), 37:549, 559; Reich, supra note 164, at 719–20.

170. T. Emerson, supra note 144, at 10.

171. Emerson wrote, "[I]t is necessary to recognize the powerful forces that impel men towards the elimination of unorthodox expression. Most men have a strong inclination, for rational or irrational reasons, to suppress opposition." T. Emerson, supra note 144, at 9; see id. at 9–11; Emerson, Toward a General Theory of the First Amendment, *Yale L.J.* (1963), 72:877, 887–93.

172. See T. Emerson, supra note 144, at 6,21; Cahn, supra note 169, at 554 (Black's view that, to "preserve a dictatorship, you must be able to stifle thought, imprison the human mind and intellect"); cf. Black, supra note 169, at 880 ("Our own free system to live and progress has to have intelligent citizens who cannot only think and speak and write to influence people, but citizens who are free to do that without fear of governmental censorship or reprisal."). Both men agree, however, that actions were properly subject to government control. See T. Emerson, supra note 144, at 17; Cahn, supra note 169, at 558.

173. See supra text accompanying notes 99–137.

174. 274 U.S. 357, 375 (1927) (Brandeis, J., concurring); see Rabban, supra note 150, at 592–93 (discussing influences on Brandeis's thought); id. at 578–79 (views of prewar scholars Ernst Freund, Thomas Cooley, and Theodore Schroeder that libertarian standards for speech reduced danger of violence and crime); cf. T. Emerson, supra note 144, at 7 (freedom of expression is a method of achieving a more adaptable and hence more stable community). But see Bork, supra note 144, at 25 (safety-valve function involves solely issues of expediency or prudence, not of constitutional magnitude).

175. 274 U.S. at 375.

176. Cf. Barron, supra note 168, at 1649 ("If freedom of expression cannot be secured because entry into the communication media is not free but is confined as a matter of discretion by a few private hands, the sense of the justice of existing institutions, which freedom of expression is designed to assure, vanishes from some section of our population . . . ").

177. Mason, Louis D. Brandeis, in L. Friedman and F. Israel eds., *The Justices of the United States Supreme Court 1789–1969* (1969), 3:2043, 2044–45.

178. Several commentators have recognized that a clash of first amendment values is involved in campaign finance cases. See, e.g., Emerson, supra note 171, at 948 ("not the reconciliation of freedom of expression with another kind of interest but the reconciliation of opposing interests within the system of free expression itself"); Freund, supra note 59, at 72; Leventhal, supra note 3, at 372.

179. A. Meiklejohn, supra note 102; cf. Bork, supra note 144, at 23, 26 (political speech is only type of expression protected by the first amendment). I do not agree with Bork's narrow view of the scope of the constitutional protection of freedom of expression, but I agree with him and with Meiklejohn that self-government and free speech are inextricably interrelated.

180. A. Meiklejohn, supra note 102, at 19. As Meiklejohn noted, "The First Amendment . . . is not the guardian of unregulated talkativeness." Id. at 25; see J. Rawls, supra note 100, at 203; Meiklejohn, supra note 102, at 252, 261.

181. A. Meiklejohn, supra note 102, at 22–27. But see Karst, Equality as a Central Principle in the First Amendment, *U. Chi. L. Rev.* (1975), 43:20, 39–40 (criticizing town meeting analogy).

182. A. Meiklejohn, supra note 102, at 23.

183. Id. at 24–26, 65.

184. See L. Emerson, supra note 144, at 639–40 (contrasting limits on election campaigns, which may be permissible because they "are directed to a limited end and deal with a limited situation," and limitations on expression in other contexts, which are forbidden); Chevigny, supra note 55, at 219 ("election campaign is not an unlimited field of debate"; "the fact that a reply is theoretically possible after the election or outside the campaign is of little importance"). In contrast, in the area of general political discussion unrelated to campaigns, Brandeis's prescription holds good: "If there be time to expose through discussion the falsehood and fallacies, to avert the evil by the processes of education, the remedy to be applied is more speech, not enforced silence." *Whitney v. California*, 274 U.S. 357, 377 (1927) (Brandeis, J., concurring).

185. 336 U.S. 77 (1949).

186. Id.; cf. Freund, supra note 59, at 72 ("We are dealing here not so much with the right of personal expression or even association, but with dollars and decibels. And just as the volume of sound may be limited by law, so the volume of dollars may be limited, without violating the First Amendment.").

187. 395 U.S. (1969).

188. Id. at 390. Justice White added: "It is the purpose of the First Amendment to preserve an uninhibited marketplace of ideas in which truth will ultimately prevail, rather than to countenance monopolization of that market, whether if be by the Government itself or a private licensee. . . . It is the right of the public to receive suitable access to social, political, esthetic, moral, and other ideas and experiences which is crucial here." Id. The opinion essentially adopts Meiklejohn's view of the first amendment.

The Court has reaffirmed the general principle stated in *Red Lion* in subsequent cases. See *CBS v. FCC*, 453 U.S. 367, 395 (1981); *CBS v. Democratic Nat'l Comm.*, 412 U.S. 94, 101–02 (1973).

189. See Brief for Appellees Center for Public Financing of Elections, Common Cause, League of Women Voters of the United States, et al. 65–74, 81–88, *Buckley v. Valeo*, 424 U.S. 1 (1976); Leventhal, supra note 3, at 361–62, 367–72.

190. Justice White observed in his *Buckley* dissent that "[t]he ceiling on campaign expenditures represents the considered judgment of Congress that elections are to be decided among candidates none of whom has overpowering advantage by reason of a huge campaign war chest." 424 U.S. at 265 (White, J., dissenting).

191. In *Buckley*, the Court wrote, "In the free society ordained by our Constitution it is not the government, but the people—individually as citizens and candidates and collectively as associations and political committees—who must retain control over the quantity and range of debate on public issues in a political campaign." 424 U.S. at 57. In *Bellotti*, the Court declared, "[T]he people in our democracy are entrusted with the responsibility for judging and evaluating the relative merits of conflicting arguments." 435 U.S. at 791. The Court was apparently oblivious to the fact that the citizens, acting collectively through their elected representatives, had adopted the challenged legislation in order to protect their rights as listeners. Cf. Leventhal, supra note 3, at 368.

192. *Buckley*, 424 U.S. at 49–50 n.55.

193. See A. Meiklejohn, supra note 102, at 24–25 (comparing first amendment pro-

tection of speech by all citizens with speech or debate clause immunity for speech by legislators).

194. 435 U.S. at 809 (White, J., dissenting); see Brudney, Business Corporations and Stockholders' Rights Under the First Amendment, *Yale L.J.* (1982), 91:235, 237–38, 240–41 (discussing political influence of corporate wealth and nature of corporate entities); Note, supra note 137, at 1853–60 (arguing that *Bellotti's* emphasis on formal equality and its protection of corporate power reflect the spirit of pre-1937 economic due process jurisprudence and contending that corporate speech rights do little if anything to serve genuine speech interests).

195. Cox, Foreword: Freedom of Expression in the Burger Court, *Harv. L. Rev.* (1980), 94:1, 70.

196. Karst, supra note 181.

197. Id. at 23.

198. T. Emerson, supra note 144, at 627–30. Emerson notes that "[s]earch for the truth is handicapped because much of the argument is never heard or heard only weakly. Political decisions are distorted because the views of some citizens never reach other citizens, and feedback to the government is feeble." Under these circumstances, he urges, "it becomes essential, if the system [of freedom of expression] is to survive, that a search be made for ways to use the law and legal institutions in an affirmative program to restore the system to effective working order." Id. at 628–29.

See Z. Chafee, *Free Speech in the United States,* supra note 151, at 559–60; A. Meiklejohn, supra note 102, at 16–17, 104 (freedom of speech must not be given merely a negative meaning); Barron, supra note 168, at 1641 (marketplace of ideas is not self-operating); id. at 1654–56 ("Creating opportunities for expression is as important as ensuring the right to express ideas without fear of governmental reprisal.").

199. In the fall of 1979, the House of Representatives passed the Obey-Railsback bill, which would have lowered the permissible PAC contribution to a House candidate during an election cycle from $10,000 to $6,000 and would have created a $70,000 ceiling on the aggregate contributions from all PACs to a House candidate. A filibuster threat blocked the bill in the Senate. See Alexander, The Obey-Railsback Bill: Its Genesis and Early History, *Ariz. L. Rev.* (1980), 22:653, 663–65; Railsback, Congressional Responses to Obey-Railsback, *Ariz. L. Rev.* (1980), 22:667; Kenski, supra note 38.

200. See supra note 34, In *Bellotti* the Court was careful to distinguish the prohibition on referendum spending by corporations, which it was invalidating, from the Corrupt Practices Act's ban on corporate spending in candidate campaigns, which it did not reach. "The overriding concern behind the enactment of statutes such as the Federal Corrupt Practices Act was the problem of corruption of elected representatives through the creation of political debts. . . . The importance of the governmental interest in preventing this occurrence has never been doubted. The case before us presents no comparable problem, and our consideration of a corporation's right to speak on issues of general public interest implies no comparable right in the quite different context of participation in a political campaign for election to public office." 435 U.S. at 788 n.26.

201. See F. Wertheimer and R. Huwa, supra note 31, at 11; Chevigny, supra note 55, at 221–22 (discussing advantages and disadvantages of various public financing schemes).

The Court has held that the public must bear the cost of administering primary elections; the same policies support public funding of campaigns. "Viewing the myriad governmental functions supported from general revenues," the Court stated, "it is difficult to single out any of a higher order than the conduct of elections at all levels to bring forth those persons desired by their fellow citizens to govern." *Bullock v. Carter,* 405 U.S. 134, 148–49 (1972).

202. *Buckley*, 424 U.S. at 57 n.65 (candidate may voluntarily refuse public funding and therefore avoid subjection to spending limits); *Republican Nat'l Comm. v. FEC*, 487 F. Supp. 288 (S.D.N.Y.) (three-judge district court), aff'd mem. 455 U.S. 955 (1980) (rejecting first amendment challenge to spending limits upon presidential candidate who accepts public funds).

203. See A. Rosenthal, supra note 59, at 62; F. Wertheimer and R. Huwa, supra note 71, at 29–32 (discussing proposed reduction in maximum unit cost for political campaign ads on television).

204. See L. Sabato, supra note 75, at 327 (discussing British system of free television broadcasts on all channels for political parties during election campaigns); F. Wertheimer and R. Huwa, supra note 71, at 22–24 (discussing proposal to require television licensees to supply free time to qualifying candidates). Dean Rosenthal has concluded that such requirements would be constitutional; Congress's power to ensure that licensees used their facilities in the public interest would "undoubtedly be sufficiently broad to sustain the provision." A. Rosenthal, supra note 59, at 62–63; Rosenthal, supra note 126, at 422.

205. See Mastro, Costlow, and Sanchez, supra note 86, at 327–49 (Media Access Project's proposals for strengthening Fairness Doctrine in referendum campaigns).

The Fairness Doctrine is currently under attack by some members of the FCC. See *Broadcasting*, Nov. 2, 1981, at 36. But its repeal would eviscerate the reality, limited as it now is, of "robust, uninhibited, wide-open" debate. See Barron, supra note 168.

206. 424 U.S. at 39–59.

207. 435 U.S. at 765.

208. See, e.g., *Wickard v. Filburn*, 317 U.S. 111 (1942) (recognizing broad scope of commerce clause); *United States v. Darby*, 312 U.S. 100 (1941) (upholding Fair Labor Standards Act); *Steward Machine Co. v. Davis*, 301 U.S. 548 (1937) (upholding Social Security Act); *NLRB v. Jones & Laughlin Steel Corp.*, 301 U.S. 1 (1937) (upholding National Labor Relations Act.).

209. *Brown v. Board of Educ.*, 347 U.S. 483 (1954), overruling *Plessy v. Ferguson*, 163 U.S. 537 (1896).

210. 519 F.2d 821, 897 (D.C. Cir. 1975), rev'd in part, 424 U.S. 1 (1976).

2

NEW TORK TIMES v. SULLIVAN RECONSIDERED: TIME TO RETURN TO "THE CENTRAL MEANING OF THE FIRST AMENDMENT"

Anthony Lewis

Twenty years ago a professor at this law school brought to the Supreme Court of the United States a case that became a landmark of our constitutional freedom. In *New York Times v. Sullivan*[1] the Court held for the first time that an award of damages for libel violated the freedoms of speech and press guaranteed by the first amendment. The decision had from the first the ring of a great occasion in the law, sensed not only in the result but in the bold sweep of the Court's opinion, by Justice Brennan. And the occasion was in large part shaped by Professor Herbert Wechsler. It takes nothing from Justice Brennan to recognize, as anyone who looks into it must, that his transforming analysis of what that libel judgment meant for freedom of expression was based on the brief and argument of Professor Wechsler.[2]

This is an appropriate time to think again about that great case. It is a time of growing libel litigation, of enormous judgments and enormous costs. The press and its lawyers are deeply worried; the protection that they thought was won for free expression in *New York Times v. Sullivan* seems to them to be crumbling. Some would say that libel actions are a more serious threat than ever. Now the American press is addicted to self-pity. Although it is the freest in the world, and freer now than it ever has been, it often cries that doom is at hand.[3] But this time even someone as skeptical of press claims as I am must admit that there is something to the concern.

I propose to begin at the beginning: with the *Sullivan* case. For some, that will mean a restatement of the familiar. But I do not apologize for that. A landmark such as *Sullivan* becomes a set of symbols. What brought it to life originally dims in our perception. At least that is true for me. So let me remind you how it was when Herbert Wechsler filed his petition for a writ of certiorari on November 21, 1962.

The *New York Times* had carried an advertisement under the heading "Heed Their Rising Voices."[4] It was what would be called message advertising: an exhortation on behalf of the civil rights movement in the South and especially of its leading figure, Dr. Martin Luther King, Jr., then a minister in Montgomery, Alabama. It said that "Southern violators" had hounded Dr. King, arrested him seven times, persecuted black students after they stood on the steps of the State Capitol in Montgomery and sang "My Country, 'Tis of Thee." Mr. Sullivan was an elected commissioner of Montgomery, in general charge of the police; although he was not named in the advertisement—no one was criticized by name—he claimed that it reflected on him. He also showed that there were factual mistakes in the text: Dr. King had been arrested only four times, for example, not seven; the students on the Capitol steps had sung, not "My Country, 'Tis of Thee," but the National Anthem, and the students dining hall had never been padlocked, as the advertisement said, "in an attempt to starve them into submission."[5] Mr. Sullivan sued for $500,000, an Alabama jury awarded him that amount, and the state supreme court affirmed.[6] Other Montgomery officials and the Governor of Alabama had also sued over the advertisement, asking for another $2.5 million, and there was every reason to think that they would get all they sought.[7] That was where things stood when review was sought in the United States Supreme Court.

Seen from twenty years later, the case may look easy. A state libel rule that allows an official to recover large damages for trivial errors of fact in a publication that does not mention his name seems grotesque. But the *New York Times* was far from confident of victory in 1962. The very existence of any question for the Supreme Court to review was in doubt: any question, that is, of federal constitutional law. The Court had gone for 170 years without finding in the first amendment any limits on libel judgments, however tenuous their logical bases or outlandish the amount of damages awarded.[8] Moreover, local lawyers had been held to have inadvertently given away what the *Times* then thought might be its only good defense, objection to the in personam jurisdiction of the Alabama courts over it, waiving that objection when they raised it by making what was held to be a general appearance.[9] Were *Times* executives worried? A former vice president and general counsel of the paper said recently of the jury verdicts in the *Sullivan* case and other libel cases of that time in Alabama: "Without a reversal of these verdicts, there was a reasonable question of whether the *Times*, then wracked by strikes and small profits, would survive."[10]

What was at stake on the facts of the *Sullivan* case was more than the fate of one newspaper. It was the ability, or the willingness, of the American press to go on covering the racial conflict in the South as it had been doing. Those were very different times in Alabama and Mississippi and large parts of other states in the Deep South: Blacks could not vote, much less attend school or eat a restaurant meal or ride a bus on a nonracial basis.[11] To challenge the racial system was dangerous; physical violence and threats were common. The national press, print and broadcast, played an extremely important part in bringing all this to the attention of the rest of the country, in arousing the federal government to corrective action and hence in changing the ways of the South.[12] Of course those who wished to preserve what was then called "the Southern way of life" did not like the press when it intruded into that life. Justice Black, who was from Alabama, observed in his concurring opinion in the *Sullivan* case that white Southern feelings were especially hostile "to so-called 'outside agitators' "—a term, Justice Black dryly added, that "can be made to fit papers like the *Times,* which is published in New York."[13]

In short, the libel suit brought by Commissioner Sullivan was a weapon in a political struggle. And it was in those terms that Professor Wechsler analyzed the case when he briefed and argued it in the Supreme Court. Calling something libel, he said, gives it no automatic insulation from the Constitution; like expression given such provocative labels as contempt, breach of the peace, and obscenity, libel "must be defined and judged in terms that satisfy the First Amendment."[14] And whatever else the amendment does, it protects *political* expression: the right of Americans to write and speak as they will about politics and public affairs.[15] Such expression does not lose its immunity because it "diminishes the reputation of the officers whose conduct it deplores"; like judges, they must be " 'men of fortitude, able to thrive in a hardy climate.' "[16] Nor is the freedom limited "by any test of truth, to be administered by juries, courts, or by executive officials, not to speak of a test which puts the burden of establishing the truth upon the writer."[17] Professor Wechsler quoted Justice Roberts's opinion in *Cantwell v. Connecticut,*[18] reversing the conviction of a Jehovah's Witness who went through a Catholic neighborhood preaching the iniquity of the Catholic Church. Our Constitution, Roberts said, allows us to resort to "exaggeration, to vilification of men who have been, or are, prominent in church or state, and even to false statement."[19]

Then came what I think was the heart of the Wechsler brief. If criticism of official conduct may not be repressed,

> upon the ground that it is false or that it tends to harm official reputation, the inadequacy of these separate grounds is not surmounted by their combination. This was the basic lesson of the great assault on the short-lived Sedition Act of 1798, which first crystallized a national awareness of the central meaning of the First Amendments.[20]

What he was saying was that this was really akin to a case of seditious libel—of punishment for agitating against authority. And for reasons deep in English and American history, that is a concept particularly suspect under the first amendment. The Sedition Act of 1798 made it a crime to defame the President, Congress, or the federal government as a whole: to bring them "into contempt or disrepute."[21] The act made truth a defense, a liberalizing change from the English law of seditious libel, and provided that juries should decide both facts and law. But despite those reformist features, the law was denounced by the Jeffersonians as a violation of the first amendment—and the criticism carried the day. The act was allowed to expire after two years, and Congress repaid the fines of those convicted under it. "[T]he verdict of history," Professor Wechsler said, had found it unconstitutional.[22]

Justice Brennan made the seditious libel analysis the crux of his opinion. "If neither factual error nor defamatory content" removes the constitutional shield from political expression, he said, no more do the two in combination.[23] "This is the lesson to be drawn from the great controversy over the Sedition Act of 1798, . . . which first crystallized a national awareness of the central meaning of the First Amendment."[24] The attack on the Act's constitutionality, Justice Brennan said, had "carried the day in the court history."[25]

That was the reasoning in *New York Times v. Sullivan.* I think it remains as persuasive today, and as elegant, as it was then. If there are doubts in the light of experience, they relate, not to the Court's analysis of the threat that libel actions pose to first amendment freedoms, but to the remedy adopted: the formula laid down by the Court to protect constitutional values in libel cases.

In suggesting remedies in his brief, Professor Wechsler had argued first that criticism of official conduct should be absolutely protected: not subject to penalty at all. Using the language of the clear-and-present-danger test, he said that a threat to official reputation was not a " 'substantive evil' that a State has the power to prevent by the suppression of the critical expression."[26] Nor was concern for official reputation a governmental interest of the kind that requires balancing against protected freedoms.[27] Under questioning at the oral argument, Professor Wechsler made clear that this reasoning would bar any libel action by an official over a critical comment, however false and personal it was. If a citizen falsely and maliciously charged a mayor with taking a bribe, for example, a public reply by the mayor would be his only "avenue of retaliation."[28]

But Professor Wechsler also offered, in the alternative, rules that would leave some room for protection of official reputation but limit the harm to freedom of expression. One possibility, he said, was to require proof of special damages by an official who complained of defamation—that is, to limit recovery to the amount of actual, proved financial injury.[29] Another was to make "the aggrieved official prove the critic's malice" by showing that he had made "an accusation known to be unfounded."[30] A number of states had adopted this requirement of "actual malice," the brief said, and scholarly opinion favored it.[31]

Justice Brennan chose the last of those options. He said:

> The constitutional guarantees require, we think, a federal rule that prohibits a public official from recovering damages for a defamatory falsehood relating to his official conduct unless he proves that the statement was made with "actual malice"—that is, with knowledge that it was false or with reckless disregard of whether it was false or not.[32]

That is the rule of *New York Times v. Sullivan*. It is what most of us remember from that great case.

Three members of the Court—Justices Black, Douglas, and Goldberg—were not satisfied with that result. They would have prohibited any libel suit directed at criticism of official conduct: Professor Wechsler's first alternative.[33] The first amendment, Justice Black said, provided "absolute immunity for criticism of the way public officials do their public duty."[34] He predicted that the majority's requirement of proof of actual malice would prove to be "an evanescent protection" for freedom of criticism.[35] Judges and juries would get around it, he said: "This record certainly does not indicate that any different verdict would have been rendered here whatever the Court had charged the jury about 'malice,' 'truth,' 'good motives,' 'justifiable ends,' or any other legal formulas. . . ."[36] No doubt in answer to that warning, Justice Brennan took an extraordinary step to make sure that the Alabama courts would not find some new way to punish the *Times* when the case went back down to them. He reexamined the facts and found that they could not support a finding of actual malice.[37]

The decision in *New York Times v. Sullivan* had an immediate and large impact on the law. For years there were virtually no recoveries by public officials in libel actions. The Supreme Court extended the rule to criminal libel[38] and then to public figures, as well as officials.[39] Alexander Meiklejohn, who for so many years had argued that the first amendment must assure absolute freedom for political speech, said the decision was "an occasion for dancing in the streets."[40]

But I need hardly say that publishers are not dancing in the streets today. In July of 1982 a jury in Washington, D.C., awarded more than $2 million to the president of the Mobil Oil Corporation, William Tavoulareas, for a *Washington Post* story stating that he had "set up his son" in a shipping management firm that did business with Mobil.[41] Carol Burnett, the actress, won $1.6 million from the *National Enquirer*.[42] A former Miss Wyoming won $26.5 million from *Penthouse* magazine, reduced by the trial judge to

$14 million, but the entire award was set aside on appeal.[43] Newspapers in San Francisco and Oklahoma City and Alton, Illinois, have faced judgments in the millions.[44]

And it is not just judgments that worry publishers and reporters and others concerned with freedom of expression. It is the cost of defending libel actions: the cost not only in money but also in time and in the psychological burden on editors and reporters. To try to convey what may be involved nowadays in a libel action, I thought I might chronicle the future of a case just launched, one that promises to be a grand example. That is the case of *Westmoreland v. CBS.*

Westmoreland is General William Westmoreland, the American commander in Vietnam. On January 23, 1982, CBS broadcast a ninety-minute documentary that charged him and others with "a conspiracy, at the highest levels of American military intelligence, to suppress and alter critical intelligence on the enemy" in the year leading up to the Tet Offensive of 1968.[45] The intelligence involved was estimates of the number of North Vietnamese infiltrating into South Vietnam. The program, called "The Uncounted Enemy: A Vietnam Deception," produced as witnesses several former military officers and intelligence analysts who said the command, in reporting to Washington, had deliberately understated the infiltration figures it had.[46] General Westmoreland criticized the program as unfair.[47] Then, in May, the magazine *TV Guide* attacked it in a long article entitled "Anatomy of a Smear." CBS had violated its own rules, the article said, by using a paid consultant as a witness and rehearsing him before he was interviewed on camera, and by treating witnesses who supported the conspiracy theory gently while grilling others.[48] CBS then conducted an internal investigation, producing a sixty-one-page report that was not made public; CBS said the inquiry found that there had been mistakes, but it stood by the documentary's conclusions.[49] CBS announced that it would do a follow-up broadcast giving General Westmoreland and other critics an opportunity to air their views. It offered the General fifteen minutes of unedited air time. But he rejected that idea, saying it would serve only "to dignify a lie."[50] On September 13 he sued for libel, asking $120 million in compensatory and punitive damages.[51]

The first thing that is going to happen in the *Westmoreland* case is discovery: intensive, prolonged, enormous discovery. The General's lawyers will try to learn everything about the preparation and editing of the documentary. They will ask for all the film shot in the making of the program, of which of course only a small portion went on the air; it is routine for commercial networks to spend hours on a filmed interview for such a documentary, for example, and then use only minutes or even seconds. The lawyers will ask for scripts from all stages of the enterprise and for internal memoranda among reporters, editors, and producers. The effort will be to show what General Westmoreland and his friends have already charged: that CBS had material in hand disproving its conspiracy theory about the infiltration figures but deliberately chose not to use it—in other words, that CBS could and should have made a different program. The lawyers will surely ask for the report of the CBS internal investigation. They will depose the producers and reporters. They will depose the witnesses who made the charges on the program, asking them for their sources.

CBS's lawyers will be at least as ingenious and determined. They will turn to all imaginable public and private sources to explore the accuracy of what the program said—and of what General Westmoreland says it said. They will depose the General, taking him in infinite detail over the conduct of the war in Vietnam. They will depose men who were with him there, army officers and CIA agents and diplomats, and they will depose high Washington officials of that time: everyone involved in the estimates of enemy strength, from the field to the White House. They will no doubt also look into the *TV Guide* article that may have provoked the libel suit. The article relied on confidential sources inside CBS, who leaked unedited transcripts of the full interviews from which editors put the program together. Who were those sources?

The prospect of discovery in the *Westmoreland* case is so endless that a cynic might suspect a conspiracy by lawyers. And the irony is that discovery has become as massive as it has in libel cases in large part because of *New York Times v. Sullivan.* So we learned when the Supreme Court dealt with the discovery problem in the case of *Herbert v. Lando.*[52] It arose from another CBS documentary, this one scouting the claims of Colonel Anthony Herbert that he had tried to report massacres in Vietnam and had been punished for doing so. CBS resisted discovery of the kind I have predicted in *Westmoreland:* requests for unedited film, questions about why this footage was used instead of that. Such questions, CBS argued, cut deeply into the editorial process and compromised its independence: Editors would do their work with an eye to possible legal second-guessing later, and there would be self-censorship of the very kind that *New York Times v. Sullivan* was supposed to prevent. But a privilege not to answer those questions would effectively turn the *Sullivan* rule into a virtually insurmountable barrier for plaintiffs: They would have to prove what the publisher knew when he published—was he aware of probable falsehood?—but would not be able to find out from those who knew by asking them and looking at their notes and drafts. That is what the Supreme Court said in rejecting the claim of privilege. In the old days, Justice White said, before *Sullivan,* when the only issues in a libel case were really publication and truth, most of the questions about the editing process would have been irrelevant, but now they got at essential elements of what the plaintiff must prove.[53]

Notwithstanding the *Lando* decision, there will undoubtedly be claims of privilege in the *Westmoreland* case—by both sides. Former officials may well assert a claim of state secrets or intelligence privilege. A demand for the report of CBS's internal investigation could raise the lawyer-client privilege. Any attempt to get at confidential sources would renew the old claim of a first amendment right to keep them secret.[54] Each of these attempts to avoid discovery will no doubt be litigated. If the trial judge overrules a claim of privilege and orders the party to produce documents or answer questions, or for that matter if he rules the other way, his decision may be appealed. That happened in the *Lando* case, which went all the way to the Supreme Court in the middle of the discovery process.[55]

How long will discovery take in *Westmoreland,* and how much will it cost? We cannot know, but we have some depressing clues from the *Lando* case. Mr. Lando was the producer of that CBS documentary; he was deposed on and off over more than a year, at twenty-eight lengthy sessions generating almost 3000 pages of transcript and 240 exhibits.[56] The last two sessions, after the Supreme Court decision, were devoted exclusively to Lando's thought processes and editorial judgments as he made the program;[57] in others he was taken over volumes of his handwritten notes. Also produced by CBS were videotapes and transcripts of all interviews done for the program,[58] notes of interviews conducted with 130 people, all of Lando's files, all documents in CBS's files from the relevant period relating to Colonel Herbert, whether or not Lando and the others connected with the program ever saw them, and transcripts and tapes of all of Herbert's radio and television appearances from 1971 to 1981.[59] At the request of CBS's lawyers, Colonel Herbert produced more than 12,000 pages of documents, including the Army's material on its investigation of Herbert's charges. Defense counsel deposed Herbert at length, as well as his literary agent and his ghostwriter.[60]

The lawyers will not say how much all that discovery has cost. But Mike Wallace on CBS, who is a defendant in both the *Lando* and the *Westmoreland* cases, was quoted in mid-1982 as estimating that CBS had so far spent between $3 and $4 million for legal fees in *Lando.*[61] The good news is this: On September 24, 1982, the defendants filed motions for summary judgment in the *Lando* case. Discovery had ended—eight years after the suit was filed.

What has happened in Colonel Herbert's lawsuit, and almost certainly will in General Westmoreland's, illustrates how the pretrial phase of a major libel action works today under the regime of *New York Times v. Sullivan.* Another case gives us a remarkable insight into the trial itself. That is Mr. Tavoulareas's lawsuit against the *Washington Post.*[62] The trial took more than three weeks. The executive editor of the paper, Benjamin Bradlee, was there all day every day, as were one of his deputies, Bob Woodward, and the reporter who wrote the story, Patrick Tyler. Testimony showed that the *Post* had devoted exceptional care to the piece about Mr. Tavoulareas and his son, checking and rechecking it.[63] The plaintiff was able to point to only a few mistakes in the story—modest errors, and in my opinion none reflecting negligence on the part of the editors, much less knowing or reckless falsification. Yet the jury, after three days of deliberation, brought in a verdict of $250,000 for William Tavoulareas in compensatory damages. And after a further brief hearing it went out again and awarded him $1,800,000 in punitive damages. What happened?

Unusually, we know a good deal about what went on in the jury room. For an article on the Tavoulareas case the editor of the *American Lawyer*, Steven Brill, interviewed five of the six jurors, and his piece presented a detailed and convincing picture of their deliberations.[64] The key figure was the foreman, a twenty-seven-year-old reference librarian in the Library of Congress law library, Geoffrey Mott, who Brill says was ardently interested in the law and was to enter law school shortly after the trial. When the jurors took a first vote, it was four to two in favor of the *Post* on all counts. Mott was one of the two in the minority. He said he agreed with the majority that Tavoulareas had in fact "set up" his son in business. "But the article has to prove it," he said. "And it doesn't."[65] Mott stuck rigidly to that line through all the deliberations: that under the law, the *Post* had the burden of proving that the story supported its headline. The trial judge, Federal District Judge Oliver Gasch, had found Tavoulareas to be a public figure and told the jury, in the middle of a long charge, that the plaintiff must prove knowing or reckless falsehood to win the case. But nothing was said about any of that in the jury room. The issue, as framed by foreman Mott, was whether the story proved its charge against Tavoulareas. Mott made much of an internal *Post* memorandum, produced in discovery, which questioned the value and persuasivenes of the story as first drafted by Tyler. He also dwelt on testimony showing that Tyler had used as a source a vindictive former son-in-law of Tavoulareas's and had had some help from a gung-ho freelance writer who kept notes of a crack by Tyler about how rare it would be to "knock off one of the Seven Sisters"—testimony that might show ill will but not "actual malice" within the *Sullivan* definition. Brill quotes a juror as saying: "[N]one of us thought big Tavoulareas had *not* set up his son. It's just we couldn't prove it." Brill asked that juror: What if you had just been asked to decide whether the *Post* had been recklessly or deliberately inaccurate or unfair? He answered: "Oh, in that case, there's no way the plaintiff would have won. We all, even Mott, I think, conceded they hadn't done anything careless or on purpose."[66]

The leaked secrets of the jury room are not admissable evidence on appeal. But they give us dramatic evidence in support of a conclusion that libel lawyers had already reached: When a case goes to a jury, the *Sullivan* rule means little or nothing. All those phrases designed by the Supreme Court to protect freedom of speech and press may not in fact be applied. When a judge's charge lasts an hour or more, and one sentence speaks of the need to find "reckless disregard," it rolls right past the jury—it would roll past any of us. In the real world, too, jurors are part of a public that is not very fond these days of the institutions that are usually libel defendants: big newspapers and magazines and broadcasters. They think those media giants can afford hefty damages and might as well pay. In the brief hearing that Judge Gasch held after the return of the $250,000 compensatory judgment for Tavoulareas, the jury heard testimony about the healthy profits of the Washington Post Company, and Tavoulareas testified that he had spent $1.8 million on lawyers' fees in this case. The jury took a few minutes to fix punitive damages at $1.8 million.[67]

It is not just the Tavoulareas case that informs us about juries in libel cases. A study just carried out by the Libel Defense Resource Center[68] analyzes cases decided by judges on motions for summary judgment: most commonly, motions by libel defendants claiming that plaintiffs could not meet the constitutional standard. Defendants prevailed in 75 percent of those summary judgment decisions. But of forty-seven cases that went to a jury, the plaintiffs won 89 percent. If judges usually decide on summary judgment the cases in which plaintiffs' evidence is weakest, it is not surprising that plaintiffs do better in the remaining cases—those that go on to a jury. But the staggering difference in the figures must also in part reflect who made the decision: judge or jury.

Now recall the concern that moved the Supreme Court to its decision in *New York Times v. Sullivan.* Justice Brennan said the old common law rule, the Alabama rule, making the critic of official conduct guarantee the truth of his factual assertions, was unconstitutional because it led to self-censorship. Would-be critics, he said, "may be deterred from voicing their criticism, even though it is believed to be true and even though it is in fact true, because of doubt whether it can be proved in court or fear of the expense of having to do so."[69] But the *Sullivan* rule, as it is in fact working today, may have precisely that effect: It may discourage the voicing of criticism that is believed to be true and may indeed be true.

Any sensible publisher of comment on official conduct must worry today about the legal process and its expense. If there is a libel action, he knows there will be a massive discovery process. Apart from cost, his writers and editors may be tied up for months or years. Their editorial decisions will be re-examined, their thoughts probed. A good system of editorial checking may actually prove damaging, because internal criticism of an article or broadcast may become evidence of fault in publishing. The *Sullivan* rule remains a very useful defense before judges. But if the defendant cannot persuade a judge to dispose of the case on summary judgment, the rule may not make a difference to jurors. The jury will be free to award compensatory damages unrelated to actual financial loss, and punitive damages on any theory that strikes its fancy.

Freedom of expression is not the only value involved in libel cases: not for me, at any rate. There is also reputation, a characteristic close to the sense of self—to the integrity of one's personality. But is the libel action as it now works in the United States an effective remedy for a wounded reputation? I doubt it. The person who feels injured has to summon huge resources to wage the fight, and go through what may be an agonizing experience. Can General Westmoreland have any idea what it will be like to be questioned day after day in the discovery process, very likely week after week, about the course of the war in Vietnam? To be shown and asked about documents that were handled by some remote subordinate a dozen years ago or more? And then, if there is a trial, to go through it all again on the witness stand, having his judgment critically questioned in a war that, after all, was lost? It is not a process designed to burnish reputation.[70]

The question—by now the urgent question—is how the great promise of *New York Times v. Sullivan* can be redeemed. It is a question that the Supreme Court should be asking. And I think there are some practical steps that may commend themselves even to justices with no burning passion for freedom of speech and press.

A first essential is to recognize that damages awarded without effective limit in libel may violate the first amendment. Damages unconstitutional? The idea must at first seem startling. Like other traditional tort actions, libel is premised on the understanding that law may not be able to restore a wronged party to exactly the position he had before the wrong was done; instead he is to be compensated for the harm suffered. Even if libel litigation may not repair a wounded reputation, that is, it may salve the purse. But the Supreme Court has already suggested that, in doing so, unrestricted damages engage the guarantees of free expression. In *Gertz v. Robert Welch, Inc.*[71] in 1974 Justice Powell, writing for the Court, noted that common-law defamation was an oddity of tort law in presuming injury and allowing "recovery of purportedly compensatory damages without evidence of actual loss."[72] The doctrine was not just odd, he suggested, but constitutionally dubious. It allowed juries to "punish unpopular opinion" under the guise of compensating individuals for injury, and it compounded "the potential of any system of liability for defamatory falsehood to inhibit the vigorous exercise of First Amendment freedoms."[73] Moreover, he said, "the States have no substantial interest in securing for plaintiffs . . . gratuitous awards of money damages far in excess of any actual injury."[74] Accordingly, *Gertz* held that the first amendment limited private libel plaintiffs who do not meet the *Sullivan* test of knowing or reckless falsehood to "compensation for actual injury."[75] That was a first step—but a very modest one, because Justice Powell said that "actual injury" could include such intangibles as "mental anguish" and that there need be no evidence that "assigns an actual dollar value to the injury."[76]

It is time now to take the logical next step and limit compensatory damages, constitutionally, to just that: compensation for proved injury. Beyond perhaps a symbolic sum, the injury would have to be tangible and measured by evidence of financial loss, because allowing recovery for "mental anguish" or other unmeasurable harm would allow juries to speculate at large and in effect bring back presumed damages. Such a rule would not at all compromise the true interest in defamation actions that alone justifies restraints on expression: the interest of reputation. The vindication of one's good name does not require colossal damage verdicts. Indeed, in countries far less concerned with freedom of expression, and more sensitive to interests of reputation, damage awards on the scale of recent American libel verdicts are simply unknown. Britain, for example, is feared by American journalists for its tough libel rules, yet the largest libel judgment known to have been paid in Britain was for 100,000 pounds—about $150,000 at current rates.[77] The Supreme Court should adopt the first suggestion made by Professor Wechsler twenty years ago to accommodate the interests of reputation and freedom of expression: require proof of special damages in all libel cases.[78]

Punitive damages are an even more anomalous feature of common-law libel. As Justice Powell said in *Gertz*, they amount to "private fines levied by civil juries to punish reprehensible conduct and to deter its future occurrence."[79] Such punishment and deterrence are the business of the criminal law, with all the safeguards surrounding it—safeguards lacking when a jury imposes punitive damages on any theory that strikes its fancy. When the Supreme Court decided *Sullivan* it noted that the maximum fine for criminal libel in Alabama was $500: one-thousandth of what the jury awarded Mr. Sullivan. It is hard to imagine any state legislature today fixing a fine of $1.8 million for criminal libel, the amount imposed by the *Tavoulareas* jury to punish the *Washington Post.* No more can one imagine a legislature introducing for libel cases alone in this country the British rule that winning parties in civil cases have their legal fees paid by losers, as the Tavoulareas jury in effect required. Justice Powell recognized in *Gertz* that punitive damages are "wholly irrelevant" to the state interest in vindicating reputation and that jury discretion to award them "in wholly unpredictable amounts . . . unnecessarily exacerbates the danger of media self-censorship."[80] But as on compensatory damages, he shied away from the logic of ruling them out entirely. *Gertz* held that the states may not allow punitive damages "at least when liability is not based on a showing of knowledge of falsity or reckless disregard for the truth."[81] In short, if the actual malice standard is met, punitive damages may still be awarded.

The wiser rule was suggested in 1971 by Justice Marshall, dissenting in *Rosenbloom v. Metromedia, Inc.*[82] In a scholarly opinion, he said the Constitution barred punitive damages in all libel cases and limited compensatory damages to "proved, actual injuries."[83] That rule would largely eliminate press fears that lead to self-censorship, he said, yet at the same time it would respect "society's interest in protecting individuals from defamation."[84] Justice Powell's opinion for the Court in *Gertz* in fact relied on that earlier analysis of the damage problem. If it did not go all the way with Justice Marshall, that may be because Justice Powell preferred to test the question by further experience. His phrase "at least" in the holding[85] seems to leave open the possibility that punitive damages may in time be found too intimidating to free expression to be allowed at all. By now the evidence is surely in. Experience in the near-decade since *Gertz* has made dramatically clear the threat of punitive damages awarded on a jury's whim. Punitive damages have no place in the defamation law of a country with a first amendment.[86]

A second step to redeem the promise of the *Sullivan* case can be taken as a matter of judicial management rather than constitutional interpretation. That is for judges to play a fuller part in libel cases. Experience has shown that the protective benefits of the *Sullivan* rule may be mythical if juries are given unregulated discretion. Unless judges oversee the process rigorously, Justice Black will have been correct in his prediction that sophisticated legal theories would not protect the critics of official conduct.

There are a number of ways in which judges can be more active. One is to hold juries to the *Sullivan* test by special verdicts. That is, a jury would be required, in addition to returning a verdict in damages, to answer specific questions: Was the challenged statement false? Did the publisher know it was false when he published, or did he publish in reckless disregard of its truth? Such questions might well have exposed the faulty basis of jury deliberations reported in the *Tavoulareas* case.[87] Judges should also be prepared to review jury verdicts rigorously to see that they square with the *Sullivan* rule. Appellate courts already evidence a good deal a skepticism toward libel juries; reversals in such cases as that of Miss Wyoming[88] relieve some of the concern about megaverdicts. But trial judges on motions for directed verdicts or judgments notwithstanding jury verdict,[89] as well as appellate judges, should be prepared to scrutinize facts and law. After all, there is persuasive precedent: the Supreme Court's examination of the evidence in *Sullivan*.

The most important point for application of judicial control is on motions for summary judgment. A number of lower federal courts, concerned about the burden of libel actions on freedom of expression, had spoken of the need to resolve the cases on summary judgment if possible.[90] Then, in a much-discussed 1979 dictum, Chief Justice Burger expressed "some doubt" about what he called the view that summary judgment "might well be the rule rather than the exception" where the issue was the existence of knowing or reckless falsehood. Since the *Sullivan* standard called a defendant's state of mind into question, he said, it did "not readily lend itself to summary disposition."[91]

It is true that libel comes within the ordinary civil rules, which allow summary judgment to be granted only when there is no disputed material issue of fact.[92] But the Supreme Court could properly, and meaningfully, remind trial judges of the particular need to dispose of cases promptly when the very existence of prolonged litigation threatens first amendment values. Judges vary greatly in the rigor with which they press for early disposition of civil cases. And that can make a great difference in the practical burden of libel litigation, as a recent case shows.

In 1979 the *Washington Post*, in a story on the Philadelphia police, described an incident in which policemen had beaten a black man, "breaking nightsticks on his head and shoulders, after he had run a stop sign."[93] Three police officers sued for libel. They were not named in the story, but they had previously been charged with federal civil rights violations over that incident—and acquitted. On December 9, 1981, the trial judge denied a motion for summary judgment by the *Post.*[94] "It is clear," he wrote, "that the author of the offending article conducted a very thorough investigation. . . . It is also reasonably clear that the reporter was and is convinced that his account of the incident was accurate. . . ."[95] But the judge said that the plaintiffs might still be able to convince a jury that "the reporter was motivated by actual malice."[96] How could someone be "motivated" by "actual malice"? As used by Justice Brennan in *Sullivan,* the phrase was a term of art meaning knowledge of falsehood or reckless disregard of truth or falsity. The trial judge was evidently using the term, wrongly, in the dictionary sense of malice: meaning ill will. Accordingly the *Post* asked him to reconsider his decision. In a memorandum of June 15, 1982,[97] he denied the motion, saying: "To state that the reporter made a thorough investigation does not readily translate into an assertion that the reporter accurately incorporated the results of his investigation in his newspaper article, without bias or malice."[98]

The case went to trial on October 18, 1982. The next day, at the close of plaintiffs' evidence, the judge dismissed the case.[99] He said there could be "no doubt" that the reporters "thoroughly investigated" the incident. The plaintiffs themselves conceded, he said, that the writer of the *Post* article "sincerely believed, and still believes," that the alleged victim of police brutality "was mistreated"[100] He concluded: "From plaintiffs' own evidence, it is simply impossible to conclude that the article was written either with actual knowledge of its falsity, or with reckless disregard of the truth."[101]

By all appearances, the judge stopped the trial to do what he could just as well have done on the motion for summary judgment—and should have done. Of course it may be said that he wanted to give the plaintiffs a further chance to come up with evidence of actual malice, but the summary judgment procedure should not allow such wishful possibilities—especially not in libel cases. Nor can deference to jury fact-finding have been a decisive consideration, since the judge's ultimate decision indicated that he would have overruled a jury verdict for plaintiffs. And the delay was costly. Preparation for trial, including lawyers' time and bringing witnesses to Philadelphia, cost the *Post* around $170,000[102]—which would pay the salaries of five or six reporters for a year.[103] If judges do not face the issues on summary judgment in libel cases, the litigation burden grows, and with it the in terrorem effect on potential critics.

Limitation of damages and a more active judicial role would help restore reason to our libel law. But those steps would not really vindicate the philosophy of *New York Times v. Sullivan.* Remember what Justice Brennan said: that in the field of political speech the first amendment allows no test of truth to be administered by judges or juries. Justice Harlan put it beautifully in another case. "[I]n many areas which are at the center of public debate," he said, " 'truth' is not a readily identifiable concept, and putting to the pre-existing prejudices of a jury the determination of what is 'true' may effectively institute a system of censorship."[104]

The wisdom of those warnings against putting "truth" to a jury in political matters is perfectly demonstrated in the *Westmoreland* case. If it goes to trial, jurors will hear testimony from many witnesses about the "truth" of what General Westmoreland and others did in Vietnam—utterly conflicting testimony. Like Justice Harlan, I put "truth" in quotation marks because I do not believe there can be any such absolute in debates over Vietnam, even debates about ostensibly measurable things such as infiltration. There is a scene in a novel, *In the City of Fear,* by Ward Just, who was a reporter in Vietnam. The President of the United States is being briefed on Vietnam, and he begins to worry about the figures he gets. Are they cooked? he asks. One adviser replies, "Not *cooked* exactly. . . . All of the statistics are accurate, I'm sure." Another says: "That is the point about them. They are accurate, of course. Beautiful, in their way. And so numerous."[105]

In the Vietnam War a statistic could be true in a limited sense and false in another—in suggesting that what it measured pointed to a particular conclusion. And that is true not only of Vietnam but potentially of any public issue. The stuff of governmental decisions cannot be subject to a legal test of truth in our constitutional system.[106] One man's truth is not another's. That is the central meaning of the first amendment: the right to differ about political truth, the right to criticize those who govern us without being held to a standard of temperateness or truth.

New York Times v. Sullivan rested on that proposition. But the Court shied away from its own logic when it said in the end that critical statements about public officials could be penalized if they were knowingly or recklessly false. The whole premise of Justice Brennan's opinion, its analysis in terms of seditious libel and the historical rejection of the Sedition Act of 1798, pointed to the conclusion that Americans may criticize the public actions of public men without fear of any penalty. If there can be no test of truth in political debate, then there can be no libel actions as a result of anything said in such debate.

A personal note is required here. What I am saying now represents a judgment reached in hindsight. When the *Sullivan* case was decided, I did not think Justice Black's view was persuasive. I still find his absolutist language uncongenial. But it is no longer possible to escape the realization that, in calling for "absolute immunity for criticism of the way public officials do their public duty,"[107] he was carrying out the logic—the compelling logic—of Justice Brennan's constitutional analysis. The result for which Professor Wechsler first argued in *New York Times v. Sullivan* should be the law. The first amendment permits no libel actions against the critics of official conduct.

The suggested new rule, sweeping as it is, would not eliminate the need for judges to draw lines; few rules do. But I think it would free a very broad area of debate about politics and public life from the threat of litigation. Consider, for example, the distinction often drawn between general attacks on "policy" or "ideas" on the one hand and, on the other, particularized charges of personal wrongdoing by an official. Justice Harlan made the point that truth is especially hard to define when it comes to ideas. "Any nation which counts the *Scopes* trial as part of its heritage," he said, "cannot so readily expose ideas to sanctions on a jury finding of falsity."[108] Justice Powell in *Gertz* distinguished ideas, which he said could never be punishably false under the first amendment,[109] from "false statements of fact," which had no constitutional value.[110] But the distinction is not so easy to draw. The *Westmoreland* case shows that. The infiltration statistics are "facts," but they are political facts not suitable for nice weighing to determine "truth." That will be so in many libel actions arguing facts in a political context. Similarly, many charges of "personal" wrongdoing may bear on a public official's fitness for office: Is it irrelevant to public concern that a legislator is found publicly drunk?[111] Of course there may be an extreme end of the spectrum at which charges are so personal that they lose their connection to Professor Meiklejohn's business of governance. But public officials should be fair game for most comment, under the first amendment. Their recourse is not litigation but rebuttal. As Professor Wechsler told the Court, the mayor falsely charged with taking a bribe has verbal reply as his only "avenue of retaliation."[112]

Speech can be a highly effective weapon in reply to criticism, as the *Westmoreland* example reminds us. There is every indication that General Westmoreland was able to give his critics as good as he got. From the moment the CBS documentary was shown he denounced it, and he found many platforms: *TV Guide,* broadcasts, newspapers. He succeeded to the point that the public may well have thought better of him after than it did before the documentary. He did not need a legal forum. He used the marketplace, and that is where the debate belongs.

Private persons are in a very different position when they are criticized. They have not chosen the rigors of public life: assumed the risk of injury, as it were. And their opportunities to rebut criticism are slimmer. Justice Harlan had them in mind when he said the marketplace was the best testing ground for truth "where it functions."[113] It does not function for the private person, because no one is interested in listening to him, and Justice Harlan warned against "the dangers of unchallengeable untruth."[114] For these reasons the Supreme Court seems to me to have got the balance of interests about right when it decided in *Gertz* that the states could allow private plaintiffs to recover for libel on any standard except liability without fault: The publisher, that is, must be shown at least to have been negligent in publishing a falsehood.[115]

The hard problem of line-drawing is how to define and treat those who are more than private persons but less than official: public figures. The question may well be unanswerable by any formula. But I think we can see, now, that there have been flaws in the judicial attempts to draw the lines.

The *Sullivan* rule was rooted in our historical antipathy to seditious libel. Yet the Supreme Court quickly—and too glibly, I believe—extended the rule to nonpolitical situations. In *Time, Inc. v. Hill,*[116] which was a specialized privacy case but really engaged the developing constitutional principles of libel, a majority applied the *Sullivan* rule to a private citizen who had been victimized years earlier by criminals and then had that episode put in a false light by *Life* magazine. Justice Brennan, speaking for the Court, said the first amendment guarantees were "not the preserve of political expression or comment upon public affairs, essential as those are to healthy government."[117] Nowadays, he said, a vast range of published matter exposed "persons to public view, both private citizens and public officials. Exposure of the self to others in varying degrees is a concomitant of life in a civilized community."[118] That last statement makes me bristle, because I agree with Justice Brandeis that civilized men value the right to be let alone[119]—the value should not need explanation in this totalitarian century. But putting aside the interest of privacy, what did a *Life* magazine article on Mr. Hill have to do with Professor Meiklejohn's first amendment? With the Sedition Act of 1798? With the citizen's right to criticize his official servants?

The first amendment in my view protects not only political but artistic expression. But its primary concern must be political speech, because in some measure the "core purpose"[120] of the amendment relates to self-government. Professor Meiklejohn, even while urging an "absolute" first amendment,[121] drew a sharp distinction between "private defamations," in which the verbal attack has "no relation to the business of governing," and a political attack "properly regarded as a citizen's participation in government."[122] The *Sullivan* opinion itself spoke of the right to criticize government, as identified in the Sedition Act controversy, as "the central meaning of the First Amendment."[123] And when the Supreme Court extended the *Sullivan* rule to criminal libel, it said that "speech concerning public affairs is more than self-expression; it is the essence of self-government."[124] To try to spread the protections of the rule too broadly over matters beyond the scope of public affairs runs the risk of diluting it.

In *Rosenbloom v. Metromedia, Inc.*[125] a plurality opinion by Justice Brennan said the crucial consideration was not the status of the plaintiff in a libel action but the character of the issue treated in the challenged publication: "If a matter is a subject of public or general interest, it cannot suddenly become less so merely because a private individual is involved, or because in some sense the individual did not 'voluntarily' choose to become involved."[126] The holding that the *Sullivan* rule applied whenever there was an issue of public or general interest drew a strong dissent from Justice Marshall. Deciding what was a legitimate subject of public interest was not a proper role for judges, he warned, and that test would threaten "society's interest in protecting private individuals from being thrust into the public eye by the distorting light of defamation."[127] Then, in *Gertz,*[128] a majority abandoned the issue test and went back to the plaintiff's status. The Court held that "public figures" had to meet the *Sullivan* standard and defined them as either persons so prominent that they are public figures for all purposes or those who have thrust themselves into particular public controversies. But that definition produces an irony. The best known public figures in this country, those most likely to fall into the Court's all-purpose category, are movie stars—and what do they have to do with "the central meaning of the First Amendment"?

If the plurality in *Rosenbloom* went too far in weakening the private person's remedy for defamation when he is involved in a matter of "public interest," as I believe, the majority in *Gertz* overreacted in removing the subject matter of controversy from the test altogether. Whether speech is relevant to public affairs must always be a critical question in determining the level of constitution protection from libel actions. Justice Marshall had a point when he argued in dissent in *Rosenbloom* that judges would have difficulty defining what was a subject of "public or general interest."[129] But as long as the values of reputation and free expression both command our respect, judges will have to draw lines somewhere. And relevance to "public affairs" or "government" is a more meaningful line to draw than whether something is of "public or general interest"—really a bootstrap expression, since anything publicized by a newspaper may be said to be of general interest.

It seems to me that nonofficials come within the philosophy of *New York Times v. Sullivan,* and should like officials be barred from bringing libel actions, only when they meet two tests: prominence in the community *and* relevance to public affairs.[130] Carol Burnett and William Westmoreland are both prominent; both have assumed the risk of fame and can command a forum to answer their critics. But the subject of Miss Burnett's libel action, an attack on her personal behavior, was unrelated to public affairs. Hence the first amendment bars General Westmoreland's suit but not hers. And William Tavoulareas? He is close to the line, but because the story raised issues of public policy and specifically concerned the Securities and Exchange Commission, I think his action should be barred. As I said, judges will still have to draw lines. But it is better to base the judgment on the reality of influence in public affairs than on an abstract definition of "public figure" that in practice is often abandoned because the plaintiff is remote from political concerns.[131]

Libel is not the only form of litigation afflicted in this country today by endless discovery, high costs, and extravagant jury verdicts. But it does not follow that the critics of official conduct must wait for general reforms in our law to get relief from burdens that induce self-censorship. It was the point of *New York Times v. Sullivan* that libel actions against public officials are not like other lawsuits: They invoke the first amendment. Justice Brennan was cautious in laying down a remedy in 1964. "We think,"[132] he said, "that the Constitution requires the test of knowing or reckless falsehood." Time has shown that the test does not work well enough. The Court is free, and I think obligated now, to find a new remedy.

New York Times v. Sullivan remains, for me, a thrilling case. There is a grandness to the opinion from the opening sentence: "We are required in this case to determine for the first time. . . ."[133] At its heart is a concern to protect the function of "the citizen-critic of government," as Justice Brennan called him—called us. "It is as much his duty to criticize as it is the official's duty to administer."[134] That view reflects not just the first amendment but the premise of our whole constitutional system: the belief that the citizen is sovereign. It is, we might say, the central meaning of the Constitution. It is time once again for the law to vindicate that understanding.

ENDNOTES

1. 376 U.S. 254 (1964).

2. Professor Wechsler represented petitioner *New York Times;* a report of the argument before the Court appears at 32 U.S.L.W. 3249 (U.S. Jan. 14, 1964).

3. Editors and commentators, reacting to the Supreme Court's decision in *Herbert v. Lando,* 441 U.S. 153 (1979), that journalist defendants in libel cases must answer questions on discovery about the editorial process that led to publication of the offending matter, spoke of "judicial Agnewism" and "an Orwellian domain" and said the decision "has the potential of totally inhibiting the press to a degree seldom seen outside a dictatorial or fascist country." See Brennan, Address, *Rutgers L. Rev.* (1979), 32:173, 179. (quoting from various newspapers).

4. See *N.Y. Times,* March 29, 1960, at 25 (reproduced as Appendix to the Opinion of the Court in *Sullivan,* 376 U.S. at 292).

5. *Sullivan,* 376 U.S. at 257–59.

6. 273 Ala. 656, 144 So. 2d 25 (1962).

7. *Sullivan,* 376 U.S. at 278 n.18. One other suit had gone to trial by the time the Supreme Court decided *New York Times v. Sullivan,* and the jury had once again awarded $500,000, the full amount claimed. Id.

8. The first amendment speech and press clauses are made applicable to the states by the fourteenth amendment, *Gitlow v. New York,* 268 U.S. 652 (1925); the Court had found no limits there either.

9. A claim by the *Times* that the Alabama jurisdictional ruling denied it due process of law was dismissed by the Supreme Court, *Sullivan,* 376 U.S. at 264 n.4.

10. Goodale, Is the Public 'Getting Even' With Press in Libel Cases?, *N.Y.L.J.,* Aug. 11, 1982, at 1, col. 2; id. at 2, col. 2.

11. See generally A. Lewis, *Portrait of a Decade* (1964).

12. Professor Alexander Bickel credited television coverage of the riots over desegregation in Little Rock and elsewhere with changing Northern attitudes on segretation. "Compulsory segregation, like states' rights and like "The Southern Way of Life," is an abstraction and, to a good many people, a neutral or sympathetic one. These riots, which were brought instantly, dramatically, and literally home to the American people, showed what it means concretely. Here were grown men and women furiously confronting their enemy; two, three, a half dozen scrubbed, starched, scared, and incredibly brave colored children. The moral bankruptcy, the shame of the thing, was evident." A. Bickel, *The Least Dangerous Branch* (1962), 267.

13. *Sullivan,* 376 U.S. at 293, 294 (Black, J., concurring).

14. Brief for Petitioner at 41. Compare id. with *Sullivan,* 376 U.S. at 269 ("Like . . . the various other formulae for the repression of expression that have been challenged in this

Court, libel can claim no talismanic immunity from constitutional limitations. It must be measured by standards that satisfy the First Amendment.").

15. Brief for Petitioner at 41–43.

16. Brief for Petitioner at 44 (quoting *Craig v. Harney,* 331 U.S. 367, 376 (1947). Compare id. with *Sullivan,* 376 U.S. at 272–73 (relying on Wechsler's analysis).

17. Brief for Petitioner at 43. Compare id. with *Sullivan,* 376 U.S. at 271.

18. 310 U.S. 296 (1940).

19. Id. at 310.

20. Brief for Petitioner at 45–46.

21. Sedition Act of 1798, ch. 73, § 2, 1 Stat. 596 (1798) (expired 1801). See *Sullivan,* 376 U.S. at 273–74.

22. Brief for Petitioner at 47.

23. *Sullivan,* 376, U.S. at 273.

24. Id.

25. Id. at 276.

26. Brief for Petitioner at 51 (citing Justice Holmes' first formulation of the clear-and-present-danger test in *Schenck v. United States,* 249 U.S. 47, 52 (1919), and its application in *Dennis v. United States,* 341 U.S. 494, 506–07, 508–10 (1951).

27. Brief for Petitioner at 51–52 (citing *Konigsberg v. State Bar,* 366 U.S. 36, 50 n.11 (1961)).

28. 32 U.S.L.W. 3250 (U.S. Jan. 14, 1964).

29. Brief for Petitioner at 52–53.

30. Id. at 53–54.

31. Id. at 54 n*. The note said that *Coleman v. MacLennan,* 78 Kan. 711, 723, 98 Pac. 281, 285 (1908), had frequently been cited as a leading case requiring proof of actual malice.

32. *Sullivan,* 376 U.S. at 279–80 (citing *Coleman v. MacLennan* as an "oft-cited statement of a like rule").

33. See *Sullivan,* 376 U.S. at 293 (Black, J., concurring); id. at 297 (Goldberg, J., concurring).

34. Id. at 295 (Black, J., concurring).

35. Id. at 293.

36. Id. at 295.

37. See id. at 284–88 (opinion of the Court).

38. *Garrison v. Louisiana,* 379 U.S. 64 (1964).

39. *Curtis Publishing Co. v. Butts,* 388 U.S. 130 (1967).

40. Quoted in Kalven, The *New York Times Case:* A Note on "The Central Meaning of the First Amendment," 1964 Sup. Ct. Rev. 191, 221 n.125.

41. See *N.Y. Times,* July 31, 1982, at 1, col. 1.

42. *N.Y. Times,* March 27, 1981, at 1, col. 5.

43. *Pring v. Penthouse Int'l, Ltd.,* 695 F.2d 438 (10th Cir. 1982).

44. See *Miskovsky v. Oklahoma Publishing Co.,* 654 P.2d 587 (Okla. 1982) (reversing jury verdict; held trial court erred in submitting matter to jury); *Green v. Alton Tel. Printing Co.,* 107, 111. App. 3d 755, 438 N.E.2d 203 (1982) (appeal of $9.2 million judgment dismissed; defendants removed case to bankruptcy court, and that court has jurisdiction over appeal); Kupferberg, Libel Fever, *Colum. Journalism Rev.,* Sept./Oct. 1981, at 36.

45. Quoted in *N.Y. Times,* Sept. 14, 1982, at C9, col. 5.

46. *N.Y. Times,* Jan. 27, 1982, at All, col. 1; *N.Y. Times,* Jan. 21, 1982, at A9, col. 1.

47. *N.Y. Times,* Jan. 27, 1982, at All, col. 1.

48. *N.Y. Times,* May 27, 1982, at C15, col. 3.

49. *N.Y. Times,* July 17, 1982, at 44, col. 2.

50. Quoted in *N.Y. Times,* Sept. 14, 1982, at C9, cols. 5–6.

51. The suit was filed in the United States District Court for South Carolina. But on motion by CBS, the court transferred it to the Southern District of New York. *N.Y. Times,* Nov. 19, 1982, at C34, col. 1.

52. 441 U.S. 153 (1979).

53. Id. at 175–76.

54. See *Branzburg v. Hayes,* 408 U.S. 665 (1972).

55. See *Herbert v. Lando,* 441 U.S. 153, 157–58 (1979).

56. The discovery that took place before the Supreme Court decision is described in *Herbert v. Lando,* 568 F.2d 974, 982 (2d. Cir. 1977); the sessions that took place afterward are described in Affidavit of Carleton G. Eldridge, Jr., *Herbert v. Lando* (S.D.N.Y. Sept. 24, 1982) (accompanying Defendants' Motion for Summary Judgment) (on file at the offices of the *Columbia Law Review*) [hereinafter cited as Affidavit].

57. See Affidavit, supra note 56, at 3–5.

58. See id.; *Herbert v. Lando,* 568 F.2d 974, 982 (2d Cir. 1977), rev'd, 441 U.S. 153 (1979).

59. See Affidavit, supra note 56, at 3–5.

60. Id.

61. Kahn, Profiles—"60 Minutes": The Candy Factory (pt. 2), *New Yorker,* July 26, 1982, at 38, 42.

62. Substantial reports of the *Tavoulareas* case have appeared in *Am. Law.,* Nov. 1982, at 1, and in Hanson, What Went Wrong at *The Washington Post?*, *Colum. Journalism Rev.,* Jan./Feb. 1983, at 31.

63. The *Sullivan* standard, as the Supreme Court has explained it, does not even require an editor to check a story unless he is on notice that it is probably false. See *St. Amant v. Thompson,* 390 U.S. 727 (1968).

64. See *Am. Law.,* Nov. 1982, at 1.

65. Id. at 93.

66. Id. at 94.

67. Id. at 94. The profits of the Washington Post Company were more than $32 million on revenues of more than $750 million in 1981. *N.Y. Times,* Feb. 4, 1982, at D4, col. 1.

68. Libel Defense Resources Center, Summary Judgment in Libel Litigation: Assessing the Impact of *Hutchinson v. Proxmire* (Oct. 15, 1982).

69. *Sullivan,* 376 U.S. at 279.

70. Of course there is hope of large jury verdicts to keep the plaintiff's spirits up. But megadamages in libel cases raise other questions: constitutional questions. See infra notes 71–85 and accompanying text.

71. 418 U.S. 323 (1974).

72. Id. at 349.

73. Id.

74. Id.

75. Id.

76. Id. at 350.

77. The case, unreported, was decided by a jury in 1982. It awarded 100,000 pounds to a British football player, Billy Bremner, who had sued the *Sunday People* newspaper for a story accusing him of rigging the results of matches. There was no appeal. Confidential letter from Queen's Counsel to author (Jan. 17, 1983) (summarizing recent libel judgments) (on file with author). See also Browne, The Pound and the Jury, *Washington Journalism Rev.,* Jan./Feb. 1983, at 52.

78. Some civilized legal systems, for example, West Germany's, do away with libel damages altogether and merely provide a legal forum for establishment of the truth when someone claims to have been defamed. See A. Davila, *Libel Law and the Press* (1971), 35 (citing Strafgesetzbuch [StGb] art. 186 (86 (W. Ger)). The British House of Commons considered a private member's bill to require publication, in equally prominent position, of replies to statements found incorrect by a panel of press and public representatives chaired by a judge. The bill was supported by a vote of ninety to seven but failed for lack of a quorum. *The Times* (London), Feb. 19, 1983, at 4, col. 1. Justice Brennan has suggested the possibility of legislation to the same effect in the United States: The successful libel plaintiff would win not damages but a judicial declaration of falsehood and an order that the publisher of the defamatory statement publish a correction. (The only issue, then, would be truth; there would be no need to explore the publisher's original awareness of falsehood.) See *Miami Herald Publishing Co. v. Tornillo,* 418 U.S. 241, 258 (1974) (Brennan, J., concurring); *Gertz v. Robert Welch, Inc.*, 418 U.S. 323, 368 n.3 (1974) (Brennan, J., dissenting). But it is hard to see how such legislation would square with the *Tornillo* holding that a newspaper cannot constitutionally be required to publish a reply by a political candidate criticized in its columns.

79. *Gertz v. Robert Welch, Inc.*, 418 U.S. 323, 350 (1974).

80. Id.

81. Id. at 349.

82. 403 U.S. 29, 78 (1971) (Marshall, J., dissenting).

83. Id. at 84.

84. Id.

85. See supra text accompanying note 81.

86. In *Wheeler v. Oregon,* 286 Ore. 99, 593 P.2d 777 (1979), the Oregon Supreme Court held that a state constitutional prohibition of laws "restraining the free expression of opinion" forbade the award of punitive damages for defamation even though another clause of the constitution assured those defamed a legal remedy. The court distinguished the obligation to provide civil relief for the injury from a power to punish the author of the defamation, even by proxy through the plaintiff.

87. See supra notes 64–66 and accompanying text.

88. See supra note 43 and accompanying text.

89. Cf. *Gertz,* 418 U.S. at 327–30 and n.2 (trial court submitted case to jury on incorrect theory but entered judgment for defendant notwithstanding the verdict on the ground that the plaintiff had not shown falsity or reckless disregard).

90. See, e.g., *Oliver v. Village Voice,* 417 F. Supp. 235, 237 (S.D.N.Y. 1976); *Guitar v. Westinghouse Elec. Corp.*, 396 F. Supp 1042 (S.D.N.Y. 1975), aff'd, 538 F.2d 309 (2d Cir. 1976).

91. *Hutchinson v. Proxmire,* 443 U.S. 111, 120 and n.9 (1979).

92. See Fed. R. Civ. P. 56(c); Wright, Miller, and Kane, Federal Practice & Procedure: Civil 2d § 2725 (2d ed. 1983).

93. Quoted in *Casper v. Washington Post Co.*, No. 79-3997, slip op. at 1 (E.D. Pa. Dec. 9, 1981) (denying motion for summary judgment).

94. Id. at 3 (citing Chief Justice Burger's statement in *Hutchinson v. Proxmire,* 443 U.S. 111 (1979), discussed supra text accompanying note 91).

95. Id. at 2.

96. Id.

97. *Casper v. Washington Post Co.*, No. 79-3997 (E.D. Pa. June 18, 1982) (denying reconsideration of Dec. 9, 1981, order).

98. Id., slip op. at 2.

99. *Casper v. Washington Post Co.*, 549 F. Supp. 376 (E.D. Pa. 1982) (granting motion for rule 41(b) dismissal).

100. Id. at 378.

101. Id.

102. Confidential interview with *Washington Post* executive (Feb. 9, 1983).

103. The minimum salary at the *Post* for reporters with four years of experience or more was $557 per week. Telephone interview with Jim Griffin, collective bargaining and research assistant, The Newspaper Guild (Mar. 15, 1983).

104. *Time, Inc. v. Hill,* 383 U.S. 374, 406 (1967) (Harlan, J., concurring in part and dissenting in part).

105. W. Just, *In the City of Fear* (1982), 83.

106. An example of the folly likely when judges try to define political "truth" is to be found in *Gilbert v. Minnesota,* 254 U.S. 325 (1920). Defendant was convicted of injuring the war effort in violation of a state statute by saying, during World War I, "We were stampeded into this war by newspaper rot to pull England's chestnuts out of the fire for her." Id. at 327. A majority of the Supreme Court, indignantly rejecting the speaker's view, said of the war: "It was not declared in aggression, but in defense, in defense of our national honor. . . . This was known to Gilbert for he was informed in affairs and the operations of the Government, and every word that he uttered in denunciation of the war was false, was deliberate misrepresentation of the motives which impelled it. . . ." Id. at 333.

107. *Sullivan,* 376 U.S. at 295 (Black, J., concurring).

108. *Time, Inc. v. Hill,* 385 U.S. 374, 406 (1967) (Harlan, J., concurring in part and dissenting in part).

109. *Gertz v. Robert Welch, Inc.*, 418 U.S. 323, 339 (1974).

110. Id. at 340.

111. In *Miskovsky v. Oklahoma Publishing Co.*, 654 P.2d 587 (Okla.), cert. denied, 103 S. Ct. 235 (1982), plaintiff, a candidate for the United States Senate, repeated charges made by a second candidate about a third candidate's sexual preferences. The defendant newspaper publisher printed several items about the plaintiff's actions, including an editorial comment that "George Miskovsky has sunk to a new low in Oklahoma political rhetoric—and for him that takes some doing." Id. at 594. A libel jury awarded plaintiff $35,000 in compensatory and $965,000 in punitive damages. The Oklahoma Supreme Court reversed, holding inter alia that the offending comments were "judgmental" and "opinionative," like calling someone a scoundrel, rather than factual, and hence could not be false. Id. at 593. Justices Rehnquist and White dissented from the United States Supreme Court's denial of certiorari, 103 S. Ct. at 235. They said that the Oklahoma court, misled by Justice Powell's "dicta" in *Gertz,* may have thought that expressions of "opinion" could not be the subject of defamation actions under the first amendment. Id. at 236. But quite apart from "opinion," such expressions of political abuse as those directed at Mr. Miskovsky are surely akin to the seditious libel that the Jeffersonians thought the first amendment removed from legal concern—and hence squarely within the protective theory of *New York Times v. Sullivan.*

112. See supra note 28 and accompanying text.

113. *Time, Inc. v. Hill,* 385 U.S. 374, 406 (1967) (Harlan, J., concurring in part and dissenting in part).

114. Id. at 408.

115. *Gertz v. Robert Welch, Inc.*, 418 U.S. 323, 347 (1974).

116. 385 U.S. 374 (1967).

117. Id. at 388.

118. Id.

119. *Olmstead v. United States,* 277 U.S. 438, 478 (1928) (Brandeis, J., dissenting).

120. *Richmond Newspapers, Inc. v. Virginia,* 448 U.S. 555, 575 (1980) (plurality opinion). Some have argued that the first amendment should be read to protect *only* expression related to government. See, e.g., Bork, Neutral Principles and Some First Amendment Problems, *Ind. L.J.* (1971), 47:1.

121. See Meiklejohn, The First Amendment Is an Absolute, 1961 Sup. Ct. Rev. 245.

122. Id. at 259.

123. *Sullivan,* 376 U.S. at 273.

124. *Garrison v. Louisiana,* 379 U.S. 64, 74–75 (1964).

125. 403 U.S. 29 (1971).

126. Id. at 43 (plurality opinion).

127. Id. at 79 (Marshall, J., dissenting).

128. *Gertz v. Robert Welch, Inc.,* 418 U.S. 323 (1974).

129. *Rosenbloom,* 403 U.S. at 79 (Marshall, J., dissenting).

130. In the Virginia Resolutions of 1798, the General Assembly of Virginia attacked the Sedition Act for attempting to exercise a power forbidden by the first amendment—"a power which, more than any other, ought to produce universal alarm, because it is levelled against the right of freely examining *public characters and measures,* and of free communication among the people thereon, which has ever been justly deemed the only effectual guardian of every other right." 4 Elliot's Debates 553–54, quoted in *Sullivan,* 376 U.S. at 274 (emphasis added).

131. See, e.g., *Time, Inc. v. Firestone,* 424 U.S. 448 (1976) (member of a socially prominent family involved in a notorious divorce case was not a public figure).

132. *Sullivan,* 376 U.S. at 279.

133. Id. at 256.

134. Id. at 282.

3

NICARAGUA, THE UNITED STATES, AND THE WORLD COURT

Abram Chayes

THE SETTING

On April 9, 1984, Nicaragua commenced an action against the United States in the International Court of Justice at the Hague. The Application charged that the policy and actions of the United States in supporting a mercenary army, the contras; in launching attacks on the territory of Nicaragua; and in seeking to overthrow the government constitute the use of armed force against Nicaragua in violation of the international obligations of the United States under the U.N. Charter, the O.A.S. Charter, and general international law.[1] These are the most sweeping charges of violation of fundamental international legal norms ever brought by one state against another in the history of the Court.

Three times the government of the United States sought to avoid participating in this litigation on the merits. First, on April 6, 1984, three days before the application was filed, and clearly in anticipation of Nicaragua's action, Secretary of State Shultz delivered a letter to the Secretary General of the United Nations purporting to withdraw this country's consent to the jurisdiction of the Court for a period of two years with respect to disputes arising out of the situation in Central America.[2] Then, on January 18, 1985, after the Court, on the basis of extended written and oral submissions, had upheld its jurisdiction to hear the complaint, the government of the United States announced that it would not participate further in the case, and, specifically, that it would not appear in the proceedings on the merits.[3]

Finally on October 9, 1985, the State Department announced that the United States had terminated its Declaration of August 26, 1946, submitting to the compulsory jurisdiction of the International Court of Justice. It was a sad day for America. And it was especially distressing for anyone who is trying to teach international law to American law students. Nevertheless, the Court will survive this wanton act. And President Reagan did not, any more than President Truman, speak the last word for the United States on this subject.

The editorial reaction to the decisions by our government was negative.[4] There was an apparent consensus that the United States should have been prepared to present its case before a duly constituted tribunal like any other defendant and to abide by the judgment of law. Such a response was especially called for from the United States, for we pride ourselves on being a nation that is ruled by law. We are a nation that has played a major role in the establishment of the World Court and the international legal order,[5] a nation that frequently calls others to account in terms of the precepts of international law. The obligation, it was argued, weighed even more heavily after the Court, as it is authorized to do by its statute,[6] decided by overwhelming majorities after full and fair hearing in which the United States *did* participate, that it had jurisdiction over the parties and that the subject matter was appropriate for judicial consideration.[7]

Despite these instinctive reactions, as lawyers we are bound to try to evaluate the reasons that the government of the United States has advanced in justification of its refusal to proceed in the case. Although my stance is inevitably partisan, I hope to contribute to such a fair and professional evaluation.

We need not spend very much time on the administration's effort to disparage the judicial character and integrity of the Court.[8] Presidents Hoover, Roosevelt, Truman, Eisenhower, Kennedy, and Carter all sought in one way or another to increase the use of the Court by the United States and to broaden our acceptance of its jurisdiction. During the last forty years the United States has called upon the Court many times, most recently in the Iranian hostages case[9] and in the dispute with Canada about the boundary between the two countries in the Gulf of Maine.[10] Not until the present case, when it appeared that the United States was likely to lose, has it ever questioned the professional quality of the Court's judicial work. The history and tradition of the Court stretch back to 1920, when its predecessor, the Permanent Court of International Justice, was established in the wake of World War I. The statute of the present Court, its rules, composition, mode of judicial selection, and even its seat at the Hague are substantially the same as the earlier body's, with technical adjustments to account for the disappearance of the League of Nations, to which the former Court was an adjunct, and for the organization of the United Nations, of which the International Court of Justice is "the principal judicial organ."[11]

Anyone familiar with the history and work of the Court knows that it displays very high standards of professional craftsmanship. It is said that the Court is "political," and of course it is, in the sense that all courts, including our own Supreme Court, are "political." That is to say, courts often deal with cases involving important political issues and affecting the course of political affairs. In such cases the legal materials are far from determinate. Indeed, they are not even the only relevant materials. They shed light on the matters in issue and provide points of departure, a vocabulary, a methodology, and a mode of analysis. But in the end, the decision of a court in such cases cannot help but be informed by the background and outlook, and the political and moral philosophy of the judges. In that sense, the World Court is a political institution.

But if what is implied by "political" is that the judges of the International Court of Justice vote their preferences in the manner of senators or that they are instructed by their governments as are delegates to the United Nations, that is simply not the case. Like their counterparts in domestic legal systems, they exercise a judicial judgment within an amorphous but familiar framework of professional and institutional constraints. The World Court is a court, immediately recognizable as such to practitioners before the courts in this country.

I do not propose here to examine the question of the Court's jurisdiction in the technical sense (in which I include the validity of Secretary Shultz's attempt to modify the United States' consent to jurisdiction). The United States claimed before the Court, and it still claims, that the Court was without power to entertain the case.[12] Nicaragua supported jurisdiction on two different grounds. The questions presented were intricate and technical, and turned upon documentation and actions specific to the parties in this case.[13] They were exhaustively briefed and argued to the Court by both sides. All but one of the judges were satisfied that the Court had power to adjudicate on one ground or the other.[14] The reactions of the American international law community to the decision ranged from former legal adviser Monroe Leigh's "preposterous,"[15] to Professor Herbert Briggs' "great satisfaction in a Judgment in which patient and careful legal analysis . . . resulted in upholding legal obligations voluntarily assumed."[16] The statute of the Court, following the usual rule that the tribunal is judge of its own jurisdiction, provides that "in the event of a dispute as to whether the Court has jurisdiction, the matter shall be settled by the decision of the Court."[17] That should be the end of the matter. No purpose would be served by rearguing here these narrow jurisdictional questions, without either significant effects beyond the immediate parties to the case or general jurisprudential significance.[18]

The matters that are the focus of this article stand on a somewhat different footing. The basic public justification given by the United States government for its refusal to participate in the case is not narrowly technical. It is that the questions presented are inappropriate for judicial resolution. This position was first advanced when Secretary Shultz attempted to withdraw the United States' consent to the jurisdiction of the Court.[19] Again in January, in announcing its decision not to participate further in the case, the United States maintained that the dispute "is an inherently political problem that is not appropriate for judicial resolution" and that the World Court is "patently unsuited" to decide it.[20] As Dean Acheson said, the law "simply does not deal with such questions of ultimate power—power that comes close to the sources of sovereignty."[21] These issues of "admissibility," as they are called, were also presented to the Court, and here too the Court again held against the United States—this time by a unanimous vote.[22]

Unlike the technical jurisdictional objections, the challenge to the propriety of judicial resolution *does* have a larger significance. It raises the question of what kinds of issues are appropriate for courts and in particular what role the International Court of Justice can properly play in the field of international peace and security. Such questions sound familiar enough to American lawyers, weaned on the mysteries of article III of the Constitution. In those terms, the objection goes to the issue of justiciability. The contention is that the questions presented in the *Nicaragua* case are not "legal" or "judicial" questions. They are "political" questions.[23]

Professor Louis Henkin has said: "The 'political question' doctrine, I conclude, is an unnecessary, deceptive packaging of several established doctrines that has misled lawyers and courts to find in it things that were never put there and make it far more than the sum of its parts."[24] But despite his efforts to extirpate it, the language of the political question doctrine still reverberates in the Supreme Court reports.[25] The United States argument, both before the World Court and to the public, appropriates that language and that conception.

In elaborating its basic position, the United States has drawn on three standard political question arguments:

1. It argues that the questions presented by the application show "textually demonstrable commitment," in the language of *Baker v. Carr,*[26] to a different international organ for determination.[27] Article 39 of the U.N. Charter provides that "the Security Council shall determine the existence of a threat to the peace, breach of the peace or act of aggression. . . ."[28] The use of force in violation of international law falls within that rubric. Thus, the Court is simply disempowered from adjudicating Nicaragua's application because the issues are consigned to the Council by the relevant language of the Charter.

2. Again in the familiar language of *Baker v. Carr,* there is no "judicially discoverable and manageable standard"[29] on the basis of which the legal obligations of the parties can be adjudged.[30] The

substance of the case is an on-going armed conflict. The question of what is a "threat or use of force" within the relevant conventional and customary norms is too amorphous for judicial determination, given the spectrum of possible kinds of armed actions, direct and indirect, and the highly colored ideological context of contemporary international life. It may be acknowledged that these norms remain relevant to national decisionmaking and in other forums, but it was never intended that the World Court should adjudicate such cases. Moreover, the factual basis of the charges is such that the procedures of the Court and its capacity for taking and evaluating evidence cannot be relied on for an accurate result.[31]

3. The problems of Central America are wide ranging and multifarious, implicating not only Nicaragua and the United States, but neighboring countries as well. The political organs of the United Nations and the Organization of American States are already seized of these problems. They can develop a solution for the entire conflict, not just the limited set of bilateral issues tendered in the Nicaraguan application. These political bodies and other interested parties have endorsed the Contadora process as the appropriate forum for settlement of these all-encompassing and interconnected issues. Considerations of prudence, of sound judicial administration, and of the appropriate relations between judicial and political institutions dictate that the Court should not interfere with these political processes.[32]

I propose, first, to examine these contentions on their own terms and to argue that, even on the basis of traditional article III conceptions, adjudication of Nicaragua's claims should not be barred. But concern with the decision of political questions by judges is not just a derivative of the special domestic tradition of separation of powers. Consequently, second, I want to consider the more general objections against resort to the Court in these circumstances, based on the objections' implications both for the Court and for international law.

FROM THE PERSPECTIVE OF ARTICLE III

Textual Commitment

The first category of political questions listed by Justice Brennan in *Baker v. Carr* is that in which there is "a textually demonstrable constitutional commitment of the issue to a coordinate political department."[33] The words "textual commitment" occur more than once in the U.S. Counter-Memorial, although without citation to the Supreme Court opinion.[34] The United States propounds a kind of syllogistic argument based on this conception:

1. Under article 39 of the Charter, "[t]he Security Council shall determine the existence of a threat to the peace, breach of the peace or act of aggression. . . ."
2. A "threat or use of force" in violation of article 2(4) is inevitably a threat to the peace, breach of the peace, or act of aggression.[35]
3. Therefore, the power to "determine" whether there has been an article 2(4) violation is "textually committed" to the Security Council to the exclusion of the Court, by the quoted language of article 39.
4. Since Nicaragua's application, in its central aspect, would require the Court to make such a determination, it has asked for a decision that the Court is powerless to grant.

It seems almost self-evident that in an institution operating under a constitutive charter, language of that instrument assigning a function or process to one organ of the institution rather than another should be decisive. Yet for all its common sense appeal, Justice Brennan cited no cases in support of his first category, and it has not been often applied as such by the Supreme Court. The most likely candidate was *Powell v. McCormack.*[36] The House of Representatives had refused to seat Adam Clayton Powell, duly elected by the voters of New York's eighteenth Congressional district, on the grounds that he had misappropriated public funds and abused the process of New York courts. The Supreme Court invalidated this action despite the provision of article I, section 5 of the Constitution that "[e]ach House shall be the Judge of the Elections, Returns and Qualifications of its own Members. . . ." The "textual commitment" criterion is not as robust as it may at first appear.

A weaker form of the claim of constitutive allocation of competence on particular kinds of questions between judicial and political organs focuses on some of Justice Brennan's other criteria: the need for a prior discretionary policy decision, the appropriate respect for a coordinate institution, and the potential for embarrassment from conflicting pronouncements on the same issue.[37] In United States practice, these considerations, separately and together, have been especially applicable to the field of foreign affairs, where arguably the executive must be able to respond flexibly to the exigencies of occasions and to speak with one voice on behalf of the nation.[38]

Since the United Nations is itself an international entity, there is no direct analogy from the requirements of a national government of divided powers in the conduct of foreign relations. Nevertheless, it is at least arguable that these same considerations would be applicable where different parts of the system might get in each other's way and disrupt the effective functioning of the whole—a possibility the Charter expressly recognizes in the case of relations between the General Assembly and the Security Council.[39] Even in its weaker form, however, the argument about exclusive allocation of competences must rest on a careful juxtaposition of the functions or activities said to be irreconcilable to determine just how much overlap or potential interference there is. It requires, in Justice Brennan's words,

> a discriminating analysis of the particular question posed, in terms of the history of its management by the political branches, of its susceptibility to judicial handling in the light of its nature and posture in the specific case, and of the possible consequences of judicial action.[40]

The United States finds support for its position in the negotiating history of the Charter, which reveals that the Council was expected to play the major role in resolving situations that threaten international peace and security.[41] Of this there can be no doubt. From Dumbarton Oaks to San Francisco, the record is replete with examples of the effort to ensure that nothing would prevent the Security Council from taking prompt and effective measures to resolve political disputes.[42] Thus, article 24 "confer[s] on the Security Council primary responsibility for the maintenance of international peace and security."[43] And, although the General Assembly is empowered to "discuss any questions relating to the maintenance of international peace and security" and to "make recommendations with regard to any such questions,"[44] article 12 provides that "[w]hile the Security Council is exercising in respect of any dispute or situation the functions assigned to it in the present Charter, the General Assembly shall not make any recommendations with regard to that dispute or situation unless the Security Council so requests."[45]

The Court has had occasion to remark that the responsibility of the Security Council is "primary," not "exclusive,"[46] and that the strictures explicitly placed on the General Assembly by articles 11(2) and 12(1) are not applied to the Court.[47] Still, as noted in the United States Counter-Memorial, this allocation of principal responsibility for the maintenance of international peace and security to a single compact organ was designed to avoid a repetition of the paralysis of the League of Nations.[48]

It does not follow from all of this, however, that article 39 gives the Security Council exclusive power to make determinations concerning violations of article 2(4)—except perhaps, by virtue of article 12, vis-á-vis the

Assembly, when the Council is actually considering a dispute. Article 2(4) provides:

> All Members shall refrain in their international relations from the threat or use of force against the territorial integrity or political independence of any state, or in any other manner inconsistent with the Purposes of the United Nations.[49]

It is cast in the language of a straightforward prohibitory legal norm[50] and was intended as such by the draftsmen.[51] Professor Henkin says that "[t]he Charter contains little else of a general normative character. . . ."[52] From this it might equally follow that the essentially legal issue of interpreting the norm is committed to the Court.[53] The result of the textual analysis would be a standoff—concurrent jurisdiction, with authority in each institution to decide the question as it arises in matters otherwise properly before it. The argument against judicial power would have to retreat to other ground.

In fact, however, a more discriminating analysis of the two articles and the functions they envision for the Court and the Council shows that there is no essential inconsistency between them. Obviously, as in the present case, both bodies might find themselves addressing the same general situation. But each has a different task to perform and can do so without any inherent institutional conflict.

The Security Council is expected to provide political solutions for political imbroglios, not to conduct exercises in legal taxonomy. What then is the significance of the words: "The Security Council shall determine the existence of any threat to the peace, breach of the peace or act of aggression"? The position of this language is important. It appears at the beginning of chapter VII of the Charter, entitled "Action with Respect to Threats to the Peace, Breaches of the Peace, and Acts of Aggression." The immediately following words of article 39 authorize the Council, after making the determination, to "decide what measures shall be taken in accordance with Articles 41 and 42, to maintain or restore international peace and security."[54]

Articles 41 and 42 empower the Council to impose mandatory economic and diplomatic sanctions[55] or to "take such action by air, sea, or land forces as may be necessary to maintain or restore international peace and security."[56] Such Council decisions are binding on members of the United Nations by virtue of article 25. This was the great departure from earlier practice, particularly that of the League of Nations.[57] Through the new organization, the international community, for the first time, was to be empowered to make binding decisions to save the world from "the scourge of war."[58]

The determination under article 39 functions as a predicate necessary to bring into play the powers of the Security Council under articles 41 and 42 of the Charter. These powers to impose mandatory sanctions or take military action were regarded as extraordinary, to be used only in situations of great urgency.[59] The Charter is concerned to maintain a bright-line distinction between "action" under chapter VII and all other activities of the United Nations. The function of the solemn determination called for by article 39 is to mark the crossing of that bright line. It demonstrates in formal terms that the Council has put itself in a position to exercise these extraordinary powers. It has the same character as the presidential declaration of emergency or formal findings that are sometimes required by statute in the domestic legal system to ensure that extraordinary executive powers are invoked only after due deliberation and with appropriate political accountability.[60]

A decision to invoke chapter VII powers will not ignore the legal situation or the legal claims of the parties to the dispute. Legal argumentation commonly forms a large part of the debates of the Council on such occasions. But it is not decisive. There is no suggestion in the Charter or anywhere else that every violation of article 2(4) calls for a determination by the Council under article 39 or action under chapter VII. On the contrary, the draftsmen of the Charter were at pains to avoid any suggestion of "automaticity" in bringing chapter VII into play. Significantly, they did not carry the language of article 2(4) forward to article 39. And, as the United States Counter-Memorial amply demonstrates, they resisted all efforts to define aggression or to set up rules that would automatically call for action by the Council.[61] And all subsequent efforts to define such rules have failed.[62]

The power to take mandatory action binding on members of the United Nations is reserved for those rare occasions when the Security Council, in the exercise of political, not legal judgment, determines that the situation requires it. Until the Council makes such a determination under article 39, the Charter consigns the situation, not to chapter VII, concerning "Action with Respect to Threats to the Peace, Breaches of the Peace, and Acts of Aggression," but to chapter VI on "Pacific Settlement of Disputes." Until the Security Council so determines, the situation, no matter how grave or inflamed, is, for the purposes of the Charter, a "dispute, the continuance of which is likely to endanger the maintenance of international peace and security" under article 33. It remains to be dealt with by the methods of peaceful settlement enumerated in that article, including judicial settlement.[63]

The understanding of the Charter derived from careful analysis of the text and drafting history is borne out by the subsequent practice of the United Nations. It is elaborated most fully in the response of the Security Council to the purported "Unilateral Declaration of Independence" (UDI) of the Smith regime in Rhodesia in November 1965, culminating in the imposition of economic sanctions. The draft resolution first put forward by the African states employed the canonical language of an article 39 determination:

> *The Security Council*
>
> . . . .
>
> 1. *Determines* that the situation resulting from this declaration of independence constitutes a threat to international peace and security;
>
> . . . .
>
> 9. *Decides* to take all the enforcement measures provided for under Articles 42 and 43 of the Charter against the racist minority settler regime. . . .[64]

Great Britain, with the support of the United States and other countries, opposed the resolution on the ground that the situation could be resolved without enforcement action, and thus resort to chapter VII was unnecessary.[65] Ultimately, the draft resolution was withdrawn in favor of a negotiated text, in which the Security Council "[d]etermines that the situation . . . is extremely grave . . . and that its continuance in time constitutes a threat to international peace and security."[66] This language deliberately approaches the formula of an article 39 declaration but does not reach it. Indeed, the United States emphasized in the debate that the resolution had been adopted under chapter VI.[67] Consequently, all the operative paragraphs in the resolution are recommendatory.

In the spring of 1966, oil tankers were discharging cargoes at Beira in Mozambique for transshipment to Rhodesia, and the United Kingdom asked the Security Council for authorization to use force to intercept such ships on the high seas. In the United Kingdom draft resolution, which was ultimately adopted, the Security Council "[d]etermines that the resulting situation constitutes a threat to the peace" and "[c]alls upon the Government of the United Kingdom . . . to prevent, by the use of force if necessary, the arrival at Beira of vessels reasonably believed to be carrying oil destined for Southern Rhodesia."[68] This is an even closer approximation to the article 39 formula than the earlier resolution and was thought to legalize British naval interception of tankers on the high seas that would otherwise have been forbidden by international law. In the hope "at long last" of moving "from the application of Chapter VI of the Charter to the application of Chapter VII," the Africans sought to substitute a determination that the situation prevailing in Southern Rhodesia "constitutes a threat to international peace" and "security."[69] But the United Kingdom and its allies successfully resisted the amendment.[70] The resolution that was eventually adopted was referred to in the corridors of the United Nations as a chapter VI-and-one-half action.[71]

Finally, after negotiations between the Wilson government and the Smith regime collapsed in November 1966, the Security Council moved unequivocally to chapter VII. In Resolution 232 of December 16, 1966, the Security Council "[d]etermines that the present situation in Southern Rhodesia constitutes a threat to international peace and security" and "[d]ecides" to impose comprehensive economic sanctions against Rhodesia.[72] The Resolution expressly called attention to the binding force of the action under article 25.[73] This was the first time that article 41 was invoked in its mandatory form in the United Nations.

In the entire year of Security Council consideration, there was no military action in or against Rhodesia, aside from desultory guerilla encounters that were readily contained by the Smith forces. There was certainly nothing that could be deemed an armed attack or an act of aggression in the traditional sense. Nor was there any change in the situation on the ground from the adoption of the first Security Council resolution under chapter VI to the one under chapter VII, more than a year later.

What changed was the Security Council's political willingness to use mandatory economic sanctions. Very little time was spent in debating whether the situation was really, in some "legal" sense, a threat to peace and security.[74] The issue to which the delegates addressed themselves was whether the time had come to impose sanctions, or whether to give the United Kingdom more leeway to seek a voluntary solution.[75] When time ran out, the Council made the determination under article 39, not because of anything that had happened in Rhodesia, but to give effect to its political will.

The same understanding of the effect and meaning of article 39 appeared the first time the issue arose, in connection with the Palestine problem in 1948. There, the United States expressly recognized the empowering function of an article 39 determination. When its draft resolution was amended to delete a reference to article 39 and to "call upon" rather than "order" the parties to observe a cease fire, the United States objected that the amendment would transfer the case from chapter VII of the Charter into chapter VI.[76] Some time later, the Security Council invoked chapter VII but only after first warning the parties that the situation in Palestine would be reconsidered "with a view to such further action under Chapter VII of the Charter" if they rejected the terms of its earlier recommendatory resolution.[77]

Not only in the Security Council but also in its pleadings before the World Court, the United States has not hitherto taken the purist view it now maintains of the separation of functions between Court and Council. In the 1950s this country brought seven cases to the Court involving armed attacks by military aircraft of the Soviet Union or its allies against United States military aircraft, and one, the *Aerial Incident* case, where an Israeli civil aircraft carrying United States citizens, among others, was downed.[78] Presumably, all these attacks raised a question of the use of force within the meaning of article 2(4). Since none of the respondents had submitted to the jurisdiction of the Court, the cases never went to judgment. Nevertheless, the United States had no compunction about pursuing the judicial route and perceived no difficulty about invading the exclusive competence of the Security Council. Indeed, it may be imagined that the reason the United States chose the Court rather than the Council was the certain knowledge that relief in the Council was precluded by the Soviet veto—a situation not unlike that in which Nicaragua finds itself today.

Thus, the uniform experience under the Charter, as well as its structure and language, shows that a determination under article 39 is a procedural prerequisite for transferring a dispute from the ordinary course of business under chapter VI to chapter VII, so as to provide the basis for invoking the extraordinary powers to order enforcement action. Indeed, the Court itself long ago intimated that without such a determination the Council could not authorize "military action against any State."[79]

This legal distinction between judgments of the Court and actions of the Council was emphasized by Sir Humphrey Waldock in his authoritative early analysis:

> Aggression as a legal concept now has significance in two related but distinct contexts:
>
> (1) When the Security Council makes a "determination" of an "act of aggression" under Article 39 of the Charter in order to bring into being its powers to take enforcement action. . . .
>
> (2) When a State or an individual in a State is charged before a tribunal with having committed the criminal offence of "aggression" under international law.[80]

The existence of a threat or use of force in violation of article 2(4) is not a condition for a determination under article 39. In the Rhodesian case, the most important recent instance of the use of chapter VII powers, there was nothing resembling such a threat or use of force.[81] Conversely, as is demonstrated by the infrequent use of article 39—only twice despite the many armed conflicts that have wracked the world since 1945—by no means does every violation of article 2(4) require action by the Security Council under article 39.

If, in a case properly before it, the Court should conclude that the respondent has violated article 2(4), the decision would not give rise to any consequent duty of the Security Council to act under article 39. Even if the applicant were to seek enforcement of a Court decision under article 94(2), the Security Council would still be required to make an independent determination under article 39 before it could take enforcement action. And the Council would be free to do so or not, as "it deems necessary," in accordance with its independent judgment about the requirements of the situation.[82] By the same token, the failure of the Court to find a violation of article 2(4) in a case before it cannot preclude the Security Council—if "it deems necessary"—from making a determination under article 39 with respect to the situation out of which the case arose.

Thus, article 2(4), prohibiting the threat or use of force, and article 39, empowering the Security Council to take enforcement action, are distinct in their nature and functions: article 39 established a political process; article 2(4) defines a legal obligation.[83] Both are supremely important to the regime of the Charter. But the structure would be severely compromised by ignoring the difference between them or collapsing the one into the other.

Judicially Manageable Standard

Like other tests propounded by Justice Brennan in *Baker v. Carr* for identifying political questions, the lack of a judicially manageable standard is elusive.[84] Perhaps it was a response to the concern expressed in Justice Frankfurter's dissent that the absence of accepted legal standards would enmesh judicial review of apportionment decisions in a web of "non-legal factors," leaving judges to "make their private views of political wisdom the measure of the Constitution."[85] Transposed to the present context, the argument would be that coercive activity of various forms, undertaken for a variety of political and ideological reasons, is endemic to the contemporary conduct of relations between states. Coercive measures of a military, economic, or political character and material or moral support of insurgents are the everyday stuff of international affairs. Such situations do not lend themselves to classification in neat legal categories that a court could confidently apply by traditional judicial methods to distinguish permissible from prohibited coercion.

Ultimately, the Supreme Court's response to the problem in the reapportionment setting was to reject a "rule of reason" approach and to enunciate a requirement of one-person-one-vote,[86] which has proved eminently manageable. Similar possibilities lie open to the World Court in fashioning a rule in the present case. Although it would be inappropriate at this time to comment on the merits of issues still pending before the Court, some discussion of the legal theory underlying Nicaragua's claims may be warranted to illuminate this manageability question.

The question of the meaning of "use of force" under article 2(4) is surely one of the most exhaustively considered topics in international law. True, there is not a great deal of case law, although the Court has made some trenchant observations, notably in the *Corfu Channel* case.[87] But a dearth of cases is the general condition of international law. On the other hand, the writings of publicists here are voluminous.[88] The drafting history of the U.N. Charter is helpful.[89] And attention to the question at the United Nations and elsewhere since 1945 has resulted in a number of clarifying resolutions and conventional instruments,[90] culminating in Resolution 3314(XXIX) on the Definition of Aggression, adopted by the General Assembly in 1974.[91] There is thus plenty of legal material for a judicial body to work with.

It is true that these efforts have not resulted in unanimity. And it is true that many of these pronouncements embrace very broad conceptions of prohibited coercion. But as Professor Schachter has pointed out, norms against the use of force, like other legal rules, have a core of tolerably clear meaning,[92] surrounded by what H. L. A. Hart called a penumbra, in which applications may grow increasingly problematic.[93]

Nicaragua's case, as defined by the facts alleged in its application,[94] is pitched on the core meaning of the rule. It does not depend on any attenuated or recondite theory of the use of force. In the first place, Nicaragua charges that officials and employees of the United States government acting under color of office and in the line of duty, have themselves committed acts of force against Nicaragua in violation of article 2(4).[95] Many such instances are in fact admitted: for example, the mining of Nicaraguan ports, the destruction of the oil storage facilities at Cornito, and other attacks on the port facilities.[96]

Nicaragua also alleges that the actions of the United States, in recruiting, organizing, financing, training, supplying, directing, and controlling the contra forces, have violated the law of the Charter.[97] The theory on this branch of the case—the cause of action asserted—is that the relation of the United States to the contra activities is such that they can for legal purposes be attributed to the United States. They are, in law, the acts of the United States.[98] As a legal matter, Nicaragua accepts the burden of showing something more than merely that the United States has provided material and financial resources to an indigenous rebel movement.[99]

One of the ironies of the case is that this theory of the law was developed and urged by United States international lawyers, scholars, and diplomats. The United States has argued repeatedly in all available international law forums that the prohibition against the use of force could no longer be confined to old-fashioned transborder aggression by uniformed military forces of the offending country. The United States took the lead in urging that in the conditions of modern international life the most common use of force occurs through the medium of irregulars, directed by an outside power against the legitimate government of a state. The United States was the chief proponent of the view that "indirect aggression," as thus conceived, was within the purview of article 2(4).[100] These efforts generated a broad consensus for the United States view, reflected in numerous international legal instruments. In particular, article 3 of the U.N. Resolution 3314(XXIX) on the Definition of Aggression, strongly supported by the United States,[101] includes among the actions constituting armed attack:

> [t]he sending by or on behalf of a State of armed bands, groups, irregulars or mercenaries, which carry out acts of armed force against another State . . . or its substantial involvement therein.[102]

And, of course, ever since 1948, the O.A.S. Charter has provided:

> No State or group of States has the right to intervene, directly or indirectly, for any reason whatever, in the internal or external affairs of any other State. The foregoing principle prohibits not only armed force but also any other form of interference or attempted threat against the personality of the State or against its political, economic, and cultural elements.[103]

The sweeping character of this formulation is rooted in a long and bitter history of unilateral intervention by the United States in the affairs of Latin American countries.[104] The surrender by the United States of any claim of right to unilateral intervention is widely regarded as the quid pro quo for the enlistment of the Latin American countries in a defensive alliance against external aggression.[105]

These repeated provisions of treaties and other international instruments defining the use of force are no more opaque or indeterminate than others that judges, certainly American judges, manage to deal with every day. Particularly since the Court in this case is not asked to explore the outer reaches of the concept but can decide on the basis of the central meaning, the "manageability" of the standard is not a serious problem.

As to the facts, the burden of proof in the case rests on the applicant,[106] whether or not the United States appears.[107] Thus, Nicaragua must adduce evidence to convince the Court that the factual allegations defining its cause of action are well founded. In this case, the evidence is largely documentary. The essential elements of the proof are official statements of officers of the United States government, starting with the President.[108] Although, as in the *United States Staff* case (the Iranian hostages case), the Court will have to take account of matters of common knowledge,[109] there is no rule, as Justice Frankfurter used to say, that judges must pretend to be ignorant of what everyone else knows.

It might be thought that issues relating to self-defense are exceptions to the statements just made about the evidentiary basis of the case and the Court's fact-finding capabilities. Perhaps a word on that point is in order.

Of course, there has been no pleading by the United States to the merits of the case, and thus self-defense has not technically been put in issue. If it had been, the President, by his recent pronouncements about the true purpose of his Nicaraguan policy, has made it clear that the United States involvement in Nicaragua is not founded on self-defense.[110]

But even if it were otherwise, the applicability of the defense can be determined as a matter of law. Article 51 of the Charter preserves "the inherent right of individual or collective self defense" only "if an armed attack occurs against a Member of the United Nations."[111] Nicaragua's position is that, even if the United States charges about supply of the El Salvador guerillas are assumed to be true, which Nicaragua denies, they do not add up in law to an "armed attack," necessary to bring the right of self-defense into play.[112] Nor do the admitted actions of the United States meet the procedural and substantive limitations of the defense.[113]

Thus, on examination, the claimed inability of the Court to manage the legal and factual issues presented by the case disappears. The Court is presented with a set of familiar judicial tasks well within the reach of the traditional methodologies and arts of judging.

Noninterference with Political Agencies

The United States argues that, apart from any general division of competence and jurisdiction as between judicial and political institutions in the international system, in this particular case, the political bodies were already seised of the issues raised in Nicaragua's application and had acted on them before the application was filed. These exercises of political jurisdiction provide another compelling reason for the Court to stand aside.

Again, this argument has a stronger and a weaker form. In the strong form, the position is that Nicaragua presented to the Security Council substantially the identical issues tendered in its application to the Court, and requested the Council to condemn the United States actions. The Security Council considered such a resolution, but adoption failed owing to the negative vote of the United States. According to the United States, this amounts to a Security Council decision to take no action, the implication being that it considered Nicaragua's position to be without merit. The Court, said the United States, was being asked, in effect, to "review" this action, and of course, the United Nations system contains no provision for judicial review of Security Council decisions. Thus, it was inappropriate for the Court to hear the case.[114]

In this extreme form the argument falls of its own weight. In the first place, failure to adopt a resolution because of a veto by the Permanent Member concerned cannot be regarded as a "decision" of the Council against the aggrieved state. It is a nonaction. We have been repeatedly warned of the dangers of attributing affirmative significance to the failure of a deliberative body to adopt or enact a given measure.[115] Certainly no intimation can be drawn from such a failure about the merits of the issues involved.

Second, and more important, Nicaragua's application does not in any sense require the Court to reexamine any action of the Council or to decide whether or not it was proper in the light of some "higher law" precept asserted to be binding on the Council. It simply asks the Court, as an independent matter, to do something the Council has never done or purported to do: to adjudicate the propriety of United States conduct under international law.

In its weaker form, the United States argument relies on actions and pronouncements that undoubtedly have been taken by international political bodies. The United Nations—both through the General Assembly and the Security Council—and the Organization of American States have adopted resolutions endorsing the efforts of the Contadora process to resolve the complex and many-faceted situation in Central America.[116] In these circumstances, it is urged, the Court should, as a prudential matter, step aside and let the political processes run their course.[117]

But none of the resolutions in question suggest that Contadora is to be the exclusive modality for approaching the Central American situation. None of the bodies involved, including the Contadora states themselves, have made any objection to the proceedings in the Court.[118] As a practical matter, Contadora has made at least as much progress since April 1984, when Nicaragua's application was filed, as before.[119]

The United States position in this respect is at odds with the uniform prior practice of the Court and its predecessor, the Permanent Court of International Justice, in their relationships with international political organs. And here again, the United States has contradicted its own previous positions, put forward as recently as 1980 in the *United States Staff* case.

The earlier practice on the issue of concurrent jurisdiction is summed up in the *South West Africa* case, where the Court went forward even though the dispute had been continuously on the agenda of the General Assembly since 1946 and was being debated there while the case was pending before the Court.[120] After a full analysis of this case, Dr. Shabtai Rosenne, the paramount expert on the Court's procedures, concluded "it is now clear that the fact that a dispute is simultaneously being dealt with by the General Assembly and by the Court is not in itself regarded in either organ as a bar to its further action."[121] This necessarily follows because the two bodies deal with different aspects of the problem: "while in the General Assembly the political facets have priority, the Court may only decide the issues before it on the basis of law."[122]

Dr. Rosenne is at pains to show that in *South West Africa* the Court was following the general lines marked out by the Permanent Court in *Minority Schools*[123] and *Interpretation of the Statutes of the Memel Territory.*[124] In each of these cases, the Court was construing a special convention vesting the Council of the League of Nations with powers over the subject matter of the convention and providing for reference of legal disputes to the Permanent Court. In *Minority Schools,* the Court refused to find that a prior ruling of the Council on the matter in issue precluded the Court's consideration of the legal questions involved.[125] And in the *Memel Statutes* case, it held that submission of the matter to the Council was not a precondition to proceedings before the Court, nor could such an interpretation be given unless "the intention of the contracting Parties to stipulate such a condition [is] clearly established."[126] In each situation Court and Council were carrying out different functions.

If these earlier cases can be distinguished because they dealt with the General Assembly or the Council of the League of Nations (which exercised, as we have seen, only limited powers in the field of peace and security), in the *United States Staff*[127] case the Court applied the same approach to a question of judicial action concurrent with Security Council deliberation. In that case, the Council remained "actively seized of the matter" during the pendency of the Court proceedings.[128] Moreover, Iran had stated in a communication to the Court:

> The problem involved in the conflict between Iran and the United States is thus not one of the interpretation and the application of the treaties upon which the American Application is based, but results from an overall situation containing much more fundamental and more complex elements. Consequently, the Court cannot examine the American Application divorced from its proper context, namely the whole political dossier of the relations between Iran and the United States over the last 25 years.[129]

The Court on its own motion examined the impact of these matters on its competence to decide the case. As to the general political context, it said:

> [L]egal disputes between sovereign States by their very nature are likely to occur in political contexts, and often form only one element in a wider and long-standing political dispute between the States concerned. Yet never has the view been put forward that, because a legal dispute submitted to the Court is only one aspect of a political dispute, the Court should decline to resolve for the parties the legal question at issue between them. If the Court were, contrary to its settled jurisprudence, to adopt such a view, it would impose a far-reaching

> and unwarranted restriction on the role of the Court in the peaceful resolution of international disputes.[130]

On the question of concurrent Security Council consideration, the Court noted that no member of the Security Council saw "anything irregular in the simultaneous exercise of their respective functions by the Court and the Security Council."[131] It concluded that despite the pendency of the matter before the Council,

> [i]t is for the Court, the principal judicial organ of the United Nations, to resolve any legal questions that may be at issue between parties to a dispute; and the resolution of such legal questions by the Court may be an important, and sometimes decisive, factor in promoting the peaceful settlement of the dispute.[132]

The *United States Staff* case contains a further parallel with that of Nicaragua. There, the Secretary General had appointed a special fact-finding and mediating commission, somewhat analogous to the Contadora process in the present case. The Court concluded that the operation of the Commission had no effect on "its competence to decide the present [*United States Staff*] case or the admissibility of the present proceedings." The Court stated:

> The establishment of the Commission by the Secretary General with the agreement of the two States cannot, therefore, be considered in itself as in any way incompatible with the continuance of parallel proceedings before the Court. Negotiation, enquiry, mediation, conciliation, arbitration and judicial settlement are enumerated together in Article 33 of the Charter as means for the peaceful settlement of disputes.[133]

On all these points, the Court adopted positions put forward and urged upon it by the United States.

FROM THE PERSPECTIVE OF THE WORLD COURT

To this point, I have deliberately used headings and tag lines that are familiar in American constitutional parlance: "textual commitment," "judicially manageable standard," "primary jurisdiction." The United States Counter-Memorial follows the same pattern. It reflects our tendency, as I suggested earlier, to think about the World Court in terms and conceptions drawn from our own constitutional jurisprudence. But the previous section of this article demonstrates, I think, that any such effort at systematic transposition overlooks fundamental differences between the domestic and international institutional contexts.

As the Supreme Court has repeatedly recognized, our conceptions of justiciability, in particular the political question doctrine, derive from the unique American version of the separation of powers.[134] The argument of the United States that the *Nicaragua* case is inappropriate for judicial determination is an attempt to project American separation of powers thinking upon the very different set of institutions and organs that comprise the international system. The tendency, as I have said, is not uncommon among American lawyers, and I must confess to having indulged in it myself, not only in an earlier appearance before the Court,[135] but in academic publication as well. In 1965, in an article seeking guidance in American experience for the role of the International Court, I wrote:

> I suggest that most great disputes between states, even when they involve important legal elements, are not justiciable—and for much the same reason that most disputes between organs of our government not involving invasions of private right are not justiciable. Courts do not exist to answer legal questions just for the sake of having an answer. They are specialized institutions. Acceptance of their judgments depends on a subtle complex of factors. Institutional characteristics limit the range in which they can effectively exercise authority. If judges go beyond those limits, the result is likely to be not vindication of the law, but erosion of judicial authority.[136]

As you may well imagine, I have already made a meal of those words in the Hague. But longer and more careful reflection, both on the capacities of the judiciary[137] and on the structure of the international system, has convinced me that the traditional American conception of the proper judicial function is not applicable, certainly not in an undiluted form, to international adjudication.

The American Constitution was an explicit effort to allocate all the powers of a single sovereign government among three major departments. In theory, the powers do not overlap. The main structural principle of the Constitution is that no branch should invade or exercise powers belonging to the others. Each branch was given powers to defend itself against the encroachments of the others.[138] It was a Newtonian scheme of checks and balances, keeping each element within its appointed sphere of power.[139] In practice over two centuries, of course, the system has not operated in any such rigid and abstract way. But that was the architectural plan, and it has decisively conditioned our thinking about the degree of separation to be maintained between the appointed spheres of governmental institutions and about the powers that lie within them.

The architectural plan of the contemporary international system is very different. The problem facing the framers at San Francisco, unlike that at Philadelphia, was not how to divide the whole body of governmental powers among the branches of one sovereign government. It was to provide an institutional framework within which a multitude of sovereigns could work cooperatively on matters of common concern and could adjust the inevitable frictions and disputes arising in a community of formally sovereign and equal states. The solution was not to distribute powers in a number of watertight compartments. It was to provide a broad menu of institutional forms that states could use as they saw fit in the pursuit of their own purposes.

It is tempting for Americans to see in the United Nations the shadow of a bicameral legislature and in the International Court of Justice a reflection of our own Supreme Court. But that is to distort institutional reality. The Charter establishes a Secretary General, a Secretariat, an Economic and Social Council, a Trusteeship Council. Beyond these, there is a multiplicity of specialized international agencies, each with its own charter and history and its peculiar set of legal and political relations with the United Nations. There are no analogues to these in the American constitutional scheme. The notion of exclusive institutional competences does not fit well in such an environment.

If criteria of justiciability deriving from the separation of powers are not applicable, it does not follow that there are no limits to what the International Court can properly do. We start with the proposition that the World Court is, after all, a court. Its function is not to make generalized political pronouncements. It is supposed to decide cases, brought before it by parties to a dispute, in conformity with the methods and using the materials familiar to the professional discipline of the law. Article 36, defining the jurisdiction of the Court in contentious cases, divides it into two broad categories: (1) "all cases" referred by agreement of the parties or arising under compromissory clauses of treaties;[140] and (2) for States accepting the "compulsory" jurisdiction, all legal disputes concerning:

a. the interpretation of a treaty;

b. any question of international law;

c. the existence of any fact which, if established, would constitute a breach of an international legal obligation;

d. the nature or extent of the reparation to be made for the breach of an international legal obligation.[141]

Are there other limits—positive or prudential?[142] What weight should be attached to the absence of any coercive power backing the pronouncement of the Court? Can such a court really make a contribution to the settlement of the problems before it? What good is a judgment of a court that cannot be enforced?

It was Stalin who asked: "How many divisions has the Pope?" We should not make the mistake of asking: "How many divisions has the Court?" I think we make too much, in general, of the coercive elements of the legal system.[143] No such system could survive for long if it depended on coercive power to make good its norms. On this question, there is wisdom to be found in our own experience. When the Supreme Court issued its subpoena against Richard Nixon,[144] it had no power to enforce its judgment. The armed forces, the national guard, the United States marshals, all were under the control of the President as Commander in Chief or as head of the executive branch. The Supreme Court commanded only the force of the law. That proved to be enough.[145]

We cannot say how the United States will respond to an adverse judgment in the *Nicaragua* case. The answer must await the event. And the answer will be more complex than is commonly thought. Although the President has large powers to establish and carry out United States foreign policy, he is not the United States. Especially where policy requires funds to carry it out, he shares power with the Congress. I think it is evident that the actions of the Court to date and the efforts of the Administration to escape adjudication have already influenced the debate about whether and on what terms to continue financial assistance to the contras.

And beyond the Congress are the American people. As has been remarked many times, we are, at bottom, a law-abiding nation.[146] We believe in government under law. In my opinion, it will be impossible to sustain a controversial policy over a long period, requiring continuous financial support and public justification, if that policy has been declared unlawful by a duly constituted and authoritative tribunal. That may be a handicap for a superpower in today's world. We may labor under a burden of constraint that does not apply symmetrically to others. Perhaps that is "not fair." But I think that it is the kind of country we are, and I would not have it any other way.

The question of compliance is related to, but does not conclude, the larger question: What impact will the decision to adjudicate have on the future of the Court itself and on the future of international law? It is said, for example, that this case could mark the end of the "compulsory jurisdiction" of the Court. The United States has now terminated its Declaration, leaving only forty-six countries that still accept jurisdiction under article 36(2), many of them subject to severe reservations. Great Britain is now the only Permanent Member of the Security Council among them. States may be quicker to follow the United States example in withdrawing than they were in acceding to the Court's jurisdiction. Or they may make reservations with respect to cases involving armed conflict or national security. Does not all this weaken the Court and undermine its legitimacy—at least in regard to pronouncements involving peace and security? Is not the whole edifice of international adjudication, already fragile, put at risk?

Moreover, as I said in the beginning, this case is unprecedented in the nature and sweep of its charges. Although the Court has occasionally pronounced on matters involving the use of force,[147] it has never been asked to adjudicate on an armed conflict of the scale set forth in Nicaragua's application, nor with a superpower, in effect, the party in the dock. Can the Court with such small opportunity for sustained elaboration of the legal questions involved really make a contribution to the development of international law in this field? Or will not a single utterance, perhaps ignored, erode rather than enhance respect for the norms that limit the use of force in international affairs?

These are penetrating and difficult questions. Although the Court could not refer to them in its decision on jurisdiction, I have little doubt that they weighed as heavily on the judges. But in addressing these questions, we should not forget that the legitimacy of the Court and the prospects for the rule of law in international affairs are at stake whether the Court decides or refuses to decide the case before it. It is true that, given the consensual character of the Court's jurisdiction, the appearance of this case on its docket is, in a sense, accidental. Still, the case is there. And in the circumstances, it is only in the Hague that Nicaragua can face the United States on equal terms. It is the only forum where the outcome is not predetermined by the disparities of military and economic power between the parties. In the countries of the world that are "possessed of neither the purse nor the sword,"[148] it would be a severe blow to the legitimacy and moral authority of the Court, as well as to the claims for international law, if the door to that forum were closed.

What are the costs and the opportunities if the Court does speak? That depends, of course, on what the Court says. Justice Frankfurter often spoke of the Supreme Court's "self-inflicted wounds."[149] He was referring to cases like *Lochner v. New York*[150] and *Dred Scott.*[151] He thought the Supreme Court was wrong to intervene in those cases to attempt to solve by judicial fiat when he saw as political problems. No doubt he would have pointed to the withdrawal of the United States from the compulsory jurisdiction as an example of the consequences of disregarding these strictures. But we must ask whether it is the Court or the United States that has suffered the self-inflicted wound. The damage from *Lochner* and *Dred Scott* came not *because* the Supreme Court decided those cases, which it could hardly have refused to do, but because of *what* it decided.

Let me offer, by way of contrast, *Brown v. Board of Education,*[152] now just more than twenty years old. If we consider only the concrete results of *Brown* in the field of school desegregation, we might conclude that not much has been accomplished. Although de jure desegregation has been abolished, there are still millions of children being educated in predominantly minority schools.[153] It may be that what progress there has been is being eroded by demographic trends and population movements.[154] It is certainly the case that in the major urban areas, schools populated by minority children predominate and segregation is actually on the rise.[155]

Does that mean that the Court was wrong to decide *Brown* as it did? Would those who worked so long and hard to achieve the reversal of *Plessy v. Ferguson*[156] now conclude that the effort was a failure? I think not.

The significance of *Brown* was not solely, or even chiefly, in the field of school desegregation. To see it that way is to ignore the power of the Court as spokesman, as a uniquely weighty participant in a continuing discourse on our deepest values.[157] The real importance of *Brown* is that it changed the terms of the discourse on the question of how we treat blacks in our society. It wrought a seismic change in our ways of thinking on those issues that will continue to reverberate as far into the future as we can imagine.

The current discourse on the question of the use of force in international affairs is in a state of serious disrepair. We have recently witnessed a debate between the Secretary of State and the Secretary of Defense about the circumstances in which the United States should use force in the conduct of its foreign policy. It was common ground between them that we should do so whenever it could be successfully used to forward United States interests. The difference between them was that Secretary Weinberger argued we should not use force unless domestic popular support could be assured. Secretary Schultz was not willing to accept even that constraint.[158] The current official United States position thus seems to be that the use of force is a legitimate instrument of foreign policy. That position turns its back on the long and costly effort, in large part led by this country, to establish the contrary.[159]

Can the World Court judgment in the *Nicaragua* case do anything to change the state of discourse, not only in the United States, but elsewhere in the world? And as I noted above, it depends a good deal on what the Court says and how it says it. The paucity of cases on its docket means that the Court cannot proceed by elaborating legal rules, case by case over time, as common law courts do. That has never been the way in which the World Court has contributed to the development of international law. On the contrary, just because the Court's pronouncements are few, they command extraordinary attention and authority among international lawyers and government officials who must deal with international legal problems. So whatever the Court says will have great importance for the development of international law.

But in rendering judgment in the *Nicaragua* case, the Court will also exercise its function as a spokesman for universal values. As Alexander Bickel said about our own Supreme Court:

> Even when it is ultimately constrained to yield to necessity, however—to yield, that is to say, to the judgment of political institutions—the Court can exert immense influence. It may be unable to wield its ultimate power as the organ of government charged with translating principle into positive law; but it need not abandon its concomitant role of "teacher to the citizenry." . . . [T]he Court can explain the principle that is in play and praise it, and thus also guard its integrity.[160]

Will the World Court in *Nicaragua v. United States* fulfill its role as "teacher to the citizenry?" Will its judgment have any of the extended resonance that *Brown* has had? It may seem hopelessly romantic to think that it might. But if it should, the result will have been well worth the risk—for the Court, for Nicaragua, for the United States, for the world.

ENDNOTES

I owe special thanks to my students Anne-Marie Burley, Richard De Natale, Thomas M. Kellenberg, Kathleen M. Milton, and H. Marshall Sonenshine.

1. See Application of Nicaragua, Military and Para-military Activities in and Against Nicaragua (*Nicar v. U.S.*), filed April 9, 1984.

2. See Letter from Secretary of State Shultz to the Secretary General of the United Nations (April 6, 1984), *I.L.M.* (1984), 23:670 [hereinafter cited as Secretary Shultz's letter]. The letter purported to modify the U.S. Declaration submitting to the Court's jurisdiction of August 14, 1946, 61 Stat. 1218, T.I.A.S. No. 1598.

3. See Statement of United States Department of State concerning "U.S. Withdrawal from the Proceedings Initiated by Nicaragua in the International Court of Justice," Jan. 18, 1985, 85 Dep't St. Bull. No. 2096, at 64 (March 1985) [hereinafter cited as U.S. Statement].

4. See, e.g., *Wash. Post*, Jan. 22, 1985, at A18, col. 1 (editorial condemning United States withdrawal); *N.Y. Times*, Jan. 20, 1985, at E22, col. 1, (same); American Society of International Law Resolution, *Am. Soc'y Int'l L. Newsletter*, May–June 1984, at 1 (condemning Secretary Shultz's letter, supra note 2).

5. The Senate Foreign Relations Committee report on the resolution, which first accepted the Court's jurisdiction, demonstrates an awareness of a special United States responsibility: "The ultimate purpose of the resolution is to lead to general world-wide acceptance of the jurisdiction of the International Court of Justice in legal cases. The

accomplishment of this result would, in a substantial sense, place international relations on a legal basis, in contrast to the present situation, in which states may be their own judge of the law." S. Rep. No. 1835, 79th Cong., 2d Sess. 3 (1946).

6. Statute of the International Court of Justice art. 36, ¶ 6, 59 Stat. 1055, 1060, T.I.A.S. No. 993 (1945); see infra text accompanying note 17.

7. Military and Paramilitary Activities in and Against Nicaragua (*Nicar. v. U.S.*), 1984 I.C.J. 392 (Judgment of Nov. 26 on Jurisdiction and Admissibility) [hereinafter cited as Judgment on Jurisdiction]. Other proceedings in the case are reported in Military and Paramilitary Activities in and Against Nicaragua (*Nicar. v. U.S.*), 1984 I.C.J. 169 (Provisional Measures, Order of May 10) [hereinafter cited as Provisional Measures]; Military and Paramilitary Activities in and Against Nicaragua (*Nicar. v. U.S.*), 1984 I.C.J. 215 (Declaration of Intervention, Order of Oct. 4).

8. See *N.Y. Times,* April 13, 1984, at A3, col. 1 (report of a speech by Mrs. Kirkpatrick to the American Society of International Law on April 12, 1984); cf. U.S. Statement, supra note 3, at 65 (expressing concern for the potential "politicization" of the Court).

9. United States Diplomatic and Consular Staff in Tehran (*U.S. v. Iran*), 1980 I.C.J. 3 (Judgment of May 24).

10. Delimitation of the Maine Boundary in the Gulf of Maine Area (*U.S. v. Can.*), 1984 I.C.J. 246 (Judgment of Oct. 12, 1984).

11. U.N. Charter art. 92. The Statute of the Court is appended as a part of the Charter, and every member of the United Nations is automatically a party to it.

12. In its statement on January 18, 1985, the United States asserted that the Court's decision on jurisdiction "is erroneous as a matter of law and is based on a misreading and distortion of the evidence and precedent." U.S. Statement, supra note 3, at 64.

13. Nicaragua argued, first, that its Declaration of November 29, 1929, is a valid acceptance of the Court's jurisdiction even though it had not perfected its ratification of the Protocol of Signature of the Statute of the Permanent Court of International Justice. Because the 1929 Declaration was unconditional and unlimited in duration, it became effective when Nicaragua ratified the U.N. Charter in 1945, under article 36(5) of the Statute of the present Court, which provides:

> Declarations made under Article 36 of the Statute of the Permanent Court of International Justice and which are still in force [French text: *pour une durée qui n'est pas encore expirée*] shall be deemed, as between the parties to the present Statute, to be acceptances of the compulsory jurisdiction of the International Court of Justice for the period which they still have to run and in accordance with their terms.

Memorial of Nicaragua (Jurisdiction and Admissibility), Military and Paramilitary Activities in and against Nicaragua (Nicar. v. U.S.), (Memorial submitted June 30, 1984), hereinafter cited as Nicaraguan Memorial.

The United States argued that article 36(5) extended only to binding acceptances of the jurisdiction of the Permanent Court of International Justice (PCIJ). See Counter-Memorial of the United States (Jurisdiction and Admissibility), Military and Paramilitary Activities in and against Nicaragua (Nicar. v. U.S.), at 1–61 (Counter-Memorial submitted August 17, 1984) [hereinafter cited as U.S. Counter-Memorial]. In addition, the United States asserted that jurisdiction was barred by the "multilateral treaty reservation" in its acceptance of compulsory jurisdiction of August 26, 1946, and by Secretary Shultz's letter, supra note 2. See U.S. Counter-Memorial, supra, at 103–21, 131–73.

As its second ground of jurisdiction, Nicaragua contended that the activities charged in the Application violate the Treaty of Friendship, Commerce and Navigation, 9 U.S.T. 449,

367 U.N.T.S. 3, concluded between the United States and Nicaragua on January 21, 1956 (the FCN Treaty), and thus gave rise to jurisdiction under article XXIV(2), submitting disputes arising under the Treaty to the jurisdiction of the Court. See Nicaraguan Memorial, supra, at 85–90.

The United States in turn argued that the FCN Treaty was a "commercial" treaty inapplicable to the matters in issue between the parties. See U.S. Counter-Memorial, supra at 67–71.

14. Eleven judges found that the Court had jurisdiction on the basis of article 36(2) and (5) of the Statute of the Court. Fourteen judges found that the Court had jurisdiction on the basis of article XXIV of the FCN Treaty. Only Judge Schwebel of the United States held that there were no grounds for jurisdiction. See Judgment on Jurisdiction, supra note 7, at 442.

15. Leigh, Judicial Decisions, *Am. J. Int'l L.* (1985), 79:442, 446.

16. Briggs, *Nicaragua v. United States:* Jurisdiction and Admissibility, *Am. J. Int'l L.* (1985), 79:373, 378.

17. Statute of the International Court of Justice art. 36, ¶ 6, 59 Stat. 1055, 1060, T.I.A.S. No. 993 (1945).

18. As Professor Briggs and others have pointed out, that is not quite true of the Court's discussion of the reciprocity principle in relation to the formal aspects of declarations under article 36. See Briggs, supra note 16, at 376–78; Judgment on Jurisdiction, supra note 7, at 419–21.

19. See *N.Y. Times*, April 9, 1984, at Al, col. 2.

20. U.S. Statement, supra note 3, at 64.

21. Remarks by the Honorable Dean Acheson, 1963 Proc. Am. Soc'y Int'l L. 14.

22. Judgment on Jurisdiction, supra note 7, at 442.

23. See U.S. Counter-Memorial, supra note 13, at 177–237.

24. Henkin, Is There a "Political Question" Doctrine? *Yale L.J.* (1976), 85:597, 622.

25. The doctrine in its modern form traces to Justice Brennan's opinion in *Baker v. Carr,* 369 U.S. 186 (1962); see also, e.g., *Gilligan v. Morgan,* 413 U.S. 1 (1973) (congressional and executive authority to prescribe and regulate training and weaponry of National Guard precludes any form of judicial regulation). The doctrine is discussed, but ultimately not applied, in *United States v. Nixon,* 418 U.S. 683 (1974), and *Powell v. McCormack,* 395 U.S. 486 (1969); see also Justice Powell's separate opinion in *Goldwater v. Carter,* 444 U.S. 996, 997 (1979) (judicial branch should not decide issues affecting the allocation of power between the President and Congress until the political branches reach a constitutional impasse).

26. 369 U.S. 186, 217 (1962).

27. See U.S. Counter-Memorial, supra note 13, at 186–90.

28. U.N. Charter art. 39.

29. 369 U.S. at 217.

30. See U.S. Counter-Memorial, supra note 13, at 225–26.

31. See id. at 223–25.

32. See id. at 229–37.

33. 369 U.S. at 217.

34. See U.S. Counter-Memorial, supra note 13, at 188, 189; see also id. at 190 (discussing "textual evidence").

35. Or, at least, every threat to the peace, or breach of the peace, or act of aggression within the meaning of article 39 involves a threat or use of force in violation of article 2(4).

36. 395 U.S. 486 (1969).

37. See 369 U.S. at 217.

38. Justice Brennan himself, however, was careful to point out: "[I]t is error to suppose that every case or controversy which touches foreign relations lies beyond judicial cognizance." Id. at 211.

39. See U.N. Charter art. 11 ¶ 2; id. art. 12, ¶ 1; infra text accompanying notes 44–45.

40. 369 U.S. at 211–12.

41. See U.S. Counter-Memorial, supra note 13, at 192–200 (citing United States Tentative Proposals for General International Organization (July 18, 1944)).

42. See, e.g., Report of the Rapporteur of Commission III to the Plenary Session, Doc. 1170, III/13, 11 U.N.C.I.O. Docs. 232 (1945). The Rapporteur summarizes the efforts of Commission III to this end: "It seems clear that the enforcement of peace and security requires arrangements to ensure the speedy assembling of forces of such magnitude as to deter or to repress aggression. The general plan for the application of force adopted by the Commission embodies a wide grant of authority to the Security Council. Thus, it is empowered to determine the existence of a threat to the peace, to decide in general what measures shall be taken to cope with the danger, to adopt necessary provisional measures, and to call upon the member states of the Organization to apply various categories of measures not involving the actual employment of force." Id. at 233–34.

43. U.N. Charter art. 24, ¶ 1.

44. Id. art. 11, ¶ 2.

45. Id. art. 12, ¶ 1; accord id. art. 11, ¶ 2.

46. Certain Expenses of the United Nations (art. 17, para. 2, of the Charter), 1962 I.C.J. 151, 163 (Advisory Opinion of July 20) [hereinafter cited as Certain Expenses]. The Court reiterated this finding in its Judgment on Jurisdiction, supra note 7, at 434.

47. See United States Diplomatic and Consular Staff in Tehran (*U.S. v. Iran*), 1980 I.C.J. 3, 22 (Judgment of May 24).

48. See U.S. Counter-Memorial, supra note 13, at 193 n.1.

49. U.N. Charter art. 2, ¶ 4.

50. See H. Briggs, *The Law of Nations* 964 (2d ed. 1952); I. Brownlie, *International Law and the Use of Force by States* (1963), 112–13; L. Goodrich and E. Hambro, *Charter of the United Nations* (2d ed. 1949), 102–03; L. Henkin, *How Nations Behave* (2d ed. 1979), 135; Bishop, General Course of Public International Law, *Recueil des Cours* (1965), 115:147, 427; Jiménez de Aréchaga, International Law in the Past Third of a Century, *Recueil des Cours* (1978), 159:1, 87; Lachs, The Development and General Trends of International Law in Our Time, *Recueil des Cours* (1980), 169:1, 159; Schachter, The Right of States To Use Armed Force, *Mich. L. Rev.* (1984), 82:1620 1632; Waldock, The Regulation of the Use of Force by Individual States in International Law, *Recueil des Cours* (1952), 81:451, 492. There is virtually unanimous agreement that this prohibition against the use of force is the fundamental provision, indeed the great achievement, of the Charter.

51. The records of the committee charged with drafting article 2(4) at the San Francisco Conference reveal that numerous proposed amendments were voted down for fear that they would sully the clarity of the original text. According to the delegate of the United States, the authors' intention was "to state in the broadest terms an absolute all-inclusive prohibition." Summary Report of Eleventh Meeting of Committee I/1, Doc. 784, I/1/27, 6 U.N.C.I.O. Docs. 331, 335 (1945).

52. L. Henkin, supra note 50, at 136.

53. The Court has held that the interpretation of the Charter presents a legal question. See Certain Expenses, supra note 46, at 156; Conditions of Admission of a State to Mem-

bership in the United Nations (art. 4 of the Charter), 1947–1948 I.C.J. 61 (Advisory Opinion of May 28, 1948).

54. U.N. Charter art. 39.

55. See id. art. 41.

56. Id. art. 42.

57. Dr. Herbert Evatt, Australian Minister for External Affairs and a key figure at the San Francisco Conference, recalls that "[t]he Dumbarton Oaks draft centered mainly round the Security Council, and it is in the Chapters dealing with this body . . . that the major powers made a real attempt to fill in the 'gap' in the League of Nations Covenant which made enforcement action and the application of sanctions so difficult. . . ." H. Evatt, *The United Nations* (1948), 11; see also L. Goodrich and E. Hambro, supra note 50, at 205, 208 (the "association of responsibility with power" in article 24 is one of "the major advances" of the Charter over the Covenant; and article 25 is a "logical consequence of . . . article 24"); H. Kelsen, *The Law of the United Nations* (1950), 276–77 (Article 25 is an attempt to improve on the Covenant by "conferring upon the Security Council a power almost equal to that of a government."); cf. E. Jiménez de Aréchaga, *Derecho Constitutional de las Naciones Unidas* (1958), 24–27 (criticizing Great Power dominance but recognizing the central importance of article 25).

58. U.N. Charter, Preamble.

59. Chapter VII powers have been explicitly invoked only twice in the history of the Organization: in connection with the Palestinian question in July 1948, see 3 U.N. SCOR Supp. (July 1948) at 76, U.N. Doc. S/902 (1948); infra notes 76–77 and accompanying text, and again 18 years later in imposing economic sanctions on Rhodesia, see S.C. Res. 232, 21 U.N. SCOR, Resolutions and Decisions, at 7, U.N. Doc. S/INF.21.Rev. 2 (1966). Only in these two cases has the operative Security Council resolution recited that the situation "constitutes a threat to international peace and security." The various formulae used in the steps leading up to the final Rhodesian sanctions resolution are discussed infra notes 65–74 and accompanying text; and, e.g., the Korean resolution of June 25, 1950, reciting that "*The Security Council* . . . [*d*]*etermines* that this action constitutes a breach of the peace," did not invoke the mandatory powers of article 39. S.C. Res. 82, 5 U.N. SCOR (473d mtg.) at 7, U.N. Doc. S/Inf/21/Rev. 1 (1950).

The Council's resolution in response to charges of aggression in Indonesia in 1947 referred to the existence of "hostilities" but expressly omitted any mention of article 39. See 2 U.N. SCOR (172d mtg.) at 1700–02, U.N. Doc. 268 (1947); 2 U.N. SCOR (171st mtg.) at 1626, U.N. Doc. 264 (1947). India pressed similar charges against Pakistan in 1948, see 3 U.N. SCOR Supp. (Nov. 1948) at 139, U.N. Doc. S/628 (1948), as did the People's Republic of China against the United States concerning the invasion of Taiwan in 1950, see 5 U.N. SCOR (490th mtg.) at 9 U.N. Doc. S/1715 (1950), but in neither situation was action under article 39 proposed or taken.

60. See, e.g., International Emergency Economic Powers Act, 50 U.S.C. §§ 1701–1706 (1982).

61. See U.S. Counter-Memorial, supra note 13, at 195–99.

62. See id. at 202–07, The United States contended that, in the lengthy efforts by the General Assembly and the International Law Commission to define aggression, the legal and conceptual issues "were addressed in an institutional context that went virtually unquestioned, namely, that the purpose and utility of any such definition of 'aggression' would be as guidance to the political organs in the exercise of their respective responsibilities under the Charter. . . ." Id. at 203. Nicaragua countered that the difficulties encountered in reaching consensus on the issue were a direct result of the Security Council's determination to avoid being hamstrung by a legal definition that would automatically

commit it to action under chapter VII. See Military and Paramilitary Activities in and Against Nicaragua (*Nicar. v. U.S.*), CR 84/15 at 54–55 (Oral Proceedings of Oct. 10, 1984). These efforts are discussed infra notes 90, 101.

63. The Court unanimously agreed with this view of the relationship between chapter VI and chapter VII. It disposed of the United States argument in the following passage: "'[I]t has to be noted that, while the matter has been discussed in the Security Council, no notification has been given to it in accordance with Chapter VII of the Charter, so that the issue could be tabled for full discussion *before a decision were taken for the necessary enforcement measures to be authorized.* It is clear that the complaint of Nicaragua is not about an ongoing armed conflict between it and the United States, but one requiring, and indeed demanding, the peaceful settlement of disputes between the two States. Hence, it is properly brought before the principal judicial organ of the Organization for peaceful settlement." Judgment on Jurisdiction, supra note 7, at 434 (emphasis added). Even after an article 39 determination, as we shall see later, there is no necessary inconsistency between Security Council action and adjudication by the Court. See infra notes 114–33 and accompanying text. The only power exclusively committed to the Security Council is the power to take "action" within the meaning of chapter VII. See Certain Expenses, supra note 46, at 163.

64. 20 U.N. SCOR (1259th mtg.) at 20–21, U.N. Doc. S/P.V. 1259 (1965) (emphasis in original).

65. See id. at 5–10.

66. S.C. Res. 217, 20 U.N. SCOR, Resolutions and Decisions at 8–9, U.N. Doc. S/RES/217 (1965).

67. See 20 U.N. SCOR (1265th mtg.) at 15, U.N. Doc. S/P.V. 1265 (1965).

68. S.C. Res. 221, 21 U.N. SCOR, Resolutions and Decisions at 5–6, U.N. Doc. S/P.V. 1277 (1966).

69. 21 U.N. SCOR (1276th mtg.) at 11, U.N. Doc. S/P.V. 1276 (1976).

70. See id. at 5–7, 14–18; 21 U.N. SCOR (1277th mtg.) at 36–38, U.N. Doc. S/P.V. 1277 (1966).

71. See 2 A. Chayes, T. Ehrlich, and A. Lowenfeld, *International Legal Process* (1969), 1365.

72. S.C. Res 232, 21 U.N. SCOR, Resolutions and Decisions at 7–9, U.N. Doc. S/P.V. 1340 (1966) (emphasis deleted).

73. See id. § 3.

74. As the Jordanian representative said, "The determination of the situation as one falling within the meaning of Article 39 is not a question of legal interpretation, it is a question of evidence, a question of proof, a question of fact." 20 U.N. SCOR (1264th mtg.) at 5, U.N. Doc. S/P.V. 1264 (1965); see also *Repertory of Practice of United Nations Organs* (1955), 2:353–54 (discussion of the report of the Security Council subcommittee established in April 1946 to determine whether the activities of the Franco regime in Spain posed a danger to international peace and security) [hereinafter cited as 2 U.N. Practice].

75. See, e.g., 21 U.N. SCOR (1332d mtg.) at 13, U.N. Doc. S/P.V. 1332 (1966); 21 U.N. SCOR (1331st mtg.) at 5–6 U.N. Doc. S/P.V. 1331 (1966); 21 U.N. SCOR (1276th mtg.) at 5–7, U.N. Doc. S/P.V. 1276 (1966); 20 U.N. SCOR (1258th mtg.) at 21–22, U.N. Doc. S/P.V. 1258 (1965).

76. See 3 U.N. SCOR (296th mtg.) at 6 (1948).

77. 2 U.N. Practice, supra note 74, at 350.

78. See Application of the United States (*U.S. v. U.S.S.R.*), 1959 I.C.J. Pleadings 8–11 (Application dated June 8, 1959) (Aerial Incident of Nov. 7, 1954); Application of the

United States (*U.S. v. Bulg.*), 1959 I.C.J. Pleadings 22–24 (Application dated Oct. 24, 1957) (Aerial Incident of July 27, 1955); Application of the United States (*U.S. v. U.S.S.R.*), 1958 I.C.J. Pleadings 8–10 (Application dated July 25, 1958) (Aerial Incident of Sept. 4, 1954); Application of the United States (*U.S. v. U.S.S.R.*), 1956 I.C.J. Pleadings 9–11 (Application dated May 26, 1955) (Aerial Incident of Oct. 7, 1952); Application of the United States (*U.S. v. Czech.*), 1956 I.C.J. Pleadings 8–10 (Application dated March 22, 1955) (Aerial Incident of March 10, 1953); Applications of the United States (*U.S. v. Hung., U.S. v. U.S.S.R.*), 1954 I.C.J. Pleadings 8–10, 42–44 (Applications dated Feb. 16, 1954) (Treatment in Hungary of aircraft and crew of United States of America.

79. Certain Expenses, supra note 46, at 177.

80. Waldock, supra note 50, at 506.

81. See supra text following note 73.

82. U.N. Charter art. 94, ¶ 2.

83. The Court adopted this view of the matter in the *Nicaragua* case. It said: "The Council has functions of a political nature assigned to it, whereas the Court exercises purely judicial functions. Both organs can therefore perform their separate but complementary functions with respect to the same events." Judgment on Jurisdiction, supra note 7, at 435.

84. See *Baker v. Carr,* 369 U.S. 186, 217 (1962).

85. Id. at 301 (Frankfurter, J., dissenting).

86. See *Reynolds v. Sims,* 377 U.S. 533 (1964).

87. Corfu Channel (*U.K. v. Alb.*), 1949 I.C.J. 4 (Judgment on the Merits of April 9, 1949).

88. See, e.g., I. Brownlie, supra note 50; R. Falk, *Legal Order in a Violent World* (1968); C. Rousseau, *Le Droit des Conflits Armés* (1983); Baxter, The Legal Consequences of the Unlawful Use of Force Under the Charter, *Am. Soc'y of Int'l L. Proc.* (1968), 62:68; McDougal and Feliciano, Legal Regulation of Resort to International Coercion: Aggression and Self-Defence in Policy Perspective, *Yale L.J.* (1959), 68:1057; Schachter, supra note 50; Waldock, supra note 50. For a complete bibliography of books and articles on the subject through 1963, see I. Brownlie, supra note 50, at 475.

89. The record of the San Francisco Conference is quite clear that article 2(4) was intended to refer to military rather than political or economic force. See Doc. 784, I/1/27, 6 U.N.C.I.O. Docs. 334 (1945); Doc. 215, I/1/10, 6 U.N.C.I.O. Docs. 559 (1945) (rejecting a Brazilian amendment that would have prohibited "the threat or use of economic measures"). Second, the addition of the phrase "against the territorial integrity or political independence of any state" to the draft text was in no way intended to limit the basic prohibition against the use of force. See Doc. 20, P/6, 1 U.N.C.I.O. Docs. 165 (1945); Doc. 272, I/1/11, 6 U.N.C.I.O. Docs. 286 (1945); Doc. 810, I/1/30, 6 U.N.C.I.O. Docs. 342 (1945); Doc. 337, I/1/A/2, 6 U.N.C.I.O. Docs. 646 (1945); Doc. 382, I/1/19, 6 U.N.C.I.O. Docs. 303 (1945).

The most succinct statement of the intended import of article 2(4) is contained in the report of the Rapporteur of Committee 1 to Commission I: "The Committee wishes to state . . . the unilateral use of force or similar coercive measures is not authorized or admitted. The use of arms in legitimate self-defense remains admitted and unimpaired. The use of force, therefore, remains legitimate only to back up the decisions of the Organization at the start of a controversy or during its solution in the way that the Organization itself ordains." Doc. 944, I/1/34(I), 6 U.N.C.I.O. Docs. 446–449 (1945).

90. For a comprehensive documentation of the work of the International Law Commission and various United Nations special committees on a definition of aggression, see B. Ferencz, *Defining International Aggression, the Search for World Peace: A Documentary*

History and Analysis (1975). Precursors of the definition finally adopted in 1974 include, e.g., Essentials of Peace Resolution, G.A. Res. 290(IV), U.N. Doc. A/1251, at 13 (1949); Draft Declaration on the Rights and Duties of States, adopted by the International Law Commission in 1949, 7 U.N. GAOR Supp. (no. 10) at 10, U.N. Doc. A/925 (1949); Peace Through Deeds Resolution, G.A. Res. 380(V), 5 U.N. GAOR Supp. (No. 20) at 13, U.N. Doc. A/1775 (1950); International Law Commission, Draft Code of Offenses Against the Peace and Security of Mankind, 9 U.N. GAOR Supp. (No. 9) at 11, U.N. Doc. A/2693 (1954); Declaration on the Inadmissibility of Intervention in the Domestic Affairs of States and the Protection of Their Independence and Sovereignty, G.A. Res. 2131(XX), 20 U.N. GAOR Supp. (no. 14) at 11, U.N. Doc. A/6014 (1965); Declaration on Principles of International Law Concerning Friendly Relations and Co-operation Among States in Accordance with the Charter of the United Nations, G.A. Res. 2625(XXV), 25 U.N. GAOR Supp. (No. 28) at 121, U.N. Doc. A/Res/2625 (1970).

91. 29 U.N. GAOR Supp. (No. 31) at 142, U.N. Doc. A/9631 (1974).

92. See Schachter, supra note 50, at 1633.

93. See H. Hart, *The Concept of Law* (1961), 119.

94. The discussion in the text analyzes Nicaragua's legal theories in terms of the facts alleged in its application. These allegations must be proved by Nicaragua in the merits phase of the proceedings. See infra notes 106 and 107.

95. See Nicaraguan Memorial, supra note 13, at 116–22.

96. President Reagan's personal authorization of the mining of the Nicaraguan harbors was revealed by Senator Goldwater, the Chairman of the Senate Intelligence Committee, on the floor of the Senate. See *Cong. Rec.* 130:S4198 (daily ed. April 10, 1984); see also Letter from Senator Barry Goldwater, Chairman, Senate Select Committee on Intelligence, to William J. Casey, Director of Central Intelligence (April 9, 1984), reprinted in *Wash. Post,* April 11, 1984, at A17, col. 1 (expressing his anger over the mining). Congressional sources further revealed that United States military and intelligence personnel had directed and participated in the attack on the port of Corinto on October 10, 1983. See *N.Y. Times,* April 18, 1984, at Al, col. 5; *Wash. Post,* Apr. 18, 1984, at Al, col. 4; see also News Conference by President Ronald Reagan, October 19, 1983, *Dep't. St. Bull.* (Dec. 1983), 83:(2081):6 (Reagan suggests that some covert activity is a "part of government's responsibilities"); CIA Internal Report Details U.S. Role in Contra Raids in Nicaragua Last Year, *Wall St. J.*, March 6, 1985, § 1, at 20, col. 1 (recounting United States direction and participation in 19 separate attacks against Nicaraguan economic installations between January 1 and April 10, 1984, using helicopters and speedboats launched from C.I.A. "mother ships").

97. See Nicaraguan Memorial, supra note 13, 122–67.

98. Article 8 of the draft Articles on State Responsibility prepared by the International Law Commission provides: "The Conduct of a person or group of persons shall also be considered as an act of the State under international law if (a) it is established that such persons or group of persons was in fact acting on behalf of that State. . . ." Report of the International Law Commission to the General Assembly, [1974] 2 *Y.B. Int'l L. Comm'n* (pt. 1) 283 U.N. Doc. A/9610/Rev. 1. The principle involved is essentially a straightforward application of the law of agency to the international realm.

99. This theory would not cover United States aid to the Afghan rebels, for example.

100. Numerous instances of United States support for these views are collected in 5 M. Whiteman, *Digest of International Law,* ch. XIII, § 22 (1965). A few salient examples are given in this note.

As early as 1947, United States Representative Austin, in urging the Security Council to condemn external support for the guerrillas in Greece, said: "I do not think that we should interpret narrowly the Great Charter of the United Nations. In modern times, there are many ways in which force can be used by one State against the territorial integrity of another. Invasion by organized armies is not the only means for delivering an attack against a country's independence. Force is effectively used today through devious methods of infiltration, intimidation and subterfuge." 2 U.N. SCOR (147th & 148th mtgs.) at 1120 (1947).

In 1958, commenting on the situation in Lebanon, Secretary of State Dulles said: "[W]e do not think that the words 'armed attack' preclude treating as such an armed revolution which is fomented from abroad, aided and assisted from abroad." Secretary Dulles' News Conference of July 1, 1958, 39 Dep't St. Bull., No. 995, at 104–05 (July 21, 1958), reprinted in 5 M. Whiteman, supra, at 320.

Speaking to the Organ of Consultation of the OAS in 1964 on the question of Cuban-sponsored subversion in Venezuela, Secretary of State Rusk invoked the same principle: "Awareness that subversion, supported by terror, sabotage, and guerrilla action, as practiced by the international Communist movement, is as dangerous a form of aggression as an armed attack has been very slow in developing in this hemisphere, as well as in other parts of the world. I think it is fair to say that until very recently there has been a lack of sufficient understanding of this point everywhere, and this has led to uncertainty in some quarters as to whether our regional security system possesses an adequate mechanism for dealing with Communist subversion." Statement of July 22, 1964, at the 9th Meeting of Consultation of Ministers of Foreign Affairs, serving as Organ of Consultation in Application of the Inter-American Treaty of Reciprocal Assistance, *Dep't St. Bull.* (Aug. 10, 1964), 51 (1311):174, 178.

The United States representatives to the United Nations Special Committee on the Question of Defining Aggression unwaveringly maintained this view of indirect aggression and ultimately succeeded in incorporating it into the United Nations Definition of Aggression. See infra note 101.

101. The General Assembly began debate on a proposed definition of aggression in the late 1940s, and in 1952 referred the matter to a Special Committee. See G.A. Res. 688(VII), 7 U.N. GAOR Supp. (No. 20) at 63, U.N. Doc A/2361 (1952); supra note 90. Whether the definition should distinguish direct from indirect aggression was an issue in the Special Committee from its early days. See, e.g., Report of the 1956 Special Committee on the Question of Defining Aggression, 12 U.N. GAOR Supp. (No. 16) at 8, U.N. Doc. A/3574 (1956). The U.S. representatives to the Special Committee consistently asserted that it should not. For example, Judge Schwebel, then United States Representative to the Special Committee, argued that "the Charter of the United Nations makes no distinction between direct and indirect use of force" and that the "most pervasive forms of modern aggression tend to be indirect ones." Schwebel, Aggression, Intervention and Self-Defence in Modern International Law, *Recueil des Cours* (1972), 136:458.

102. 29 U.N. GAOR Supp. (No. 31) at 142, U.N. Doc. A/9631 (1974). The final language of 3(g) was a compromise between the position of the United States, which wanted a still broader definition, and the Third World countries, which were concerned that too wide a sweep would inhibit support of independence struggles. 2 B. Ferencz, supra note 90, at 40; J. Stone, *Conflict Through Consensus* (1977), 75.

103. Charter of the Organization of American States art. 15.

104. Although the story is well known to Latin Americans, it may not be amiss to set forth the highlights here. It begins in 1823 with the Monroe Doctrine, *Messages and Papers of the Presidents of the United States,* (J. Richardson ed. 1897), 2:776–89, which, in its original context, was intended and received as a statement of the principle of nonintervention, directed at the European powers. Yet as time went on, the United States

interpreted the Doctrine as authorizing a very broad range of unilateral United States intervention in the affairs of Latin American countries, whether in response to European involvements or conflicts among Latin American States themselves or internal developments thought inimical to United States interests. In 1904 this practice was formalized in the Roosevelt Corollary to the Doctrine, asserting a general United States police power in the Western Hemisphere. See J. Moore, *A Digest of International Law* (1906), 6:596–97.

As the United States assumed a larger role in world affairs in the twentieth century, Colombia, Cuba, the Dominican Republic, Haiti, Honduras, Mexico, and Nicaragua were all victims of occupation by United States armed forces at one time or another. Treaties with Cuba, Panama, and other countries purported to authorize future interventions.

The Latin American reaction is summed up by Luis Quintanilla, a Mexican diplomat and representative to the Organization of American States: "In the previous fifty years [before 1933], the United States had intervened some sixty times in the affairs and territories of its Latin American neighbors—especially in the Caribbean. . . . How could one speak seriously of inter-American solidarity, Pan Americanism, or Good Neighborliness when the stumbling block in the path of the good relations was nothing less than the most powerful republic of the Hemisphere? The situation could change only if and when the United States decided to abandon once and for all its imperialistic interventionism." L. Quintanilla, *A Latin American Speaks* (1943), 156.

105. See, e.g., Fenwick Intervention: Individual and Collective, *Am. J. Int'l L.* (1945), 39:653–59; Supulveda, The Reform of the Charter of the Organization of American States, *Recueil des Cours* (1972), 137(3):83, 96.

106. See Judgment on Jurisdiction, supra note 7, at 437 (Judgment on the merits "will be limited to upholding such submissions of the Parties as have been supported by sufficient proof. . . . [I]t is the litigant seeking to establish a fact who bears the burden of proving it; and in cases where evidence may not be forthcoming, a submission may in the judgment be rejected as unproved. . . .").

107. The World Court cannot give a default judgment. It may render a decision in the absence of the respondent, but it must "satisfy itself . . . that the claim is well founded in fact and law." Statute of the International Court of Justice art. 53, ¶ 2, 59 Stat. 1055, 1062, T.I.A.S. No. 993 (1945).

108. See, e.g., sources cited infra note 110.

109. See Corfu Channel (*U.K. v. Alb.*), 1949 I.C.J. 4, 248 (Judgment on the Merits of April 9, 1949). The Court relied upon this precedent in the *U.S. Staff* case, where it accepted the contentions of the United States concerning the evidence: "The essential facts of the present case are, for the most part, matters of public knowledge which have received extensive coverage in the world press and in radio and television broadcasts from Iran and other countries." United States Diplomatic and Consular Staff in Tehran (*U.S. v. Iran*), 1980 I.C.J. 3, 9 (Judgment of May 24, 1980). The Court concluded that in light of the consistency and amount of the information available, and given the absence of any denial or rebuttal by the Iranian government, the requirements of article 53 were satisfied. See id. at 10.

110. See, e.g., the notorious exchange with a reporter: Q. [A]ren't you advocating the overthrow of the present government? If—. . . . A. Not if the present government would turn around and say, all right, if they'd say Uncle." Radio Address to the Nation by President Ronald Reagan, March 30, 1985, *Dep't St. Bull.*) (June 1985), 85 (2099):11.

This exchange was part of a series of statements made by President Reagan after the United States had announced its withdrawal from the case in early 1985, in which he affirmed openly that the United States sought to use the contras to force a change in the structure of the Nicaraguan government. See Interview of President Ronald Reagan by the *New York Times,* February 11, 1985, *Weekly Comp. Pres. Doc.* (Feb. 15, 1985), 21:169; Radio Address to the Nation by President Ronald Reagan, February 16, 1985, *Dep't St. Bull.* (April 1985), 85 (2097):10; accord Address to Conservative Political Action Conference, March 1, 1985, *Weekly Comp. Pres. Doc.* (March 11, 1985), 21:243; Interview with the President, *Bus. Wk.*, March 11, 1985, at 68; News Conference by President Ronald Reagan, February 21, 1985, *Dep't St. Bull.* (April 1985), 85 (2097):11 [hereinafter cited as News Conference]. The same basic purpose is reflected in numerous earlier presidential statements and news interviews. See, e.g., Interview with the *New York Times* (March 28, 1984), *Weekly Comp. Pres. Doc.* (April 12, 1984), 20:440 Question-and-Answer Session with Reporters, May 4, 1983, *Weekly Comp. Press. Doc.* (May 9, 1983), 19:645; News Conference of October 19, 1983, *Dep't St. Bull.* (Dec. 1983), 83 (2081):6.

111. The majority of commentators adopt this reading of article 51. See, e.g., I. Brownlie, supra note 50 at 278; L. Henkin, supra note 50; E. Jiménez de Aréchaga, supra note 57, at 401; L. Oppenheim, *International Law* (7th ed. 1952), 156; Bishop, supra note 50, at 436–37; Verdross, Idées directrices de l'organisation des Nations Unies, *Recueil des Cours* (1953), 83:1, 14–15; Wright, The Prevention of Aggression, *Am. J. Int'l L.* (1956), 50:514, 529. A number of authors take a broader view, equating self-defense under article 51 with the right of self-defense under customary law. But even these would not stretch the concept to include military action over a long period of time to force a state to change its government or general policies. See, e.g., D. Bowett, *Self-Defence in International Law* (1958); Higgins, The Legal Limits to the Use of Force by Sovereign States: United Nations Practice, *Brit. Y.B. Int'l L.* (1961), 37:269, 301–02; Schachter, supra note 50, at 1634–35; Schwarzenberger, The Fundamental Principles of International Law, *Recueil des Cours* (1955), 87:191, 332–33.

112. Note that a claim of self-defense would have an important bearing on the issue discussed above of United States responsibility for contra activities. See supra text accompanying notes 97–99. Whatever the formal rules about inconsistent pleading in the International Court, it would hardly be possible to maintain at the same time that the contras are not surrogates of the United States and, on the other hand, that they are being used by us in an exercise of the inherent right of self-defense.

113. The key procedural requirement is set out in article 51 itself: "Measures taken by Members in the exercise of this right of self-defence shall be immediately reported to the Security Council. . . ." U.N. Charter art. 51.

It is universally agreed that the legitimate exercise of the right of self-defense under both customary law and the Charter is subject to the requirement of proportionality. See, e.g., Lachs, supra note 50, at 164. Even assuming arguendo the truth of the United States allegations of arms shipments to El Salvador, the United States response is on a completely different scale. Finally, even those authors who favor a broad interpretation of article 51, see supra note 111, would subject a government to the requirements of Daniel Webster's famous formulation in the *Caroline* case: "A necessity of self-defense [that is] instant, overwhelming, and leaving no choice of means, and no moment for deliberation." Waldock, supra note 50, at 496–98.

114. U.S. Counter-Memorial, supra note 13, at 218–19.

115. See, e.g., H. M. Hart and A. Sacks, *The Legal Process* (tent. ed. 1958), 1381–1400.

116. See S.C. Res. 530, 38 U.N. SCOR (2437th mtg.) at 10, U.N. Doc. S/Res./530 (1983); G.A. Res. 38/10, 38 U.N. GAOR Supp. (No. 47) at 21, U.N. Doc. A/38/47 (1983); OAS General Assembly Resolution of November 18, 1983, on Peace Efforts in

Central America, AG/Res. 657 (XII-O/83), attached to 38 U.N. SCOR (7th plen. mtg.) at 5–6, U.N. Doc. S/16208 (1983).

The Contadora process takes its name from the site in Panama of a January 1983 meeting of the foreign ministers of Colombia, Mexico, Panama, and Venezuela devoted to a general review of common problems, particularly the deteriorating situation in Central America. The communique of January 9, 1983, began by expressing profound concern at the direct or indirect involvement of foreign forces in Central America. It called urgently for dialogue among the States of the region, reaffirmed the obligation to refrain from the threat or use of force and called on the States concerned to do nothing to aggravate the situation or increase the danger of a general war in the region. See *N.Y. Times,* Jan. 10, 1983, at A3, col. 1.

From this beginning, the Contadora powers were successful in establishing arrangements, with the agreement of the five Central American States, for general negotiations about the problems of the region, in which Colombia, Mexico, Panama, and Venezuela would continue to participate by way of good offices and mediation. By virtue of its location in the region, Nicaragua has been a participant since July 1983, but the United States has not.

117. See U.S. Counter-Memorial, supra note 13, at 209–12, 223, 229–37. The United States insistence that the Court "act with due regard for the functional responsibilities of its co-ordinate organs," id. at 210, echoes Justice Brennan's concern in *Baker v. Carr* for the "respect due coordinate branches of government," 369 U.S. 186, 217 (1962).

118. But see Communication to the Registrar of the Court from Costa Rica, April 18, 1984 (expressing concern that adjudication of the Nicaragua case could jeopardize the Contadora process); Communication to the Registrar of the Court from El Salvador, April 19, 1984 (same); Note from Honduras to the Secretary General of the United Nations, April 18, 1984 (same).

119. On May 15, 1984, after the Court's Provisional Measures order in the *Nicaragua* case, supra note 7, Contadora-sponsored negotiations resulted in an agreement between Nicaragua and Costa Rica for the establishment of border supervision to suppress armed incursions across their common boundary. See Nicaraguan Memorial, supra note 13, Annex IV, Exhibits H and I. On September 7, 1983, the four Contadora nations signed a draft treaty, entitled "Contadora Act for Peace and Cooperation in Central America (Revised)," and invited comments from the participating countries. See *Wash. Post,* Oct. 4, 1984, at A30, col. 1. Although Nicaragua expressed its willingness to sign two weeks before the release of the draft, Costa Rica, El Salvador, and Honduras bowed to United States pressure and requested further revisions. See *N.Y. Times,* Oct. 18, 1984, at Al, col. 3.

120. See South West Africa Cases (*Ethiopia v. S. Afr., Liberia v. S. Afr.*), 1962 I.C.J. 319 (Judgment on Preliminary Objections of Dec. 21, 1962); id. 1966 I.C.J. 6 (Second Phase Judgment of July 18, 1966).

121. 1 S. Rosenne, *The Law and Practice of the International Court* (1965), 87.

122. Id. at 86.

123. German Minority Schools in Upper Silesia (*Ger. v. Pol.*), 1928 P.C.I.J., ser. A, No. 15 (Judgment of April 26).

124. Interpretation of the Statute of the Memel Territory (*Gr. Brit. v. Lithuanian Republic*), 1932 P.C.I.J., ser. A/B, No. 47 (Preliminary Objection, Judgment of June 24).

125. See (*Ger. v. Pol.*), 1928 P.C.I.J., ser. A, No. 15, at 29.

126. (*Gr. Brit. v. Lithuanian Republic*), 1932 P.C.I.J., ser. A/B, No. 47, at 248.

127. United States Diplomatic and Consular Staff in Tehran (*U.S. v. Iran*), 1980 I.C.J. at 16.

128. Id. at 20.

129. Id. at 19.

130. Id. at 20.

131. Id. at 21. The Court referred to this passage in its decision in the *Nicaragua* case and concluded: "[T]he Court is of the view that the fact that a matter is before the Security Council should not prevent it being dealt with by the Court and that both proceedings could be pursued *pari passu*." Judgment on Jurisdiction, supra note 7, at 433.

132. 1980 I.C.J. at 22.

133. Id. at 23.

134. See, e.g., *Baker v. Carr,* 369 U.S. 186, 217 (1962); Henkin, supra note 24, at 598.

135. See Oral Proceedings, 1962 I.C.J. Pleadings (Certain Expenses of the United Nations) 413 (Memorial dated May 21, 1962).

136. Chayes, A Common Lawyer Looks at International Law, *Harv. L. Rev.* (1965), 78:1396, 1409.

137. See Chayes, The Role of the Judge in Public Law Litigation, *Harv. L. Rev.* (1976), 89:1281.

138. See, e.g., *The Federalist No. 10* (J. Madison); id. *No. 47* (J. Madison); id. *No. 51* (J. Madison).

139. For an analysis of the way in which the allocation of powers within the state derives from the protections of the "absolute rights" of "personal security, personal liberty, and private property," see Kennedy, The Structure of Blackstone's Commentaries, *Buffalo L. Rev.* (1979), 28:205, 272–311.

140. Statute of the International Court of Justice art. 36, ¶ 1, 59 Stat. 1055, T.I.A.S. No. 993 (1945).

141. Id. ¶ 2.

142. In an early case brought under the advisory jurisdiction, see id. art. 65, ¶ 1, the Permanent Court exercised its discretion to decline to adjudicate, apparently on the ground that what was presented as a request for an advisory opinion in reality asked the Court to adjudicate a contested boundary dispute when one of the parties, the Soviet Union, had not accepted the jurisdiction of the Court. See Reply to the Request for an Advisory Opinion Concerning the Status of Eastern Carelia (*Fin. v. U.S.S.R.*), 1923 P.C.I.J., ser. B., No. 5 (Resolution of April 21). Even in advisory cases, however, where there is a discretionary element in the jurisdictional grant, the present Court has not been reluctant to decide assertedly political cases. For example, in Advisory Opinion on Conditions of Admissions of a State to Membership in the United Nations (Article 4 of the Charter), 1948 I.C.J. 57, 58 (Advisory Opinion of May 28), the Soviet Union contended that the question presented—whether a member voting on admission of another state is "juridically entitled to make its consent to the admission dependent on conditions not expressly provided by paragraph 1 of [Charter Article 4]"—was essentially a political question and ought not to be resolved by adjudication. See id. The Court replied: "The Court cannot attribute a political character to a request which, framed in abstract terms, invites it to undertake an essentially judicial task, the interpretation of a treaty provision. It is not concerned with the motives which may have inspired this request, nor with the considerations which, in the concrete cases submitted for examination to the Security Council formed the subject of the exchange of views which took place in that body. It is the duty of the Court to envisage the question submitted to it only in the abstract form which has been given to it; nothing which is said in the present opinion refers, either directly or indirectly, to concrete cases or to particular circumstances." Id. at 61.

143. It is hardly original to assert that the law operates by incentives as often as by

sanctions. Even where the law is cast in the form of clear prohibition, obedience to its precepts "is most often not perceived as response to an external constraint, but as the affirmation of valued and desired objectives." A. Chayes, *The Cuban Missile Crisis* (1974), 26; see L. Fuller, *The Morality of Law* (1964), 145–51; H. Hart, supra note 93, at 197; see also L. Tribe, *American Constitutional Law* (1978), 52 (describing the valued objectives in desegregation and in one person, one vote).

144. See *United States v. Nixon,* 418 U.S. 683 (1974).

145. Dissenting in *Baker v. Carr,* Justice Frankfurter observed: "The Court's authority—possessed of neither the purse nor the sword—ultimately rests on sustained public confidence in its moral sanction." 369 U.S. 186, 267 (1962) (Frankfurter, J., dissenting). He was arguing *against* deciding *Baker v. Carr.* Yet in retrospect it seems clear that the decision strengthened the Supreme Court's moral authority.

146. The locus classicus is de Tocqueville, who commented on the unusual "respect for the law in the United States," attributing it to the fact that as a member of a democracy, "the American . . . regards . . . [a law] as a contract to which he is one of the parties," or, at worst, "as a self-imposed evil." A. de Tocqueville, *Democracy in America* (G. Lawrence trans., 1969), 240–41. His oft-cited paragraph is worth quoting in full here: "There is hardly a political question in the United States which does not sooner or later turn into a judicial one. Consequently the language of everyday party-political controversy has to be borrowed from legal phraseology and conceptions. As most public men are or have been lawyers, they apply their legal habits and turn of mind to the conduct of affairs. Juries make all classes familiar with this. So legal language is pretty well adopted into common speech; the spirit of the law, born within schools and courts, spreads little by little beyond them; it infiltrates through society right down to the lowest ranks, till finally the whole people have contracted some of the ways and tastes of a magistrate." Id. at 270.

147. See United States Diplomatic and Consular Staff in Tehran (*U.S. v. Iran*), 1980 I.C.J. 3 (Judgment of May 24, 1980); Nuclear Tests (*Austl. v. Fr., N.Z. v. Fr.*), 1974 I.C.J. 253, 457 (Judgment of Dec. 20, 1974; Corfu Channel (*U.K. v. Alb.*), 1949 I.C.J. 4 (Judgment on the Merits of April 9, 1949).

148. *Baker v. Carr,* 369 U.S. 186, 267 (1962) (Frankfurter, J., dissenting); see also *The Federalist No. 78* (A. Hamilton).

149. See Frankfurter, Supreme Court, United States, 14 *Encyclopaedia of the Social Sciences* (1934), 474, 477.

150. 198 U.S. 45 (1905).

151. *Dred Scott v. Sandford,* 60 U.S. (19 How.) 393 (1857).

152. 347 U.S. 483 (1954).

153. See *N.Y. Times,* May 17, 1984, at B18, col. 1; see also Symposium: Educational Equality Thirty Years After *Brown v. Board of Education, U. Colo. L. Rev.* (1984), 55:487 (examining the legal, political, and educational issues raised in seeking equal access and opportunities for those previously discriminated against by the educational system).

154. See Rossell, Desegregation Plans, Racial Isolation, White Flight, and Community Response, in C. Rossell and W. Howley, eds., *The Consequences of School Desegregation,* (1983), 13.

155. A report submitted to Congress in 1983 by the Joint Center for Political Studies concluded that the segregation of black and hispanic students in inner-city schools, particularly in the Northeast, was increasing. See *N.Y. Times,* May 17, 1984, at B18, col. 1.

156. 163 U.S. 537 (1896).

157. See Bickel, Foreword: The Passive Virtues, *Harv. L. Rev.* (1961), 75:40, 50; Tribe, Constitutional Calculus: Equal Justice or Economic Efficiency? *Harv. L. Rev.* (1985), 98:592, 595.

158. Compare Excerpts from Address of Weinberger, *N.Y. Times,* Nov. 29, 1984, at A5, col. 1 (Address to National Press Club, Nov. 28, 1984) (Weinberger lists six tests to be used in weighing the use of military force abroad, one of which is the reasonable assurance of support of the American people and their representatives), with G. Shultz, The Ethics of Power, *Dep't. St. Bull.* (Feb. 1985), 85 (2095):1–3 (Address delivered at the Convocation of Yeshiva University, December 9, 1984) (Shultz notes that there can be no guaranteed public support in advance of military action but that wise and effective action will win public support for actions to which the United States must respond); see also, Halloran, Shultz, and Weinberger: Disputing Use of Force, *N.Y. Times,* Nov. 30, 1984, at B6, col. 3 (comparing Shultz's and Weinberger's views).

159. The United States first undertook an obligation to "renounce the use of force as an instrument of national policy" in the Kellogg-Briand Pact of 1928, 46 Stat. 2343, T.S. No. 796, 94 L.N.T.S. 57, which was named after United States Secretary of State Kellogg. This obligation was incorporated in article 2(4) of the United Nations Charter, see I. Brownlie, supra note 50, at 112–13, and is generally recognized by the United States, as well as others, as "a peremptory norm of international law," Press Release USUN-156(76), Nov. 22, 1976 (statement of the United States Representative in the Sixth Committee (Legal) at the United Nations); see A. McNair, *The Law of Treaties* (1961), 217.

160. A. Bickel, *The Least Dangerous Branch* (1962), 187–88.

4

FURTHER REFLECTIONS ON THE CONSTITUTIONAL JUSTICE OF LIVELIHOOD

Charles L. Black, Jr.

The first words uttered by the new American people claimed, for all humankind, equality in creation, and acknowledged the rights to life, to liberty, and to the pursuit of happiness, as gifts of God to His human creatures.[1] It is not wonderful that Catherine the Great grew troubled in mind, and mounted a diplomatic offensive designed to bring about the failure of our Revolution. And the ghost of La Rochefoucauld must have smiled, for his most famous maxim, published about a century before, had attained quintessential illustration.

But in less than another century—for only eighty-nine years, a length of human life recorded every day or two in the obituary pages, elapsed between the Declaration of Independence and the thirteenth amendment—La Rochefoucauld might have been moved to add unto his maxim yet a codicil. Hypocrisy is indeed the homage that vice renders to virtue. But hypocrisy may commit itself beyond easy retraction. The thirteenth amendment had lain latent in the Declaration of Independence.

Indeed, the hypocrisy that commits itself may undergo metamorphosis as the commitment is acted upon. It may turn out that what seemed hypocrisy was commitment all the while; no more than persons do nations fully know their own minds all at once. The choice for this metamorphosis can be made only over the lapse of generations. The generation that abolished slavery made such a choice, as to the matter wherein the hypocrisy of the Declaration had seemed most startling.

But the Declaration of Independence is still here. Later generations, yours and mine and others to come, have much work to do, if we, and those who follow us, choose to change *all* the assertions in the second sentence of the Declaration from hypocrisy to commitment.

Kenneth Stampp has said that the imperishable accomplishment of the Reconstruction was the utterance of the fourteenth and fifteenth amendments.[2] Placed where they were, these amendments were sure sooner or later to bear fruit. The words stayed there, through decades wherein the fifteenth amendment was laid open to frustration by mere monkey tricks, and wherein the segregation regime made snickering nonsense of the fourteenth. Then, at last, the words would not be denied. There is no reason why the remaining unredeemed words of the Declaration, which likewise cannot be expunged, may not come to have a like history. It wasn't very long ago that national commitment to those words was recorded. Here I stand in front of you, full of fight. Yet just three lives, each the length of mine to now, take you back to the summer of 1774, nearly two years before the Declaration was uttered. It is in awareness of this scale of time that I am trying to move any who will listen toward acceptance of the proposition that there is, "and of Right ought to be,"[3] a constitutional justice of livelihood.

Breuer, the early collaborator with Freud in that work on hysteria that led at last to the full development of psychoanalysis, remarked that when any subject is much in the intellectual air, it becomes impossible to separate out lines of influence.[4] Anybody who in these days writes about the justice of livelihood must feel the force of Breuer's saying. I desire to make no claim of originality in may own throughts on this. Nor can I with knowledge disclaim all originality; maybe I could if I were a wider reader than I am.

I am calling this lecture "Further Reflections on the Constitutional Justice of Livelihood." Since I cannot assume that everybody here this afternoon has been eagerly following my recent writing, I have to sketch what I have been up to.[5]

I have committed myself to drawing from the ninth amendment[6] an irresistibly implied legitimation for our doing something we have in fact been doing for quite a long time—first seeking and then protecting rights not named in the constitutional text. I see the amendment not as in itself *referring* to any particular right or rights, but rather as commanding us to use the methods available within our legal system in an ongoing *search* for "unenumerated" rights, with a view to their taking their place, without denial or disparagement, in a rational and therefore productive system. I have proposed, as one general method for that search (besides the ancient methods of analogy and of inference from structure), the use of a test of gross disproportionality—between private human loss and public gain—as marking the governmental act that is discernibly incompatible with a serious commitment to liberty, such as that expressed in the Declaration of Independence and in the preamble to the Constitution. With that general method I shall not deal in this lecture. At this time I want to elaborate on a special derivation—the derivation of a constitutional right to a decent material basis for life—from the Declaration, from the preamble, and from certain parts of the Constitution proper.

If any human rights at all are shielded against denial or disparagement by the command of the ninth amendment, then there could be no third place as good to begin a search for their ground as in the Declaration or in the preamble. Let me say, however—and so perhaps spare a few or many of you some anxiety—that if you just cannot bring your mind around to the ninth amendment, if the two-century prescriptive silence about the ninth amendment irreversibly taboos it in your estimation, then one can also say, with equal truth, that the Declaration and the preamble are the most clearly indicated places for starting a search for those "fundamental values" whose identification has seemingly turned out to be necessary for explicating that quaint paradox, now at home in the black-letter, "sustantive due process," as well as for a start toward assaying the quantities of suspiciousness in "suspect classifications" under the "new" equal protection clause. You can transpose into those keys, if they are to your taste, any derivation of rights from the Declaration or the preamble. I hope you will allow me to stick with the ninth amendment, in whose words unenumerated rights actually are spoken of and somehow dealt with in the Constitution.

We start with the Declaration: "Life, Liberty, and the pursuit of Happiness."[7] Well, many people do die, quickly sometimes, sometimes more slowly, of poverty; poverty may be the leading cause of death. Liberty is very often made into a mocking simulacrum by poverty. But I would lay stongest stress on the phase, "the pursuit of happiness." Can we, the inheritors of the Declaration, of the treasure of its words, dare to treat *these* words as semantically blank, as mere burnished orotundity without reference?

This latter effect may be achieved by treating the phrase as a truism. It follows from the very existence of consciousness and will that everybody can pursue happiness, in the sense of electing between alternatives, however unpleasant, as these present themselves. A galley slave could pursue happiness by continuing to row, thus avoiding a whipping. Or the galley slave might sometimes make the decision that relief from the tedium and exertion of rowing was worth a little whipping now and again—with the consequence that the pursuit of happiness would for the nonce take a different tack.

But the trouble with this line of thought—aside from its general absurdity as an interpretation of such a document as the Declaration—is that it would have been specifically absurd, an implicit contradiction, to use the word "right" in regard to this truism. As a right, and not as a truism, the right to the pursuit of happiness is the right to be in a situation where that pursuit has some reasonable and continually refreshed chance of attaining its goal—or of moving toward its goal, as one may move eastward, though "east" itself will never be attained.

The possession of a decent material basis for life is an indispensable condition, to almost all people and at almost all times, to this "pursuit." The lack of this basis—the thing we call "poverty"—is overwhelmingly, in the whole human world, the commonest, the grimmest, the stubbornest obstacle we know to the pursuit of happiness. I have suggested that poverty may be the leading cause of death; it is pretty certain that it is the leading cause, at least amongst material causes, of despair in life. Of course some few people, through extraordinary talent or rabbit's-foot luck (and the possession of talent is itself a kind of luck), do clamber over the obstacle. But the right to the pursuit of happiness is going to be, for all but a small minority of those in poverty, the palest grinning ghost of a right.

Now to the preamble, and to an echoing of the preamble in article I, section 8. I am going to deal with this quite schematically here, because the arrangement of topics further on will suggest a return to this theme.

The preamble declares that a purpose of the Constitution is to "promote the general Welfare."[8] Then, in a phrasal echo that can hardly be accidental, means are furnished for serving this very purpose, in the article I, section 8 empowerment of the Congress to tax and spend "for the . . . general Welfare."[9] Do not these twinned phrases pick up and carry forward the very themes of the pursuit of happiness, and of the duty of government to aim at maximizing happiness, that are found in the Declaration? And does not the possession of the *power* to seek and to support the general welfare generate a resulting *duty* to do these very things—even without the Declaration, strongly corroboratory though that document be?

Now of course there will always be incertitudes about the boundaries of the concept "general welfare." But our American generation is in the happy position of not having to worry about these peripheral and penumbral problems. It is a clarifying metaphor, pointing to ugly truth, to say that our country contains two countries—a country wherein everybody has plenty of good food to eat, and a country wherein nutrition is a bad problem and getting worse. In one country, infant mortality, the death of babies, is going down; in the other country it is going up. A house thus divided against itself is not a penumbral case on the general-welfare question. It is a classic case—I ought better say *the* classic case—of welfare diffused not *generally* but instead *partially*—with, as we all know, scandalously strong streaks of racism and sexism in that partiality.

Ideas like these cannot be accepted or rejected on the spot; they have to be around, to be revisited in different moods, to be talked over and over. I think one of the most important jobs just now is to deal with certain objections that impede the mind's motion to such plenary consideration. I have been writing and speaking on this matter long enough to have some sense of these objections. I have found it natural to organize today's "further reflections" as replies to a number of them, as I have heard and sensed them, to wit:

1. The Declaration and the preamble are not ordinarily treated as sources of law.
2. The right to a decent livelihood is not named in the Constitution.
3. The constitutional law of human rights is traditionally conceived as being a set of prohibitions only, rather than as containing as well a set of claims to affirmative duties.
4. There is no way to "draw the line" as to the components of a decent material basis for life.
5. Courts, commonly considered the protectors of constitutional rights, cannot form or enforce adequate programs to wipe out poverty.

It will be handy to treat the first and second of these points separately. Then I have found it best to group the last three objections together, in an answer that will say: "The courts probably cannot do very much herein—certainly not enough—though perhaps we will know more about this later, through trial. But Congress too is bound by the Constitution; that instrument imposes many affirmative duties on Congress. Of course no exhaustive and detailed blueprint of constitutionally required action can be laid out, now or ever, but this fact is not to be taken to make impossible the discernment of legal duty, including constitutional duty."

Now, to go back, it is true that the Declaration of Independence and the preamble to the Constitution have not ordinarily been thought to be of avail in the forming of lawyers' law. But to approve of this is to embrace a technical incompetence that would be shocking in a lawyer who had to deal with the interpretation of a will or a contract. It is an especially inane canon in a system of constitutional law that has been groaning and travailing for generations after the discovery and authentication of its "fundamental values"—a quest, I remind you, joined in by some of the most conservative and restrained justices of our century.[10] The Declaration and the preamble are not the only places wherein such fundamental values can be located. But there can be no sense at all in our failing to seek in those documents whatever help they can give in this quest—taking them seriously, getting from them all we can. We will find no higher charter of legitimation for our fundamental values or rights than the organic act that made us a separate nation, and the explicit statement of the purposes of our Constitution.

To proceed to the second objection: the right to a decent livelihood, the right to be rescued from poverty, is not named in the Constitution. It is perhaps not needful, in just this professional atmosphere, to say that this fact is not even close to dispositive of the question whether such a right can validly be derived in the American system. But a lot of people do gain a lot of ground, in other atmospheres, out of the astonishing myth, defiant of all readable reality, that American constitutional law has been and is formed entirely by tracing out the references of words and phrases in the text. The proposition that this is not so is the *pons asinorum* of our subject, a bridge that I am sorry to say some people never have been able to cross and to put quite behind them. But our constitutional regimes of governmental empowerment, of federal relations, of interbranch structure, and of human rights, are all saturated with norms—accepted norms—that cannot with a real straight face be said to be mandated by their naming in the text. I will, however, confine myself to the individual rights field and choose two of the commonest and most luxuriantly developed illustrations—the use of the so-called "dormant" commerce clause as a source of individual immunity from some restrictions, imposed by state regulation and taxation, on transactions having other than local ties, and the protection of freedom of speech against action by state or local authority.

For well over a century, case after case, exhibiting the assertion by private persons of this interstate-commerce immunity, has been decided by the Supreme Court, often in favor of the natural peson or corporation claiming the immunity. The regime constituted by these cases has been the subject of ample panegyric; indeed, it has been more than hinted that the putting in place of this shield was the chief purpose of the adoption of the Constitution.[11] Is this a "named" right?

Well, it might just barely, just possibly, do to say that the commerce clause, in giving Congress the power to regulate commerce among the several states, implied that the states might not at all regulate the thing that Congress was given power to regulate. That's an unnecessary and most impractical use of the always optional *expressio unius* schema, and even so not quite a direct naming of the immunity. But maybe it's close. We need not worry about how close, because that is not what the force of the dormant commerce clause has really been held to be, at any time, by any Supreme Court. Instead, formulation has succeeded metaphysical formulation, line after tormented line has been drawn, to mark out the areas of permissible and impermissible state interference with interstate commerce—as to migration,[12] as to mudguards,[13] as to milk,[14] as to minnows.[15] Take any one of these formulas—the one in the *Cooley*[16] case or any in later cases—and see whether you can say that it is something the Constitution actually "names" in the commerce clause. Now maybe some people can; the human mind is all-powerful—at least as to perversity. But they will thereby have undermined the very concept of naming rights, robbing it of all intelligibility. Most people, I think, on putting any of these structural and functional formulations alongside a text that says nothing about any restriction on the states, will have to say forthrightly that the set of immunities referred to in these formulations is not named or in any way expressly commanded in the Constitution.

The guaranty of free speech is sometimes pointed to as the paradigm of the named right. In most of its applications, it is the paradigm of the unnamed right. Most of its applications have been against state and local authority. As against these authorities, the protection of free speech is not named and has had to be pushed through the generalities of the fourteenth amendment.[17] Since the privileges and immunities generality has even yet not become functional,[18] the gate that has had to be passed, or, perhaps better, climbed over at dark of moon, is the phrase "without due process of law." The celebrated *Gitlow*[19] case held, to be sure, that liberty of speech was one of the liberties of which you could not be deprived without due process of law;[20] how could anybody have thought otherwise? But the rest of the road was toilsome for Gitlow; the Court held that his liberty had *not* been impermissibly taken away—that he was not being deprived of it without due process of law—when he was put in prison for publishing a pamphlet about revolution, with neither statutory requirement of nor showing of danger, or of any effect at all. The tone of the *Gitlow* opinion is set by the sentence: "Every presumption is to be indulged in favor of the validity of the statute."[21] In hindsight we know that much flowed from—mostly away from—*Gitlow*. But the case as it stood in 1925 was not much more than one big toe in the door for the turning of the first amendment against the states, and it was quite unclear whether the door or the toe would win.

By about 1937, as a result of a process never adequately explained in any opinion of the Court or in any dissent, the right to first amendment freedom of speech as against the states—a right nowhere named—is pretty much taken for granted.[22] In that year Justice Cardozo tried to say why. It was because, in his famous words, "neither liberty nor justice would exist" if this right were lacking.[23] "Of that freedom," he goes on, "one may say that it is the matrix, the indispensable condition, of nearly every other form of freedom."[24]

Now, come on! Is that the way you name a right? By saying in effect that "without due process of law" means "not at all," or "only with very strong reason," when the right is one you think to be "the matrix of nearly every other right"? Or by short-circuiting altogether the phrase "without due process of law"? When that phrase fades out, then of course freedom of speech is a generically named right. But so are all other freedoms or liberties, and order becomes chaos. What makes the due process words fade at some times and not at other times? We have to do here not with namings but with radical glosses written over the text by later scholiasts for reasons extrinsic to the text itself. In the rough-and-ready world of law, the truth is that freedom of speech, as against state and local authority, is a right not named in the Constitution.

(Parenthetically, I would like to look Cardozo straight in his gentle eyes and ask him to consider whether the rights to freedom from gnawing hunger and from preventable sickness may not form "the matix, the indispensable condition, of nearly every other form" of freedom.)

The freedom of speech has, moreover, generated in its field of force many smaller unnamed rights; these, where they prevail against state and local power, might be called unnamed rights of the second degree. The 1981 case of *Citizens Against Rent Control v. Berkeley*[25] will do as an illustration of an exceedingly profuse development. The city ordinance prohibited anyone's giving more than $250 in connection with a referendum campaign. Giving money is not speech, except in an extended metaphorical sense. Speech may accompany the giving of money, or it may not. The Court, speaking through the now incumbent Chief Justice,[26] knocked out the ordinance. He said, "The restraint . . . plainly contravenes both the right of association and the speech guarantees of the First Amendment."[27] He also stated that "regulation of First Amendment rights is always subject to exacting judicial scrutiny."[28] Think about those utterances, from such a man as we know our Chief Justice to be. The fourteenth amendment is no longer even a formal bridge; now it's just the first amendment *proprio vigore* against the City of Berkeley. The presumption that set the tone of *Gitlow* now runs strongly the other way. And now there's a "right of association" that is not mentioned in the first amendment, though very free use of functional equivalence or similarity arguments might connect the peaceable assembly and petition clauses to the act of slipping somebody $300. But, *da capo,* these assembly and petition clauses are limits, expressly, only on Congress, a textual fact that would strongly have supported a *Barron v. Mayor of Baltimore*[29] holding as to the first amendment,[30] quite apart from the more general arguments Marshall adduced in that case.

I have picked these two clusters of well-weathered and copiously litigated unnamed rights because, regardless of the patency of the record, some of us tend to forget the actual derivation of unnamed rights, once they have been around a long time. We get so used to them that even calling them "unnamed" seems captious. They have, as it were, acquired named status *honoris causa,* or by prescription, or perhaps by the fiction of a lost constitutional clause. Then, when yet another unnamed right is added to the large unclosed class of such rights, lots of people—naive, disingenuous, or a little of the worst of both—point aghast to the fact that the Constitution does not say anything about the new subject.

I believe there has been no Supreme Court Justice in this century who has not voted to support some right that could on no common-sense basis be said to be named in the Constitution; the great majority have cast such votes in some numbers over a wide range. I should think well over half the cases in any good casebook concern the often successful invocation of unnamed rights or of other norms without evident textual basis. The fact that the right to a decent livelihood is not named cannot be a valid objection, unless we are prepared to rewrite our constitutional law in all its branches (in the words of the old Texas judge) "*de novo*—from the egg." And it would have to be a sterile egg.

Now I shall treat together the last three of the objections I set out a little way back. I go on to the affirmative constitutional duty of Congress diligently to devise and prudently to apply the means necessary to ensure, humanly speaking, a decent livelihood for all.

We have been brought up on the largely unspoken concept of constitutional human-rights law as a set of limitations on governmental power. This concept contains in abundance both truth and health. But a serious thirst for human rights, and so for human-rights law, cannot be slaked with no more than a canon of "thou shalt not's." Sins against human rights are not only those of commission but also those of omission. Other nations seem to have gotten ahead of us in explicit and detailed recognition of this; herein the papacy has outstripped the United States of America.

But since we are talking about human rights as a part of our own constitutional law, it might be useful to ask whether affirmative duties are exotic in that law. We closely study the empowerments of the national government, the distributions of power within it, and the limitations that lie upon it, devoting little attention to the Constitution as a source of affirmative obligation to act, sometimes on a very grand scale.

If we start at the beginning, we read no further than article I, section 2, before we find that Congress lies under the mandated duty of providing for a decennial census.[31] Failure to make such provision would be plainly unconstitutional. Congress is under an affirmative duty to assemble at least once a year.[32] Each House must keep a journal.[33] Congress must provide a compensation for its own members,[34] for the President,[35] and for the article III judges.[36]

The President lies under the highly general affirmative duty to "take Care that the Laws be faithfully executed."[37] Here is exhibited a characteristic that may be seen to inhere in some degree in all the most important duties mandated by the Constitution. The President cannot do everything imaginable to bring it about that the laws be faithfully executed; he is limited by his own physical and mental powers, by other claims on these, and by the amplitude of the means put at his disposal by Congress. The duty has to be a duty to act prudently within these limits, without ulterior motive, sensitive to the force of the powerful conscience-stirring word "faithfully."

It cannot be any more—or, I should think, any less—than that. But is it not a duty?

Let us take a closer look at some of the mandated congressional duties. The duty to provide for the decennial census must be a duty to commit reasonable resources, in a prudent way, to producing a serviceably accurate count; to produce a wholly accurate count, as of any given moment, is rigorously impossible. Yet who can doubt that a congressman who openly refused to vote for any census, or who would vote only for a census-taking procedure that he knew to be grossly flawed, would be in flagitious breach of constitutional duty?

Something like this must be said of Congress' affirmative duty to appropriate money for compensating the President, the judges, and indeed its own members. The words "a compensation" must mean an amount of money that reasonably compensates; otherwise the provision, thrice carefully set out in respect of all the principal officers of the United States, could easily be brought to nothing. Nobody can say, with any show of reason, that there is a duty to compensate the President at one exactly calculable level. Yet a Congress that refused to appropriate a reasonable compensation for the President would be in breach of constitutional duty.

All or most of the constitutional duties expressly set out combine two characteristics. They are, on one hand, real duties. But they can be fulfilled by good-faith action, over a pretty wide and indistinctly bounded range. In these respects they resemble a very great many duties in law outside constitutional law.

I rather guess that my self-chosen task, for the rest of my years as a constitutionalist, is going to be arguing, in all weathers, the case for the proposition that a constitutional justice of livelihood should be recognized and should be felt by the President and Congress as laying upon them serious constitutional duty. In the early phases of this work, I find I am most often asked the question, "How much?" or "Where will you draw the line?" I think it well to try to suggest, at the beginning, that the establishment of a duty is one thing, while the specification of prudent quantities and means is another—though it must be remembered as well that the decently eligible range of means and measures is one thing when you are under no duty at all to act, and quite another when you are under a serious duty to act effectively.

This characteristic continues to be visible as we consider constitutional duties that arise from structural and relational considerations. Congress is literally commanded, as to the support of the other branches of government, only to provide for compensation for the President and the judges. Yet the Constitution assigns to the President duties and functions that require the spending of money—for people, space, travel, supplies, and so on. Since, under article I, section 9, clause 7, Congress alone can provide this money,

Congress must lie under a constitutional duty to appropriate such money in reasonable amounts, and even to levy taxes, or to borrow, so that the money will be there to appropriate. The same duty is discernible, *mutatis mutandis,* as to the judiciary. These duties, derived from the Constitution, cannot be given exact arithmetical shape but are nonetheless constitutional duties.

I go now to a higher level of magnitude. The preamble to the Constitution says that one of the purposes of that instrument is to "provide for the common defence."[38] Congress is then given the power to lay and collect taxes to "provide for the common Defence,"[39] as well as several other powers over military concerns. Now is it doubtful that the *power* to provide for the common defense generates a resulting *duty* to provide for the common defense—that a Congress that embarked on a course of making knowably insufficient provision for the common defense would be in breach of constitutional duty? The power is a power held in trust—hardly a difficult concept within the legal regime of a Constitution that, even on the judicial side, is looked on as capable of generating cases both in law and in equity.

Even this one huge instance establishes that the systematic frame of constitutional rights and duties can comfortably contain, and quite evidently does contain, a duty not expressly declared as such, but of vast scope and highest essentiality, a duty derived from the grant of a power that is held in trust, a duty, moreover, that can be (because it has to be) fulfilled by prudential choice over a wide range of means—but over a range to be located by good faith acknowledgment of the duty as a duty. That is exactly what I want as to the duty of Congress continually to move, by the general diffusion of welfare, to give life to a constitutional justice of livelihood, and so to prepare the way for the "Pursuit of Happiness—thus taking on, as to all the people, *both* of the tasks allotted to government in the Declaration of Independence: "to *effect* their Safety and Happiness."[40]

When we are faced with these difficulties of "how much," it is often helpful to step back and think small and to ask, not, "What is the whole extent of what we are bound to do?" but rather, "What is the clearest thing we ought to do first!" When we descend to that level, one reasonable answer occurs. Somebody's count is that a million and a half people in the State of New York are undernourished;[41] somebody else's count is that 13% of the American people live in poverty,[42] which pretty much always implies hunger more or less serious. This hunger is disproportionately high among children;[43] about half our black children under six lived in poverty in 1984.[44] Some helpless old people eat dog food when they can get it; it is not recorded that any Cabinet member has yet tried this out on elderly persons in his own extended family. Now you can bog down in a discussion about the exact perimeter of "decent livelihood," or you can cease for a moment from that commonly diversionary tactic and note that, wherever the penumbra may be, malnourished people are not enjoying a decent livelihood.

In a constitutional universe admitting serious attention to the Declaration of Independence, a malnourished child is not enjoying a "*right* to the pursuit of happiness."

And we are very lucky herein, because we know pretty much what to do. We suffered chronic, endemic malnutrition in America. We got rid of it, humanly speaking, by food stamps, school lunches, and a few smaller measures. Then we just let it come back, because we wanted our own taxes lowered. The Great Society nutrition programs, widely spoken of as having somehow failed, in fact succeeded brilliantly[45]—a thing that often happens when you attack a problem directly and simply, giving hungry people more food the shortest way, instead of feeding them rancid metaphors about boats that rise when the tide rises. All we have to do is to reinstitute adequate funding for these programs. Then we can think about the next thing. We won't have to think very long.

Now I know that I'm talking into the political wind. The country is now infatuated with an idol call "the economy," which most high priests seem to agree is doing real well, though millions of children are not getting enough to eat, and millions of adults who want work cannot find it. But winds change; they always have, and doubtless they always will. A period of no power is a period for the reformation of thought, to the end that when power returns it may be more skillfully, more fittingly, used. The way I want to see thought reformed is by our ceasing to view the elimination of poverty as a sentimental matter, as a matter of compassion, and our starting to look on it as a matter of justice, of constitutional right.

Now I want to make two last general points—inspirational points if you like, because this theme, the constitutional justice of livelihood, inspires my age as I wish it to inspire the youth of the young among you.

I will make the first point by reminding you of the prolificity of application of the free speech guaranty against state and local actions. Remember? The *Berkeley* case? The present Chief Justice[46] (no reckless innovator he) in 1981 wrote for a Court that by that time felt itself, so far as concerned state and local subjection to first amendment norms, to be travelling *super vias antiquas*—almost in an ancient and even comfortable rut.

In 1922, fifty-nine years before the *Berkeley* case, the Chief Justice-to-be was a lad of fifteen springs. In that year the Court decided *Prudential Insurance Co. of America v. Cheek.*[47] The insurance company assailed the federal constitutionality of a state statue that required employers to furnish discharged employees with letters stating the grounds for discharge. Argument was multifarious and ranging, but the Court made short work of one contention:

> But, as we have stated, neither the Fourteenth Amendment nor any other provision of the Constitution of the United States imposes

> upon the States any restrictions about "freedom of speech" or the "liberty of silence"; nor, may we add, does it confer any right of privacy upon either persons or corporations.[48]

When those words were uttered in an opinion of the Court, the fourteenth amendment had been around for fifty-four years—substantive due process" had already strongly come on the scene. By 1937, just fifteen years after *Cheek,* Mr. Justice Cardozo, in the famous *Palko* passage that I have quoted,[49] was explaining, after the fact, why it was that the free speech guaranty of the first amendment had been held binding on the States. The rest of the way to the *Berkeley* case was only a matter of filing in detail.

In 1922, the *Cheek* year, Hugo Black was thirty-six, a seasoned though not yet grizzled general practitioner in Birmingham, just over half the age promised in the Bible. Now what do you think his Alabama friends would have said if someone had read out this brush-off sentence in the *Cheek* case and had added, "Now do I prophesy: It won't be long before the States *are* held subject to the first amendment guaranty, and Hugo here, by twenty years hence, will have played a big part in all that"! I guess such a person would have been judged crazy—about as crazy as somebody who this afternoon insists that this nation is permanently committed, as a matter of constitutional right, to a generous use of its oceanically overabundant resources to keep all its people out of poverty, all the time.

History does not always repeat itself. But history does show what is possible. The movement from the *Cheek* brush-off to the Chief Justice's opinion in the *Berkeley* case shows that a vast revolution in legal doctrine and action, a revolution to astound and bewilder the old people, can take place in a very short time and that revolutionary doctrine may after not very much more time be looked upon as ancient doctrine by a Chief Justice who was almost fully grown when the revolution started.

As the lifeline of Hugo Black shows, such a total turnabout can comfortably be contained in the span of one professional career in law, with years to spare at both ends, and a good deal of time left over for playing tennis. I stress this because I am talking to young people, who need to form some first-approximation estimate of how much they may accomplish if they decide to fight. You have time; just add the other ingredients.

In closest connection, I want to resay something I believe I said somewhere earlier,[50] and cannot now find because I somehow have not prepared an index to my fugitive writings.

Holmes once remarked of the first Justice Harlan that the latter's mind resembled a powerful vise, the jaws of which could not be brought closer than two inches apart.[51] This was a much-admired remark among the mandarins, though it ought to have lost a bit of its savor when one reflected, after 1954, that the first Justice Harlan, in *Plessy v. Ferguson,*[52] wrote the lone dissent—a dissent full of passion and of common wisdom—that became the law of the land in *Brown v. Board of Education,*[53] while Holmes, as far as I can find, never showed any irresistible discontent with *Plessy*.

What I said (and I hope I said it in the *Harvard Law Review*) was that, in constitutional-law work, jewelers' vises are well enough for tasks of detail, but the lack tremblingly to be feared is the lack of a vise whose jaws can be got *more* than two inches apart, because if you lack such a vise you cannot handle the big beams. I exhort each of you young people (and I mean to include the young in spirit of any age): In thinking about the constitutional justice of livelihood, ask of your mind that it be a vise that can handle the big beams. We have to do with some big ones here. If we succeed in cutting them to fit and in joining them for the ages, we will once again have given the world a new thing—this time a constitutionally based system of human rights that takes into account at last *all* the needs of humanity for life spiritual and physical—these two together, just as they occur in nature. We will once again be the City on the Hill; our achievement, promised in our beginning, will be seen to be moving toward completion. If we fail in this cutting and joining, all our brave words about human rights will slowly or soon come to be seen as fatally flawed, it will grow too late to transmute hypocrisy into commitment, and such part of the hope of earth as we still guard and cherish will be found one morning to have flickered out in the night.

ENDNOTES

1. The Declaration of Independence, para. 2 (U.S. 1776).
2. See K. Stamp, *The Era of Reconstruction, 1865–1877* (1965), at 214–15.
3. The Declaration of Independence para. 32 (U.S. 1776).
4. See J. Breuer and S. Freud, *Studies in Hysteria* (A. Brill trans. 1937), 133.
5. The work immediately preceding the present lecture is my "On Reading and Using the Ninth Amendment," in M. McDougal and W. M. Reisman, eds., *Power and Policy in Quest of Law: Essays in Honor of Eugene Victor Rostow* (1985), 187. For reference to my other relevant work, see id. at 209 n.*.
6. "The enumeration in the Constitution, of certain rights, shall not be construed to deny or disparage others retained by the people." U.S. Const. amend. IX.
7. The Declaration of Independence para. 2 (U.S. 1776).
8. U.S. Const. preamble.
9. U.S. Const. art. I, § 8, cl. 1.
10. See, e.g., *Poe v. Ullman,* 367 U.S. 497, 541–45 (1961) (Harlan, J., dissenting); *Wolf v. Colorado,* 338 U.S. 25, 26–28 (1949) (Frankfurter, J.); *Pierce v. Society of Sisters,* 268 U.S. 510, 534–35 (1925) (McReynolds, J.).

11. See *Hood and Sons v. Du Mond,* 336 U.S. 525, 533–34 (1949).
12. See *Edwards v. California,* 314 U.S. 160 (1941).
13. See *Bibb v. Navajo Freight Lines,* 359 U.S. 520 (1959).
14. See *Dean Milk Co. v. Madison,* 340 U.S. 349 (1951).
15. See *Hughes v. Oklahoma,* 441 U.S. 322 (1979).
16. *Cooley v. Board of Wardens,* 53 U.S. (12 How.) 299, 319–20 (1851) (commerce power of Congress exclusive where the "subjects of this power are in their nature national"; commerce power not exclusive where "the nature of the subject when examined, is such as to leave no doubt of the superior fitness and propriety, not to say the absolute necessity, of different systems of regulation").
17. See *Gitlow v. New York,* 268 U.S. 652 (1925); *De Jonge v. Oregon,* 299 U.S. 353 (1937).
18. See *Madden v. Kentucky,* 309 U.S. 83 (1940) (overruling *Colgate v. Harvey,* 296 U.S. 404 (1935), which had invalidated a state law on the basis of the fourteenth amendment priviledges and immunities clause).
19. *Gitlow v. New York,* 268 U.S. 652 (1925).
20. Id. at 666.
21. Id. at 668 (citation omitted).
22. See, e.g., *De Jonge v. Oregon,* 299 U.S. 353 (1937); *Herndon v. Lowry,* 301 U.S. 242 (1937).
23. *Palko v. Connecticut,* 302 U.S. 319, 326 (1937).
24. Id. at 327.
25. 454 U.S. 290 (1981).
26. This lecture was delivered during the tenure of Chief Justice Burger.
27. 454 U.S. at 300.
28. Id. at 298.
29. 32 U.S. (7 Pet.) 243 (1833).
30. Cf. id. (immediately concerning the fifth amendment, holding that it did not apply to the states).
31. U.S. Const. art. I, ¶ 2, cl. 3.
32. Id. art. I, § 4, cl. 2.
33. Id. art. I, § 5, cl. 3.
34. Id. art. I, § 6, cl. 1.
35. Id. art. II, § 1, cl. 7.
36. Id. art. III, § 1.
37. Id. art. II, § 3.
38. U.S. Const. preamble.
39. U.S. Const. art. I, § 8, cl. 1.
40. Declaration of Independence para. 2 (U.S. 1776) (emphasis added).
41. See Hunger Called More Prevalent in the Summer, *N.Y. Times,* July 3, 1985, at B4, col. 6.
42. See Novak and Lenkowsky, Economic Growth Won't End Poverty, *N.Y. Times,* July 24, 1985, at A19, col. 1 (prediction of Commerce Secretary Malcolm Baldridge).
43. Compare Panetta, Hunger Is Growing, But Relief Isn't, *N.Y. Times,* Sept. 9, 1985 at A19, col. 1 ("nearly one-fourth of all American children under 6 live in poverty") with Novak and Lenkowsky, supra note 42 (estimated overall American poverty rate not higher than 15.2 percent over previous eighteen years).
44. See Panetta, supra note 43.
45. See Levitan and Taggart, The Great Society Did Succeed, *Pol. Sci. Q.* (1976–77), 91:601.

46. See supra note 26.
47. 259 U.S. 530 (1922).
48. Id. at 543.
49. See supra note 23 and accompanying text.
50. This belief proved to be a realistic one. See Black, The Supreme Court, 1966 Term—Foreword: "State Action," Equal Protection, and California's Proposition 14, *Harv. L. Rev.* (1967), 81:69, 98–99.
51. *The Holmes-Pollack Letters* in M. Howe ed. (1941), 2:7–8.
52. 163 U.S. 537 (1896).
53. 347 U.S. 483 (1954).
4490

5
EXCUSING CRIME

Sanford H. Kadish

In both criminal law and everyday moral judgments the concept of excuse plays a crucial role. This is because the practice of blaming is intrinsically selective. It cannot survive if all harm-doers are to be blamed, any more than it can if none are. Excuse is one of those central concepts that serve to draw the line between the blameworthy and the blameless and so make a blaming system possible.

In this article I propose to examine the rationale and functioning of excuses in the legal system and to consider how far the law does and should follow ordinary moral conceptions in its definition of excusing conditions. Part I attempts to locate excuses in the network of rules and principles governing criminal liability, distinguishing them from other grounds of exculpation, such as justification by their grounding in some disability of the defendant. Part II surveys the excuses allowed by the criminal law, grouping them into three categories of personal disability: involuntariness, reasonable deficiency, and nonresponsibility. Part III attempts to identify the principles that underlie the law's pattern of excuses, finding them in notions of voluntarism, both literal and metaphoric, that determine when blame is justified in ordinary moral discourse. Part IV then attempts a critical assessment of the legal excuses in each category, in an effort to determine how fully legal excuses conform to the requirements of just blaming, arguing, however, that not all departures from just blaming are necessarily unjustified.

EXCUSES AND OTHER DEFENSES

My first task is to locate excuses among the possible grounds of exculpation. This requires that I sketch a kind of map of the terrain of legal defenses, a common move among criminal law theorists looking for the unities in their subject.[1] There are many equally defensible approaches to this task;

I offer mine only for its convenience in making the points I want to make.

We must start with the criminal prohibition itself. Roughly speaking, a crime is a description of certain actions in certain circumstances (the actus reus), the doing of which with designated mental states (the mens rea) is punishable. So, for example, assault is the use of force against a person with the intention to injure him; burglary is breaking and entering a structure with intent to commit a felony therein; and so on. Sometimes no mens rea is required—the action or result is enough. These are instances of strict liability. I will say more about them later.

Then there are the various grounds of exculpation. One ground is simply that the person did not do the acts constituting the crime, or did not act with the required mens rea—for example, "I didn't point the gun"; or "I did, but I had no intention of shooting it." We may speak of this ground of exculpation as failure of the prima facie case. Another category of exculpation is different. Here, although I do not deny doing the action prohibited, I claim I may not be punished even so because I have grounds for exculpation. These grounds of exculpation I will refer to as defenses.

There are two kinds of defenses of this character. The first kind is grounded, not on notions of moral guilt or innocence, but rather on policies of law enforcement—that the statute of limitations has run, for example, or that the police obtained the evidence to be used against me by unlawful methods. We may put this kind of defense aside. The other kind of defense constitutes a claim of personal innocence, which I may assert on one of two possible grounds.

One ground is justification. My claim here is that I did nothing wrong even though I violated the prohibition. This is so, I argue, because the crime's definition of the forbidden conduct is incomplete. The law allows what the crime as defined prohibits where circumstances, specified elsewhere in the law, make may action the right thing to do: I killed, but only to keep an assailant from killing me or another; I entered another's cabin in the wilderness, but only to obtain food and water to keep myself alive.

The other ground for asserting my innocence is excuse. Here again, I deny my culpability even while admitting the criminal harm, but not, as before, because I did the right thing after all. Rather, I argue, some disability in my freedom to choose the right makes it inappropriate to punish me.

LEGAL EXCUSES DESCRIBED

The disabilities of choice that ground excuse in our law seem to fall into one of three groups, depending on the particular disability of which they take account.

Involuntary Actions

The first group of excuses includes situations in which in the most literal sense the person had no control over his bodily movements. Cases of physical compulsion are obvious examples; others are tumbling downstairs or being pushed. These are easy to deal with because we can see the external force being applied. But the law recognizes some excuses as belonging to this category even when the source of the lack of control is internal, as in the case of reflex movements or epileptic seizures.

If involuntariness is the touchstone of excuse, then literal involuntariness, of course, represents the paradigm case. But such extreme instances of involuntariness may also be viewed as raising a bar to liability more fundamental even than excuse—namely, that there is no *action* at all, only bodily movement, so that there is nothing to excuse. Under this view, which represents the conventional characterization of the involuntary act defense, the defense comes to an "I-didn't-do-it" defense, a failure of the prima facie case.

Thus, there are two ways to classify cases of physical compulsion or involuntariness. On the one hand, these cases can be interpreted as exculpatory because there was no actus reus, and hence, no crime to excuse. This interpretation rests on the distinction between genuine human actions, which are susceptible of praise and blame, and mere events brought about by physical causes, which happen to involve a human body. Such events can be harmful or harmless, but they are not human actions and therefore are not subject to moral judgment. On the other hand, there is bodily movement in these cases, and it may have done harm. To that extent the involuntary-act exculpation is not identical with the failure of the prima facie case. When a person denies doing the act the usual expectation is that if he did not do it, someone else must have. When a person claims the involuntary-act defense he is conceding that his own body made the motion but denies responsibility for it. Therefore, however we characterize the involuntary-act exculpation, whether as a failure of the prima facie case or as a defense, the reason it exculpates belongs to the rationale of excuse: the defendant had no choice in the matter.

Deficient but Reasonable Actions

In the second group of excusing conditions there is power to choose in a literal sense—nothing prevents the person from making a choice—but the choice is so constrained by circumstances that ordinary law-abiding persons would not have chosen otherwise. The constraining circumstances are of two kinds. In the first, the constraint arises from defect of knowledge; in the second, from defect of will.

Cognitive Deficiency

The law's excuses based on reasonable lack of knowledge are commonly spoken of as cases of mistake or accident, the same terms used in blaming discourse outside the law. But to constitute an excuse it is not enough that the person lacked knowledge of some relevant feature of his action. His lack of knowledge must itself be excusable, in the sense that it would be reasonable for any person in his situation not to have known.

For example, if I shoot at a firing range target and kill a person sitting behind it, who I had no reason to think was there, I have killed by accident. If I shoot at an object in the forest reasonably thinking it is a game animal, when in fact it is a person dressed in animal costume, I have killed by mistake. In both cases, I had the choice not to shoot at all. But once it is accepted that shooting in the circumstances, as I reasonably took them to be, was a proper action, the accidental or mistaken killing was effectively beyond my control. Indeed, for this reason, Aristotle regarded an action taken under mistake as involuntary in the same sense that a compelled action is involuntary.[2]

Explaining accident and mistake as excuses is today somewhat unconventional. Like the involuntary-act defense, accident and mistake are more likely to be viewed as precluding liability, not because of excuse, but because the elements of the crime have not been proven, resulting in a failure of the prima facie case. After all, homicidal crimes are defined to require a mens rea of at least culpable negligence. Under this view reasonable mistake and accident should be defenses, not because they excuse what otherwise would be a crime, but simply because they negate the required culpable mens rea, without which there is no crime to excuse. But such a view fails to distinguish different functions of a mens rea requirement in definitions of crimes.

Some mens rea requirements are essential elements in the definition of the wrong made criminal. Take loitering with criminal intent, or reckless driving: without the intent in the first case or recklessness in the second, there is only standing around or driving a car. Hence there is nothing to excuse, since we would not want the person to have acted otherwise. This is the case with all crimes, like loitering with intent and reckless driving, whose definition does not require occurrence of the ultimate harm the crime seeks to prevent. The concern of such crimes is the danger of further action or events that will produce the ultimate harm. The mens rea serves to identify that danger. This is characteristically true of all inchoate crimes, both those explicitly inchoate, like attempt and conspiracy, and those implicitly so, like burglary and larceny.

Other mens rea requirements, on the other hand, are excuses in mens rea clothing. They are excusing conditions because they serve to deny blame for a harm done. That they are cast in the form of mens rea requirements does not change their character. Thus, in my shooting examples, my defense would not be put in terms of a formal excuse. It would be that I have not committed culpable homicide, because that crime is defined to require that I intentionally or negligently kill, and I have not. Nonetheless, the reasons these particular mentes reae are required are the very reasons for excusing conditions: we could not expect a person to have chosen otherwise, even though we might wish he had done otherwise. This is why accident and mistake are excuses, despite their formal character as definitional mens rea requirements. Indeed, before the clarifying analysis of mens rea by the Model Penal Code, this was how accident and mistake were traditionally thought of.[3]

Volitional Deficiency

The law's excuses based on defect of will are not as well developed as those based on defect of knowledge. Duress is the best established defense of this kind, and even its status is not free of doubt. Duress is generally established when a person commits a crime under the command of another backed by such threats of physical injury that even a person of reasonable fortitude would have done the same. It is often subject to restrictions; for example, in some jurisdictions it is not available as a defense to major crime, and in some there must be a threat of immediate and serious bodily injury.[4] There is also authority for the view that duress is not available as an excuse at all, but only where the choice to commit the crime is justified as the choice of the lesser evil.[5] Nevertheless, partly due to the influence of the Model Penal Code, duress in some circumstances is generally available as a defense, even when not justified by the lesser evil principles.

Nonresponsibility

The excuses in my third category, unlike those in the first, do not involve involuntary actions. And unlike those in the second, they do not rest on circumstances that would lead a person of normal capacities to make the choice the defendant made. The grounds for excuse are simply that this particular person could not have been expected to act otherwise than as he did, given his own inadequate capacities for making judgments and exercising choice.

Our law is niggardly with excuses of this kind. The individual's difficulty in complying with the law is a common ground for mitigation, but it is rarely a ground for a total excuse. Infancy or legal insanity are the only two excuses of this kind the law allows, and since the juvenile court laws have made the defense of infancy in practice redundant, legal insanity is the only significant defense remaining in this category.[6]

While the basis for excuses in the second category is that the actor has shown himself no different from the rest of us, the basis of the insanity excuse is that he has shown himself *very* different from the rest of us. But how different and in what respects? After all, those who commit atrocious crimes are certainly very different from the rest of us. That fact alone scarcely excuses them.

The various competing formulations of legal insanity seek to answer this question. The *M'Naghten* and Model Penal Code rules are the most common today. Both rely on the concept of mental disease to distinguish the legally nonresponsible person from the rest of us. *M'Naghten* asks whether as a result of mental disease the defendant was unable to know the nature of his act or that the act was wrong.[7] The Model Penal Code expands *M'Naghten* to ask as well whether a mental disease prevented the defendant from conforming his conduct to the requirements of the law.[8] However formulated, the defense seeks to identify those who may not be regarded as moral agents, that is, persons who are not necessarily incapable of choice, but who are incapable of making choices that count as such because of impaired reasoning and judgment. I will say more about the theory of legal insanity later when I attempt to assess the adequacy of the law's excuses.[9]

WHY EXCUSES

Why we have excuses is less obvious than why we have other defenses. Let us start with Jeremy Bentham's explanation. He saw the point of excuses to be that they identified situations in which conduct is nondeterrable, so that punishment would be so much unnecessary evil. For since only the nondeterrable are excused, withholding punishment offers no comfort to those who are deterrable.[10] The trouble is, as is now widely appreciated, that this does not follow, for punishing all, whether or not they happen to be deterrable, closes off any hope a deterrable offender might otherwise harbor that he could convince a jury that he was among the nondeterrable.[11] Moreover, without excuses, prosecutions would be faster and cheaper, convictions more reliable, and the deterrent threat more credible. Indeed, we have in our law a class of offenses, strict liability offenses, that dispenses with mens rea requirements on just these grounds. Have we not given up something of value for the increased effectiveness that strict liability arguably provides, something that is not captured in Bentham's rationale?[12]

Professor Hart, in one of his essays, offered a different account of excuses. He argued that by confining liability to cases in which persons have freely chosen, excuses serve to maximize the effect of a person's choices within the framework of coercive law, thereby furthering the satisfaction people derive in knowing that they can avoid the sanction of the law if they choose.[13]

This rationale is an improvement over Bentham, inasmuch as Hart gives us a reason why we might want to put up with the loss of deterrence caused by excuses. But does this account capture the full force of a system of excuses? Suppose we preferred the risk of accidentally being victims of law enforcement to the increased risk of being victims of crime. That would be a plausible choice, particularly for a public obsessed with rising crime rates. Would we then feel there was nothing more problematic in giving up excuses than that we would be trading one kind of satisfaction for another? I think not. Something is missing in this account.

Hart's account focuses on the interests and satisfactions of the great majority of us who never become targets of law enforcement—our security in knowing we will not be punished if we do not choose to break the law. What is missing is an account of the concern for the innocent person who is the object of a criminal prosecution. Hart's essay does refer to the satisfaction of the lawbreaker in knowing the price he must pay to get what he wants by breaking the law.[14] But it is doubtful that this is a satisfaction the law has any interest in furthering, for the point of the criminal law is surely to keep people from engaging in prohibited conduct, not to give them a choice between complying with the law or suffering punishment.[15] The law's concern is for the person accused who has not made a culpable choice to break the law, not with furthering the interests of persons who would like to.

To blame a person is to express a moral criticism, and if the person's action does not deserve criticism, blaming him is a kind of falsehood and is, to the extent the person is injured by being blamed, unjust to him. It is this feature of our everyday moral practices that lies behind the law's excuses. Excuses, then, as Hart himself recognized in a later essay,[16] represent no sentimental compromise with the demands of a moral code; they are, on the contrary, of the essence of a moral code.

It may be argued that though this may be true of excuses in everyday moral judgment, it is not true of the criminal law, because it is not intrinsic to judgments of criminality in our society that they express a moral fault. But this view is surely mistaken. Certainly not all criminal conduct is independently immoral. In some cases the law attaches criminal penalties as well to conduct that, apart from its being prohibited, is not immoral.[17] But in either case criminal conviction charges a moral fault—if not the violation of a moral standard embodied in the criminal prohibition, then the fault of doing what the law has forbidden. The same principle that compels excuses in moral criticism also compels them in the criminal law.

Of course, one might escape excuses altogether by withdrawing the element of blame from a finding of criminality. Indeed, there are some—though not so many as there were a generation ago—who would prefer that the criminal law reject all backward-looking judgments of punishment, blame, and responsibility and concern itself exclusively with identifying and treating those who constitute a social danger.[18] Whether it would be desirable to loosen punishment from its mooring in blame is a large and much discussed question.[19] I will confine myself here to two observations. First, such a dissociation would not likely succeed. People would continue to see state coercion as punishment, notwithstanding official declarations that the state's only interest is the individual's welfare and social protection. Second, it is very doubtful that we should want it to succeed, since blame and punishment give expression to the concept of personal responsibility, which is a central feature of our moral culture.[20]

The three categories of legal excuses that I described in the previous part suggest the common rationale behind excuses in both law and everyday moral judgments—namely, that justice requires the preclusion of blame where none is deserved. In the first category, the person is not to blame because he has no control over his movements; in the second, because though he breached a legal norm, he acted in circumstances so constraining that most people would have done the same; and in the third, because though there is action in breach of a norm in circumstances in which most people would *not* have done the same, the person, because of a fundamental deficiency of mind, is not a responsible moral agent.

What principle lies behind these categories of excuse? I find it convenient to develop an answer to this question in the next part in the context of an assessment of legal excuses, but it may be helpful to state it briefly here. I suggest that the underlying principle is that of voluntarism, in two senses, literal and metaphorical.

By literal voluntarism I mean the principle that requires choice as a condition of blame: the person must have chosen to do the action and have had the capacity to choose otherwise. When this is not so there is no basis for attributing fault to the person, who is no less a victim of the event than those who have been injured by it.

This principle expresses the rationale of legal excuses of the first and third categories. This is most obvious in the first, because the very feature that marks these excuses is the absence of choice. But it is also true of the third, because there is here only the outward show of choice; the person's fundamental deficiency of mind makes it in appropriate to count his seeming choices as true choices.

Voluntarism in a metaphorical sense lies behind excuses of the second category. It is "metaphorical" because, literally, the actor has made a choice to do an act that is criminal. But the choice is nonetheless not blameable, because of two considerations: First, he has acted either under ignorance of significant features of the situation or under constraining pressures of his will; and second, those circumstances would have led even a reasonable, normally law-abiding person to act in the same way. This being so, his action does not merit blame, because it fails to distinguish him from the common run of humankind., It may be said in these cases that the person had no *effective* choice or that no reasonable and upright person *could* have done otherwise.[21] But as I said, these usages are only metaphorically, not literally, accurate.

LEGAL EXCUSES ASSESSED

So much for the sketch of the excusing conditions in our law and what seems to lie behind them. But what shall we say of the excuses the law does not allow? Is our legal system too ungenerous with excuses? Are there excuses good in morals that should be, but are not, good in law? Is the law always at fault in imposing blame where it is unjust to do so? These questions are the agenda for the remainder of my discussion of excuses. I will deal with the three categories of legal excuses in turn.

Involuntary Actions

Legal excuses of the first kind, involuntary actions, generally parallel moral excuses. A problem arises only when one asks whether this category can fairly be limited to movements produced by external physical force and internal physiological reactions or whether it should be extended to include conduct produced by psychological forces, like addiction, that seem to make resistance hopeless or very difficult. I will return to this issue when I reach the subject of addiction in my last category.

Deficient but Reasonable Actions

In the second class of excuses—those based on some deficiency of cognition or volition that is the common lot of humankind—we find significant gaps between what is legally and morally excusable. I will deal first with excuses based on lack of knowledge.

Cognitive Deficiency—Strict Liability

Strict liability imposes guilt without regard to whether the defendant knew or could reasonably have known some relevant feature of the situation. The defendant did an act that, judged from his or her perspective, is blameless:

she drove a car; she rented her home in another city[22]; he presided over a pharmaceutical company that bought packaged drugs and cosmetics and reshipped them under its own label.[23] But the facts were not as they thought. The driver could not see a stop sign at the intersection, because it was obscured by a bush. The homeowner's otherwise respectable tenants decided to throw a marijuana party. The drugs and cosmetics the pharmaceutical company reshipped were mislabeled by the manufacturer and there was nothing the defendant officer could practically have done about it. These circumstances would surely be a defense to a charge of moral fault, and usually, under the requirement of mens rea or the doctrine of reasonable mistake, they would be a legal defense as well. But in the three cases I described many jurisdictions would disallow the excuse of reasonable mistake because, it would be explained, these are instances of strict liability. If a principle is at work here, it is the principle of "tough luck."

Another gap is created by the rule that ignorance of the law is no excuse. This rule presents no problem where the law embodies a moral wrong. There is usually little injustice when the law turns a deaf ear to a defendant who claims that he did not know it was against the law to mug a stranger or steal from his employer's till.[24] It is another matter to deny a defense to a defendant, engaged in an otherwise lawful activity, who claims he was unaware of one of the numerous regulations governing the conduct of his business. If no reasonable person in the defendant's situation could be expected to know of the existence of the regulation (not likely but still possible), he could not be morally faulted, and neither, it would seem, should he be legally blamed. Yet, with few exceptions, the law gives the same answer: in the Latin the law often uses for lofty sentiments, *ignorantia legis neminem excusat.* Or, in not very lofty English, "tough luck" again.

The injustice of blaming a person despite reasonable mistake or reasonable ignorance of the law does not derive from the principle of voluntariness in its literal sense. In these cases, unlike the cases of involuntary actions, people's capacity to exercise choice is intact—literally they do choose to do what they do. And the fact that reasonable persons in their situation would have been as ignorant of the relevant facts or law as they were does not itself necessarily demonstrate a lack of opportunity to choose, rendering their acts involuntary in the Aristotelian sense. This is because it is always (or, at least, usually) theoretically possible for them to have found out. This is the point sometimes made in defense of strict liability. So it has been argued, for example, that though a person may have acted in altogether reasonable ignorance of the factual circumstances or law that made her action criminal, nothing compelled her in the first place to engage in the activity during which she faultlessly committed the harmful action. She could have chosen another line of activity, and might well have if, as is often the case, she was aware that the general line of activity, like the food and drug industry, for example, was subject to a myriad of strict liability regulations.[25]

The reason this argument is inadequate is that the source of the injustice is not the violation of the voluntarism principle in its literal sense but that the person did nothing meriting blame in originally venturing into the general line of activity.[26] Driving a car, letting a premises, and running a drug packaging business are lawful and socially useful activities; they are unlike leaguing oneself with a criminal group, for example. Engaging in these activities cannot, therefore, justly serve as a basis for blame. The defendant did only what it was reasonable to do. Later she did something harmful, but only in virtue of circumstances of which even a thoroughly reasonable person would have been ignorant. We may say that holding her liable in these circumstances would violate the voluntarism principle, but only in the sense that the opportunity to know, which otherwise would make her choice voluntary, is not one we regard as genuinely open, because it is right and reasonable for her not to act on it.

In strict liability and conventional ignorance-of-law doctrine, therefore, there is a gap between legal and moral blaming. Can it be justified? The usual attempt to do so rests on the need to protect the public interest, which would be imperiled by allowing the normal excuse. In defense of the doctrine that ignorance of law is no excuse, Holmes wrote:

> It is no doubt true that there are many cases in which the criminal could not have known that he was breaking the law, but to admit the excuse at all would be to encourage ignorance where the law-maker has determined to make men know and obey, and justice to the individual is rightly outweighed by the larger interests on the other side of the scale.[27]

The defense of strict liability runs along similar lines. So Justice Frankfurter, upholding the conviction of the pharmaceutical company president in the drug mislabelling case I referred to earlier, echoed the views of Holmes:

> [Strict liability] legislation dispenses with the conventional requirement for criminal conduct—awareness of some wrongdoing. In the interest of the larger good it puts the burden of acting at hazard upon a person otherwise innocent but standing in responsible relation to a public danger.[28]

I do not believe these responses are sufficient, even on their own terms. It is not at all obvious that eliminating the defenses of nonculpable mistake is necessary for social protection. Other legal systems allow the defenses and seem to get along well enough.[29] Moreover, there are other ways to improve enforcement. One is to shift the burden of proving reasonable mistake to the defendant.[30] Another is to impose criminal liability for negligence in failing to be aware of the law or the danger.[31] A third is to permit only civil sanctions.[32] These arguments are well known and well taken.

Justifying Departures from the Blame Principle

But this is a natural place to raise a question that has more theoretical interest and that has to be addressed in an enterprise like this that attempts to assess legal blaming by the measure of moral blaming. Suppose these arguments were not right—that compromising the principle of blameworthiness was actually necessary to maintain a credible level of law enforcement. If this were the case, could punishment possibly be morally justified?

There are those who seem to say no, on the ground that no social gain can justify an injustice to an individual.[33] Again in lofty Latin, *fiat justitia, ruat coelum.* This response is appealing in many ways. It has the virtue of clarity and simplicity. All we need to know to do the right thing is that some injustice will otherwise be done to an individual. But I doubt that the absolutism of this position is a part of our common intuition of what morality requires.

Surely an individual's claimed right not to be blamed in the absence of fault carries great weight, quite apart from its social uses. But it does not follow that this claim must prevail in all circumstances and whatever the costs. On one level, the very existence of a system of formal blame and punishment entails some compromise, since that system requires the establishment of the factual grounds for blaming. We know that a system of this kind will probably result in punishing some innocent people because of the inevitability of error. We can adopt procedures designed to minimize punishing the innocent, such as the requirement of proof beyond a reasonable doubt. But we know this will only reduce error, not preclude it, and we know that we could, if we chose, reduce the chance of error still further by, for example, requiring proof beyond a doubt, always allowing retrial where further evidence is adduced, and so on. We do not, because we think it necessary and right to accept some compromise with a commitment not to punish the innocent in the interest of the practical needs of a functioning criminal justice system.

Similar considerations govern the formulation of the substantive law of excuses. The criminal law, in contrast to social mores, must serve as a clear explicit guide to lawful conduct. It must also discourage the belief that a "loophole" can always be found to escape prosecution. Further, it must be suited to fair and uniform application and restrain as much as possible the biases of individual judges and jurors. Hence, instead of permitting any excuse that the court deems relevant, the law defines the elements of available excuses. It is the nature of such definition that they cannot always accommodate subtle moral distinctions or novel situations. For these reasons the law sacrifices complete accord between moral and legal excuses.

Suppose that under a strict liability rule, the total amount of injustice would be slight, because it will be rare that an individual will have a good excuse for not knowing the law or for being unaware of some relevant factual feature of his action. Suppose also that the penalty is slight (a fine rather than imprisonment) and that a great deal is riding on compliance (for example, the safety of foods and drugs). I suggest that in these circumstances there is a reasonable argument that disallowing the excuse would not merely be the practical thing to do, it would be the right thing to do as well.

The argument is that though justice to the individual has great and usually determinative weight, it need not have absolute weight. We would expect John Stuart Mill, as a utilitarian theorist, to hold this view.[34] But one need not wholly embrace utilitarianism to conclude, as Professor Feinberg has, that a "practice can be right even though to some extent unjust, and that we can sometimes be *justified,* all things considered, in treating some persons to some extent unjustly."[35] This represents a general moral intuition and a common ground for practical judgment. In this view, justice is regarded as one among other prima facie social values. As such it must be weighed against such other values as social peace and security or the indispensable practical requirements of administering a system of law. While justice is a fundamental value, and hence usually paramount, it may on occasion be outweighed by these other values. What is right is what is right all things considered. This position finds support in constitutional adjudication, where even the fundamental guarantees of the Bill of Rights do not stand as absolutes.[36] In short, doing the right thing, all things considered, might justify—"rightify" would better convey the sense—some departure from the requirements of just blaming.

Another reason why justice for the individual is not an absolute is that it can conflict with the moral claims of other individuals. Consider, for example, the claim of the law-abiding for some reasonable governmental protection against crime.[37] A legal system so scrupulous that nearly every defendant was acquitted would not only be inefficient and ineffective, it would be unfair to the citizens who rely on it to articulate and enforce standards of conduct. Thus, there are moral, as well as pragmatic, reasons why a perfect correspondence between an individual's moral fault and criminal liability is not an absolute value.

Volitional Deficiency—The Necessity-Coercion Principle

I turn now to excuses based on reasonable deficiency of will. Here, too, there is an apparent gap between excuses allowed by the law and the requirements of just blaming. Professor Fletcher has done much to illuminate this gap,[38] which arises in situations in which the law affords no excuse for a defendant's act even though a person of reasonable, law-abiding capacities and inclinations would have chosen to violate the law. The common law and the law of most states excuse in only one situation of this kind: duress, where the coercive predicament facing the defendant arises from the threats of another; and even then, under the common law and the law of most jurisdictions, the act is excused only when the threat is immediate and the crime is not a homicidal one.[39] But, of course, coercive predicaments capable of breaking the will of persons of average fortitude can arise in other circumstances as well. To take familiar examples, consider the shipwrecked castaways who kill, reasonably concluding there is not other way to survive,[40] or a prisoner who escapes in the reasonable belief that it is the only way to avoid repeated sexual assaults and threats of violence.[41]

Our law excuses, therefore, only in some circumstances in which persons of common fortitude would break the law. Even the Model Penal Code, while eliminating the common law restrictions on duress,[42] declined to establish a necessity-coercion defense,[43] which would generalize the principle underlying duress,[44] as some foreign and a few American jurisdictions have done.[45]

I conclude, therefore, that the narrow recognition of the necessity-coercion excuse creates a gap between what the law allows and what just blaming requires. But what principle of just blaming is violated? It is not simply the principle that blame may not be imposed in the absence of voluntary choice—not, at least, without qualification. It is true that the defense of duress is often explained in terms of the threat overpowering the will, rendering the person unable to choose otherwise.[46] But the sense of disability of will present in duress situations is plainly not the same as when we say that a physically or physiologically compelled movement is beyond the control of the person.[47] Why, then, is it unjust to blame a person in this situation? The answer is parallel to the answer I offered in the case of reasonable mistake: in yielding to a threat to which most of us would yield, the person has not shown herself to be more blameable than the rest of us. All that distinguishes her is the accident that produced her predicament. As the Model Penal code is commentary observes:

> [L]aw is ineffective in the deepest sense, indeed . . . it is hypocritical, if it imposes on the actor who has the misfortune to confront a dilemmatic choice, a standard that his judges are not prepared to affirm that they should and could comply with if their turn to face the problem should arise. Condemnation in such a case is bound to be an ineffective threat; what is, however, more significant is that it is divorced from any moral base and is unjust.[48]

It is not, then, that there is literally no choice in these cases but that there is not effective choice given the limits of moral fortitude, not just of the defendant, but of humankind generally. In other words, the choice exhibits no defect of character meriting blame.

The law, then, departs from the requirements of just blaming by failing to include a general necessity-coercion defense. As with other such departures, however, it is potentially justifiable on an "all things considered" view of rightness.[49] The case would have to be that a general necessity-coercion defense would open nearly every prosecution to the claim that even reasonable and lawful persons would have done the same in the defendant's circumstances and that this burden, with its potential for delay and jury mistakes, is too great for the criminal justice system to bear. Moreover, even when properly applied, the defense might be thought, as in the prison escape cases, to provide too great a weakening of the deterrent discipline of the criminal law.[50] The central issue is whether these considerations warrant condemning people who behave no differently than most of us would in the extraordinary situations in which they find themselves. I am not inclined to think so, but there is little ground for certitude.

The Adequacy of the Reasonableness Standard

I turn now to a different challenge to excuses in this second category: not that the standard of common humanity is rejected but that it is inadequate. The argument is that the standard of what most of us are capable of, or would do, is unjust, because it fails to take into account what the particular defendant was capable of.[51] So, for example, a person might raise the following defense to a charge of being an accessory to a burglary: "I only helped out because the other fellow, a person of violent reputation, threatened to seek me out one day and bloody my nose if I refused. Though I concede that a person of reasonable fortitude would have refused anyway, I am not such a person. I am a coward, and weakness in the face of physical danger is just what distinguishes us."[52]

Or he claims self-defense: "I concede that a person with normal judgment and nerves would never have mistaken the gesture of the deceased as the start of a deadly attack. But I did make that mistake, because I am a nervous, fearful, and apprehensive person. I should therefore be excused."

I fear these examples may not be sufficiently sympathetic. Let me try to do better with an actual case.[53] Defendants are charged with involuntary manslaughter in the death of their infant. Their lawyer argues: Yes, my clients should have realized their child was seriously ill and needed medical attention. It would have been obvious to you or me, but my clients are not like us. They are Native Americans, living on a reservation, with little formal education and little acquaintance with modern medicine. They loved the baby, staying up with it night after night trying to comfort it. They were crushed by its death. But they never realized how badly the baby needed medical attention; they thought it was only a toothache. If only they had known. Most people would have; but they didn't. They should be excused.

One response to these claims might be the all-things-considered view of what is right; namely, that allowing defects of self-discipline and judgment to excuse would cut too wide a swath through the criminal law, which has to coerce people of all degrees of capacities and varieties of inclination to conform. Indeed, this is the usual defense of the objective standard—the standard of what can be expected of reasonable persons—that our law imposes on excusing conditions.[54] But I want to take a different tack: I want to argue that in these cases the law does not commit injustice in imposing blame.

The first point to be made is that in applying its objective standard, the law does not abstract all of the circumstances in which the defendant acted. To some extent it does individualize. A relevant physical defect of the defendant—that she was blind or deaf, for example—surely would be seen as part of the circumstances in which we imagine the ordinary person to be acting when the law asks what her response would be. So would some less obvious features of the actor's situation. Suppose in my duress case the defendant were in such poor health that the threat of a bloody nose took on more than its usual significance; or suppose that in the mistaken self-defense case, the defendant had recently received anonymous threats. These circumstances, presumably, would be seen as a part of the situation facing our reasonable person when we consider how she would act.[55]

Now the line is hazy between those special circumstances that are relevant and those that are not, but surely it is a very different thing to individualize completely. For that would be to abandon altogether the very point of excusing in the second category of excuses I have described. What could be expected of the ordinary run of individuals would be irrelevant. All that would count would be the behavior of this very person. But what, then, could be the reason for excusing him? That he is the kind of person he is? That, in the duress case, the defendant is unnaturally cowardly? That, in the mistaken self-defense case, the defendant is unnaturally apprehensive? These are most peculiar excuses. Presumably, to say that a person is cowardly, or apprehensive, or whatever, is to say that his actions tend to be deficient in certain ways. It is certainly not to say that the person has no choice but to act in those ways. That he has once again acted in this way is the very ground for blaming him. It could hardly serve as an excuse. Such defenses are not accorded in moral judgments any more than in legal ones.[56]

Nonetheless there is a case for considering the deficiencies of the particular defendant in one circumstance: where negligence is the basis of liability. So, for example, Professor Hart has argued that while punishing for negligence may justly rest on an objective standard (which he prefers to describe as an invariant standard of care), the law is obliged in justice to adopt an individualized condition of liability.[57] That is, while it is not necessary, to justify blaming the defendant, to show that she was aware of the objectively unreasonable risk her action created, it is necessary to show that she could have been aware and could have taken the necessary precautions. Only if this is so do we avoid the injustice of holding liable "unfortunate individuals who, through lack of intelligence, powers of concentration or memory, or through clumsiness," could not have acted in conformity with the required standard.[58]

This is an appealing argument. The case of the backward parents who failed to realize their child's need for medical attention vividly illustrates its force. Nonetheless, Hart's argument cannot easily escape the objection I just raised to a requirement of a completely individualized standard in all situations. If we excuse parents for ignorance of the medical needs of their child on the ground that they are ignorant people, must we not also excuse a person for yielding to a trivial threat of future harm on the ground that he is a cowardly person? If it is a defense to a crime of negligence that the defendant could not have known and taken care because that's the kind of person he is, why would it not also be a defense to a crime of intention that the defendant could not help choosing to act as he did because that is the kind of person *he* is: aggressive, self-centered, brutal, and so on?

If this objection is to be met, it would have to be by distinguishing between incapacities of cognition and incapacities of volition. An argument for such a distinction would be the following: We can accept that some people cannot help being deficient in intelligence, power of concentration, or memory and that this deficiency, despite all the good will in the world, may keep them from adverting to a danger that others would attend to. To excuse such people for actions they could not have helped does not seriously erode the concept of blame. On the other hand, we do not accept that otherwise normal people who are uncompelled cannot control their intentional actions. That would be incompatible with the way we view human actions. That the defendant is the kind of person who has yielded to his antisocial inclinations in the past does not show him to be incapable of resisting on this occasion. To hold otherwise would undermine the practice of blaming altogether, in common moral discourse, as well as in law.

This distinction, then, would lead to the conclusion that the law commits no injustice by refusing excuses of incapacity for intentional crimes, but that it is a condition of just liability for unintentional crimes that the capacity of this defendant to have known and done otherwise be open to inquiry in every case. But before we too quickly judge the law deficient in not allowing such a defense to unintentional crimes, we should understand the practical difficulties in administering it.

For example, in the infant neglect case, how could it be shown that the parents were unable to know enough to call a doctor? They did not, this time. But in the actual case, they had visited a doctor some months before. And they knew their baby was sick. No doubt they did not appreciate how sick the baby was. But what does it mean to say they could not have? Would the excuse simply function as a message to the jury to acquit in any case of criminal negligence when they sympathize enough with the defendants? And could the excuse be confined to sympathetic cases like the infant neglect case? Consider the case of unreasonably mistaken self-defense I put earlier. Would we be obliged to allow as an excuse that the defendant's abnormal fearfulness (which he would show, presumably, by a long record of such behavior) disabled him from discriminating a hostile gesture from a friendly wave?[59] We might want to say that such a defect of judgment in deciding to shoot and kill someone is blameworthy. But could it be distinguished from the infant neglect case? Isn't deficient judgment in appraising reality at issue in both cases?

These kinds of practical difficulties were no doubt in the minds of the Model Penal Code framers when they concluded that "the heredity, intelligence or temperament of the actor would not be held material in judging negligence."[60] Further, these practical problems reveal that the moral distinction between ability to know and ability to will is not entirely clear. Someone's purposes and concerns can influence how he develops and uses his cognitive abilities and how hard he tries to overcome his intellectual shortcomings. In this sense, his intentions may be relevant even in unintentional crimes. In view of both the practical and moral complexities raised by an excuse of incapacity to know better, it is understandable that our law does not recognize it.

Nonresponsibility

This brings us to the last category of excuses: cases of nonresponsibility, represented primarily by the defense of legal insanity. To assess the justification for and the adequacy of the excuse of legal insanity it is necessary to explicate further the principle of justice that lies behind it.

A Rationale of Nonresponsibility

The modern tests of legal insanity are varied and controversial, but they all rest on the view that the claim of incapacity to comply with the law because of defects of understanding or self-control[61] is an excuse only if it is the result of a mental disease. Here, then, it is precisely the individual's personal incapacities that serve as the basis of the excuse, whereas, in other cases, saving cases of physical and physiological compulsion, the law declines to permit individualized inquiries into the capacities of the defendant. Why should the presence of mental disease make all this difference?

One answer is a wholly practical one. We cannot allow personal incapacity as an excuse generally without unduly compromising the deterrent effectiveness of the law. Proof would be too speculative and uncertain, acquittals would be invited based on the jury's subjective attitudes toward the defendant, there would be too great a chance of erroneous acquittals, and less incentive would be given potential violators to make every effort to comply. Narrowing the excuse to those who can be identified, through medical testimony, as having a mental disease helps to meet these practical concerns. There is support for this explanation in the efforts from time to time (and certainly in these times) to limit or abolish the defense, precisely on the ground that the requirements of a mental disease is inadequate to meet these concerns.[62]

Without denying that this practical explanation plays a part, I suggest it is not the heart of the matter. The explanation seems to accept that the reason for disallowing an unqualified defense that the defendant could not understand or control his conduct is wholly a matter of expediency. But neither in moral judgments nor in legal ones do we ask of a person who wrongs another whether he could have helped choosing to do so. Being responsible for our characters means that we are responsible for our choices, even if in some sense they have their causes, like any other events, in the world.[63]

What, then, is different about a person whose disabilities result from mental disease? The answer, I believe, is that the concept of mental disease serves to identify so complete a breakdown of the normal human capacities of judgment and practical reason that the afflicted person cannot fairly be held liable. That concept, it should be emphasized, is not synonymous with the varieties of mental illness identified for therapeutic purposes. Categories developed with regard to whether and how a person can be helped by psychiatry are not designed to determine whether a person may be justly punished. They have some evidentiary relevance to the questions of judgment and moral responsibility, which are the law's concern, but that is all.

Though the prevailing tests of legal insanity speak in one way or another of inability of the defendant, because of mental disease, to know the nature or wrongfulness of his action or (sometimes) to choose to comply with the law, it is apparent that "know" and "choose" in these tests mean more than what those terms signify in casual discourse. Many defendants acquitted on grounds of legal insanity, particularly those with psychoses, "knew" what they were doing and "meant" to do it in a literal sense.

Consider the facts of a famous California case, *People v. Wolff*[64]: A schizophrenic teenager, after previous failed attempts, killed his mother with an axe because he saw her as an obstacle to fulfilling his bizarre sexual fantasies. He kept a list of seven girls he had not met whom he planned to chloroform and kidnap and bring back to his home, where he would rape them and photograph them nude. In such a case, surely the defendant knows well enough what he is doing and acts with deliberate choice. But he may nonetheless be excused if his disease of the mind has so far impaired his rationality that he has ceased to be a moral agent.[65] As Professor Moore puts it:

> [S]everely diminished rationality preclude[s] responsibility . . . because our notions of who is eligible to be held morally responsible depend on our ability to make out rather regularly practical syllogisms for actions. One is a moral agent only if one is a rational agent. Only if we can see another being as one who acts to achieve some rational end in light of some rational beliefs will we understand him in the same fundamental way that we understand ourselves and our fellow persons in everyday life. We regard as moral agents only those beings we can understand in this way.[66]

Seen in this way, it is apparent why the excuse of legal insanity is fundamental. No blaming system would be coherent if it imposed blame without regard to moral agency. We may become angry with an object or an animal that thwarts us, but we cannot blame it.

Of course, being beyond the reach of moral responsibility, not being a moral agent, is not the same as being nonhuman. The acts of insane people are usually ambiguous between deliberate actions and pointless, unreasoned behavior; they are not mere events, like rocks falling. Insane people are *just* beyond responsibility, and that is why they are so disturbing. Nevertheless, blaming them commits an anomaly (we would say an "injustice" as applied to people) similar to that entailed in blaming a rock for falling or a dog for barking.

This, then, explains the distinctive and fundamental character of the defense of legal insanity. It also explains the central objection to recently revived proposals to abolish the defense[67]: To do so would open a dramatic gap between moral and legal requirements of blaming. Whether abolishing the defense could nonetheless be justified by an all-things-considered view of what is right[68] is another question, although, for reasons that are beyond the purview of these comments. I doubt that the case can be made.[69]

Volitional Disability

I have so far discussed the moral significance of the legal insanity defense without attending to its proper formulation, just as I have with respect to the other excuse defenses. But one long-standing and basic issue in defining the defense has received considerable attention as part of the current reassessment of the defense and therefore merits comment. This is whether the insanity defense should extend beyond cases in which a mental disease has impaired a person's cognitive abilities to cases in which it has impaired his ability to control his conduct.

One reason not to extend legal insanity to cases of volitional disability is the practical difficulty of administering an insanity defense so extended. It has been urged with force that there is no way objectively to establish that a person could not refrain from a criminal action, rather than would not,[70] and that therefore such a test "involves an unacceptable risk of abuse and mistake."[71] These considerations may justify eliminating that feature of the defense, particularly if most cases of substantial volitional impairment are accompanied by cognitive impairment sufficient to establish the defense independently.[72] They do not, however, settle the question I am most concerned with here: whether legal insanity must include a volitional disability feature in order to meet the moral requirement of blaming.

This question involves the defensibility of treating cognitive and volitional disabilities differently for the purpose of assessing blame. I considered this issue earlier in connection with Professor Hart's argument for an individualized standard of negligence.[73] He argued, it will be recalled, that the requirements of just blaming compel allowing an inquiry in each case into the cognitive capacity of the defendant. I concluded that this argument could not succeed without making the case for treating negligent and intentional conduct differently. While just blaming might require proof of the defendant's capacity to know, it could not require proof of his capacity to have intended other than he did without seriously threatening the whole concept of moral blame.

In the context of the legal insanity defense we again face the cogency of this distinction between cognitive and volitional capacity. In defining legal insanity, are we equally constrained to disallow inquiry into the capacity of the person to control his intentional, uncompelled conduct? There is perhaps some support for an affirmative answer in the traditional formulation of the insanity defense, still vigorously defended in some quarters, which allows inquiry into the ability of the defendant to know what he was doing but not into his ability to do other than what he chose to do. But there is also ground to believe that for purposes of defining legal insanity, an inquiry into volitional capacity has a special claim.

The idea that a normal actor, who commits a crime intentionally and under no physical or physiological compulsion, might have been unable to choose to act otherwise threatens to undermine blame at its foundation.[74] But the notion is less threatening as applied to those suffering from a mental disease,[75] not simply in the sense of a medically recognized psychological disorder, but as reflecting the common sense moral judgment that the person lacks the minimal capacities for rational action required to be a moral agent.[76]

It seems apparent that distorted reality perceptions are not the only ground on which we may come to such a judgment. Bizarre, senseless, and unintelligible motivations may manifest lack of moral agency even where the person is literally aware of what he is doing. The teenage schizophrenic in the *Wolff* case is an example.[77] Lack of the minimal capacity for rational action required for moral agency may be manifested, not only by the inability to know the nature and wrongfulness of one's actions, but also by the performance of knowing and intentional actions that are motivated by bizarre and unintelligible purposes.[78]

In this sense volitional incapacity is a morally relevant element of a concept of legal insanity. I should want to distinguish it, however, from a different sense of volitional incapacity that is grounded, not on the standard of general capacity to be a moral agent, but on the more literal notion of a "psychic" compulsion, a desire so strong and urgent that the person is unable to resist it. Here is where the greatest difficulties lie in determining whether a person was unable to resist or simply did not resist and, indeed, in even knowing what the distinction means. A jury can judge whether a person was physically compelled by another or physiologically compelled by a reflex. But (putting drug addiction aside for a moment) how can a jury distinguish between a psychic compulsion and a strong desire that the person lacks the character to resist? Indeed, how is the psychiatrist to know? Using Greek nouns to describe repetitive stealing or fire setting is hardly an explanation. I do not believe that the proper ground of excuse in these cases is the person's inability to choose not to steal or not to set fires. Such persons choose not to do such acts on many occasions. Nor, in *Wolff,* was it that the young man was unable to choose not to kill his mother. Indeed, he held back on an earlier occasion when it appeared too risky. The ground of excuse is not inability to choose, but rather the senseless and absurd character of the behavior—its bizarre repetitiveness in the first case, its wildly unrealistic motivation in the second. In other words, it is not that the defendant is not capable of choosing, but that his choosing is so irrational that he manifests a lack of moral agency.

Expansion of Nonresponsibility—Social Deprivation and Addiction

I have so far tried to make the case for the fundamental importance of the defense of legal insanity and against proposals to eliminate it. I turn now to arguments that take the opposite view: not that the defense should be abolished but that the concept of legal nonresponsibility must be expanded beyond legal insanity if legal and moral blame are to be brought into line.

One such proposal is to establish a defense of social deprivation.[79] The argument proceeds this way: If the law recognizes that mental disease can have the effect of so far interfering with the capacity of the defendant to conform that he is excused, why should it not recognize other influences that have the same effect? Consider a defendant who has, from birth, led a life of grinding poverty and deprivation, who suffered from defective parenting and little family support, who spent his childhood and youth mostly in the streets under the tutelage of older youngsters similarly situated, and who, naturally enough, turned to crime. This demonstrably criminogenic background, it is argued, itself should serve as the basis for an excuse, without a need to show that this history of cultural deprivation produced a mental disease. In short, a defendant who has been subjected to such a life may have as little effective control over his conduct as one with a mental disease.

Courts have resisted this line of argument,[80] and I think with good reason. One strong counterargument is practical: The defense would be difficult to administer, it would weaken the law's deterrent effect, and, once recognized, it would be hard to justify punishing anyone, for even evil has its casual roots somewhere. But I am here concerned with the defense as a matter of principle, that is, whether the principle of just blaming requires it.

Social deprivation may well establish a credible explanation of how the defendant has come to have the character he has. But it does not establish a moral excuse any more than a legal one, for there is a difference between explaining a person's wrongful behavior and explaining it away. Explanations are not excuses if they merely explain how the defendant came to have the character of someone who could do such a thing. Otherwise, there would be no basis for moral responsibility in any case where we knew enough about the person to understand him. And that would mean every case, because ignorance about a person could hardly stand as a justification for blaming him.[81]

The reason the argument fails to make out a moral excuse, as insanity does, is that it fails to establish the breakdown of rationality and judgment that is incompatible with moral agency. It may be conceded that cultural deprivation contributed to making the defendant what he is (though, of course, only some people so brought up end up committing crimes). But what is he? He is a person with wrong values and inclinations, not a human being whose powers of judgment and rational action have been so destroyed that he must be dealt with like an infant, a machine, or an animal. Those who propose this defense are plainly moved by compassion for the downtrodden, to whom, however, it is nonetheless an insult.[82]

The strongest case for the social deprivation defense is that a state which fosters or tolerates such deprivation forfeits its right to condemn its victims. But the question "Who has the legitimate authority to judge and punish?" is a different question from "Who should be blamed for individual crimes?" The social deprivation defense may be a fair vehicle for accusing the society responsible for the deprivation, but it is not a ground for excusing the deprived defendant, because by itself it fails to establish the defendant's lack of responsibility.

Other proposals to expand the concept of legal irresponsibility are tied to special conditions that it is argued, substantially impair the capacity of the person to conform in certain ways. On this basis narcotics addiction has been urged as a defense to narcotics crimes,[83] and even to other crimes driven by the need to support the addiction[84]; chronic alcoholism has been raised as a defense to crimes involving public drunkenness[85]; and compulsive gambling has been raised as a defense to theft offenses.[86] Very rarely have courts been receptive.[87]

Courts have chiefly emphasized the threat to the social control functions of the criminal law that allowing these defenses would pose.[88] This is plausible enough, considering that drugs and alcohol figure prominently in the commission of many of the crimes the public fears most. Perhaps these concerns justify departing from the requirement of moral blame, as I said earlier. But the issue that concerns me here is whether denial of the excuse in those cases is indeed a violation of those requirements.

It has been argued that the principles of responsibility and blame underlying the legal insanity defense require a legal defense of addiction.[89] One defense of this view is that the crimes of an addict are symptoms of a sickness and therefore require treatment, not punishment.[90] But this is surely a non sequitur. To find that criminal conduct is causally related to persistent patterns of behavior which are to some extent medically treatable (for this is what sickness here presumably connotes) does not establish that punishment is unjust. Being "sick" in this sense does not mean or imply that the person is irresponsible and not morally culpable.[91] Just as a psychiatric diagnosis of mental illness does not itself establish a defense of legal insanity, neither does a diagnosis of addiction establish that the addict is not responsible for his actions. The concept of disease of the mind as it functions in the insanity defense does not simply represent a medical treatment category. As I said before, it is rather a judgment that the person suffers from such a persistent distortion of his powers of judgment and practical reasoning that he lacks moral agency.

It is hard to see how addiction could qualify as a disease of the mind in the sense of a condition negating moral agency. There is nothing irrational in the conduct of a person who engages in addictive behavior. Distortion of reality is not a necessary feature of addiction. Nor is there anything bizarre or unintelligible in the desire to achieve either the gratification the conduct affords (gratification that nonaddicted people seek in large numbers in drink, drugs, or gambling) or in the avoidance of the negative effects of not gratifying the desire.

What distinguishes addiction is that it constitutes a powerful motivation to engage in certain kinds of conduct. The argument for a defense of irresponsibility is better seen, therefore, as a claim that the motivation of the addict goes so far beyond strong temptation, which itself can hardly constitute a full excuse in morals or law, that it must be thought of as utterly overwhelming behavior controls. The argument that such overwhelming motivation should constitute an excuse could proceed by analogy to two well-established grounds of exculpation—the defense of an involuntary act and the excuse of duress or, more generally, the necessity-coercion principle.

There is some looseness in the concept of an involuntary act. Even the Model Penal Code eschews a definition and resorts to an enumeration of examples, plus a general reference to other bodily movements that are not "a product of the effort or determination of the actor, either conscious or habitual."[92] But the characteristic actions of an addict could hardly be made to fit. They are movements he chooses to make to achieve his purposes and therefore have nothing in common with falling or being pushed or with reflexive or convulsive movements, or even with sleepwalking or hypnotic movements.[93] There is a substantial difference between those movements and the complex and varied activities involved in obtaining and using alcohol and other drugs. There are enough conscious, purposive actions in the characteristic behavior of addicts (including abstinence when the motivation is great enough) that it cannot possibly be considered involuntary. The same objections apply a fortiori to crimes, such as theft, committed to support addiction, which are even less like mere reflexes than crimes of possession and use.

A second possible argument is one that draws support from the principle of duress. Just as a defendant may be excused if he commits a crime under the imminent threat of bodily injury by another, so, it may be argued, should the addict be excused if he commits a crime in order to avoid the acute suffering of withdrawal. While duress is technically distinguishable because it is limited to threats by another person, in principle the excuse can hardly be so contained. Indeed, the defense of necessity-coercion, better recognized in other legal systems than our own, constitutes just such an extension.[64]

Nevertheless, the argument for an addiction defense based on the rationale of the necessity-coercion principle confronts significant difficulties. That principle, it will be recalled, does not excuse simply because the will of the defendant was overwhelmed by pressures he lacked the fortitude to resist.[95] There is always an objective qualification, which requires that in like circumstances a person of reasonable firmness would not have resisted and that the defendant was not at fault in producing his predicament.[96] The addiction defense fails both of these requirements.

As to the latter, anyone can suddenly and without fault because the victim of a terrorist's threats. Not so a victim of addiction. Save in the rarest of cases, he must have voluntarily consumed narcotics over a period of time before becoming addicted. Therefore his problem is almost always in some sense of his own making. However powerful the pressures once the person becomes addicted, they were not present in the steps along the way.

Concerning the former, the first difficulty is the same as that just discussed—persons of reasonable firmness do not become addicted. Therefore the standard would have to be construed to refer to the *addicted* person of reasonable firmness. But even if this much concession were made to an individualized standard, there is the further difficulty of demonstrating this standard is met. The evidence makes it appear doubtful that it could be.

The once popular view was that the addict was enslaved to his habit, irresistibly hooked in ways beyond his capacity to alter, and in the thrall of the body-and-soul-wracking experiences of withdrawal. Recent reviews of what is known about narcotic addiction tell a different story.[97] The great majority of heroin addicts do not experience extraordinary suffering when they stop using drugs. And even in classic form, withdrawal symptoms seem closer to those of the one-week flu than to the horrors of the popular myth.[98] Further, the distress of withdrawal can be kept relatively moderate and bearable by gradual withdrawal under professional care, which is widely available.[99] Recent data concerning patterns of addiction and withdrawal also refute the bondage myth. Addiction is not an inevitable result of use. There appears to be a sizable population of nonaddicted but regular heroin users who succeed in controlling its use and leading normal lives.[100] Nor does addiction appear to be either continuous or permanent. Many addicts succeed in giving up heroin at an early stage and never return to using it.[101] Finally, social and psychological inducements to begin and to continue using narcotics appear to have a large role in accounting for addiction patterns.[102]

Of course, to show that the theory of existing legal excuses does not support an addiction defense does not show that exculpating addicts is not a requirement of moral blame. That theory may be insupportable or wholly a reflection of practical requirements of law enforcement. But I believe neither is the case.

Sometime during the gradual process of conditioning himself to drugs—before the addiction reached its greatest force—the addict could have desisted but did not. These early voluntary actions constitute a sufficient predicate for blaming him. There may well be ground for mitigation in a long lapse of time between the voluntary action and the addiction or in the unawareness of the defendant that his actions would lead to addiction. But this is not to say there are no grounds for blame.

As for the requirement of an objective standard, I have already tried to develop the case for it.[103] A wholly individualized standard would look only to the condition of the defendant-addict before the court. But what would be the question: Could this defendant have resisted committing the crime? But no one compelled him, and he was not incapable of choice. Was it too hard for this defendant to resist in light of his desires and fears? But absent some objective measure of "too hard," what could the measure be? Presumably it would have to be the capacity of this individual to prefer to choose doing the right thing, under varying conditions of temptation and pressure. But this is simply a way of talking about character, and it would lead to the paradoxical result that the worse the person's character, the stronger the case for excusing his conduct. We need some standard of responsibiity external to the make-up of the person to maintain our practices of blame. The law's objective standard has, therefore, significant roots in the very logic of blaming itself.

I must emphasize that I am speaking only of excuse as a complete negation of blame. Of course there is room for compassion and mitigation based on special elements in the background of the individual. The difference is that compassion and mitigation are not incompatible with blame. Excuse is.

ENDNOTES

1. See, e.g., Moore, Causation and the Excuses, *Calif. L. Rev.* (1985), 73:1091.
2. Aristotle, *Nichomachean Ethics* (W. D. Ross trans. 1915) 1110a–111b; Irwin, Reason and Responsibility in Aristotle, in A. Torty, ed., *Essays on Aristotle's Ethics* (1980), 133.
3. The dual character of accident and mistake defenses may be seen in Cal Penal Code § 26 (West 1987), enacted in 1872.. "All persons are capable of committing crimes except those belonging to the following classes: . . . *Three*—Persons who committed the act or made the omission charged under an ignorance or mistake of fact, which disproves any criminal intent. . . . *Five*—Persons who committed the act or made the omission charged

through misfortune by accident, when it appears that there was no evil design, intention, or negligence." This formulation follows Blackstone in including accident and mistake (along with duress, infancy, and insanity) as instances of excuse based on defect of will. 4 W. Blackstone, Commentaries *20–*32.

4. The various approaches to duress are reviewed in Model Penal Code and Commentaries § 2.09 commentary at 368–71 (1985).

5. W. LeFave and A. Scott, *Criminal Law* (2d. ed. 1986), 432–33.

6. A word needs to be said about intoxication. It is not an independent excuse; it is irrelevant that what the defendant did drunk he would not have done sober. It may provide the evidentiary basis for a mens rea or legal insanity defense, but it is the absence of mens rea or the condition of insanity that are defenses, not simply that the defendant is intoxicated. There is some authority for recognizing intoxication itself as an independent excuse if it is involuntary, but the Model Penal Code and most states allow the defense only if the incapacitation is of the kind and degree that would constitute a defense of legal insanity if it had been caused by a mental disease. "The actor whose personality is altered by intoxication to a lesser degree is treated like others who may have difficulty in conforming to the law and yet are held responsible for violation." Model Penal Code and Commentaries § 208 commentary at 363 (1985).

7. M'Naghten's Case, *Eng. Rep.* (1843), 8:718.

8. Model Penal Code § 4.01 (1985).

9. See infra text accompanying notes 61–78.

10. J. Bentham, *An Introduction to the Principles of Morals and Legislation* in J. Burns and H. L. A. Hard ed. 1970, 160–62; see discussion in H. L. A. Hart, Legal Responsibility and Excuses, in *Punishment and Responsibility* (1968), 41–43. For a modern version of the utilitarian argument, see Spriggs, A Utilitarian Reply to McCloskey, in M. Boyles, ed., *Contemporary Utilitarianism* (1968, 261, 291–92.

11. See Legal Responsibility and Excuses, in H. L. A. Hart, supra note 10, at 43; G. Fletcher, *Rethinking Criminal Law* (1978), 813–17.

12. Legal Responsibility and Excuses, in H. L.A. Hart, supra note 10, at 40–44.

13. Id. at 28–53.

14. Id. at 46–48.

15. But see G. Newman, *Just and Painful: A Case for the Corporal Punishment of Criminals* (1983), 141–42: "[T]he greatest consequence of this de-emphasis in prisons is that fewer persons will come under the direct control of the State (which is what we mean by prisons), and that the major portion of criminal punishment (that is, corporal punishment) will be conducted with the view that it is not criminals *per se* who are being punished at all, but free citizens who have exercised their right to break the law. In this way the most basic of all freedoms in a society is preserved: the freedom to break the law."

16. Punishment and the Elimination of Responsibility, in H. L. A. Hart, supra note 10, at 174–77.

17. See Legal Responsibility and Excuses, in H. L. A. Hart, supra note 10, at 37.

18. See B. Wootton, *Crime and the Criminal Law* (1963) 51; B. Wootton, *Social Science and Social Pathology* (1959), ch. 8.

19. See Punishment and the Elimination of Responsibility, in H. L. A. Hart, supra note 10, at 177–85; H. Packer, *The Limits of the Criminal Sanction* (1968), 27; Hart, Book Review, *Yale L. J.* (1965), 73:1325 (reviewing B. Wootten, *Crime and the Criminal Law* (1963)).

20. See Kadish, The Decline of Innocence, *Cambridge L. J.* (1968), 26:273. This is not, of course, to embrace the retributive view that responsibility for law violation itself requires punishment, only that responsibility is necessary, but not sufficient, for punish-

ment. See W. D. Ross, *The Right and the Good* (1930), 60–61; Prolegomenon to the Principles of Punishment, in H. L. A. Hart, supra note 10, at 9–10.

21. Compare Model Penal Code § 2.09(1) (1985), where duress is defined as follows: "It is an affirmative defense that the actor engaged in the conduct charged to constitute an offense because he was coerced to do so by the use of, or a threat to use, unlawful force against his person or the person of another, which a person of reasonable firmness in his situation *would have been unable to resist*" (emphasis added).

22. *Sweet v. Parsley,* 1970 App. Cas. 132 (H.L. 1958).

23. *United States v. Dotterweich,* 320 U.S. 277 (1943).

24. There may be injustice, however, in rare cases of foreign defendants reared in an ethically alien culture. See Note, The Availability of the "Cultural Defense" as an Excuse for Criminal Behavior, *G. J. Int'l. & Comp. L.* (1986), 16:335.

25. See, e.g., Kelman, Strict Liability: An Unorthodox View, in S. H. Kadish, ed., *Encyclopedia of Crime and Justice* (1983), 4:1512; Wasserstrom, Strict Liability in the Crimincal Law, *Stan. L. Rev.* (1960), 12:731, 735–39; Note, Criminal Liability Without Fault: A Philosophical Perspective, *Colum. L. Rev.* (1975), 75:1517, 1543–46.

26. See Johnson, Strict Liability: The Prevalent View, in 4 *Encyclopedia of Crime and Justice,* supra note 25, at 1518.

27. O. W. Holmes, *The Common Law* (1881), 48; see also J. Selden, *Table Talk of John Selden* (1927), 68 ("Ignorance of the Law excuses no man, not that all Men know the Law, but 'tis an excuse every man will plead & no man can tell how to confute him.").

28. *United States v. Dotterweich,* 320 U.S. 277, 281 (1943).

29. Germany does not employ strict liability. See H.-H. Jescheck, *Strafrecht im Dienste der Gemeinschaft* (1980), 320–22. It does allow the defense of reasonable mistake of law. See S. H. Kadish, S. J. Schulhofer, and M. G. Paulsen, *Criminal Law and Its Processes* (4th ed. 1983), 314.

30. *Regina v. City of Sault Ste. Marie,* 85 D.L.R. 3d 161 (Can. 1978); *Proundman v. Dayman,* 67 C.L.R. 536 (Austl. 1941);. see also Kadish, Book Review, *Harv. L. Rev.* (1965), 78:907, 910–13.

31. C. Howard, *Strict Responsibility* (1963), 36, 79.

32. Model Penal Code § 2.02(1) (1985). Cf. H.-H. Jescheck, supra note 29.

33. See, e.g., H. M. Hart, The Aims of the Criminal Law, *Law & Contemp. Probs.* (1958), 23:301, 422–23.

34. See J. S. Mill, Utilitarianism, in J. B. Schneewind, ed., *Mill's Ethical Writing* (1965), 337–38: "[J]ustice is a name for certain moral requirements, which, regarded collectively, stand higher in the scale of social utility, and are therefore of more paramount obligation, than any others; though particular cases may occur in which some other social duty is so important, as to overrule any one of the general maxims of justice. Thus, to save a life, it may not only be allowable, but a duty, to steal, or take by force, the necessary food or medicine, or to kidnap, and compel to officiate, the only qualified medical practitioner. In such cases, as we do not call anything justice which is not a virtue, we usually say, not that justice must give way to some other moral principle, but that what is just in ordinary cases is, by reason of that other principle, not just in the particular case. By this useful accommodation of language, the character of indefeasibility attributed to justice is kept up, and we are saved from the necessity of maintaining that there can be laudable injustice."

35. Feinberg, Justice, Fairness and Rationality (Book Review), *Yale L. J.* (1972), 81:1004, 1005 (reviewing J. Rawls, *A Theory of Justice* (1971)).

36. Another analogy is the principle of the choice of the lesser evil as a defense to what otherwise would be a crime. See Model Penal Code & 3.02 (1985).

37. See Kadish, Respect for Life and Regard for Rights in the Criminal Law, *Calif. L. Rev.* (1976), 64:871, 884–85.

38. See Fletcher, supra note 11, at 818–33.

39. See Model Penal Code and Commentaries § 2.02 commentary at 368–71 (1985).

40. *Regina v. Dudley and Stephens,* 14 Q.B.D. 273 (1884).

41. E.g., *People v. Lovercamp,* 43 Cal. Appl. 3d 823, *Cal. Rptr.* (1974), 118:110. Escape might be justified on the view that suffering the bad conditions is a greater evil than violating prison discipline. The question here is whether the prisoner would have an excuse if the court found escaping to be the greater evil. See Fletcher, Should Intolerable Prison Conditions Generate a Justification or an Excuse for Escape? *UCLA L. Rev.* (1979), 26:1355.

42. Model Penal Code § 2.09 (1985).

43. This awkward term is needed to distinguish the excuse of necessity based on coercion from the justification of choice of the lesser evil, which is often also termed necessity.

44. Model Penal Code and Commentaries § 2.02 and commentary at 377–79 (1985); see S. H. Kadish, S. J. Schulhofer, and M. G. Paulsen, supra note 29, at 797–98.

45. The Criminal Codes of Queensland and Western Australia provide: "[A] person is not criminally responsible for an act or omission done or made under such circumstances of sudden or extraordinary emergency that an ordinary person possessing ordinary power of self-control could not reasonably be expected to act otherwise." Queensl. Crim. Code § 25; W. Austl. Crim Code § 25; see also G. Fletcher, supra note 11, at 833 (quoting the German Criminal Code); Calif. Joint Leg. Committee for Revision of the Penal Code, Penal Code Revision Project § 520 (Tent. Draft No. 1, 1967) ("[I]t is an affirmative defense that the defendant engaged in the conduct otherwise constituting the offense in order to avoid death or great bodily harm to himself or another in circumstances where a person of reasonable firmness in his situation would not have done otherwise."). Three states (Ind. Code Ann. § 35-41-3-8 (West 1986); N.D. Cent. Code § 12.1-05-10 (1985), Tex. Crim. Proc. Code Ann. § 8.05 (Vernon 1977)) have adopted a version of this proposal suggested by the Brown Commission. *Working Papers of the National Commission on Reform of Federal Criminal Laws* (1970), 1:276–77.

46. See, e.g., Model Penal Code and Commentaries § 2.09 commentary at 373 (1985); *Regina v. Hudson* [1971] 2 Q.B. 202, 207 (Crim. App. 1971) (duress consisted of "threats sufficient to destroy [the defendant's] will").

47. This was Aristotle's view. Speaking of actions under threats he says: "Now the man acts voluntarily; for the principle that moves the instrumental parts of the body in such actions is in him, and the things of which the moving principle is in a man himself are in his power to do or not to do. Such actions, therefore, are voluntary, but in the abstract perhaps involuntary; for no one would choose any such act in itself." Aristotle, supra note 2, at 1110a.

48. Model Penal Code and Commentaries § 2.09 commentary at 374–75 (1985).

49. See supra text accompanying notes 34–36.

50. See MacCaulay and Other Indian Law Comm'rs., *A Penal Code* (London 1838), 82–84.

51. For a strong statement of the case for individualization, see Fletcher, The Individualization of Excusing Conditions *S. Cal. L. Rev.* (1974), 47:1269.

52. Professor Williams had doubted the desirability of confining the duress defense to cases in which the defendant acted reasonably. See G. Williams, *Textbook of Criminal Law* (2d ed. 1983), 633. For a contrary view, see Model Penal Code and Commentaries § 2.09 commentary at 373–74 (1985).

53. *State v. Williams,* 4 Wash. App. 908, 484 P. 2d 1167 (1971).

54. See O. W. Holmes, supra note 27, at 48–57, 108–10.

55. See Model Penal Code and Commentaries § 2.02 commentary at 242 (1985).

56. There is, of course, the great issue of whether we are responsible for our characters: whether our characters are made for us rather than by us. But I think I am not obliged to take a position on the issue, since my subject is a comparison of moral and legal blame. All I need to point out is that to the extent we are not so responsible, the ground beneath the whole concept of blame, moral as well as legal, is eroded.

57. Negligence, Mens Rea and Criminal Responsibility, in H. L. A. Hart, supra note 10, at 152–57.

58. Id. at 154. The German law of criminal negligence seems close to what Professor Hart argues ours should be. See The Case of the Gable Wall (Giebelmauer), 56 RGSt 343, 349 (1922); H. H. Jescheck, *Lehrbuch des Strafrechts* (1969), 379; Fletcher, The Theory of Criminal Negligence: A Comparative Analysis, *U. Pa. L. Rev.* (1971), 119:401, 406.

59. Cf. *People v. Goetz,* 68 N.Y. 2d 96, 111, 497 N.E. 2d 41, 50, 506 N.Y.S. 2d 18, 27 (1986): "To completely exonerate such an individual, no matter how aberrational or bizarre his thought patterns, would allow citizens to set their own standards for the permissable use of force. It would also allow a legally competent defendant suffering from delusions to kill or perform acts of violence with impunity, contrary to fundamental principles of justice and criminal law."

60. Model Penal Code and Commentaries § 2.02 commentary at 242 (1985).

61. I am assuming, of course, a concept of legal insanity that extends to volitional, as well as cognitive, incapacities. The original *M'Naghten* rules and rules recently developed to tighten the defense eliminate the volitional feature of the defense. See *United States v. Lyons,* 731 F.2d 243, 248 (5th Cir.), cert. denied, 469 U.S. 930 (1984); Bonnie, The Moral Basis of the Insanity Defense, *A.B.A.J.* (1983), 69:194. I shall return shortly to the case for eliminating volitional incapacity as a feature of the insanity defense.

62. See generally Slovenko, The Insanity Defense in the Wake of the Hinckley Trial, *Rutgers L. J.* (1983), 14:373.

63. See Moore, supra note 1, at 1092.

64. 61 Cal. 2d 795, 394 P.2d 959, *Cal. Rptr.* (1964), 40:271.

65. The California Supreme Court reversed a first degree murder conviction on the ground that "the true test [of premeditation and deliberation] must include consideration of the somewhat limited extent to which this defendant could *maturely and meaningfully reflect* upon the gravity of his contemplated act." Id. at 821, 394 P.2d at 975, *Cal. Rptr.* (1964), 40:287. In view of the psychiatric evidence of the defendant's diminished capacity, the court concluded that the defendant could not be found to have met this test. Id. It declined to reverse a second-degree murder conviction, however, because of the absence of a volitional disability feature in the California definition of legal insanity, which the court felt it had no authority to revise without legislative authorization. Id. at 803, 394 P.2d at 963, *Cal. Rptr.* (1964), 40:275.

66. M. Moore, *Law and Psychiatry* (1984), 244–45. Although Professor Moore develops the argument most fully, others have also identified the defense of legal insanity with incapacity for rational conduct. E.g., H. Fingarette, *The Meaning of Criminal Insanity* (1972), 175–215; Morse, Excusing the Crazy: The Insanity Defense Reconsidered, *S. Cal. L. Rev.* (1985), 58:777, 782.

67. See N. Morris, *Madness and the Criminal Law* (1982), 53–87.

68. Professor Hart's concession that it might be desirable to eliminate the defense can be understood only on this ground, given his otherwise consistent defense of the blame principle. See Changing Conceptions of Responsibility, in H. L. A. Hart, supra note 10, at 204–05.

69. See Kadish, supra note 20; Greenawalt, "Uncontrollable" Actions and the Eighth Amendment: Implications of Powell v. Texas, *Colum. L. Rev.* (1969), 69:927, 944.

70. See *United States v. Lyons,* 731 F.2d 243, 248 (5th Cir.) (en banc), cert. denied. 469 U.S. 930 (1984); American Psychiatric Association, *Statement on the Insanity Defense* (1982), 11; Morse, Failed Explanations and Criminal Responsibility: Experts and the Unconscious, *Va. L. Rev.* (1982), 68:971.

71. Bonnie, supra note 61, at 196–97.

72. Id.

73. See supra text accompanying notes 57–60.

74. See *State v. Sikora,* 44 N.J. 453, 475–79, 210 A.2d 193, 205–07 (1965) (Weintraub, C. J., concurring)I.

75. See *United States v. Lyons,* 739 F.2d 994, 997–98 (5th Cir. 1984) (Rubin, J. dissenting): "Our concept of responsibility . . . is not limited to observable behavior; it embraces *meaningful* choice, and necessarily requires inferences and assumptions regarding the defendant's unobservable mental state. . . . The difference between the concepts of excusing circumstances such as coercion and the insanity defense is that the former is based on objective assumptions about human behavior and is tested against hypothetical-objective standards such as the reasonable person. The insanity defense [on the other hand] marks the transition from the adequate man the law demands to the inadequate man he may be" (emphasis in original) (quoting A. Goldstein, *The Insanity Defense* (1967) 18).

76. See M. Moore, supra note 66, at 244–45.

77. See supra notes 64–65 and accompanying text. The court thought otherwise, however. *People v. Wolff,* 61 Cal. 2d 795, 807, 394 P.2d 959, 966, *Cal. Rptr.* (1974), 40:271, 278.

78. Cf. H. Fingarette, supra note 66, at 240: "[T]he reference in the original M'Naghten rule to the defect as one involving knowledge (cognition) is not of the essence so far as the central meaning of criminal insanity is concerned. The defect of reason may show up primarily as a cognitive, a volitional, an emotional, or a behavior-control defect, or for that matter as any other specific mental sort of defect or any combination of defects."

79. See *United States v. Alexander,* 471 F.2d 923, 960–61 (D.C. Cir.) (Bazelon, J.) cert. denited, 409 U.S. 1044 (1972); Bazelon, The Morality of the Criminal Law, *S. Cal L. Rev.* (1976), 49:385; Delgado, "Rotten Social Background": Should the Criminal Law Recognize a Defense of Severe Environmental Deprivation? *Law & Inequal.: J. Theory & Prac.* (1985), 3:9.

80. See, e.g., *United States v. Brawner,* 471 F.2d 969 (1972).

81. See Moore, supra note 1, at 1092–93.

82. See Morse, The Twilight of Welfare Criminology: A Reply to Judge Bazelon, *S. Cal. L. Rev.* (1976), 49:1247, 1267–68.

83. *United States v. Moore,* 486 F.2d 1139 (D.C. Cir.) (en banc) (plurality opinion), cert. denied, 414 U.S. 980 (1973); *People v. Davis,* 33 N.Y.2d 221, 306 N.E.2d 787, 351 N.Y.S.2d 663 (1973), cert. denied, 416 U.S. 973 (1974).

84. *Commonwealth v. Sheehan,* 376 Mass. 765, 383 N.E.2d 1115 (1978).

85. *Powell v. Texas,* 392 U.S. 514 (1968).

86. *United States v. Torniero,* 735 F.2d 725 (2d Cir. 1984), cert. denied, 169 U.S. 1110 (1985); *United States v. Gould,* 741 F.2d 45 (4th Cir. 1984); *United States v. Llewellyn,* 723 F.2d 615 (8th Cir. 1983).

87. See *Easter v. District of Columbia,* 361 F.2d 50 (D.C. Cir. 1966); *Driver v. Hinnant,* 356 F.2d 761 (4th Cir. 1966); *State v. Lafferty,* 192 Conn. 571, 472 A.2d 1275 (1984); see also Annotation, Drug Addiction or Related Mental State as a Defense to a Criminal Charge, *A.L.R. (1976),* 73:3d 16.

88. See, e.g., *Moore,* 486 F.2d at 1147–48 (Wilkey, J.) (plurality opinion) ("[T]he particular nature of the problem of heroin traffic makes certain policies necessary that should not be weakened by the creation of this defense.").

89. See, e.g., *Powell,* 392 U.S. at 559–61 (Fortas, J., dissenting); *Moore* 486 F.2d at 1235–50, 1258–60 (Wright, J., dissenting).

90. See, e.g., *Moore,* 486 F.2d at 1178–80 (Leventhal, J., concurring) (stating and rejecting argument); *Torniero,* 735 F.2d at 730–32 (same).

91. M. Moore, supra note 66, at 124–26.

92. Model Penal Code § 2.01 (1985).

93. *Fain v. Commonwealth,* 78 Ky. 183 (1879); Model Penal Code and Commentaries § 2.01 commentary at 220–21 (1985).

94. See supra note 45.

95. Model Penal Code and Commentaries § 2.09 commentary at 375–76 (1985).

96. Id. at 379–80.

97. H. Fingarette and A. Hasse, *Mental Disabilities and Criminal Responsibility* (1979), 155–72; J. Kaplan, *The Hardest Drug—Heroin and Public Policy* (1983), 15–51; Fingarette, Addiction and Criminal Responsibility, *Yale L. J.* (1975), 84:413, 427.

98. J. Kaplan, supra note 97, at 21–22, 35.

99. Id. at 35; see also Fingarette, supra note 97, at 436–37 (treatment facilities are increasingly available).

100. J. Kaplan, supra note 97, at 33.

101. Id. at 37.

102. Id. at 43–51; Fingarette, supra note 97, at 431–33. The phenomenon of alcohol addiction presents a pattern different in many ways from narcotics addiction but affords even less ground for the claim of compulsion. See H. H. Fingarette and A. Hasse, supra note 97, at 173–90; Fingarette, The Perils of Powell: In Search of a Factual Foundation for the "Disease Concept of Alcoholism," *Harv. L. Rev.* (1970), 83:793.

103. See supra text accompanying notes 51–60.

6

LOCHNER'S LEGACY

Cass R. Sunstein

Constitutional law tends to define itself through reaction to great cases. The defining case for the last several decades was *Brown v. Board of Education*[1]—an example of social reorganization, in the interest of a racial minority, brought about through the judiciary. *Roe v. Wade*[2] has to some extent played this role for the past decade, and its status as a defining case may grow larger in the next generation. But for more than a half-century, the most important of all defining cases has been *Lochner v. New York.*[3] The spectre of *Lochner* has loomed over most important constitutional decisions, whether they uphold or invalidate governmental practices.[4] In the different answers to the question, what was wrong with the decision in *Lochner*?, can be found the various positions on most of the major constitutional issues of the modern era.[5]

The received wisdom is that *Lochner* was wrong because it involved "judicial activism": an illegitimate intrusion by the courts into a realm properly reserved to the political branches of government. This view has spawned an enormous literature[6] and takes various forms.[7] The basic understanding has been endorsed by the Court in many cases taking the lesson of the *Lochner* period to be the need for judicial deference to legislative enactments.[8]

The principal purpose of this descriptive article is to understand *Lochner* from a different point of view. For the *Lochner* Court, neutrality, understood in a particular way, was a constitutional requirement. The key concepts here are threefold: government inaction, the existing distribution of wealth and entitlements, and the baseline set by the common law. Governmental intervention was constitutionally troublesome, whereas inaction was not, and both neutrality and inaction were defined as respect for the behavior of private actors pursuant to the common law, in light of the existing distribution of wealth and entitlements. Whether there was a departure from the requirement of neutrality, in short, depended on whether the government had altered the common law distribution of entitlements. Market ordering under the common law was understood to be a part of nature rather than a legal construct, and it formed the baseline from which to measure the constitutionally critical lines that distinguished action from inaction and neutrality from impermissible partisanship. This understanding of the *Lochner* period is faithful to what the Court said when it both engaged in and abandoned *Lochner*-like reasoning, and it points to an important element in the *Lochner* Court's approach, one that has little to do with an aggressive judicial role in general.[9]

Understood in this way, however, *Lochner* has many descendants in current law. Numerous decisions depend in whole or in part on common law baselines or understandings of inaction and neutrality that owe their origin to *Lochner*-like understandings. And if *Lochner* is understood in these terms, its heirs are not *Roe v. Wade*[10] and *Miranda v. Arizona*[11] but instead such decisions as *Washington v. Davis,*[12] *Buckley v. Valeo,*[13] *Regents of California v. Bakke,*[14] and various cases immunizing those who are thought not to be "state actors" from constitutional constraints. These and other decisions can be understood from a unitary perspective through the lens of the *Lochner* period. Such a perspective may or may not justify dramatic departures from current law. It may be that modern doctrine, insofar as it shares *Lochner's* premises, is entirely unobjectionable.

The second purpose of the essay is normative. To some degree, *Lochner*-like themes are so deeply ingrained in the constitutional order, indeed in the very concept of constitutionalism,[15] that it would be hopeless to attempt to abandon them even if it were desirable to do so. But in some settings, the modern progeny of *Lochner,* like *Lochner* itself, depend on false premises and lead to unfortunate results. Most important, the baselines selected by the Court and the use of the key concepts—"neutrality" and "inaction"—are often a mistake, for the same reasons that originally led to the rejection of *Lochner* and the common law system of regulation generally. The eventual task is to design a set of constitutional doctrines that does not derive from common law rules but that instead builds on still-emerging principles that might be roughly associated with the New Deal. In the final section I venture some thoughts on how to accomplish that task.

Almost eighty years since the case was decided, the lesson of the *Lochner* period has yet to be settled. I suggest that the case should be taken to symbolize not merely an aggressive judicial role but also an approach that imposes a constitutional requirement of neutrality and understands the term to refer to preservation of the existing distribution of wealth and entitlements under the baseline of the common law. Thus understood, *Lochner* has hardly been overruled.

THE RISE AND FALL (?) OF *LOCHNER*

It will be useful to begin with excerpts from two important decisions associated with the *Lochner* period. The first excerpt is from *Adkins v. Childrens Hospital,*[16] a 1923 decision invalidating minimum wage legislation for women and children. The Court said:

> To the extent that the sum fixed [by the minimum wage statue] exceeds the fair value of the services rendered, it amounts to a compulsory exaction from the employer for the support of a partially indigent person, for whose condition there rests upon him no peculiar responsibility, and therefore, in effect, arbitrarily shifts to his shoulders a burden which, if it belongs to anybody, belongs to society as a whole.[17]

The next excerpt is from the case generally thought to spell the downfall of *Lochner.* In the 1937 decision of *West Coast Hotel v. Parrish,*[18] the Court upheld a minimum wage law for women. The Court said:

> The exploitation of a class of workers who are in an unequal position with respect to bargaining power and are thus relatively defenceless against the denial of a living wage . . . casts a direct burden for their support upon the community. What these workers lose in wages the taxpayers are called upon to pay. . . . The community is not bound to provide what is in effect a subsidy for unconscionable employers.[19]

The notion of subsidy is of course incoherent without a baseline from which to make a measurement. Both of these excerpts refer to subsidies, but by the time of *West Coast Hotel,* the concept has been turned on its head. In *Adkins,* the Court saw minimum wage legislation as requiring a subsidy to the public from an innocent employer. Such legislation was thus a kind of "taking" from A to B. According to the Court, if B is needy, it is not A, but the public at large, who should pay. In *West Coast Hotel,* it is the failure of a state to have minimum wage legislation that amounts to a subsidy—this time, from the public to the employer.[20] The common law system, for the *West Coast Hotel* Court, turns out to subsidize "unconscionable employers." In the fifteen-year period between *Adkins* and *West Coast Hotel,* the baseline has been shifted. What accounts for the shift? In answering that question, it will be useful to turn to *Lochner* itself.

Lochner involved a regulation enacted by the state of New York prohibiting employers from permitting or requiring bakers to work for more than sixty hours in a week. The Court's analysis came in several steps. The Court said that the right of contract—in particular, the right to buy and sell labor—is part of the liberty protected by the due process clause. But the Court recognized that the "police power" was available to justify intrusions on liberty of contract; thus, for example, the government could protect health or morals by restricting contractual agreements. Here, however, the Court concluded that maximum hour legislation was not permissible as a "labor law," because bakers were of full legal capacity and "in no sense wards of the State."[21] Only wards could be protected through labor legislation.

The Court also concluded that the statue could not be defended as a health law. The problem was that the state could not demonstrate a close connection between maximum hour regulation and the protection of health. There was not sufficient showing that a maximum hour law was necessary to protect health, and if the evidence brought forth here were thought sufficient, the state's power would be unlimited. The Court concluded that the statue was "in reality, passed from . . . motives"[22] other than protection of health—motives that were illegitimate but that the Court did not specify.

For the contemporary observer, two features of the Court's approach are especially distinctive. The first is the sharp limitation of the category of permissible government ends. Efforts to redistribute resources and paternalistic measures were both constitutionally out of bounds. They did not fall within the "police power"; the employer had committed no common law wrong, and regulatory power was largely limited to the redress of harms recognized at common law. This limitation of the category of permissible ends had important implications, excluding a wide range of measures enacted by majorities. The scope of the "police power," as understood in the *Lochner* era, has never been entirely clear.[23] But there can be no doubt that most forms of redistribution and paternalism were ruled out.

The second step in the Court's approach consists of careful scrutiny of the relationship between the permissible end invoked by the state to support the statute and the means chosen by the state to promote that end. The Court was unsatisfied by the claim that limitations on working hours contributed to the health of bakers, notwithstanding the plausible nature of the claim—hence Justice Harlan's powerful dissent.[24] It would thus be possible to accept, as Justice Harlan did, the limitation of police power and at the same time to uphold the legislation attacked in *Lochner*. On the other hand, one could reject both features of the Court's approach, as Justice Holmes did in his famous dissent.

There is, moreover, a close relationship between the two elements of the Court's approach; the one reinforces the other. The careful scrutiny of means-ends connections operates to "flush-out"[25] impermissible ends. If there is no class of impermissible ends, means-ends scrutiny is incoherent.[26] And by impermissible ends, the Court appeared to be referring to what we may call "raw" interest-group transfers.[27] Because the only available public justifications were insufficient, the minimum wage statute was invalidated as an interest-group deal, reflecting nothing other than political power. Above all, the Court's concern was that maximum hour legislation was partisan rather than neutral—selfish rather than public-regarding.[28] It was neutrality that the due process clause commanded,[29] and neutrality was served only by the general or "public" purposes comprehended by the police power. If the statute could be justified as a labor or health law, it would be sufficiently public to qualify as neutral. Since no such justification was available, it was invalidated as impermissibly partisan—what might now be called special-interest legislation. The legislative result was thus unprincipled; it depended on "whose ox is gored." Under this framework, the common law categories were taken as a natural rather than social construct. The status of the common law as a part of nature undergirded the view that the common law should form the baseline from which to measure deviations from neutrality, or self-interested "deal."[30]

Justice Holmes' celebrated dissenting opinion is a rejection of neutrality altogether. It comes close to modern interest-group pluralism, which treats the political process as an unprincipled struggle among self-interested groups for scarce social resources.[31] Under this view, *Lochner's* means-ends scrutiny, examining whether there is a "public" and hence neutral justification for the statute, is difficult to understand. Holmes' opinion treats the political process as a kind of civil war, in which the powerful succeed; if courts interfere, they will be bottling up forces that will express themselves elsewhere in other and more destructive forms.[32] Thus for Holmes, the Constitution does not prevent "the natural outcome of a dominant opinion."[33]

Holmes' opinion is probably best known for its apparent humility: the rejection of Spencer's *Social Statics,*[34] with which Holmes was sympathetic as a matter of personal predilection; the proposition that the Constitution does not embody any particular social and economic theory; and its author's apparent willingness to disregard his personal views in the process of constitutional interpretation. But the opinion is best understood as an outgrowth of the very species of constitutional social Darwinism that it purports to reject. Holmes' market-oriented conception of politics and his skepticism about normative argument are the very personal building blocks for his enthusiasm for judicial deference.[35]

The decline of the *Lochner* understanding was slow wavering. In some cases the Court upheld statutes by deferring to claims of plausible means-ends connections. Elsewhere the Court seemed gradually to conclude that redistributive goals were permissibly public and thus in some sense neutral, even if there was a departure from the common law; the common law categories thus broke down.[36] But it was in *West Coast Hotel* that the Court rejected the theoretical foundations of the *Lochner* period. The case involved a statute providing minimum wages for women. Perhaps oddly, at least to modern readers, the emphasis of the opinion was not on the undemocratic character of the Court's previous approach or on the value of judicial deference to legislative determinations.[37] Instead the Court stressed the need for minimum wage regulation, referring to "the exploiting of workers at wages so low as to be insufficient to meet the bare cost of living" and the fact that "the exploitation of a class of workers who are in an unequal position with respect to bargaining power casts a direct burden for their support upon the community."[38] In perhaps the most striking passage of the opinion, the Court referred to the subsidy problem and added, "[t]he community may direct its law-making power to correct the abuse which springs from [employers'] selfish disregard of the public interest."[39]

In the *Lochner* era itself, of course, the police power could not be used to help those unable to protect themselves in the marketplace.[40] The expansion of the police power in *West Coast Hotel* signaled a critical theoretical shift, amounting to a rejection of the *Lochner* Court's conception of the appropriate baseline. The key lies in the notion that failure to act would amount to "a subsidy for unconscionable employers." The idea that what appears, in the *Lochner* framework, to be government "inaction," or neutrality, might amount to a subsidy is at first glance quite puzzling. The Court's claim is that the failure to impose a minimum wage is not nonintervention at all but simply another form of action—a decision to rely on traditional market mechanisms, within the common law framework, as the basis for regulation.[41] *West Coast Hotel* rests on an understanding that in any case, government—through minimum wage laws or the common law system—is making a choice. The common law could not be regarded as a natural or unchosen baseline. The traditional treatment of the police power was unable to survive this understanding.[42] For the Court in *West Coast Hotel,* the baseline for analysis was instead a system in which all workers had a living wage.

Similar developments occurred in other areas of the law. Consider for example, the law of eminent domain, with which *Lochner* must be closely associated: both involved perceived "takings" from A to B, and an underlying framework built on common law baselines.[43] *Miller v. Schoene*[44] tested the constitutionality of a statute requiring the destruction of ornamental cedar trees infected with a disease damaging to local apple orchards. The owners of the cedar trees complained that the statute amounted to a "taking" of their property for which compensation was constitutionally required. The Court responded that "the state was under the necessity of making a choice between the preservation of one class of property and that of the other wherever both existed in dangerous proximity. It would have been nonetheless a choice if, instead of enacting the present statute, the state, by doing nothing, had permitted serious injury to the apple orchards within its borders to go unchecked. When forced to such a choice the state does not exceed its constitutional powers by deciding upon the destruction of one class of property in order to save another. . . ."[45] This was so notwithstanding the fact that the injury at issue was not tortious at common law. In *Miller* as in *West Coast Hotel,* adherence to common law baselines no longer seemed neutral, and departures from those baselines were no longer impermissibly partisan. The same phenomenon occurred under the contracts clause, as the Court expanded the range of justifications that would allow the state to assert its "police power" in order to abrogate private agreements.[46] In these circumstances it should be unsurprising that *Erie v. Tompkins,*[47] the principal case recognizing the constructed rather than prepolitical character of the common law, was decided only one year after *West Coast Hotel.*

We may thus understand *Lochner* as a case that failed because it selected, as the baseline for constitutional analysis, a system that was state-created, hardly neutral, and without prepolitical status. Once the Court's baseline shifted, its analysis became impossible to sustain. As every student of the law of torts is aware, one cannot treat as a "taking" from A to B a decision to transfer resources to which A had no entitlement in the first place. The whole notion of "taking" depends on a belief in an antecedent right to the property in question.[48] Once the common law itself was seen to allocate entitlements and wealth, and the allocation seemed controversial, a decision to generate a new pattern of distribution could not be for that reason impermissible.

The defect of the *Lochner* era might, then, be understood in three ways that are closely related but that have some significant differences as well. In its narrowest form, the problem was the Court's decision to take market ordering under the substantive standards of the common law as the baseline from which to decide constitutional cases.[49] In this formulation, the difficulty lay in the use of the common law as the starting point from which to administer the critical line distinguishing action from inaction and partisanship from neutrality. More broadly, the *Lochner* Court regarded consideration of "whose ox is gored"—when those helped were the disadvantaged—as impermissible partisanship; consideration of the plight of the disadvantaged was insufficiently public or general and not neutral at all. This conclusion, reflecting a kind of legal formality, turned out to depend on the antecedent selection of a baseline grounded in the common law. More broadly still, the Court took as natural and inviolate a system that was legally constructed and took the status quo as the foundation from which to measure neutrality.[50] The use of the status quo as the foundation for measurement is of course different from similar use of the common law. We shall see both uses in the discussion to follow.

These three understandings are closely related to one another. The decision about what is partisanship and what is neutrality depends on the baseline used for measurement; thus the second defect presupposes some variation on the first. The third understanding, stressing use of the status quo, is in turn simply a generalization of the *Lochner* Court's treatment of the common law. For better or worse, these understandings of the *Lochner* era treat judicial activism as a secondary concern. The central problem of the *Lochner* Court had to do with its conceptions of neutrality and inaction and its choice of appropriate baseline.

LOCHNER AND CURRENT CONSTITUTIONAL LAW

This understanding of *Lochner* is hardly uncontroversial, but variants have been offered.[51] And if *Lochner* is understood in these terms, it has not been entirely overruled. Numerous decisions, in widely disparate areas of constitutional law, depend on *Lochner*-like baselines and similar principles of neutrality and inaction; one or more of the understandings of *Lochner* set above are reflected in many areas of current law. The areas to be covered span a wide range, including affirmative action, campaign finance regulation, gender discrimination, the state action doctrine, the distinction between de facto and de jure discrimination, and judicial review of inaction by federal administrative agencies. The discussion begins with areas using common law baselines and later shifts to areas in which the status quo is the foundation for decision.

It is important to understand that for present purposes, the goal is descriptive rather than normative. To say that a decision depends on *Lochner*-like premises is not to say that it was wrong. The normative issue is dealt with below.

Funding Limitations and the First Amendment

We begin with *Buckley v. Valeo,*[52] which involved a first amendment attack on campaign finance regulation. The regulation at issue imposed a ceiling on campaign expenditures by candidates and political parties. In defense of the regulation, the government argued that it sought to equalize the relative ability of individuals and groups to influence the outcomes of elections. Disparities in wealth, the government claimed, enabled some to drown out the voices of others. Restrictions on the speech of the wealthy served the interest of "dissemination of information from 'diverse and antagonistic sources.' "[53] By equalizing participation in the political realm, campaign finance regulation, it was said, did not undermine but instead promoted first amendment interests.

In *Buckley,* the Court concluded that this justification for regulation was illegitimate. In the Court's words, "the concept that government may restrict the speech of some elements of our society in order to enhance the relative voice of others is wholly foreign to the First Amendment."[54] The effort at equalization was not within the permissible ends of government. As far as the first amendment is concerned, the state must take disparities in wealth, and the existence of some with more "voice" than others, as part of nature for which government bears no responsibility. To do otherwise was, for the *Buckley* Court, a kind of first amendment "taking."

Buckley is a direct heir to *Lochner.* In both cases, the existing distribution of wealth is seen as natural, and failure to act is treated as no decision at all. Neutrality is inaction, reflected in a refusal to intervene in markets or to alter the existing distribution of wealth. *Buckley,* like *Lochner,* grew out of an understanding that for constitutional purposes, the existing distribution of wealth must be taken as simply "there" and that efforts to change that distribution are impermissible. Under both cases, the category of permissible legislative ends was sharply limited. To be sure, *Buckley* was a construction of the first amendment, whereas *Lochner* rested on the due process clause, and that distinction may turn out to be important.[55] But whether or not *Buckley* was rightly decided, it has much in common with *Lochner.*

Defining Liberty and Property

The due process clause accords procedural protection to "liberty" and "property," terms that the Court has had some difficulty defining in recent years.[56] The principal problems have arisen in deciding which, if any, statutory benefits—those said to be "conferred by the government"—are entitled to procedural protection.[57] For a long period the Court concluded that some benefits were "created" by the government, whereas other benefits were not. Only the latter—generally interests protected by the common law—were entitled to procedural protection. In the wake of an assault on this position, rejecting *Lochner*-like baselines deriving from common law,[58] the Court has apparently concluded that statutory benefits will sometimes be considered "liberty" or "property"—but only when there is a statutory entitlement, defined as a limitation on the administrator's discretion to provide the benefit in question.[59]

Lochner-like premises powerfully influence this debate. For the most part, liberty and property are defined by reference to the common law.[60] Interests protected at common law—including most prominently the right to private property, the right to bodily integrity, and other rights protected in the *Lochner* era—are axiomatically entitled to protection. The difficulties arise with other sorts of rights, including the right to freedom from discrimination, the right to government employment, and the right to welfare. The statutory entitlement approach is based on a partial rejection of *Lochner*-era understandings. But the Court's failure to put benefits said to be created by the government on the same footing with benefits said to be "natural" is a clear holdover from the *Lochner* period. The distinction itself treats the common law as unchosen and statutory benefits as a form of "intervention"—the same choice of baseline that affected the *Lochner* Court. An alternative approach would have been to select liberty and property interests by reference to some criterion of importance independent of the common law, or at least not determined by common law categories.[61]

Similar issues have arisen as a matter of substantive due process. In *Flemming v. Nestor,*[62] the Court concluded that social security benefits were not constitutionally protected "property."[63] The same conclusion has been reached elsewhere, as courts have concluded that government may eliminate benefits of its own creation—where that notion is defined by reference to the common law.[64] The failure to accord substantive protection to statutory benefits derives from *Lochner* era distinctions between common law interests and other benefits. Similarly, the constraints of Article III have been administered under *Lochner*-like premises. The Court is less likely to require an Article III tribunal when a right created by Congress is at stake. The common law thus defines a large amount of the territory captured by Article III requirements.[65]

State Action

The state action doctrine is a product of an (uncontroversial) understanding that the Constitution is directed to acts of government rather than acts of private individuals. But how does one decide whether government is "acting"? The legal test could in theory depend on whether government agents are involved in the process. But as the dispute provoked by such cases as *Shelley v. Kraemer*[66] makes clear, such a test would be inadequate. State officials are involved in the enforcement of private contract, tort, and property law every day, and their involvement does not subject all private arrangements to constitutional constraints. Instead, state action doctrine has always depended on a baseline establishing the legitimate or at least ordinary functions of government. And in setting forth such a theory and using it as the basis of inquiry, courts have not merely searched for state "action," but instead relied on common law baselines like those in *Lochner.* For example, the Constitution is frequently said to be a charter of "negative" rather than "positive" rights.[67] This understanding can be found in a number of areas of state action doctrine. When the government fails to provide protection against private racial discrimination, the failure is said not to be "state action" and thus raises no constitutional question.[68] Nongovernmental discrimination is created by the private rather than the public sphere. So too, no constitutional question is raised when private property owners deny the public access to their property. As the Court held in *Hudgens v. NLRB*,[69] the first amendment is not violated when landowners invoke state trespass law in order to prevent picketers from displaying their messages on private lands. All of these issues are resolved by the choice of a *Lochner*-like baseline of government "inaction," one that appears neutral and natural. Neither enforcement of the trespass law nor repeal of laws forbidding private discrimination is taken as state action—a conclusion that relies upon common law notions about the role of government.

But consider *PruneYard Shopping Center v. Robins.*[70] That case involved a decision by the California Supreme Court extending rights of free speech, under the state constitution, so as to permit people to picket on privately-owned shopping centers. The shopping center owners invoked the due process and takings clauses as a bar to the abrogation of their property rights, as those rights had been understood before the California's court's decision. The Supreme Court upheld the abrogation but left no doubt that the partial abrogation of the state law of trespass was "state action" sufficient to call for constitutional scrutiny. Indeed, a fair reading of the opinion is that some abrogations of state trespass law would amount to an unconstitutional taking—a conclusion that should be unexceptionable. Property rights are defined by state law. Abrogation of trespass law, either with respect to particular persons or across-the-board, is ordinarily the central meaning of a taking of property.

Why did the abrogation of trespass law in *PruneYard* appear uncontroversially to be state action, while application of the same law was understood to be no such thing in *Hudgens?* Indeed, which case involved "action" and which "inaction"? At first glance, the invocation of a trespass law might seem more plausibly to be action than the abrogation or removal of the very same law. The cases confirm that the state action inquiry is not a search for whether the state has "acted" but instead an examination of whether it has deviated from functions that are perceived as normal and desirable. And that examination is powerfully influenced by the common law; thus it is the abrogation rather than the enforcement of a trespass law that appears to be state action. The baseline, in short, has been defined in terms that are reminiscent of that in *Lochner.*

It will be useful to return to the treatment of private racial discrimination. There is general agreement, at least in the courts,[71] that no constitutional question is raised if a state fails to provide protection from private racial discrimination or if a state repeals a statute that had provided such protection. This understanding is made explicit in one of the most vexing of modern state action cases, *Reitman v. Mulkey.*[72] At issue in *Reitman* was a California constitutional amendment providing that no state statute may be enacted that interferes with the private right to sell property to whomever the property owner chooses. By a five-to-four vote, the Court invalidated the amendment on the ground that its purpose and effect were to encourage private racial discrimination. But the Court was careful to emphasize that the amendment stood on a very different footing from a "mere" failure to provide protection against private racial discrimination.[73] For purposes of the Constitution, *PruneYard* appeared an easy case, and the failure to provide protection against trespass was obviously state action; whereas *Reitman* was quite difficult, and the failure to provide protection against racial discrimination was obviously not state action. What accounts for this?

The answer lies in the fact that the search for state action can be made coherent only against a background normative theory of the legitimate or normal activities of government. Without such a theory, the search is unguided. It is only because of the persistence of *Lochner*-like theory that state action was uncontroversially at stake in *PruneYard* but difficult to find in *Reitman v. Mulkey.*[74] In *PruneYard,* there was a deviation from the common law baseline. In a case in which the state fails to provide protection against racial discrimination, or enforces the law of trespass, there is not. In state action doctrine, as in the *Lochner* period, the common law provides the benchmark from which to measure intervention.

Affirmative Rights: Of Welfare and Others

For the last two decades there has been considerable debate about the existence of affirmative rights against government.[75] The conventional wisdom,[76] referred to above, has it that the Constitution is a charter of negative guarantees—rights against government interference—and that "affirmative" rights are exceptional or nonexistent. Thus it is said that government may not intrude on private rights, but there is no claim against the government if it has failed to act. The basic position has resulted in rejection of claims to various public services, ranging from police protection to welfare. Perhaps the most well-known example is *Harris v. McRae,*[77] in which the plaintiffs challenged the government's failure to fund abortions needed by poor women. The Court held that government had no duty to remove barriers "not of its own creation."[78] The idea is that poverty is simply "there"; it is not a product of government action. By now it should be easy to see that this idea depends on *Lochner*-like definitions of neutrality, inaction, and appropriate baselines.

There is, however, a peculiarity in the notion that the Constitution does not guarantee "affirmative rights." We have seen that the takings clause protects against repeals, partial or total, of the trespass laws. When a state abrogates the law of trespass, it is removing what might be seen as "affirmative" protection, but its action does not become for that reason constitutionally acceptable. The protection of private contracts can be understood in similar terms. The contracts clause amounts to a right to state enforcement of contractural agreements; if the state fails to protect by refusing to enforce a contract, it is violating the clause.

Here and elsewhere, it is misleading to understand the Constitution solely as a guarantor of "negative" rights. The Constitution protects some rights and not others. Whether rights are treated as "negative" or "positive" turns out to depend on antecedent assumptions about baselines—the natural or desirable functions of government. State protection of private property and contract appears to be a "negative" guarantee because it is so usual, indeed built into the very concepts of property and contract.[79] Provision of welfare is treated differently because it is in some respects new and in any event hedged with limitations and reservations. Here *Lochner*'s premises, having to do with neutrality and inaction, account critically for current constitutional doctrine with respect to "affirmative" rights.

All this sheds some light on claims of a constitutional right to "affirmative" protection. Viewed through the lens of the *Lochner* period, claims for "positive rights" cannot be dismissed by reference to the "negative" character of constitutional guarantees or the word "deprive" in the fourteenth amendment. Whether there is a deprivation depends on antecedent conceptions of entitlement; if there were a preexisting right to welfare, the failure to provide it would in fact be a deprivation. In these circumstances one might argue that there have always been constitutional rights to certain kinds of positive guarantee and that in the modern era the right to a minimal level of material goods, like the right to protection against trespass, has constitutional status. In mature form, this argument would be quite elaborate, and for present purposes it is unnecessary to say whether the argument might be made persuasive.[80] It should suffice to suggest that cases rejecting so-called "affirmative" rights depend on *Lochner*-like premises.

Takings and Contractual Impairments

The most conspicuously *Lochner*-like provisions in the Constitution are the contracts and takings clauses, especially in their incorporation of the status quo and of common law principles. The takings clause, protecting private property, provides the analytical foundations for *Lochner* itself. And it is hard to read the provision without accepting, at least to some degree, certain premises about neutrality, inaction, and common law baselines. The contracts clause protects a species of private property; it thus grows out of the same framework as *Lochner.* But in the last fifty years, the constraints of the contracts and takings clauses have been significantly curtailed, in part for the same reasons that led to the abandonment of *Lochner* itself. These developments suggest, among other things, that text and animating purposes have been far from central to decisions about whether to rely on *Lochner*-like principles.

The decline of the contracts clause has been a subject of increasing modern controversy. The clause provides that no state shall enact any law "impairing the obligations of contracts." For a long period the clause operated as a significant barrier to government action; the clause is now for the most part[81] a dead letter. How might this development be explained?

The answer lies in the dramatic expansion of the police power—in short, from an understanding based on *Lochner* to one rooted in *West Coast Hotel.* For a long period the contracts clause has permitted states to abrogate contracts so long as they are operating within the "police power." If a state bans the sale of heroin, and the ban applies retroactively to prevent enforcement of a contract, there is no constitutional problem.[82] The reserved powers of the state, it is said, operate as an implicit limitation on the power to contract. But if the police power is understood in *Lochner*-like terms, there is still enormous room for immunity from legislative interference—a claim demonstrated by the interpretation of the contracts clause for much of the nation's history.[83] In *Home Building Loan Association v. Blaisdell,*[84] however, the Court read the police power very broadly—thus replicating the outcome in *West Coast Hotel* and rendering the contracts clause functionally identical to the due process clause.

Similar developments occurred under the law of eminent domain. Here *Lochner*-like premises might be expected in two places: the interpretation of the "public use" requirement and of the police power exception to the compensation requirement. The public use requirement traditionally meant that the property had actually to be used by the public.[85] But gradually the requirement was expanded to refer to any plausible public justification, including those that are redistributive in character.[86] Thus it is said that the public use requirement has been rendered effectively unenforceable, much like the rationality requirement of the due process clause post-*Lochner.*

Moreover, the police power exception to the eminent domain clause immunizes various regulatory measures from constitutional attack, even if they diminish the value of property. An actual physical invasion of property is often a prerequisite for a finding of a "taking."[87] All this is a product of an abandonment of *Lochner*-like baselines. It would be difficult, however, to abandon those baselines altogether without reading the contracts and takings clauses out of the Constitution; in nature, those provisions are *Lochner*-like, though their scope is uncertain.[88] The narrowing of the scope of the contracts clause has almost converted it into a constitutional redundancy; the takings clause is still important in the context of physical invasions.

Judicial Review of Agency Inaction

One of the most important issues in modern administrative law is whether inaction by administrative agencies, defined as the failure to enforce regulatory statutes, should be subject to the same standards as administrative action, defined as regulatory enforcement. Under the traditional approach, agency action is subject to a strong presumption of reviewability.[89] Much of administrative law grows out of an understanding that government may interfere with common law rights only if it has been authorized to do so by the legislature.[90] Judicial review is necessary to test the question of authorization.

Under this framework, there is little room for review at the behest of beneficiaries of statutes. In such suits, no common law right is at stake. This framework accounts for conventional limitations on the class of persons entitled to obtain "standing" to review agency action[91] and also for a long-standing presumption against reviewability of agency inaction.[92] In the last decade, there has been a substantial trend against this traditional understanding,[93] as beneficiaries of regulatory programs have been allowed to challenge unlawful agency inaction.

In its recent decision in *Heckler v. Chaney,*[94] however, the Supreme Court held that agency inaction should be presumed unreviewable. In so holding, the Court emphasized that "when an agency refuses to act it generally does not exercise its *coercive* power over an individual's liberty or property rights, and thus does not infringe upon areas that courts often are called upon to protect."[95]

This understanding is a direct modern analogue to *Lochner.* In both cases, deviations from the common law status quo demand special justification. In *Heckler,* as in *Lochner,* it is government interference with the common law allocation that is subject to legal concern. Governmental "inaction" is treated as neutral and legally unobjectionable; indeed, it does not furnish a predicate for judicial intervention. In the context of administrative law, this phenomenon is especially striking. The rise of the modern administrative state was based largely on a rejection of common law ordering. For the proponents of the administrative agency, the common law system was hardly unchosen or neutral, but was instead highly partisan[96]—a perception shared, as we have seen, by the Court in *West Coast Hotel* and also in *Erie.* Regulatory intervention was based largely on a substantive rejection of the common law system. Administrative law doctrines, rooted in traditional private law, thus continue to reflect *Lochner*-like premises despite the repudiation of those premises during the rise of the administrative state.

Standing

Similar considerations apply to the problem of standing. Originally, only those whose common law interests were at stake had standing to challenge administrative action. Thus the requirement of a "legal interest" meant, at its inception, that a litigant must be able to show that an interest protected by the common law was at stake.[97] This test was built on an analogy to private law. Those adversely affected by illegality could not always challenge it; it was necessary to show that the defendant violated some duty owed to plaintiff. Thus the issues of standing, of a cause of action, and of a persuasive claim on the merits were inextricably intertwined, in a system of public law that owed its origin and shape to common law understandings.

Eventually the Court recognized that an interest protected by statute could also form the predicate for standing.[98] Thus competitors and regulatory beneficiaries might have standing to sue if they had an interest protected by statute. Finally, in *Association of Data Processing Service Organization v. Camp,*[99] the Supreme Court rejected the legal interest test altogether, requiring only an injury "in fact" and "arguably within the zone" of statutory protection in order to test administrative action.[100] The *Data Processing* decision has been celebrated as a rejection of private property as the predicate for judicial intervention in favor of an approach that calls on courts to ensure the identification and implementation of public values.[101]

In three ways, however, modern standing doctrine still contains principles from the common law. First, the requirement of an injury in fact is often justified on the ground that officious intermeddlers ought not to be permitted to disrupt mutually advantageous relationships.[102] This idea is a direct analogue to the common law view insofar as it understands public law cases in right-duty terms. Second, the notion of judicial restraint in the law of standing often has built into it a tacit distinction between the interests of regulatory beneficiaries and those of regulated industries. The former, it is said, are for the political process rather than the courts; the judicial role is said to be the protection of traditional private rights—a *Lochner*-like understanding.[103] This reasoning is not a tribute to "judicial restraint" in the abstract but distinguishes between two categories of interests in terms of the respective roles of politics and courts.[104] This distinction should be quite controversial; it is held over from the *Lochner* era and its premises were repudiated during the New Deal.

Finally, the Court has recently used various requirements of "nexus" as a basis for denying standing.[105] Thus the plaintiff must show that his injury is attributable to the defendant's conduct and that the injury is likely to be remedied by a decree in his favor. In such cases the categorization of the injury is critical; the Court has frequently refused to recognize probabilistic or systemic harms and instead has required a showing of the sort required by traditional private law.[106] Such cases express an understanding that the distinctive judicial role is to protect traditional sorts of legal harms. In these respects, standing doctrine, even in the era following *Data Processing*, continues to be based on *Lochner*-like conceptions of the role of the courts.[107]

Racial Discrimination

The law of racial discrimination is centrally affected by *Lochner*-like premises, but here the similarity to *Lochner* lies, not in the use of the common law, but in notions of action and inaction and in the importation of the status quo and the existing distribution of wealth and entitlements.

In particular, three areas of modern discrimination law reflect a debate between conceptions that can be traced to *Lochner* and *West Coast Hotel* respectively. The same debate can be found in an earlier generation, during the discussion of the decision in *Brown v. Board of Education*,[108] and indeed in the most famous use of the term "neutrality" in constitutional scholarship. In *Toward Neutral Principles of Constitutional Law*,[109] Professor Herbert Wechsler criticized the opinion in *Brown* on the ground that the Court had not supplied a "neutral" justification for the result. In Wechsler's view, the decision provided a conflict between two sorts of associational preferences: the desire of blacks to attend school with whites and the desire of whites to attend school without blacks. So far as Wechsler was concerned, no neutral principle had been brought forward to permit a choice between these two sets of preferences.[110] The decision depended on "whose ox was gored," and was thus not shown to be neutral.[111]

This criticism has a powerful *Lochner*-like dimension. The existing distribution of power and resources as between blacks and whites should be taken by courts as simply "there"; neutrality lies in inaction; it is threatened when the Court "takes sides" by preferring those disadvantaged. Like the minimum wage legislation in *Lochner*, and for similar reasons, the attack on school segregation appeared impermissibly partisan to some of *Brown*'s critics.

In both cases, moreover, the appropriate response derives from *West Coast Hotel:* the existing distribution is not natural and does not provide a neutral baseline; it resulted in part from government decisions; efforts to improve the lot of the disadvantaged fall comfortably within the police power, should not be treated as impermissibly partisan, and may even be constitutionally compelled, especially where there is racial discrimination on the face of a statute. Indeed, the notion that the associational preferences of whites and blacks should be treated the same seems to have an other-worldly quality. To some degree, of course, Wechsler's objection was institutional. He was requiring of courts a justification of the sort that the *Lochner* Court required of legislatures. The category of neutral principles, as he understood it, was analogous to the police power as understood by the *Lochner* Court. Both forbade consideration of the plight of the disadvantaged as a sufficiently neutral or general reason for action. But the institutional differences should not deflect attention from the same basic normative foundation. In both cases, "taking sides" in favor of the disadvantaged seemed impermissibly partisan.[112]

Similar considerations can be found, in somewhat different form, in several areas of modern discrimination law.

1. *Affirmative Action.* It is now clear that "affirmative action"—discrimination in favor of traditionally disadvantaged groups—will be treated more leniently than discrimination against members of such groups.[113] But the validity of a particular affirmative action scheme will depend on a variety of factors: the nature of the institution that made the decision; the flexible or inflexible character of the scheme; the nature of the harm to members of the majority; and, perhaps most important, the existence of "findings" to the effect that the institution engaging in affirmative action has discriminated in the past.[114] The final factor has been the most sharply disputed among the justices. The dispute centers on when, if ever, past societal discrimination is a sufficient predicate for an affirmative action scheme, or whether affirmative action must be justified by a more particularized showing of discriminatory conduct on the part of the institution in question. Current indications are that societal discrimination is insufficient.[115]

The constitutional attack on affirmative action depends on a perception that the natural course is to rely on market measures. The Constitution, in this view, requires government to allocate employment and other opportunities according to criteria that have nothing to do with race. To distinguish discrimination against blacks from discrimination against whites is not neutral; it makes the issue depend on "whose ox is gored." Government intervention to redress social discrimination, or some other harm, is partisan. Indeed, the suggestion in *Adkins*—that individuals should not be singled out for burdens that ought to be placed on the public as a whole—is very close to the understanding that underlies contemporary attacks on affirmative action. But if the current position of blacks is thought not simply to be "there" but instead to be a product of past and present social choices, the argument for affirmative action becomes much more powerful.[116] No requirement of "neutrality" would be understood as mandating measures that are (or seem) indifferent to race. The constitutional arguments for and against affirmative action thus track the arguments for and against minimum wage legislation.

Indeed, the very term "affirmative action"—ironically, embraced by defenders of the practice—is based on *Lochner*-like premises. The term suggests that indifference to race (understood here as "inaction") is the natural course, that discriminatory effects deriving from colorblind rules are simply "there," and that something that counters those effects should be labeled "affirmative." The terms "affirmative" and "action" both rely on *Lochner*-like conceptions of appropriate baseline; both understand respect for the status quo and the existing distribution of power and resources as the point of departure for constitutional analysis. Moreover, racial discrimination is objectionable because of its purposes and effects; discrimination against blacks is usually accompanied by racial hostility on the part of the discriminators, and its effect is to perpetuate the social subordination of blacks. Critics of "affirmative action" take advantage of the rhetorical power of the notion of racial discrimination in a context in which the reasons for that rhetorical power—the purposes and effects of discrimination—are not at work and indeed argue in the other direction. Thus it is that *Lochner*-like premises infect the affirmative action controversy.

2. *Discriminatory Effects*. The Supreme Court has now made it clear that a showing of discriminatory intent is necessary in order to make out a violation of the equal protection clause.[117] Discriminatory effects are in themselves insufficient. Thus, for example, if a facially neutral test for police officers happens to exclude a disproportionate number of blacks, there is no equal protection problem even if the test has little relation to capacity to perform the job.

The Court has required proof of discriminatory purpose in part because of a concern that if discriminatory effects were enough, numerous government decisions would be called into constitutional doubt.[118] Wealth and opportunities correlate with race; a disproportionate number of blacks are poor, uneducated, unable to perform well on standard examinations, the perpetrators (and victims) of crimes, and so forth. Building on private law models of culpability, the Court has thus concluded that the Constitution is violated only when there is an intent to discriminate, not when discriminatory outcomes are produced by government actions that do not take race into account.

This understanding also depends on a *Lochner*-like premise that discriminatory effects are simply "there," so that the course of neutrality lies in indifference to race (what appears and is treated is inaction).[119] But if discriminatory effects were seen as partly the product of past discrimination by the state, it would be hard to treat them as natural and unobjectionable. If disproportionate harms to blacks result from a legacy of discrimination, a set of legal doctrines that treated such harms as constitutionally troublesome would hardly seem odd. Doctrine based on compensatory goals would be a permissible and perhaps mandatory course.

3. *De jure / de facto.* For a long period it was unclear whether de facto segregation was a cause for constitutional concern.[120] De facto segregation, largely in the North, is said to arise from the voluntary choices of blacks and whites; de jure segregation is the product of law. But here, as in the case of affirmative action, the terminology itself rests on *Lochner*-like premises. The notion of de facto segregation suggests that segregation simply happened; it is "just there." But if the existence of patterns of segregation were seen as an outgrowth of the legacy of racial discrimination, an attack on "de facto" segregation might have been more plausible. There may be good reasons to immunize some kinds of segregation from legal control, but the doctrinal distinction depends partly on understandings of neutrality and inaction that are close cousins of *Lochner.*

Gender Discrimination

In the last two decades, the Court has given "heightened scrutiny" to discrimination against women, invalidating a wide range of statutes. Sometimes the Court invalidates statutes because they are based on inaccurate stereotypes.[121] But the difficult cases arise when the Court faces measures reflecting differences that are in some sense real. Consider, for example, *Califano v. Goldfarb,*[122] involving a statute allowing spouses of men automatically to qualify for social security benefits but requiring spouses of women to establish dependency; Craig N. Boren,[123] invalidating a law prohibiting boys from drinking alcoholic beverages until age twenty-one but allowing girls to drink at age eighteen; *Mississippi University for Women v. Hogan,*[124] involving a nursing school limited to women; and *Rostker v. Goldberg,*[125] upholding a law requiring men but not women to register for the military draft. In all of these cases, the statute under attack responded, albeit sometimes crudely, to differences between men and women that were in some sense real. On what basis did the Court invalidate the first three measures?

A clue can be found in *Craig v. Boren,* where the Court, responding to statistics showing that boys tended to be cited for drunk driving more often than girls, said that statistical demonstrations are "in tension with the normative philosophy that underlies the Equal Protection Clause."[126] In all of these cases, the differences, even if "real," are not simply there but are at least to some degree[127] artifactual: a product of cultural forces, including the legal system, that have created and perpetuated differences between the sexes. Thus in *Goldfarb,* the fact that men tend to be wage-earners more often than women was not treated as exogenous to the legal system.

Indeed, the fact was reinforced as such, even if in a minimal way, by the very statute in *Goldfarb,* which made the package of benefits more attractive for men than for women and tended to make it more desirable for men to work. Thus in the *Hogan* case, the Court said that the statute at issue "makes the assumption that nursing is a field for women a self-fulfilling prophecy."[128]

Rostker is a striking contrast. There the Court reasoned that since Congress had excluded women from combat, the difference in registration requirements responded to "real differences" between men and women. But those real differences were a product of law; it was a statute that created them. *Rostker* is in this sense reminiscent of a wide range of earlier cases failing to recognize the constructed character of gender distinctions and upholding discrimination because of a perception that subordination of women was a part of nature.[129]

With the exception of *Rostker,* the cases under discussion derive from a partial rejection of *Lochner*-like principles that would take gender differences as exogenous variables and would understand neutrality to lie in reasonable responses to those differences.[130] To this extent, the law of gender discrimination is an outgrowth of ideas that abandon the status quo as a neutral baseline and instead rely on a baseline of gender equality operating to some extent as a criticism of the existing order. But many areas of the law of gender discrimination share *Lochner*-like premises. Consider, in addition to the *Rostker* decision, cases finding discriminatory effects insufficient for constitutional invalidation;[131] decisions permitting employers to exclude fertile women from employment when actual or potential fetuses may be endangered;[132] and *Michael M. v. Sonoma County Superior Court,*[133] upholding distinctions in age for statutory rape. Above all, cases involving discrimination on the basis of actual or potential pregnancy, or control of reproductive functions, are *Lochner*-like to the extent that they turn differences that are often regarded as natural into legal disadvantages.[134] In this sense, *Roe v. Wade* itself might be seen as profoundly anti-*Lochner* insofar as it accorded to women the power to make a decision that it had been previously thought was not theirs because of nature.[135]

To say that such cases treat gender differences as real, when the social and legal meaning of those differences is a decision of the legal system, is not necessarily to say that they were wrongly decided.[136] But it is to suggest that they depend on *Lochner*-like premises about neutrality.

Preferences and the Law

Both public and private law generally take private preferences as the appropriate basis for social choice. In private law, paternalism tends to be disfavored,[137] and the most well-known conceptions of public law understand the purpose of legislation to be the aggregation of private preferences.[138] To this degree, preferences are treated in *Lochner*-like fashion as exogenous variables; and legal interferences with those preferences are generally thought to be partisan and illegitimate. The processes of preference formation and the possibility of distorting factors are generally not a subject for legal inquiry.[139]

Sometimes, however, constitutional courts conclude that preferences are a product of some kind of distortion. Consider, for example, the constitutional hostility to freedom-of-choice plans as a remedy for school segregation.[140] At first glance it is hard to see why such plans should be objectionable, for they allow blacks and whites to send their children to whatever schools they prefer. If the result is continuing segregation, the problem might be thought to lie in private choices rather than in the legal system.

The Court's hostility to such plans depends at least in part on a conclusion that the preferences of whites and blacks are distorted by the history of discrimination.[141] Blacks may prefer not to send their children to predominantly white schools because of a fear of racial hostility and antagonism. Whites may be reluctant to send their children to black schools because of racial prejudice brought about at least in part through law. In these circumstances, the preferences are not simply "there" and to be taken as natural; they are a result of legal structures, and remedial measures must take that into account.

A similar issue is raised by *Palmore v. Sidoti*,[142] in which the Court invalidated a child custody plan giving preferences to parents of the same race as the child. The Court said that the state may not sanction racial prejudice through law, but it is unclear why the Constitution should forbid government from taking into account the reality of private racism. Here too the answer depends on a perception that racism is not simply exogenous; it is a product of public and private choices and is properly subject to legal remedy. The same considerations apply in the area of gender. What emerges is therefore a system that generally treats preferences as exogenous and a proper basis for social choice but that in certain limited contexts[143] concludes that preferences reflect relations of power brought about by, among other things, the legal system itself.

ABANDONING *LOCHNER*

We have seen that *Lochner* has many progeny in modern constitutional law.[144] Sometimes, as in *Buckley* and *Wygant*, *Lochner*-like premises are used as a basis for invalidating government measures. Sometimes, as in *Harris v.*

McRae and *Washington v. Davis,* premises of that sort are used in order to uphold such measures. Nor is the problem limited to constitutional provisions protecting individual rights. The structural provisions of the Constitution were designed partly to protect private property and liberty from government incursion.[145] The rise of the modern administrative state is based largely on a perception that aggressive governmental action, repudiating the common law, has become necessary.[146] One of the most important tasks of modern constitutional theory is to implement the original purposes of the structural provisions in a time when traditional conceptions of limited government have been repudiated.[147]

The claim that there is in many areas of current public law an analytic connection to *Lochner* is only descriptive, and it does not necessarily argue for doctrinal change. Indeed, it would be difficult to imagine a constitutional system that did not have some premises in common with *Lochner.* The framers themselves shared those premises, and versions can be found at every stage of American constitutionalism. But the argument for *Lochner*-like premises is conceptual as well as historical. It is hard to escape *Lochner* in thinking about this or any other legal system; its premises are built into our language itself.[148] Without some foundations or baselines from which to make measurements, legal analysis cannot go forward, and in some cases it is hard to dispute that understandings like those reflected in the common law or the status quo are the appropriate baseline. The point is buttressed by the fact that in any legal system, one should hope for some degree of continuity over time. The current system owes its foundations to the common law. It would be most surprising, and probably undesirable, to find those foundations entirely abandoned.[149]

But *Lochner* was wrongly decided, and one of the reasons that it was wrong is that it depended on baselines and consequent understandings of action and neutrality that were inappropriate for constitutional analysis. The New Deal to a large degree rejected those understandings, and the rejection has only partly found its way into law. Which, if any, of current doctrines should be abandoned for the same reason? How should constitutional law proceed if it is to escape its roots in *Lochner*-like reasoning? It is difficult to answer these questions in the abstract; whether and how *Lochner*-like premises should be rejected is too large a question to discuss as a whole. This section ventures some thoughts on the relevant inquiries.

Naturalness and the Problem of Baseline

The *Lochner* Court chose the status quo, as reflected in market ordering under the common law system, as the baseline for measurement of departures from neutrality and of action and inaction. There are often good reasons to abandon that baseline, at least as a general rule.[150] The common law is not prepolitical; its conception of the function of the state has been repudiated by the political branches of government, and for good reasons. Constitutional and statutory interpretation is properly informed by this repudiation.[151] Efforts to change the common law framework are not by virtue of the fact constitutionally suspect, and measures that respect that framework are not "inaction" necessarily to be immunized from legal scrutiny. Use of the status quo as a baseline is sometimes objectionable for similar reasons. Consider the fact that discrimination on the basis of race is responsible for the existing distribution of benefits and burdens along racial lines.

If the baseline provided by the common law or the status quo is abandoned, there are two principal alternatives. One possible response to the decline of *Lochner* would be to conclude that constitutional courts ought to play little or no role in deciding whether the existing distribution of wealth and entitlements should be changed. Associated with one strand in the New Deal but presaged by Holmes' *Lochner* opinion, this view appears prominently in Learned Hand's lectures on the Bill of Rights,[152] James Landis' work on administrative law,[153] and the opinions of Justice Frankfurter.[154]

Under the Holmesian view it does not matter, for constitutional purposes, whether the state is reaffirming or rejecting the common law or whether it is dramatically changing the existing allocation of entitlements and power. The abandonment of common law baselines requires an abandonment of baselines altogether, at least for purposes of constitutional law. Neutrality is not required because it cannot be achieved; all legal categories are socially constructed and irreducibly subjective.[155] Such an approach would mean that the basic terms of social life are for political rather than legal determination.[156]

Sometimes this view is founded on interest-group pluralism;[157] sometimes it is derived from skepticism about the notion of objectivity[158] and about distinctions between reason and power.[159] For those who believe in interest-group pluralism, efforts to ensure neutrality, in the form of public-regarding legislation, ignore the inevitably self-interested character of political behavior. Neutrality, however understood, is thus inconsistent with the very nature of politics.[160] The conclusion is that baselines should be rejected for purposes of constitutional law; courts should uphold legislation except in the most extreme cases. For those skeptical about objectivity, neutrality is an unacceptable effort to privilege a position that is itself contingent and likely to reflect some kind of social interest.[161] At its most general level, this concern is reflected in a wide range of work questioning the legacy of the Enlightenment.[162] This position offers obscure guidance for constitutional courts; it counsels a general rejection both of neutrality and of baselines, but at least in some forms, it offers no alternative position from which to decide cases.

Approaches that follow Holmes and abandon baselines for the purposes of constitutional law, like the approach in *Lochner,* have the advantage of easy administration; they are reflected in some of current law under the contracts, due process, and takings clauses; and they can claim as well a proper appreciation of democratic values.[163] The Holmesian abandonment of baselines is of course reflected in traditional understandings of the lesson of the *Lochner* period. The decision whether to accept those understandings is inescapably normative, and the traditional view might be defended on the foregoing grounds.

In so extreme a form, however, this position is unacceptable precisely because it is based on odd understandings of republicanism[164] and of the workings of majoritarianism.[165] The Holmesian position would result in a failure to enforce many constitutional provisions that invite judicial use of baselines, sometimes deriving from the common law, and that are self-conscious limits on the ability of government to restructure or to fail to restructure the existing order. Consider the first amendment, the takings clause, the equal protection clause, and the contracts clause, all of which impose limits on governmental power. Moreover, neutrality—understood not as preservation of market ordering or as disregard of past discrimination but as a requirement of a public-regarding justification for legislation—continues to be required, and for good reasons.[166] The Holmesian position, reflected in some traditional thinking about *Lochner,* would amount to an abandonment of constitutionalism altogether. Its crude and conclusory references to the primacy of electoral politics are insufficient to support that abandonment.[167]

A third approach would avoid the difficulties associated with both *Lochner* and the Holmesian alternative, but it would carry with it large problems of its own. That approach would attempt to generate a baseline independent of either the common law or the status quo through some theory of justice, to be derived from the language and animating purposes of the text and based to a greater or lesser degree on existing interpretations. Such an endeavor would require a theory of interpretation, a theory of institutional role, and a theory of justice. The effort would be the legal analogue to the various efforts in modern political theory to go beyond or replace classically liberal social contract theories.[168] The text would be the foundation for a theory[169] that would be independent of common law ordering, or the status quo, and would serve as a basis for evaluating it. Approaches of this sort might treat the Constitution as a unit, reflecting a single overarching theory. For reasons explored below, it would be preferable to proceed provision-by-provision,[170] constructing theories for each constitutional clause and allowing considerable variation among them. Helpful guidance can be found in republican theories of politics, which carry with them substantive constraints[171] and whose premises are highly congenial to the New Deal attack on the common law.[172] A profitable strategy would be to avoid abstraction and to examine particular areas with considerable care.[173]

Such an approach would force courts to confront the question of why and how the artifactual quality of a particular system is relevant to the legal question. The fact that a practice is artifactual hardly means that it should be changed; and the fact that it is in some sense natural is not necessarily a reason to respect it.[174] Consider here the area of gender discrimination; it is the legal system that makes relevant any biological difference, and a decision to turn a difference into a disadvantage demands independent support.[175] But a finding that a practice or system is a product of government is relevant in various respects. First, it may suggest that changes should not be regarded as "takings"; the notion of a taking depends on an antecedent baseline, and if the baseline is not natural, one needs an independent reason to respect it. Moreover, if a practice is revealed as simply an adaptation to the status quo, new legal rules will not be futile. Finally, it is sometimes thought that interferences with practices that are an outgrowth of nature infringe on liberty or on some other right. The *Lochner* era is itself an example, and the areas of race and gender discrimination might be similarly understood. A recognition that the practices in question are artifactual may weaken such objections. The fact that a practice is a creature of government thus removes some arguments for retaining it, though standing by itself, it is hardly a powerful reason to change it.

Development of a theory of justice that interprets the constitutional text but that is independent of the status quo is extremely difficult. A strong version of anti-*Lochner* thinking would make it hard to provide foundations from which to begin the inquiry; even theories of distributive justice need to accept some grounds from which to proceed.[176] Such theories must be culturally situated. The notion of a foundational theory existing entirely apart from conventions is likely to be chimerical, and in its own way reflective of *Lochner*-like premises. If so, the task is instead to be critical of existing practices without pretending to have transcended the particular culture altogether.[177]

One can point to some such efforts in current law. The first amendment prohibitions of discrimination on the basis of point of view and of government preference of particular religions are prominent examples.[178] The law of racial discrimination is a particularly helpful illustration here. Courts have developed theories that permit them to evaluate particular social practices from an independent baseline, one that prohibits intentional discrimination against blacks. Discrimination on the basis of gender, alienage, and illegitimacy is handled in similar terms. The principal effort here is to develop and justify an alternative baseline, and to imagine a world in which the illegitimate or irrelevant considerations were not at work.

In some areas, this task appears easy, but the setting of school segregation suggests why development of a baseline independent of the status quo is sometimes difficult. For a long period, the controversial questions here had to do with the constitutionality of freedom of choice and other plans in attempting to eliminate the effects of segregation.[179] Freedom-of-choice plans do not significantly reduce segregation, but court-ordered transportation plans, including racial percentages, can hardly be said to be restoring the system to what it would be if discrimination had never taken place. The problem here is to imagine a hypothetical world in which housing patterns and educational choices were unaffected by past discrimination. The search for a status quo ante in the area of school segregation has an arbitrary quality, and sometimes the Court has had to come close to requiring integration in the absence of any other plausible version of a reconstructed system.[180]

The problem is hardly limited to the area of school segregation. It arises in many cases in which courts are asked to reject the status quo as the appropriate baseline. Consider, for example, a decision to allow a showing of discriminatory effects to trigger the equal protection clause. To a greater or lesser degree, such a decision would require courts to imagine what the system of benefits and burdens across the races would look like in a world unaffected by a legacy of racism. Although inquiries of this sort are familiar in some areas of the law, in the present context they would be difficult to anchor; the causal links are so complex that a reconstruction of the past would inevitably rest on uncertain premises.[181] The area of gender discrimination poses similar problems. Imagine efforts to see how veterans' preferences or abortion would be treated in a world unaffected by sexism.[182]

This is not the occasion to set out a general theory of appropriate baselines from which to decide constitutional cases; as we will see, the answer is likely to vary across provisions. It should suffice to suggest that the common law or status quo baseline in *Lochner* will often be unacceptable; that the existing order should not be regarded as natural or inviolate; that the abandonment of baselines altogether is also unacceptable; and that generation of an independent alternative is sometimes necessary but poses large difficulties of its own. Current law is an amalgam of all three approaches. The primary purpose here is to suggest some of the ingredients in the decision why and when *Lochner*-like premises should be abandoned.

An important lesson of the discussion to follow is the need to proceed with some particularity. Abstract or general approaches are unlikely to be helpful here, at least for the foreseeable future.[183] The examination of particular areas is the starting point for extrapolating more general principles.

Swords and Shields

Even if the Holmesian approach is rejected, a less extreme version would suggest that in deciding whether *Lochner*-like premises should be accepted, it is highly relevant whether the Court is permitting government to act or prohibiting it from doing so. Courts might, in short, be inclined to uphold measures defended in terms like those in *West Coast Hotel,* even as they were disinclined to invalidate legislation under premises derived from either *Lochner* or *West Coast Hotel.* Deference to representative processes argues in favor of this result.[184] Under this view, the parallel of modern decisions to *Lochner* is closest when the Court is invalidating democratically enacted legislation. Even if one rejects the most extreme claims about the undemocratic character of judicial review, one might agree that *Lochner*-like premises should rarely be used to invalidate legislation.

The argument for upholding the statute in *Buckley v. Valeo* was therefore quite strong; the case was very close to *Lochner* itself—unless there is some difference in the nature of the right, an issue taken up below. Similarly, measures calling for "affirmative action," viewed through the lens of the *Lochner* era, should generally not be thought to raise a serious constitutional issue. When a legislature or other entity enacts an affirmative action program, it should not be treated as operating against a status quo baseline that is in some sense natural or neutral. The current distribution of benefits and burdens along racial lines is an outgrowth of a long history of discrimination. Efforts to eliminate the subordination of blacks can hardly be regarded in the same way as efforts to perpetuate it.[185]

Similar considerations apply to redistributive measures enacted under the contracts and taking clauses. Notwithstanding recent criticism under *Lochner*-like premises,[186] current law under both clauses is generally correct. It permits a wide realm of action for legislatures, an appropriate conclusion in the face of textual ambiguity, the evident desires of the majority, changed circumstances, and the growing scope of the police power.[187] In all of these contexts, an understanding like that in *West Coast Hotel* should operate, at least prima facie, as a "shield" against constitutional attacks on legislation, just as it does under the due process clause in the aftermath of *Lochner.*

Because of institutional concerns, more difficult questions are raised by the prospect of using *West Coast Hotel* as a "sword," that is, as the basis for constitutional attacks on existing social structures. In this category can be put the various arguments for a discriminatory effects test under the equal protection clause. So too, some of the arguments in the racial and gender area attempt to use an understanding like that in *West Coast Hotel* as a sword against government. In the same category can be placed the claims for welfare rights. In such cases, the fact that the plaintiff is attacking legislation enacted by a popular majority counts against recognition of the claim.[188]

All this is hardly to suggest that the issue of swords and shields should control the constitutional question; that would represent a return to Holmesian understandings about the judicial role and in its own way reflect *Lochner*-like distinctions between action and inaction.[189] But the issue is highly relevant. Constitutional law is often an uneasy mixture of substantive theory and institutional constraint.[190] The existence of institutional limits on the part of the judiciary forces the courts to limit the scope of substantive constraints on government action. This combination sometimes produces doctrinal awkwardness, but it is hard to think of an alternative. In these circumstances, it is important whether a decision would call for simple validation of a measure enacted by Congress or instead would require courts to undertake significant social change on their own.

The Nature of the Clause

The catalog of *Lochner*-like premises in modern public law spans a wide range, and it implicates a large number of constitutional provisions, including the contracts, takings, due process, and equal protection clauses, as well as the first amendment. But *Lochner*-like premises are more necessary or appropriate under some provisions than under others. A lawyer's natural reaction to the problem would be to disentangle the various provisions. The interpretive process, informed to a greater or lesser degree by the text and original purposes, might well vary across clauses; different clauses may abandon or include *Lochner*-like premises. A theory of constitutional interpretation would of course be necessary to accomplish this task.

At the most general level, it is possible to understand the original Constitution as having a substantial *Lochner*-like dimension. Both the institutional and the individual rights provisions of the document were influenced by an understanding of the naturalness of the distribution of property.[191] The Civil War Amendments were at least a partial recognition of the artifactual quality of existing distributions, and subsequent judicial interpretation carried that recognition much further. The various developments associated with the New Deal[192] were a substantial abandonment of the *Lochner*-like features of constitutionalism, in its institutional and individual rights dimensions. One of the most important tasks of modern constitutional theory is to integrate these various developments into a theory of constitutional interpretation.

Lochner, under a textual approach, was wrong above all because it was an interpretation of the due process clause. That clause may be only procedural in character,[193] it may require the government only to show some minimal justification for its decisions; it may not sharply confine the permissible ends of the state. The takings clause, by contrast, was built on a belief in the meaning and importance of private property, and it would be difficult to read that clause in the fashion of *West Coast Hotel* without reading it out of the Constitution. The same conclusion may be appropriate under the contracts clause. At a minimum, then, the takings and contracts clauses cannot easily be read to create a constitutional baseline other than that of the status quo; the notion of property itself develops and evolves from common cultural understandings that cannot easily be subject to independent judicial reconstruction.[194] The eminent domain and contracts clauses are most naturally read to embody *Lochner*-like premises about neutrality and inaction.

At the same time, it would be possible to remove both provisions from their foundations in *Lochner.* In particular, courts might recognize the social construction of property and understand the term "takings" against the backdrop set by independent theories of entitlement and an appreciation of the social functions of private ownership. Such an approach would produce difficult questions of judicial authority and competence, but some have argued in favor of an effort of that sort.[195] If such an effort is to be made, however, it should proceed slowly and incrementally in light of the history and current interpretation of the clause.

By contrast to the takings and contracts clauses, the equal protection clause is most easily read as a self-conscious rejection of *Lochner*-like premises. The purpose of the clause was, at least to some degree, to break up the system of subordination of blacks; the best interpretation of the clause recognizes that the existing allocation of power among the races is both artifactual and illegitimate, and its purpose is, to a greater or lesser extent, to equalize that allocation. It should not be surprising that insofar as understandings deriving from *West Coast Hotel* have been used as a sword against government, the equal protection clause has usually been the textual source of decision.

Much of equal protection law grows directly out of *West Coast Hotel.* Consider not only the attack on racial discrimination but also anti-discrimination law involving poverty, illegitimacy, alienage, and perhaps above all, gender. The equal protection clause is most obviously a rejection of *Lochner's* premises, just as the takings and contracts clauses are most obviously their constitutional embodiment.

What of the first amendment? In *Buckley* itself, the Court suggested that the provision disposed of the issue: the constitutional guarantee of freedom of speech prohibits the silencing of some in order to promote the speech of others. But is is much too facile to point to the text of the clause. Whether regulation of powerful private speakers might sometimes promote "freedom of speech" is the question to be decided. There was a powerful argument in *Buckley* that campaign finance regulation was necessary in order to promote freedom of speech; one could argue that such regulation was closer to being compelled than proscribed.[196] On the other hand, a wholesale abandonment of *Lochner*-like premises, requiring courts to look at the content of speech, would wreak havoc with existing first amendment doctrine—as it did earlier in the century with private property under the due process clause.

Indeed, the central commitment of the first amendment, as currently interpreted, is to neutrality on the basis of content or viewpoint,[197] and this commitment has a *Lochner*-like feature. Issues of substantive power and powerlessness do not enter into the constitutional inquiry. Government must be neutral between those viewpoints that are good and bad or those speakers that have power and those that have none.[198] A set of doctrines growing out of *West Coast Hotel* would repudiate *Buckley;* efforts to redress the distorting effects of financial contributions can be fit within the police power, especially in light of theories of free speech that grow out of republican conceptions of politics.[199] But doctrines based on *West Coast Hotel* might also be led to reject the commitment to viewpoint neutrality.[200] Under such an approach, redistributive and paternalistic goals would be permissible under the first amendment.[201] The police power under the first amendment would thus be close to the police power under the fourteenth. Such an approach would permit government to impose a wide range of regulatory restrictions, mostly on the speech of the powerful, in the interest of reassessment of the existing distribution of power.

There are reasons to be skeptical of so general an approach. The problem of deciding who is powerful and who is not is too manipulable and too likely to be skewed by impermissible factors to be the basis for first amendment doctrine. Moreover, there are good reasons to complain about restrictions on the speech of the powerful. *Buckley* itself was wrongly decided; the principle at issue there might be confined to financial expenditures without endangering the general principle of viewpoint neutrality.[202] But it should not be surprising to find *Lochner*-like premises in first amendment doctrine.

All this suggests that some constitutional provisions incorporate *Lochner*-like premises, others reject them, and still others create difficult interpretive problems. The nature of the provisions will thus be a significant factor in deciding about appropriate baselines.

The Nature of the Causal Links

Another factor has to do with the reality or perception of a close causal link between identifiable government action and the practice under attack. In the context of welfare, the link between government action and poverty may seem too attenuated to justify a claim of causation; numerous other causal factors play a role. The same conclusion is drawn in the context of de facto segregation. School and housing patterns are affected by many factors, and the relevant legal rules were not in force in the immediate past. The case of discriminatory effects may be similarly understood, for the existence of such effects is the result of a wide range of factors. Consider by contrast the courts' ready acceptance of remedial plans for actual racial discrimination in the recent past by the defendant. Here the link between state action and racially based harm is so tight that causation is unquestionable. Judgments about causation thus play a significant role in the cases.

This concern imports, however, some *Lochner*-like premises about action and inaction and is in any event secondary. In the cases under consideration, there is almost always "but for" causation. The causation issue produces difficulties when and because it is hard to imagine a status quo ante. Consider, for example, a claim that de facto segregation is unconstitutional, or even an attack on de jure segregation thirty years ago. To imagine what the system would look like if the conduct under attack had not occurred is necessarily speculative and largely unanchored. This point presents the problem of baseline in another form.

The Consequences: Utilitarian and Other Losses

Judgments about causation are not based solely on a reconstruction of history.[203] Sometimes the decision is affected by the perceived consequences of finding a causal link. Consider, for example, recognition of a constitutional right to welfare. It may be conceded here that poverty is in some sense a creation of the state. But if it were to follow that welfare was constitutionally guaranteed, the result may be to undermine incentives for productive labor. Another example has to do with discriminatory effects. If such effects were sufficient to produce invalidity, the consequences would be enormous. Affirmative action would be constitutionally mandated. Such a step would impose a severe strain on the judiciary. Moreover, it would impose costs of two kinds. The decision about which discriminatory effects were permissible and why would be enormously complex. Serious strains would be imposed on the judiciary, particularly in the remedial process.

The utilitarian and other losses—including enforcement problems—of abandoning *Lochner* are thus relevant to the constitutional inquiry. They will tend to be largest in cases in which other branches of government support the practice under attack. When, for example, Congress has enacted a statute abandoning *Lochner*-like principles, these considerations are secondary. In such cases the elected branches have decided that the utilitarian losses are properly incurred, and problems of enforcement are minimized. When the elected branches are on the other side, however, those losses and problems are properly taken into account. They are a secondary consideration, buttressing the development of substantive and institutional theories in the wake of *Lochner*.

Summary

We have seen that the question whether *Lochner*-like premises should be abandoned cannot be answered in the abstract. The issue depends on a mixture of substantive, institutional, and interpretive considerations. The substantive problems present issues of distributive justice; the institutional issues present problems of democratic theory; the interpretive questions raise problems of linguistic theory, as well as substantive and institutional issues.[204] In generating a set of constitutional doctrines in the aftermath of *Lochner,* it is necessary to proceed with considerable caution. No formula is available. But the foregoing discussion suggests some generalizations and examples that may prove helpful here. In *Lochner* itself, the textual pedigree of the decision was uncertain; and the outcome reached by the Court ran in the face of a powerful and mounting national consensus in the other direction. Similar considerations justify, at least in broad outline, the Court's current approach to the takings and contracts clauses. These provisions are necessarily *Lochner*-like in character; they cannot be read out of the Constitution, but a generous approach to the police power is appropriate under both provisions. Affirmative action for both race and gender is relatively easy. The measures in question have been adopted democratically; the equal protection clause is a repudiation of *Lochner*-like principles; utilitarian concerns cannot be said to count powerfully against affirmative action and may argue in favor of validation; the uncertainty of causation is a secondary matter. Judicial review of agency inaction and standing for regulatory beneficiaries are also relatively easy. Here Congress has created and endorsed a broad presumption of reviewability, and most important, review would serve only to vindicate constitutional and statutory provisions as against the executive branch. Some benefits that are the creature of statute should stand on the same footing as common law interests for purposes of both procedural and substantive due process. The rise of hearing rights for beneficiaries of spending programs is therefore appropriate.[205] *Buckley v. Valeo* was decided incorrectly. In the context of financial expenditures, the first amendment needs hardly be read in the *Lochner*-like fashion suggested by the Court.

The most difficult cases here involve discriminatory effects under the equal protection clause, welfare rights, and some of the state action cases, including those that raise the possibility of a right to protection against private racial discrimination. Viewed through the lens of the *Lochner* period, these decisions seem incorrect in their reasoning and questionable in their outcomes. All of them depend on premises about the appropriate baseline that were properly rejected during the *Lochner* period. But as we have seen, there are powerful prudential and institutional considerations that argue in favor of caution. The primary purpose here is not to suggest how such cases should be decided, now or in the near future, but instead to remove one of the props supporting current doctrine and to suggest some of the relevant inquiries.

CONCLUSION

The *Lochner* Court required government neutrality and was skeptical of government "intervention"; it defined both notions in terms of whether the state had threatened to alter the common law distribution of entitlements and wealth, which was taken to be a part of nature rather than a legal construct. Once the common law system came to be seen as a product of legal rules, the baseline from which constitutional decisions were made had to shift. When the *Lochner* framework was abandoned in *West Coast Hotel,* the common law system itself appeared to be a subsidy to employers. The *West Coast Hotel* Court thus adopted an alternative baseline and rejected *Lochner* era understandings of neutrality and action.

If the *Lochner* era is thought to embody less an active judicial role and more particular conceptions of baseline, neutrality, and action, it has not been entirely overruled. Numerous modern decisions reflect similar understandings. Cases distinguishing between "positive" and "negative" rights are built on *Lochner*-like premises that take the common law as the baseline for decision. Much of the law of racial discrimination can be understood similarly, though here the baseline is the status quo rather than the common law. The constitutional attack on affirmative action, indeed the very term, suggests that the current distribution of benefits and burdens along racial lines is simply "there." The state action doctrine borrows heavily from common law understandings about the proper role of government. Some of first amendment doctrine, especially that involving campaign financing, is based on similar premises.

It is one thing to identify *Lochner*-like premises in current constitutional law; it is quite another to suggest when and how they should be abandoned. One possible approach would be to reject, in the fashion of Justice Holmes, any baseline as a matter of constitutional law. Under this approach, the distribution of wealth and entitlements would be for political rather than legal determination. But we have seen that such an approach is too crude, for it would spell an end to constitutionalism. If the idea of baselines is to be retained, and if *Lochner* is at least sometimes to be abandoned, the task for the future is to develop theories of distributive justice, derived from constitutional text and purposes, that might serve as the basis for evaluating any particular practice.

Whether and how to develop and implement such theories is a mixture of substantive and institutional problems. We have seen that whether *Lochner*-like premises are used to invalidate or uphold legislation is relevant. Moreover, some provisions are most plausibly understood in *Lochner*-like terms, whereas others self-consciously reject those premises; consider the equal protection clause. Second-order considerations include whether there is a clear causal connection between identifiable social practices and the harms invoked by the plaintiff. Social consequences, including utilitarian losses, property play a role in the decision. Development and implementation of an alternative approach that would incorporate those inquiries is a large task indeed. But there is reason to reject several lines of cases that depend on *Lochner*-like premises, as in the areas of campaign finance regulation, judicial review of agency inaction, gender discrimination, and affirmative action. There is reason as well to raise questions about the reasoning and perhaps the outcome in more difficult areas, involving discriminatory effects and "positive" rights.

However these questions are resolved, the central issue in numerous areas of the law—involving campaign finance regulation, hearing rights, affirmative action, gender and race discrimination, standing, review of agency inaction, state action, and "positive" rights—is whether there is a constitutional requirement of neutrality that commands preservation of the status quo as reflected in market outcomes, or instead whether the Constitution, recognizing the artifactual quality of the market allocation, permits and sometimes demands change. One might understand the *Lochner* era as, above all, a warning about constitutional doctrine that defines neutrality in terms of the perpetuation of current practice and that treats government conduct tending to sustain it as "inaction" invariably escaping legal sanction, and government conduct proposing change as "action" tending to raise legal doubts.

ENDNOTES

I would like to thank Bruce A. Ackerman, Akhil Amar, Richard Briffault, Stephen Ellman, Richard Epstein, Richard Fallon, Terry Fisher, George Fletcher, Philip Frickey, Wendy Gordon, Kent Greenawalt, Stephen Holmes, Pamela Karlen, Andrew Kaufman, Larry Kramer, Anthony T. Kronman, Daniel Meltzer, Frank Michelman, Geoffrey Miller, Martha Minow, Henry P. Monaghan, Richard A. Posner, Steven Shiffrin, Richard B. Stewart,

Geoffrey R. Stone, David Strauss, Peter L. Strauss, Laurence H. Tribe, Mark V. Tushnet, and Roberto Unger for helpful comments. Participants in the legal theory workshops at the Harvard, New York University, University of Minnesota, and University of Pennsylvania law schools also gave valuable help. Daniel B. Rodriguez provided research assistance and useful comments.

1. 347 U.S. 483 (1954).
2. 410 U.S. 113 (1973).
3. 198 U.S. 45 (1905).
4. The most recent example is *Bowers v. Hardwick,* 478 U.S. 186 (1986), where the Court rejected a claim that a state prohibition of sodomy among consenting adults violated the due process clause. According to the Court: "The Court is most vulnerable and comes nearest to illegitimacy when it deals with judge-made constitutional law having little or no cognizable roots in the language or design of the Constitution. That this is so was painfully demonstrated by the face-off between the Executive and the Court in the 1930's, which resulted in the repudiation of much of the substantive gloss that the Court placed on the Due Process Clause of the Fifth and Fourteenth Amendments. There should be, therefore, great resistance to expand the substantive reach of those Clauses, particularly if it requires redefining the category of rights deemed to be fundamental." Id. at 2846. It is this view of the lesson of the *Lochner* period that is questioned here.
5. The view that *Lochner* was wrong is not, however, unanimously held. See R. Epstein, *Takings: Private Property and the Law of Eminent Domain* (1985), 5.
6. See, e.g., J. Choper, *The Supreme Court and the National Political Process* (1980); J. Ely, *Democracy and Distrust* (1980); M. Perry, *The Constitution, the Courts, and Human Rights* (1982).
7. Sometimes the view is based on the text of the Constitution and the "intent" of its framers, see, e.g., Monaghan, Our Perfect Constitution, *N.Y.U. L. Rev.* (1981), 56:353; sometimes it is based on conceptions of democracy, see, e.g., Bork, Neutral Principles and Some First Amendment Problems, *Ind. L.J.* (1971), 47:1; sometimes it grows out of "process-perfecting" theories, see, e.g., J. Ely, supra note 6, at 73, 228–29 n.91; sometimes it depends on distinctions between matters of policy, to be resolved by the legislature, and matters of principle, to be resolved by the courts, see R. Dworkin, *Taking Rights Seriously* (1979).
8. See, e.g., *Bowers v. Hardwick,* 478 U.S. 186 (1986); *Dandridge v. Williams,* 397 U.S. 471 (1970); *Griswold v. Connecticut,* 381 U.S. 479 (1965); *Ferguson v. Skrupa,* 372 U.S. 726 (1963); *Williamson v. Lee Optical* 348 U.S. 483 (1955).
9. Whether this understanding of *Lochner* should be accepted in place of one that stresses an active judicial role is an inescapably normative question, taken up infra notes 144–67 and accompanying text. The principal effort here is to set forth an alternative approach that fits the history at least as well and that has dramatically different implications. See infra notes 168–205 and accompanying text. Moreover, this understanding was not invented in the *Lochner* era. See *Fletcher v. Peck,* 10 U.S. (6 Cranch) 87 (1810) (using contract clause and "general principles . . . common to our free institutions" to invalidate recissions of a land grant).
10. 410 U.S. 113 (1973).
11. 384 U.S. 436 (1966).
12. 426 U.S. 229 (1976).
13. 424 U.S. 1 (1976).
14. 438 U.S. 265 (1978).
15. For general discussion, see J. Elster and R. Slagstaad eds., *Constitutionalism and Democracy* (1988).

16. 261 U.S. 525 (1923).

17. Id. at 557–58.

18. 300 U.S. 379 (1937).

19. Id. at 399.

20. To say this is not, of course, to suggest that minimum wage legislation was constitutionally required. Notably, both *Adkins* and *West Coast Hotel* involved statutes discriminating on the basis of gender; such statutes tended, in both purpose and effect, to diminish the employment prospects of women. See Landes, The Effect of State Maximum-Hours Laws on the Employment of Women in 1920, *J. Pol. Econ.* (1980), 88:476; Nelson, Women's Poverty and Women's Citizenship: Some Political Consequences of Economic Marginality, *Signs* (1984), 10:209, 228–29.

21. 198 U.S. at 57.

22. Id. at 64.

23. For an effort proceeding from similar premises, see R. Epstein, supra note 5, at 15–16.

24. 198 U.S. 65–74.

25. See J. Ely, supra note 6, at 146.

26. See Note, Legislative Purpose, Rationality, and Equal Protection, *Yale L. J.* (1972), 82:123.

27. To say this is not to say that redistribution was always impermissible. Taxation and other measures might redistribute wealth without running afoul of the due process clause, and the poor laws were generally immune from constitutional attack, Grey, The Malthusian Constitution, *U. Miami L. Rev.* (1986), 41:21. But redistribution on an ad hoc basis, of the sort represented by maximum hour and minimum wage laws, was unconstitutional if unsupported by a jurisdiction deemed "general" or "public." Cf. *Calder v. Bull,* 3 U.S. 381 (1798) (Chase, J.) (discussing natural law principles prohibiting transfers from A to B).

The preference for redistribution through taxation rather than regulation might have been the product of the broader interest in promoting generality in lawmaking. If redistribution is ad hoc, it could be perverse and in any event less visible. The requirement of generality in redistribution promotes visibility and at the same time ensures that any redistribution is to those genuinely or most in need. Compare the debate over affirmative action, discussed infra text accompanying notes 113–17. The ad hoc character of affirmative action schemes is sometimes thought to be an argument against them and in favor of more general methods of alleviating the distribution of benefits and burdens among blacks and whites. On the other hand, the requirement of generality might allow well-organized private groups to mobilize in defense of the status quo. In this sense the requirement fits comfortably with the broader hostility to redistribution.

28. Stated in this way, the requirement remains the law. Statutory classifications must be defensible as public-regarding under a wide range of constitutional provisions. See Sunstein, Naked Preferences and the Constitution, *Colum. L. Rev.* (1984), 84:1689; for various defenses, see infra note 166. In the *Lochner* era, however, the category of justifications that would count as "public" was small, excluding paternalistic and redistributive matters. Cf. *Hawaii Hous. Auth. v. Midkiff,* 467 U.S. 229 (1984) (rendering meaningless the public use requirement under the eminent domain clause).

29. Cf. Wechsler, Toward Neutral Principles of Constitutional Law, *Harv. L. Rev.* (1959), 73:1 (discussing similar requirement of neutrality imposed on judges), discussed in more detail infra notes 109–11 and accompanying text.

30. Two qualifications are in order here. First, not every common law right was, by virtue of its status as such, immunized from collective control. Marginal and not-so-mar-

ginal adjustments were permissible. Nonetheless, the basic framework of the common law formed the baseline from which to decide cases. Indeed, one can trace to this period the idea that legislative extinguishment of "core" common law rights was permissible only if the legislature furnished an adequate alternative remedy. See, e.g., *New York Cent. R.R. v. White,* 243 U.S. 188 (1917) (upholding workers' compensation in part because of quid pro quo); see also *Duke Power Co. v. Carolina Envt. Study Group,* 438 U.S. 59, 88 and n.32 (1978) (upholding liability-limiting provisions of Price-Anderson Act against due process challenge but suggesting relevance of quid pro quo).

Second, the protection of common law rights depended not merely on the fact that the rights at issue were protected by the common law but also on the (unsurprising) fact that the common law corresponded to a widely held normative theory about the proper role of government. The interests protected at common law thus tracked the category of natural rights. For a modern statement, see Epstein, A Theory of Strict Liability, *J. Legal Stud.* (1973), 2:151; R. Epstein, supra note 5.

31. See, e.g., R. Dahl, *A Preface to Democratic Theory* (1956); Stigler, The Theory of Economic Regulation, *Bell J. Econ. & Mgmt. Sci.* (1971), 2:3; see also R. Posner, *Federal Courts: Crisis and Reform* (1985) (making a similar point about Holmes).

32. See Becker, A Theory of Competition Among Pressure Groups for Political Influence, *Q.J. Econ.* (1983), 98:371 (making this argument). On Holmes, see Rogat, Some Modern Views—The Judge as Spectator, *U. Chi. L. Rev.* (1964), 31:213.

33. 198 U.S. at 76.

34. H. Spencer, *Social Statics* (1882).

35. See, e.g., Rogat, supra note 32, at 251–55; Rogat and O'Fallon, Mr. Justice Holmes, A Dissenting Opinion—The Speech Cases, *Stan. L. Rev.* (1984), 36:1349.

36. See, e.g., *Nebbia v. New York,* 291 U.S. 502 (1934); *Bunting v. Oregon,* 243 U.S. 426 (1917); *Muller v. Oregon,* 208 U.S. 412 (1908).

37. The Court did, however, refer to these themes. See *West Coast Hotel,* 300 U.S. at 397–98.

38. Id. at 399.

39. Id. at 399–400.

40. This oversimplifies a complicated framework; the scope of the *Lochner* era police power was by no means precisely defined.

41. Here the parallel to the affirmative action debate is especially striking. See infra notes 113–17 and accompanying text.

42. The point is emphasized in L. Tribe, *American Constitutional Law* §§ 8–5 to 8–7 (1978).

Why this change should have occurred is a complex matter. In part, the Depression was responsible; in a period of widespread poverty and unemployment, it became harder to see nineteenth-century market ordering as in the interest of all. In part, the partial but increasing use of government power to alleviate suffering made the common law system seem less and less natural and inviolate. See id. Consider in this regard Franklin Roosevelt's suggestion: "We must lay hold of the fact that economic laws are not made by nature. They are made by human beings," *Public Papers of Franklin D. Roosevelt* (1938), 1:657.

43. See infra notes 81–88 and accompanying text (discussing the takings clause).

44. 276 U.S. 272 (1928).

45. Id. at 279.

46. See infra notes 81–88 and accompanying text.

47. 304 U.S. 64 (1938).

48. See, e.g., Calabresi and Malamed, Property Rules, Liability Rules, and Inalienability: One View of the Cathedral, *Harv. L. Rev.* (1972), 85:1089; Michelman, Property,

Utility, and Fairness: Comments on the Ethical Foundations of "Just Compensation Law, *Harv. L. Rev.* (1967), 80:1165.

49. The terms "common law" and "nineteenth century market ordering" will be used interchangeably throughout; the reference is to the allocation of rights of use, ownership, transfer, and possession of property associated with "laissez-faire" systems and captured in the common law of the late nineteenth century. Of course common law systems have not always taken this form, and market ordering could take place under dramatically different allocations of entitlements.

50. The status quo need not, of course, be the common law.

51. See B. Ackerman, *Reconstructing American Law* (1984); L. Tribe, supra note 42, at 427–55; Kennedy, Form and Substance in Private Law Adjudication, *Harv. L. Rev.* (1976), 89:1685; MacKinnon, Pornography, Civil Rights, and Speech, *Harv. C.R.-C.L. L. Rev.* (1985), 20:1.

Similar points were made by the legal realists. See Cohen, Property and Sovereignty, *Cornell L. Q.* (1927), 13:8; Hale, Coercion and Distribution in a Supposedly Non-Coercive State, *Pol. Sci. Q.* (1923), 38:470.

A question arises here about the criteria for deciding when a particular understanding of the *Lochner* era, or of any other period, ought to be accepted. The primary requirement is, of course, that the understanding be true to the decided cases—certainly in terms of result, and, it is to be hoped, in terms of the rhetoric as well. But among conflicting understandings that fit the cases equally well, the choice has an inescapable normative dimension. R. Dworkin, *Law's Empire* (1986), 90–98. On the different implications of the approach set out here and the more conventional understanding, see infra notes 167–205 and accompanying text.

52. 424 U.S. 1 (1976).

53. Nicholson, *Buckley v. Valeo:* The Constitutionality of the Federal Election Campaign Act Amendments of 1974, *Wis. L. Rev.* (1977), 323, 336 (quoting *Buckley*, 424 U.S. at 49).

54. 424 U.S. at 48–49.

55. See infra notes 190–203 and accompanying text.

56. See, e.g., Monaghan, Of "Liberty" and "Property," *Cornell L. Rev.* (1977), 62:405; Stewart and Sunstein, Public Programs and Private Rights, *Harv. L. Rev.* (1982), 95:1193; Van Alstyne, Cracks in the New Property, *Cornell L. Rev.* (1977), 62:445.

57. See *Cleveland Bd. of Educ. v. Loudermill*, 470 U.S. 532 (1985); *Arnett v. Kennedy*, 416 U.S. 134 (1974); *Board of Regents v. Roth*, 408 U.S. 564 (1972).

58. See *Goldberg v. Kelly*, 397 U.S. 254 (1970); Reich, The New Property, *Yale L.J.* (1963), 73:733.

59. See *Cleveland Bd. of Educ. v. Loudermill*, 470 U.S. at 538–42.

60. See, e.g., *Ingraham v. Wright*, 430 U.S. 651 (1977) (bodily integrity). For a recent statement, see Easterbrook, Substance and Due Process, *Sup. Ct. Rev.* (1982), 85, which draws a sharp distinction between common law and statutory interests and which understands the distinction in *Lochner*-like terms, as responding to the differences between interests created by government and interests from some other source.

Sometimes, however, the statutory entitlement approach has been used to remove even common law interests from the category of liberty and property. See *Paul v. Davis*, 424 U.S. 693 (1976). Note also that it would be possible to treat common law interests as protected only because and to the extent that they can be classified as "entitlements"; under this view, the statutory entitlement and common law cases are closer than they might at first appear. But this sort of positivist approach to liberty and property misconceives the intended function of the due process clause, which was to protect important interests from procedural irregularity, regardless of whether there was a state-created right. See Monaghan, supra note 56, at 433–34, 442–43.

61. See Stewart and Sunstein, supra note 56, at 1257–58, for a discussion of the difficulties produced by such an approach.

62. 363 U.S. 603 (1960).

63. Id. at 608–11.

64. See *United States R.R. Retirement Bd. v. Fritz,* 449 U.S. 160 (1980).

65. The point emerges explicitly in *Northern Pipeline Constr. Co. v. Marathon Pipeline Co.*, 458 U.S. 50 (1982); see also *Commodity Futures Trading Comm'n v. Schor,* 478 U.S. 833 (1986); *Thomas v. Union Carbide Agric'l Prods. Co.* 473 U.S. 568 (1985).

66. 344 U.S. 1 (1948) (invalidating racially restrictive covenant).

67. See, e.g., Currie, Positive and Negative Constitutional Rights, *U. Chi. L. Rev.* (1986), 53:864.

68. *Reitman v. Mulkey,* 387 U.S. 369, 374–77 (1967); see Black, "State Action," Equal Protection, and California's Proposition 14, *Harv. L. Rev.* (1967), 81:69; Karst and Horowitz, *Reitman v. Mulkey:* A Telophase of Substantive Equal Protection, *Sup. Ct. Rev.* (1967), 39.

69. 424 U.S. 507, 512–21 (1976).

70. 447 U.S. 74, 82–85 (1980).

71. But see Black, supra note 68, at 83–91; Karst and Horowitz, supra note 68 (relating *Reitman* to an "expanding concept" of equality and state responsibility).

72. 387 U.S. 369 (1967).

73. Id. at 373–77.

74. The distinction may be defended, however, because of the difference between the first amendment and the equal protection clause; different provisions may repudiate or incorporate *Lochner*-like principles. See infra notes 190–203 and accompanying text.

75. See, e.g., Currie, supra note 67; Michelman, Welfare Rights in a Constitutional Democracy, *Wash. U.L. Q.* (1979), 659; Winter, Poverty, Economic Equality and the Equal Protection Clause, *Sup. Ct. Rev.* (1972), 41.

76. Currie, supra note 67; Winter, supra note 75.

77. 448 U.S. 297 (1980).

78. Id. at 316.

79. See Currie, supra note 67, at 864–67.

80. See Black, Further Reflections on the Constitutional Right of Livelihood, *Colum. L. Rev.* (1986), 86:1103; Michelman, Foreword: On Protecting the Poor Through the Fourteenth Amendment, *Harv. L. Rev.* (1969), 83;7; S. Holmes, Liberal Guilt: Some Theoretical Origins of the Welfare State, in D. Moon, ed., *Responsibility, Rights, and Welfare* (1987).

81. The qualification is necessary because of *Allied Structural Steel Co. v. Spannaus,* 438 U.S. 234 (1978) (invalidating statute on contract clause grounds).

82. See *Manigault v. Springs,* 199 U.S. 473 (1905). The Court might, however, have decided that there was a requirement of compensation.

83. See G. Gunther, *Constitutional Law: Cases and Materials* (11th ed. 1985), 487–90.

84. 290 U.S. 398 (1934).

85. See *Dunham, Griggs v. Alleghany County* in Perspective: Thirty Years of Supreme Court Expropriation Law, *Sup. Ct. Rev.* (1962), 63, 66.

86. See, e.g., *Hawaii Hous. Auth. v. Midkiff,* 467 U.S. 229, 239–48 (1984); *Poletown Neighborhood Council v. City of Detroit,* 410 Mich. 616, 304 N.W.2d 455 (1981); Dunham, supra note 85, at 66–71; Note, The Public Use Limitation on Eminent Domain: An Advance Requiem, *Yale L. J.* (1949), 58:599.

87. See, e.g., *Penn Central Transp. Co. v. New York City,* 438 U.S. 104, 130–31 (1978). An interesting example here is *Pacific Gas and Elec. Co. v. Public Util. Comm'n.* 106 S. Ct. 903 (1986), in which the Court dealt with the question of "ownership" of extra space in a billing envelope. The discussion of the plurality, id. at 912–13, assumed a prepolitical property right in the relevant utility.

88. See infra notes 193–95 and accompanying text.

89. See, e.g., *Abbott Laboratories v. Gardner,* 387 U.S. 136, 139–41 (1967).

90. See J. Vining, *Legal Identity* (1978); Stewart, The Reformation of American Administrative Law, *Harv. L. Rev.* (1975), 88:1667, 1672–73.

91. See, e.g., *Alabama Power Co. v. Ickes,* 302 U.S. 464, 478 (1938).

92. See, e.g., *Vaca v. Sipes,* 386 U.S. 171, 181–83 (1967).

93. See, e.g., *Dunlop v. Bachowski,* 421 U.S. 560 (1975); *Carpet, Linoleum and Resilient Tile Layers Local 419 v. Brown,* 656, F.2d 564 (10th Cir. 1981); *Adams v. Richardson,* 480 F.2d 1159 (D.C. Cir. 1973); *EDF v. Rickelshaus,* 439 F.2d 584 (D.C. Cir. 1971).

94. 470 U.S. 821 (1985).

95. Id. at 832. Other considerations, quite independent of *Lochner,* might be brought forth to support distinctions between review of agency action and review of agency inaction. In particular, review of inaction implicates concerns having to do with scarce prosecutorial resources, which make judicial review for arbitrariness harder to undertake. For a discussion of such considerations, see Sunstein, Reviewing Agency Inaction after *Heckler v. Chaney, U. Chi. L. Rev.* (1985), 52:653.

96. See, e.g., J. Landis, *The Administrative Process* (1938), 31–39; see also Hale, supra note 51 (criticizing the view that government's proper role is limited to protecting private property rights).

97. See *Alabama Power Co. v. Ickes,* 302 U.S. 464 (1938); Stewart, supra note 90, at 1723–24.

98. See *Chicago Junction* case, 264 U.S. 258 (1924).

99. 397 U.S. 150 (1970).

100. Id. at 153–57.

101. See J. Vining, supra note 90, at 27–33, 38–41, 179–81.

102. See Stewart, supra note 90, at 1739.

103. See *Allen v. Wright,* 468 U.S. 737, 750–52 (1984).

104. This approach is especially questionable when the legal claim is statutory rather than constitutional; in such cases, statutory beneficiaries have already won in the political process. See *Wright,* 468 U.S. at 737.

105. See id.; *Eastern Kentucky Welfare Rights Org. v. Simon,* 426 U.S. 26 (1976); *Warth v. Seldin,* 422 U.S. 490 (1975).

106. See *Wright,* 468 U.S. at 737; *Simon,* 426 U.S. at 26; *Warth,* 422 U.S. at 490.

107. There is an irony here. Case-or-controversy limitations were originally based largely on concerns, associated with Justice Frankfurter, that "progressive" programs should not readily be subject to judicial challenge; the limitations were thus rooted in anti-*Lochner* efforts to immunize from judicial challenge revisions in the common law. In recent years, such limitations have been used so as to prevent those challenging government action to do so if a common law interest is not at stake.

108. 347 U.S. 483 (1954).

109. *Harv. L. Rev.* (1959), 73:1.

110. Id. at 31–34. Consider the parallel to contemporary debates over affirmative action, where favoring blacks over whites is also said to be neutral. See generally Strauss, The Myth of Colorblindness, *Sup. Ct. Rev.* (1986), 99, for an argument that affirmative action is not in principle different from nondiscrimination.

111. Thus understood, Wechsler's view imposed sharp constraints on judges. A more

modest formulation of the requirement of neutral principles is set out in Greenawalt, The Enduring Significance of Neutral Principles, *Colum. L. Rev.* (1978), 78:982, where the requirement is understood to be a largely procedural injunction that judges conduct a kind of internal Socratic dialogue. Wechsler's view appeared to impose a substantive constraint, forbidding consideration of "whose ox is gored," in a way that borrows from *Lochner* era conceptions of neutrality. Id. at 1001–13. The relationship between the procedural and substantive versions of the requirement of neutral principles precisely parallels the relationship between the modern requirement of rationality review and the understanding of the *Lochner* Court. In both Wechsler's view and that of the *Lochner* Court, impermissible ends are ruled out.

112. Here, of course, the problem does not stem from use of common law baselines.

113. *Johnson v. Transportation Agency of Santa Clara County,* 107 S. Ct. 1442 (1987); *Wygant v. Jackson Bd. of Educ.,* 476 U.S. 267 (1986); *Fullilove v. Klutznick,* 448 U.S. 448 (1980); *Regents of the Univ. of Calif. v. Bakke,* 438 U.S. 265 (1978).

114. See cases cited supra note 113.

115. See *Wygant v. Jackson Bd. of Educ.,* 476 U.S. 267 (1986).

116. Cf. Strauss, supra note 110, at 100–08 (suggesting that the antidiscrimination principle and affirmative action are compatible rather than conflicting).

117. See *Washington v. Davis,* 426 U.S. 229 (1976).

118. The point is made explicitly in *Washington v. Davis.* See id. at 239–41.

119. The intent test, as set out in such cases as *Personnel Adm'r v. Feeney,* 442 U.S. 256 (1979), also disregards the phenomenon of selective racial care and indifference. Under *Feeney* the question is whether the government actor made the decision "because of" not merely "in spite of" its racially discriminatory effects. Id. at 279. But the equality question should be whether the actor would have made the decision *regardless of which group was helped and which hurt.* Such an inquiry would also turn on intent, but it would call into question a larger number of government decisions.

120. See G. Stone, L. Seidman, C. Sunstein, and M. Tushnet. *Commercial Law* (1986), 558–59, 567–75.

121. See *Mississippi Univ. for Women v. Hogan,* 458 U.S. 718 (1982); *Reed v. Reed,* 404 U.S. 71 (1981).

122. 430 U.S. 199 (1977).

123. 429 U.S. 190 (1976).

124. 458 U.S. 718 (1982).

125. 453 U.S. 57 (1981).

126. 429 U.S. at 204.

127. Two qualifications are necessary here. First, it is not necessary to ask to what degree gender differences have a biological component. Even if there is such a component, it hardly justifies the measures at issue in most cases; it is by no means clear that the legal system should turn biological differences into social disadvantages. The point here is that *Lochner*-like reasoning would take gender differences as a proper basis for legal differentiation, no matter their source, and that some of the current law of gender discrimination is opposed to such reasoning. Cf. C. MacKinnon, *Feminism Unmodified* (1987) (discussing ways in which legal system naturalizes discrimination against women).

The second problem lies in deciding when something is artifactual or not. A strong view of the lesson of the *Lochner* period is that everything is—precisely because government decisions not to change matters are, after all, decisions. In this view, qualifications of the sort in the text—suggesting that gender differences, poverty, and the distribution of benefits and burdens along racial lines are "partly" a product of the legal system—are unnecessary and misleading. Such qualifications themselves import *Lochner*-like premises.

128. 458 U.S. at 730. Compare the suggestion in J. Ely, supra note 6, at 153, that

prejudice is "the lens that distorts reality," an understanding that depends on the premise that there is a prepolitical reality that law should reflect. See C. MacKinnon, *Feminism Unmodified* (1987), 40–42.

129. See, e.g., *Bradwell v. Illinois,* 83 U.S. 130 (1872) (Bradley, J., concurring). Note, however, that in *Rostker* the plaintiffs had conceded the legality of the combat restriction, so the Court's conclusion was perhaps defensible in context.

130. Cf. Strauss, supra note 110, at 108–13 (exploring how rational responses to racial differences might justify racist classifications). See also the discussion of rape in Estrich, Rape, *Yale L. J.* (1986), 95:1087; MacKinnon, Feminism, Marxism, Method and the State: Toward Feminist Jurisprudence, *Signs* (1983), 8:635.

131. See *Personnel Adm'r v. Feeney,* 442 U.S. 256 (1979).

132. See generally Becker, from *Muller v. Oregon* to Fetal Vulnerability Policies, *U. Chi. L. Rev.* (1986), 53:1219.

133. 450 U.S. 464 (1981). Although the reasoning in *Michael M.* depended on *Lochner*-like premises, the outcome might be defended on quite different grounds. See Olsen, Statutory Rape: A Feminist Critique of Rights Analysis, *Tex. L. Rev.* (1984), 63:387.

134. C. MacKinnon, *Sexual Harassment of Working Women* (1979), 119–27.

135. See Tribe, The Abortion Funding Conundrum: Inalienable Rights, Affirmative Duties, and the Dilemma of Dependence, *Harv. L. Rev.* (1985), 99:330. But the general effort in the law of gender discrimination to examine whether differences are "real" or to understand gender discrimination in terms of irrational distinctions reflects *Lochner*-like reasoning.

136. Even if the differences are in some sense a product of biology, it is hardly clear that the legal system should recognize them; it is the legal system that makes such differences count, and legal ratification may itself be a form of discrimination. See C. MacKinnon, supra note 134, at 116–27 (discussing how differences are turned into disadvantages); L. Tribe, *Constitutional Choices* (1985), 238–45.

137. The most extreme views come from some law and economics and rights-based theorists. See R. Epstein, supra note 5 (presenting Lockean theory of "takings" clause); R. Posner, *Economic Analysis of Law* (3d ed. 1986).

138. See Bork, supra note 7, at 2–3; R. Dahl, *A Preface to Democratic Theory* (1956); R. Posner, supra note 137.

139. See Sunstein, Legal Interference with Private Preferences, *U. Chi. L. Rev.* (1986), 53:1129.

But note here that in the *Lochner* era, regulation of "morals" was frequently permitted even outside of the context of harm to others. In this sense, the *Lochner* Court did not take all preferences for granted. But see Epstein, Conference Proceedings, *U. Miami L. Rev.* 49, (1987), 417:49, 74 (suggesting that basis of the regulation of morals actually was harm to others).

140. *Green v. County School Bd.*, 391 U.S. 430 (1968). See Gewirtz, Choice in the Transition: School Desegregation and the Corrective Ideal, *Colum. L. Rev.* (1986), 86:728.

141. See Gewirtz, supra note 140, at 745–48. There is also a collective action problem here. Individual black families may rationally decide not to send their children to white schools, even though it would be in their interest if all black families did so.

142. 466 U.S. 429 (1984).

143. The limitation derives from a fear that if the legal system is generally permitted to intervene whenever preferences are "distorted," lines will become difficult or impossible to draw and the range of permissible interventions will be limitless. See Sunstein, supra note 139, at 1169–73, for general discussion; on the related problem of "false consciousness," see also J. Elster, *Making Sense of Marx* (1984).

144. The issue arises in private law as well. One might, for example, understand the

Coase theorem as above all a rejection of *Lochner*-like approaches to such concepts as causation, action, and inaction. Cf. B. Ackerman, *Reconstructing American Law* (1984), 46–71 (discussing effect of Coase theorem on the way lawyers structure the facts). Much private law theory in the past two decades has attempted to come to terms with the destabilizing effect of the Coase theorem—just as public law theory has had to face the confusions produced by abandonment of common law baselines.

145. See H. Pitkin, *The Concept of Representation* (1967); J. Nedelsky, Private Property and the American Conception of Representative Government (1984) (unpublished manuscript).

146. See Sunstein, Constitutionalism After the New Deal, 101 *Harv. L. Rev.* 421(1987); J. Landis, supra note 96 (rejecting traditional conceptions of separation of powers).

147. See Sunstein, supra note 146; B. Ackerman and W. Hassler, *Clean Coal/Dirty Air* (1981); Strauss, The Place of Agencies in Government: The Separation of Powers and the Fourth Branch, *Colum. L. Rev.* (1984), 84:573.

Statutory interpretation is affected by *Lochner*-like premises as well—most familiarly in the notion that "statutes in derogation of the common law should be narrowly construed," but in more modern approaches as well. See, e.g., Easterbrook, Statutes' Domains, *U. Chi. L. Rev.* (1983), 50:533, which amounts to an argument that when there are statutory "gaps," courts should resolve all doubts in favor of market ordering. See also Macey, Promoting Public-Regarding Legislation Through Statutory Interpretation: An Interest Group Model, *Colum. L. Rev.* (1986), 86:223 (defining factional tyranny in part by reference to departures from the common law). An important task is to develop approaches to statutory construction that are not based on hostility to departures from common law categories.

The same view is reflected in approaches to administrative law that distinguish between the rights of statutory beneficiaries and those of regulated class members. See Scalia, Vermont Yankee: The APA, the D.C. Circuit, and the Supreme Court, *Sup. Ct. Rev.* (1978), 345 (suggesting that ordinary concerns supporting procedural safeguards do not apply when statutory beneficiaries are the complainants); Smith; Judicialization: The Twilight of Administrative Law, *Duke L. J.* (1985), 427 (suggesting that the principal concern of administrative law is the protection of private property).

See also Stewart and Sunstein, supra note 56. Note, Intent, Clear Statements, and the Common Law: Statutory Interpretation in the Supreme Court, *Harv. L. Rev.* (1982), 95:892, for related discussions of the use of supplemental principles in statutory construction.

148. See G. Lakoff, *Women, Fire, and Dangerous Things: What Categories Reveal About the Mind* (1987).

149. Cf. Kronman, Alexander Bickel's Philosophy of Prudence, *Yale L. J.* (1985), 94:1567, 1599–1605 (suggesting a Burkean understanding of the legal system).

150. See the discussion of baselines in Kreimer, Allocational Sanctions: The Problem of Negative Rights in a Positive State, *U. Pa. L. Rev.* (1984), 132:1293.

141. I collapse a complex argument here. Cf. B. Ackerman, supra note 144 (interpreting the New Deal as a structural amendment of the Constitution). One need not accept Ackerman's view in order to recognize that the developments in the New Deal bear on the interpretation of ambiguous constitutional provisions.

152. See L. Hand, *The Bill of Rights* (1958).

153. See J. Landis, supra note 96.

154. See, e.g., *West Virginia State Board of Educ. v. Barnette,* 319 U.S. 624, 646 (1943) (Frankfurter, J., dissenting).

155. Cf. Peller, The Metaphysics of American Law, *Calif. L. Rev.* 73:1151 (1985) (discussing the constructed character of legal categories).

156. The tradition discussed here did not apply its usual skepticism to its own principles about the primacy of democratic politics; if it had, this conclusion would have been harder to reach.

157. See supra note 31.

158. See T. Nagel, *The View from Nowhere* (1986); R. Bernstein, *Beyond Objectivism and Relativism* (1983).

159. Compare M. Foucault, in C. Gordon ed., *Power/Knowledge: Selected Interviews and Other Writings, 1972–77* (1981) (suggesting that knowledge depends on particular constellations of interest) with J. Habermas, *Knowledge and Human Interests* (1971) (suggesting possibility of escaping power through communication). For recent discussion, see Nagel, supra note 158.

160. Compare Linde, Due Process of Lawmaking, *Neb. L. Rev.* (1976), 55:197 (setting forth this conception of legislation) with R. Dworkin, supra note 51 (arguing in favor of efforts to create "integrity" in law). On this approach to the interpretation of statutes, compare Easterbrook, supra note 147, at 539–44, with Posner, Legal Formalism, Legal Realism, and the Interpretation of Statutes and the Constitution, *Case W. Res. L. Rev.* (1987), 37:179.

161. See M. Foucault, supra note 159. Cf. Minow, Foreword: Justice Engendered, 101 *Harv. L. Rev.* (1987) (challenging neutrality). But see J. Habermas, *Autonomy and Solidarity* (1986) (challenging tendency to relativism and irrationalism in Foucault).

162. See J. Derrida, *Of Grammatology* (G. Spivak trans. 1976); M. Foucault, supra note 159; J. Kristeva, *Desire in Language* (1980); G. Lakoff, supra note 148; R. Rorty, *Consequences of Pragmatism* (1982). Despite the enormous differences among them, all are united in their skepticism about Enlightenment reason. J. Habermas, supra note 161, contains a brief summary at one of the most well-known responses; see also J. Habermas, *Reason and the Rationalization of Society* (1984).

163. See, e.g., J. Ely, supra note 6, at 105–34; R. Posner, supra note 137, at 581–87; Bork, supra note 7, at 18–19; Easterbrook, Legal Interpretation and the Power of the Judiciary, *Harv. J. L. & Pub. Pol'y* (1984), 7:87; Monaghan, supra note 7, 395–96.

164. Consider, for example, the interpretation of Madison in Bork, supra note 7, at 2–3, suggesting that in a Madisonian system majorities are allowed to rule in some areas of life "for no better reason than that they are majorities." Compare the interpretation in D. Epstein, *The Political Theory of The Federalist* (1984), 178 (suggesting that the system was intended to ensure a large measure of deliberation on the part of national representatives).

165. Some of the problems here include the difficulties, stressed in public choice theory, in aggregating private preferences through majority rule. See, e.g., W. Riker, *Liberalism vs. Populism: A Confrontation Between the Theory of Democracy and the Theory of Social Choice* (1982). Moreover, for various reasons some preferences should not be counted, see Goodin, Laundering Preferences, in J. Elster and A. Hylland eds., *Foundations of Social Choice Theory* (1986). Consider also the slippage between constituent pressures and legislative outcomes, and the various obstacles, captured in the collective action problem, to accurate preference-aggregation through majoritarianism, see R. Hardin, *Collective Action* (1982). On these various questions, see generally Sunstein, Constitutions and Democracies: An Epilogue, in J. Elster and R. Slagstaad eds., *Constitutionalism and Democracy* (1988).

166. That requirement has a disciplining effect, albeit a weak one, on the sorts of measures that can be proposed and enacted and also tends to transform the nature of political discourse in desirable ways. See Goodin, Laundering Preferences, in J. Elster and A. Hylland eds., *Foundations of Social Choice Theory* (1986); Sunstein, Interest Groups

in American Public Law, *Stan. L. Rev.* (1985), 38:29; Sunstein, Naked Preferences and the Constitution, *Colum. L. Rev.* (1984), 84:1689. In the area of judicial decision, the requirement of neutrality—in the form of an effort to justify differential treatment—remains important, see R. Dworkin, supra note 51 at 176–224; Greenawalt, supra note 111, at 989, 992. That requirement is the judicial analogue of the requirement of public-regardingness imposed on legislators, and in neither context should it be confused by importation of *Lochner*-like premises.

167. See supra notes 164–65 (suggesting that majoritarianism, understood in pluralist fashion, does not capture the view of the framers and is not likely to provide desirable outcomes).

A closely related approach would attempt to cabin judicial discretion by referring to the intent of the framers, the text of the Constitution, or some other limitation on judicial discretion. Such an approach would reflect a belief that because of the problems posed by democratic theory for an aggressive judicial role, constitutional courts ought not to rely on principles of distributive justice at all. See Monaghan, supra note 7, at 374; Easterbrook, supra note 163, at 91, 97.

That view cannot be dealt with in detail here; it has been amply discussed elsewhere. Partial responses are set out in Brest, The Misconceived Quest for the Original Understanding, *B.U.L. Rev.* (1986), 60:204; Dworkin, The Forum of Principle, *N.Y.U. L. Rev.* (1981), 56:469; Sunstein, Interest Groups in American Public Life, *Stan. L. Rev.* (1985), 38:29; Tushnet, Following the Rules Laid Down: A Critique of Interpretivism and Neutral Principles, *Harv. L. Rev.* (1983), 96:781. Such responses point out the difficulties of "applying" the framers' judgments in changed circumstances, the difficulties of deciding at what level of generality "intent" should be read, the problem of ascertaining the framers' intentions with respect to interpretation, the various difficulties faced by majoritarianism in aggregating private preferences, and the fact that it is by no means self-evident that a well-functioning democracy merely reflects constituent preferences. A final position on such matters is of course necessary in order to decide whether the Holmesian understanding of the *Lochner* period should be accepted in favor of the approach set out here.

168. See, e.g., B. Ackerman, *Social Justice in the Liberal State* (1980); R. Dworkin, supra note 7; J. Habermas, *The Theory of Communicative Action* (T. McCarthy trans. 1984); J. Rawls, *A Theory of Justice* (1971). For present purposes it is unnecessary to say whether and how such an approach would build on novel understandings of neutrality or generate baselines on some independent grounds. Compare various feminist approaches to the neutrality criterion, set out in A. Jaggar, *Feminist Politics and Human Nature* (1984); N. Hartsock, *Money, Sex, and Power: Toward a Feminist Historical Materialism* (1985); MacKinnon, supra note 130; Minow, supra note 161.

169. See infra note 180 and accompanying text.

170. See infra note 183 and accompanying text.

171. See Michelman, Foreword: Traces of Self-Government, *Harv. L. Rev.* (1986), 100:4, 17–24; Sunstein, supra note 166.

172. Republican approaches tend not to see rights as prepolitical; the *Lochner* understanding of the common law can thus be criticized on republican grounds, and those grounds tend to replicate the ideas described supra notes 7–8, 39–45 and accompanying text.

173. V. Held, *Rights and Goods: Justifying Social Action* (1984); Minow, Where Difference Has Its Home, *Harv. C.R.-C.L.L. Rev.* (1987), 22:111. But see the criticisms of Held in Fishkin, Book Review, *Ethics* (1987), 97: 473–74 (arguing in favor of impartiality and abstraction). This sort of approach fits comfortably with the emerging enthusiasm for various forms of contextualized practical reason in various fields. See

R. Bernstein, *Beyond Objectivism and Relativism* (1983); M. Nussbaum, *The Fragility of Goodness: Luck and Ethics in Greek Tragedy and Philosophy* (1986); Michelman, supra note 171.

174. See L. Tribe, supra note 136; C. MacKinnon, supra note 134.

175. See C. MacKinnon, supra note 134; C. MacKinnon, supra note 127.

176. See M. Nussbaum, supra note 173; Lukes, Of Gods and Demons: Habermas and Practical Reason, in J. Thompson and D. Heble eds., *Habermas: Critical Debates* (1982).

177. See P. Ricoeur, *Lectures on Ideology and Utopia* (1986) (discussing critique of prevailing ideology from within that ideology and from standpoint of "utopia"); M. Nussbaum, supra note 173 (arguing in favor of Aristotelean approach to ethics); M. Walzer, *Interpretation and Social Criticism* (1987) (urging "connected criticism"); see also R. Bernstein, supra note 173 (exploring various approaches that attempt to criticize status quo without pretending to evade convention entirely); R. Rorty, *Philosophy and the Mirror of Nature* (1980), 155–64 (criticizing foundationalism in philosophy).

178. See supra note 120.

179. See Fiss, The Fate of an Idea Whose Time Has Come: Antidiscriminatory Law in the Second Decade After *Brown v. Board of Education, U. Chi. L. Rev.* (1974), 41:742; Gewirtz, Remedies and Resistance, *Yale L. J.* (1983), 92:585.

180. See, e.g., *Dayton Bd. of Educ. v. Brinkman,* 443 U.S. 526 (1979); *Columbus Bd. of Educ. v. Penick,* 443 U.S. 449 (1979).

181. Cf. J. Vining, supra note 90 (discussing difficulties of reconstruction of past in general).

182. See *Personnel Adm'r v. Feeney,* 442 U.S. 256 (1979); see Seidman, Public Principle and Private Choice: The Uneasy Case for a Boundary Maintenance Theory of Constitutional Law, *Yale L. J.* (1987), 96:1006. Cf. C. MacKinnon, supra note 134 (proposing a test of whether legal rules prepetuate subordination of women); and compare Law, Rethinking Sex and the Constitution, *U. Pa. L. Rev.* (1984), 132:956 (criticizing that approach for not being subject to judicial management).

183. See L. Tribe, Constitution as Point of View (unpublished manuscript, January 1981).

184. To some degree this position itself incorporates *Lochner*-like premises; it distinguishes judicial action from inaction and makes the distinction turn on whether the Court is forcing dramatic changes in the status quo. Here, however, the inquiry depends on institutional concerns having to do with the role of the judiciary.

185. See Lempert, The Force of Irony: On the Morality of Affirmative Action and *United Steelworkers v. Weber, Ethics* (1984), 95:86; Strauss, supra note 110.

186. Epstein, Toward a Revitalization of the Contract Clause, *U. Chi. L. Rev.* (1984), 51:703; R. Epstein, supra note 5.

187. See Grey, supra note 27; Sax, Book Review, *U. Chi. L. Rev.* (1986), 53:279 (reviewing R. Epstein, *Takings* (1985)).

188. The relevant norms might, however, be regarded as binding on legislators and administrators even if they are not enforced by the judiciary. See Sager, Fair Measure: The Legal Status of Underenforced Constitutional Norms, *Harv. L. Rev.* (1978), 91:1212.

189. See supra note 163.

190. See Sager, supra note 188, at 1212.

191. See *The Federalist No. 10,* at 83–84 (J. Madison) (C. Rossiter ed. 1961); J. Nedelsky, supra note 145.

192. See generally Sunstein, supra note 146; Ackerman, Discovering the Constitution, *Yale L. J.* (1984), 93:1013.

193. See J. Ely, supra note 6, at 18.

194. See B. Ackerman, *Private Property and the Constitution* (1977) (comparing views

of "ordinary observer" and "scientific policymaker" in interpretation of eminent domain clause).

195. See, e.g., B. Ackerman, supra note 194; Baker, Property and Its Relation to Constitutionally Protected Liberty, *U. Pa. L. Rev.* (1986), 134:741; Michelman, Property as a Constitutional Right, *Wash. and Lee L. Rev.* (1981), 38:1097.

196. See Fiss, Free Speech and Social Structure, *Iowa L. Rev.* (1986), 71:1485.

197. See Stone, Content Regulation and the First Amendment, *Wm. and Mary L. Rev.* (1983), 25:189.

198. See MacKinnon, supra note 51.

199. See A. Meiklejohn, *Free Speech and Its Relation to Self-Government* (1948).

200. See Fiss, supra note 196.

201. See Fiss, supra note 196; Fiss, Why the State? *Harv. L. Rev.* (1987), 100:781, 790–94. Cf. R. Wolff, B. Moore, and H. Marcuse, *A Critique of Pure Tolerance* (1968) (criticizing traditional beliefs in free expression and tolerance).

202. For general discussion, see Fiss, supra note 196 (arguing against viewpoint neutrality because of maldistributions of social power).

203. See H. Hart and A. Honore, *Causation in the Law* (1984).

204. For some, the three problems, in concert, mean that judges must decide cases by reference to the "intent of the framers," or original meaning, or some other purportedly sharp constraint on judicial decisions. That approach is rejected here. See supra note 167 and accompanying text.

205. Cf. J. Mashaw, *Due Process in the Administrative State* (1985) (justifying such rights on participatory and dignatory grounds).

7

THE OVERSEAS TRADE IN THE AMERICAN BILL OF RIGHTS

Anthony Lester QC

The master builders of the Constitution of the United States, whose bicentennial we now salute and celebrate, traded freely in the ideas of seventeenth- and eighteenth-century England and of the age of enlightenment in Europe. Jefferson and Madison, Franklin and Hamilton, were steeped in the principles of the common law and in the political theories of the age of enlightenment. Their libraries were cosmopolitan and well used. The Declaration of Independence, the Constitution, and the Bill of Rights were the handiwork of men who understood the old world as well as the new world.

Over the last two centuries, the old world has returned the compliment paid to its ideas and values in the American Declaration of Independence and in the Constitution of the United States. Not only have American concepts of freedom shaped the rise of constitutionalism in Europe and elsewhere, but courts overseas refer frequently to U.S. Supreme Court precedents in constitutional cases—a phenomenon that is, I suspect, unknown and unfamiliar to most Americans. Most immediately, what happened in Philadelphia in 1776 and 1787 influenced the framing of the French Declaration of the Rights of Man and of the Citizen in 1789. The conquests of Napoleon's armies spread not only the Code Civil but also the public philosophy and public law of the American and French revolutionaries throughout the European continent. Those legal ideas and systems were also spread, through imperial rule, to other continents. Today, the many countries whose legal systems are based upon the Civil Law have constitutional guarantees of fundamental human rights and freedoms derived from seventeenth-century England, the eighteenth-century enlightenment, and the American and French Revolutions.

The United Kingdom recoiled with horror against the American and French Revolutions, rejecting even to this day, for the constitutional law of the United Kingdom, what Jeremy Bentham contemptuously derided as the rhetorical "nonsense upon stilts"[1] of natural and imprescriptible rights. But the infection of American and French ideas about fundamental rights could not ultimately be excluded from Britain's empire in its declining years, as distinct from the United Kingdom itself. From the end of the nineteenth century, demands for an enforceable Bill of Rights were repeatedly made by Indian nationalists and consistently rejected by the British Raj.[2] In 1947, the Constituent Assembly on independent India's future constitution resolved to guarantee and secure fundamental rights to all the people of India. The Indian Constitution came into force in 1950 containing enforceable fundamental rights, a feature of the United States Constitution that the British Parliament had consistently eschewed in the Constitutions enacted for Canada, Australia, and British India.

American concepts of rights have also been influential at the international level. On June 26, 1945, the United Nations Charter was signed in San Francisco.[3] A persistent lobby at San Francisco, led by United States agencies, had induced the framers of the U.N. Charter to include repeated references to human rights and to create a commission to act on them. Mrs. Eleanor Roosevelt was appointed to chair the Commission on Human Rights and to submit proposals for an International Bill of Rights.

Within a few months, the outbreak of the Cold War was to have its chilling effect. In March 1946, Winston Churchill spoke at Fulton, Missouri, of the Iron Curtain that had descended across Europe. By October 1946, when the International Military Tribunal delivered its judgment at Nuremburg, such enthusiasm as there might have been at the government level about the development of international human rights law under U.N. auspices was waning. In the aftermath of the horror, death, and devastation of the Second World War, there was still sufficient political will to enable the adoption of the Universal Declaration of Human Rights by the General Assembly of the United Nations on December 10, 1948.[4] But behind the scenes, work on the International Bill of Rights was hindered by Western fears that the project would be exploited by the Soviet bloc and by the movements for decolonization and self-determination in Asia and Africa.

Henceforth, the work was to be done with all deliberate delay. What were to become the two U.N. Covenants on Human Rights[5] were not ready for signature until December 1966, twenty years after the original proposal.[6] They did not come into force for another decade.[7] Even now, when the U.N. Covenants have been ratified by more than half the world, including the free democracies of Europe,[8] they have not been ratified by the United States, which inspired their creation. The United States remains, therefore, sadly isolated from the rapidly developing corpus of international human rights law.[9] As for Western Europe, most of the twenty-one member states of the Council of Europe have ratified the U.N. Covenants.[10] Few, however, have accepted the optional jurisdiction of the U.N. Human Rights Committee to consider claims from individuals of breaches of the Covenants.[11]

Fortunately, the weakness of international institutions has not blocked Western European efforts to strengthen protection for human rights. What has happened instead is that Western Europe has developed its own regional machinery for the protection of the human rights of its four hundred million citizens, as a supplement to national constitutional and legal mechanisms.

A second terrible war in half a century, and the Nazi Holocaust, convinced the leaders of Western Europe of the need to forge a new Europe based on a greater degree of unity and understanding. The need to guard against the rise of new dictatorships and to reduce the risk of relapse into disastrous war inspired the formation in 1949 of the Council of Europe as the first institution of Europe. One of the Council's first tasks was to work for the "maintenance and further realization of human rights and fundamental freedoms."[12]

Drawing on the Universal Declaration of Human Rights, which was itself greatly influenced by the American Bill of Rights, the Council of Europe drafted a convention less extensive in the rights it guaranteed but much stronger in their enforcement. For the first time, reasonably effective regional enforcement machinery was set up to protect human rights. Member states undertook not only to accept duties on the interstate level but also to recognize that individuals have enforceable rights against states under international law.

The work on the European Convention on Human Rights was completed in only two years. The Convention was signed in November 1950 and came into force in September 1953.[13] It has been ratified by all twenty-one member states of the Council of Europe.[14] Apart from Cyprus and Malta, all of them have now accepted the right of individuals and nongovernmental organizations within their jurisdiction to bring complaints against them to the European Commission of Human Rights in Strasbourg, France, alleging that their fundamental rights and freedoms have been breached by the state or by those for whom the state is responsible.[15] All of them, except Turkey and Malta, have agreed to accept the jurisdiction of the European Court of Human Rights in Strasbourg and are bound in international law to comply with its judgments.[16]

Decisions of the Strasbourg Court may involve findings that any of the three branches of government have violated the Convention. In practice, the Court has held not only the actions of executive officials,[17] but also national legislation[18] and decisions of national supreme courts[19] to be in breach of the Convention. Judgments of the Strasbourg Court often have important consequences for the laws and practices of member states that are not parties to the particular case under review. They also have strong persuasive authority with the younger Inter-American Commission and Court of Human Rights and the U.N. Human Rights Committee.

The twelve member states of the Council of Europe that also belong to the European Economic Community, or Common Market, have made adherence to the Convention a virtual condition of membership of the European Community. The Rome Treaty, establishing the Community, guarantees some fundamental rights, notably to equal pay and equality of treatment without sex discrimination in employment,[20] and to free movement of labor[21] and other rights without discrimination based on nationality.[22] The European Court of Justice, which sits in Luxembourg, has regard for the Convention and United States law when interpreting Community law.

Finally, during the past thirty years, the European Convention has become the model for the codes of fundamental rights that are contained in the great majority of independent Commonwealth countries and for those constitutions that give British dependent territories a substantial measure of self-government. There are some twenty-six Commonwealth countries whose independence constitutions guarantee fundamental rights and freedoms modeled on the European Convention; this is more than the total number of countries that are parties to the Convention itself. In this way, the Parliament of Westminster has exported the rights and freedoms of the Convention to the common-law countries of the new Commonwealth on a scale without parallel in the rest of the world. In those Commonwealth countries that have preserved their democracies since independence, judges review the constitutionality of legislation and administrative action against standards derived directly from the European Convention and indirectly from the American Bill of Rights. Further, in 1982, when the Westminster Parliament repatriated Canada's Constitution to the Canadians, it enacted a comprehensive Charter of Fundamental Rights many of whose concepts, like those of the European Convention and of the other Commonwealth constitutions, share their origin in the American Bill of Rights.[23]

But the Bill of Rights is more than a historical inspiration for the creation of charters and institutions dedicated to the protection of liberty. Currently, there is a vigorous overseas trade in the Bill of Rights, in international and constitutional litigation involving norms derived from American constitutional law. When life or liberty is at stake, the landmark judgments of the Supreme Court of the United States, giving fresh meaning to the principles of the Bill of Rights, are studied with as much attention in New Delhi or Strasbourg as they are in Washington, D.C., or the State of Washington, or Springfield, Illinois. My main purpose today is to sketch the contours of this phenomenon.

The trade is often brisk and vitally important. Thanks to the generous support of the Ford Foundation, the London-based International Centre for the Legal Protection of Human Rights (Interights), which I have the privilege of chairing, acts as a clearinghouse of information on international and comparative human rights law and practice, assisting individuals, nongovernmental organizations, and their legal representatives to present their cases effectively before international and national fora. Recently, an Interights workshop of Commonwealth Caribbean judges, lawyers, and public officials keenly discussed ways of making greater practical use of international and comparative human rights law in the twelve common-law countries of the Caribbean. There is a need for similar work in Africa, Asia, Europe, and elsewhere in the Americas.

It is difficult to give an accurate assessment of the influence of American constitutional law on judicial decisions overseas. Broadly speaking, the judicial activism of the Warren Court probably encouraged the European Commission and Court of Human Rights in the late 1960s and early 1970s to become stronger in interpreting and applying Convention rights and freedoms. By the same token, the more restrictive case law of the Burger and Rehnquist Courts has been matched by greater judicial restraint in Strasbourg, though this trend reflects the greater political conservatism of Western Europe in the 1980s rather than any trans-Atlantic judicial influence.

Courts overseas are not universally open to persuasion by references to American law. Sometimes, they can be isolationist and austere where fundamental rights are threatened in controversial cases. A few years ago, for example, there was a backlash by the Judicial Committee of the Privy Council against the overseas use of American constitutional law. It occurred in a case involving the unsuccessful challenge to the constitutionality of a mandatory death penalty for trafficking in heroin in Singapore.[24]

The Privy Council is notable, perhaps I should say notorious, in American history for its role in deciding appeals from the American colonies. Indeed, the Privy Council's contemptuous treatment of Benjamin Franklin in 1774 (when he was subjected to savage and sarcastic invective by the English Solicitor General, while members of the Privy Council frequently laughed aloud at Dr. Franklin's public humiliation) was described in Campbell's *Lives of the Lord Chancellors* as having "mainly conduced to the civil war which soon followed, [a reference to the American War of Independence] and to the dismemberment of the empire—by exciting over-weening arrogance on one side, and rankling revenge on the other. Had Franklin been soothed, instead of being insulted, America might have been saved."[25]

That certainly places a heavy responsibility upon the Privy Council of the late eighteenth century. I do not mean to suggest that the modern Privy Council is anti-American, still less that it behaves unjudicially like its boorish forebears. But it was scarcely in a spirit of international broad-mindedness that Lord Diplock warned, in the Singapore death penalty case, that "decisions of the Supreme Court of the United States on that country's Bill of Rights, whose phraseology is now nearly 200 years old, are of little help in construing provisions of . . . modern Commonwealth constitutions which follow broadly the Westminster model"[26]—a rare example of antiquity being regarded with judicial disfavor!

I was the advocate who attempted unsuccessfully to invoke United States authorities in the Singapore case. If I had known that the antiquity of the American Bill of Rights was regarded as a disadvantage by the Privy Council, I might have recalled Justice Brennan's statement that, "[i]n the service of the age-old dream for recognition of the equal and inalienable rights of man, the Fourteenth Amendment . . . can never be old."[27] It is, as Justice Brennan observed, like the Old Woman in Yeats' play, who had just walked out of the house.

> Peter: Did you see an old woman going down the path?
> Patrick: I did not, but I saw a young girl and she had the walk of a queen.[28]

The Privy Council will not be able to prevent Commonwealth judges and lawyers from continuing to admire the majesty of the ever-youthful American Bill of Rights. By ruling American constitutional law to be irrelevant, the Privy Council was, however, able in the particular case to discount the persuasive authority of cases such as *Lockett v. Ohio,*[29] holding a mandatory death penalty to be contrary to the eighth and fourteenth amendments. The mandatory death penalty was upheld by the Privy Council, and the appellant and many others were executed.

To be fair to the Privy Council, I should add that it did adopt a liberal interpretation of the relevant provisions of the Singapore Constitution, even though it did not apply those provisions liberally.[30] The proper approach to constitutional interpretation of provisions guaranteeing fundamental rights and freedoms had been memorably described by Lord Wilberforce in a previous Privy Council case as calling for a generous interpretation, avoiding what has been called "the austerity of tabulated legalism."[31]

Often in recent years, courts in England and elsewhere have acknowledged the relevance and persuasive authority of legal principles developed by the United States federal judiciary. In four areas, these have been of particular influence: first, in relation to procedural justice and due process of law; second, in relation to the right of equality of treatment without unfair discrimination; third, in relation to the right to freedom of expression; and fourth, in relation to the right to privacy. At times, in fact, European courts have built upon American innovations to expand human rights in ways not currently recognized by the U.S. Supreme Court, suggesting that it may be worthwhile to promote a two-way trade in the Bill of Rights.

THE TROUBLED LIFE OF DUE PROCESS

During the framing of the Indian Constitution, B. N. Rau, who was Constitutional Advisor to the Constituent Assembly, visited the United States, Canada, and Ireland for discussions with eminent persons in those countries about what India could learn from their constitutions. He was advised by Justice Frankfurter not to include the due process clause in the Indian Constitution. Justice Frankfurter was of the opinion "that the power of review implied in the 'due process' clause was not only undemocratic (because it gave a few judges the power of vetoing legislation enacted by the representatives of the nation) but also threw an unfair burden on the judiciary."[32]

Frankfurter's view was communicated to the drafting committee on the Indian Constitution, which replaced the expression "without due process of law" with the expression "except according to procedure established by law,"[33] a much narrower phrase borrowed from article 31 of the Japanese Constitution.[34] Article 22 provides specific safeguards against arrest and detention in certain cases. But there is no express reference to due process of law anywhere in the Indian Constitution.

The matter did not end there. There were debates of passionate intensity in the Constituent Assembly about the omission of a due process clause, mainly because of fears about the threat to personal liberty created by arbitrary arrests and preventive detention. The addition of more specific safeguards of the right to liberty in article 22 did not allay these fears,[35] which proved to be prophetic for the eight hundred million citizens of the world's largest democracy.

In 1950, the very first year of India's new Constitution, a challenge was made, in *Gopalan v. State,*[36] to the constitutionality of the Preventive Detention Act.[37] The Supreme Court held that "law" merely means a law enacted by a competent authority.[38] It was a literal interpretation based on legal positivism. The deliberate refusal by the drafters to include any reference to the due process of law was regarded as significant.[39]

A quarter of a century later, in June 1975, Indira Gandhi's Government invoked a state of emergency and suspended the right to move any court for the enforcement of the rights guaranteed by the Constitution. Various persons were detained without trial. Some were tortured. They applied for writs of habeas corpus. By a majority of four to one, the Supreme Court held that no person had standing to apply for habeas corpus or any other remedy to challenge the legality of an order of detention on the ground that the order was not made under or in compliance with the Maintenance of Internal Security Act,[40] or was illegal, or was vitiated by mala fides, or was based on extraneous considerations.[41] As one leading commentator observed, "In effect, if not in intent, the four judges held that in India all law was abrogated in relation to life and personal liberty."[42]

The Indira Gandhi Government soon lost power, rejected by the world's largest free electorate because of the excesses of the period of emergency. But the controversy over due process of law continued. After Mrs. Gandhi had lost power, the passport of her daughter-in-law, Maneka Gandhi, was impounded by the new Government. Maneka Gandhi was a journalist who wished to leave India in order to fulfill a speaking engagement. Her passport was impounded in what was alleged to be the "public interest," and the Government decided that it was "in the interest of the general public" not to furnish her with reasons for the making of the order.[43] In her challenge to the order impounding her passport, Maneka Gandhi complained principally that the order had been made in breach of natural justice. The Government relied both upon the absence of any express constitutional right to go abroad and also upon the Supreme Court's previous narrow case law.[44]

In a landmark decision, the Indian Supreme Court, two of whose members had been in the majority in the 1975 *Habeas Corpus Case,* held that the concept of personal liberty guaranteed by article 21 was of the widest meaning and included every aspect of personal liberty, such as travel abroad. No one could be deprived of the right to leave India except by procedure established by law. And no law could take away personal liberty unless it prescribed a procedure that was reasonable, fair, and just.[45] Mr. Justice Bhagwati, later Chief Justice, who participated in this historic decision, as well as in the *Habeas Corpus Case,* has recently noted that the Supreme Court in the *Maneka Gandhi Case,* "with a view to forging greater protection for the citizen in respect of his life and personal liberty, . . . introduced the requirement of reasonable, fair and just procedure and thus brought in the concept of procedural due process"[46]—in spite of the advice of Justice Frankfurter, the text of article 21, and the subsequent case law.

The European Court of Human Rights has reached a similar conclusion in construing similar language in the European Convention.[47] So has the Privy Council, in construing similar language in the Constitution of Singapore.[48]

However, the argument is by no means concluded. The U.N. Human Rights Committee has yet to give a normative meaning to the various references to "law" contained in the International Covenant on Civil and Political Rights.[49] The issue is far from academic. For example, when the People's Republic of China resumes sovereignty over Hong Kong in 1997, the five million people of Hong Kong have been promised that their existing human rights and freedoms will continue to be protected by law and that the provisions of the International Covenant as applied to Hong Kong will remain in force.[50] Phrases like "in accordance with law" are contained in the Covenant, as well as in the Constitution of the People's Republic of China.[51] If a due process clause (as distinct from weaker references to "in accordance with law") is omitted from the Basic Law that is currently being drafted, it may become of great importance to know whether the Hong Kong courts will adopt a literal or a purposive interpretation of such phrases.

The overseas trade in the American due process clause and in other principles guaranteeing procedural justice has been important, but its importance must not be exaggerated. For example, however much the American Supreme Court may have sought to base the *Miranda* rule[52] upon English common-law principles enshrined in the fifth amendment, such an absolute exclusionary rule has been rejected in England.[53] The same applies to the *Mapp* rule[54] on illegal searches and seizures.[55]

THE VITALITY OF EQUAL PROTECTION

I turn to a second area in which American constitutional law has been influential overseas: the promotion of equality and nondiscrimination. Landmark decisions of the United States Supreme Court on the equal protection clause of the fourteenth amendment have been adopted by the Supreme Court of India[56] and by other Commonwealth courts in interpreting the equivalent provisions of their paramount constitutions. An American constitutional lawyer would feel at home in reading their judgments in the law reports. Regrettably, I doubt whether many American judges, attorneys, or legal scholars have that experience in practice.

I will give one important example of the influence of the American Bill of Rights in this area. Two decades ago, some 200,000 United Kingdom passport holders were living in the United Kingdom's former dependencies in East Africa, notably Kenya, Tanzania and Uganda.[57] They were citizens of the United Kingdom and Colonies by virtue of their connection with those dependencies, but their ancestors had been born in what is now India, Pakistan, or Bangladesh. When the dependencies became independent, in the early 1960s, these British citizens did not automatically acquire African local citizenship. They had the right to choose to become local citizens of Kenya, Tanzania, or Uganda within two years after independence,[58] but they chose not to exercise that right. No doubt many of them realized that, as a relatively prosperous ethnic minority in the newly independent countries of East Africa, their position might become precarious, whatever their citizenship. They preferred to retain their British citizenship, which gave them the right to enter and to live in the United Kingdom.[59]

During the years following the independence of Kenya, Tanzania, and Uganda, those countries introduced policies of "Africanisation," which were designed to give preference to their citizens in many areas of trade and employment and, in due course, to require the departure of people who were not local citizens and whose right to work or trade there had, consequently, been withdrawn. The British Asians were the victims of this policy of Africanisation.[60] And they began to exercise their right to come to the United Kingdom, that is, to the country of their citizenship. Between 1965 and 1967, the annual number of such residents increased from 6,150 to 13,600. In the first two months of 1968, the number of people exercising the right was 12,800.[61] They came in greater and greater numbers because they were rightly fearful that the United Kingdom might deprive them of their rights of entry and of residence.

From the perspective of the nation of immigrants contained in these United States, it must seem incredible that the immigration of a mere 200,000 British Asian citizens to a country of some fifty-four million inhabitants was widely regarded as threatening the well-being of the British body politic. But that was the sad condition of British society in 1968 and would, for that matter, be its condition if a similar tragic situation were to arise today involving the displacement of a brown or black community from some other part of the former or remaining British Empire.

After a brief but effective populist campaign, on blatantly racial grounds, against the unrestricted immigration of these brown British citizens, who were being made destitute in East Africa, the Wilson administration panicked. It introduced emergency legislation—the Commonwealth Immigrants Act of 1968[62]—which was rushed through all its Parliamentary stages in three days and nights. The new law was neutral upon its face but racially discriminatory in intent and in effect. In broad terms, it provided that British citizens would be free of immigration control only if they, or at least one of their parents or grandparents were born, naturalized, or adopted in the United Kingdom. To the enduring shame of my country, a group of its citizens, temporarily in public office, had used their legislative majority to abridge the basic rights and freedoms of another group of citizens, because of their color and ethnic origins.

It is unnecessary to recall in detail the extent of the suffering that then ensued for the British Asians: stripped of their livelihood and possessions in East Africa; divided from members of their families in the United Kingdom; detained in prison if they sought to enter the United Kingdom; or flown here and there, across Europe, Africa, and Asia, desperately seeking a new world. Nominally, they remained citizens of the United Kingdom and

Colonies, but they became citizens without status, stateless in fact if not in law.

The United Kingdom Parliament exercises absolute power between elections, so that Acts of Parliament are not subject to judicial review on the ground that they are repugnant to the superior, paramount law of a written constitution. The only legal recourse available to these dispossessed British Asians was to complain under international law to the European Commission of Human Rights that the United Kingdom had violated their rights as guaranteed by the European Convention on Human Rights.

Unfortunately, the European Convention contains only a narrow guarantee of equality of treatment without discrimination.[63] The guarantee is breached only if there is discrimination in the enjoyment of some other right or freedom contained in the Convention, such as the right to respect for family life or the right to marry. Some British Asians could indeed complain of racial discrimination in these respects. But the crux of the British Asians' case involved racial discrimination in the enjoyment of some of the most basic rights of citizenship that are not within the scope of the European Convention—the right to enter and to live and work in one's country of citizenship. Since the guarantee of equality without discrimination, in its fourteenth article, depends upon proof of discrimination in relation to some other Convention right or freedom, and since no other Convention right or freedom covers the right to enter and to live and work in one's country of citizenship,[64] the Convention appeared to be unable to remedy the substance of the great wrong that had been done to the British Asians.

Happily, the problem was solved by Professor Charles Black, who was a vital member of the applicants' legal team. Charles Black persuaded us to argue before the Commission that racial discrimination is inherently degrading and hence contrary to the prohibition against degrading treatment contained in article 3 of the Convention.[65] He referred us to the Supreme Court's decision in *Strauder v. West Virginia,*[66] to Justice Harlan's luminous dissenting opinion in *Plessy v. Ferguson*[67] and to *Trop v. Dulles.*[68] Black's argument succeeded brilliantly. The Commission decided that

> a special importance should be attached to discrimination based on race; . . . publicity to single out a group of persons for differential treatment on the basis of race might, in certain circumstances, constitute a special form of affront to human dignity; and . . . differential treatment of a group of persons on the basis of race might therefore be capable of constituting degrading treatment when differential treatment on some other ground would raise no such question.[69]

The Commission considered that the racial discrimination to which the applicants had been publicly subjected by the application of the immigration legislation constituted an interference with their human dignity, which amounted to degrading treatment in the sense of article 3 of the Convention.[70]

To its credit, in 1974, the United Kingdom Government accepted the Commission's opinion, rather than challenge it before the European Court of Human Rights. The 200,000 British Asians were not restored to full citizenship rights, but their rate of entry into the United Kingdom was greatly accelerated. There could not be a more important example of the beneficial effects of the overseas trade in the American Bill of Rights and of heeding Charles Black's profound insights into constitutional interpretation.

I will mention one other example of the beneficial effects of Supreme Court case law in the field of equality and nondiscrimination. United Kingdom statutes on race and sex discrimination, as well as on equal pay, have been greatly influenced by United States federal legislation. In 1975, the Home Secretary, Roy Jenkins, consulted several American experts about the principles upon which our legislation should be based. One of them was Dean (now Judge) Louis H. Pollak,[71] who had written a book[72] drawing attention to the importance of the Supreme Court's decision in *Griggs v. Duke Power Co.*,[73] construing title VII of the Civil Rights Act as proscribing not only overt discrimination, but also, in Chief Justice Burger's phrase, "practices that are fair in form, but discriminatory in operation."[74] Judge Pollak's advice was that the United Kingdom Government should ensure that the civil rights legislation proscribed both intentional discrimination and discrimination in effect—the equal rule with unequal and unfair effect.

The Home Secretary, the Government, and, in due course, Parliament heeded this wise advice. The British statutes contain the *Griggs* principle.[75] The statutory definition was specifically included because it was considered unlikely that British judges would adopt the *Griggs* approach in the absence of express statutory language. However, at the very time when the United Kingdom's legislature was adopting *Griggs* in proscribing discrimination in employment, housing, education, and the provision of goods, services, and facilities, the Supreme Court held, in *Washington v. Davis*,[76] that, under the equal protection clause, as distinct from title VII, what is required is a racially discriminatory purpose.[77]

This narrow approach to the concept of discrimination is much more restrictive than the definitions of discrimination in international human rights conventions, which look to effect, as well as to purpose.[78] The *Griggs* principle has been relied upon before the European Court of Justice in arguing, in an English case, that the principle of equal pay for equal work, guaranteed by European Community law, cannot be defeated merely by proof that the employer was well intentioned. If a condition or requirement of receiving equal pay hit disproportionately at women, it had to be objectively justified.[79]

The European Court followed the *Griggs* principle in a subsequent West German case.[80] By that route, it has since been applied by the House of Lords to the British Equal Pay Act.[81] It is not yet settled whether a similar approach applies to the interpretation of the nondiscrimination guarantee in article 14 of the European Convention, but it seems likely that the Strasbourg Court of Human Rights would follow the Luxembourg Court of Justice in this respect. Overseas trade has been more profitable than American domestic consumption of that vital principle, recently derived from American federal law, but ultimately from Aristotle: that unlike cases should not be treated alike.

FREEDOM OF SPEECH: A MIXED RECEPTION

While there are many familiar examples, particularly in England, of hostility to United States free speech doctrine, these should not obscure the very real overseas trade in American first amendment values. Indeed, even when courts in England and elsewhere have imposed restrictions on speech and the press, they have often done so only after carefully considering relevant American cases in this field.

The most striking example of American influence arose because of the conflict between free speech and fair trial. It happened in this way. A company manufactured and marketed in the United Kingdom drugs containing an ingredient known as thalidomide. The drugs were prescribed as sedatives for pregnant mothers. A number of mothers who had taken the drug gave birth to children suffering from severe physical deformities. Their parents brought civil proceedings alleging negligence in the production, manufacture, and marketing of the drugs. The proceedings became dormant, and ten years after the tragedy, The Sunday *Times* began to publish a series of articles drawing attention to the plight of thalidomide in children. The Attorney General sought an injunction to restrain publication on the ground that it would be a contempt of court, in view of the pending negligence proceedings. The House of Lords unanimously held that it was a contempt of court to publish material that prejudged the issue of pending litigation or was likely to cause public prejudgment of that issue, and accordingly, the publication of an article, which in effect charged the company with negligence, would constitute a contempt.[82]

The Sunday *Times* complained to the European Commission of Human Rights that the decision of the House of Lords had interfered with the right to free expression guaranteed by article 10 of the Convention. The case came before the full European Court, which decided that the House of Lords, the supreme judicial authority of the United Kingdom, had indeed breached the applicant's rights under article 10.[83] As a result, the government was obliged to introduce legislation in effect overruling the Lords' decision.[84]

Article 10 is not drafted in the absolute language of the first amendment.[85] It guarantees the right to free expression (including imparting and receiving information and ideas), but it goes on to subject those rights to exceptions necessary in a democratic society for the protection of various interests. However, first amendment case law was extensively cited to the European Court,[86] and it seems likely that it was influential. The Court had to decide whether the interference complained of was necessary in the sense that it corresponded to a pressing social need, whether it was proportionate to the legitimate aim pursued by the Law Lords, and whether the reasons given by the national judges to justify it were relevant and sufficient.

The Court observed that:

> freedom of expression constitutes one of the essential foundations of a democratic society; subject to paragraph 2 of Article 10, it is applicable not only to information or ideas that are favourably received or regarded as inoffensive or as a matter of indifference, but also to those that offend, shock or disturb the State or any sector of the population.
>
> These principles are of particular importance as far as the press is concerned. They are equally applicable to the field of the administration of justice, which serves the interests of the community at large and requires the co-operation of an enlightened public. There is general recognition of the fact that the courts cannot operate in a vacuum. Whilst they are the forum for the settlement of disputes, this does not mean that there can be no prior discussion of disputes elsewhere, be it in specialised journals, in the general press or amongst the public at large. Furthermore, whilst the mass media must not overstep the bounds imposed in the interests of the proper administration of justice, it is incumbent on them to impart information and ideas concerning matters that come before the courts just as in other areas of public interest. Not only do the media have the task of imparting such information and ideas: the public also has a right to receive them.[87]

The Court further noted that "following a balancing of the conflicting interests involved, an absolute rule was formulated by certain of the Law Lords to the effect that it was not permissible to prejudge issues in pending cases."[88] However, the Court pointed out that it had to take a different approach. "The Court is faced not with a choice between two conflicting principles but with a principle of freedom of expression that is subject to a number of exceptions which must be narrowly interpreted."[89] As regards the right of the public to be properly informed, the Court said:

> In the present case, the families of numerous victims of the tragedy . . . had a vital interest in knowing all the underlying facts and the various possible solutions. They could be deprived of this information, which was crucially important for them, only if it appeared absolutely certain that its diffusion would have presented a threat to the "authority of the judiciary."[90]

The European Court did not go as far as the Supreme Court did in *Nebraska Press Association v. Stuart,*[91] since the near absolutist American judicial opposition to prior restraint has not been matched in Europe. But the European Court's judgment was a strong and courageous affirmation of the importance of free speech and freedom of the press even where the right to a fair trial is held by a national supreme court to be threatened by public information and discussion.

The *Sunday Times Case* was decided by a narrow margin of eleven votes to nine. However, in the recent *Lingens Case,*[92] the Court unanimously affirmed the principles enunciated in the *Sunday Times Case,* and also unanimously held that the Austrian courts had violated Mr. Lingens' right to free expression guaranteed by article 10. The applicant had published two articles in a Vienna magazine that were strongly critical of Mr. Bruno Kreisky, the retiring Chancellor of Austria. Mr. Kreisky brought private prosecutions for criminal libel. Mr. Lingens was found guilty and fined. The Vienna Court of Appeal reduced the fine but confirmed the lower court's judgment in all other respects.[93]

The Court did not go so far as to hold that *New York Times Co. v. Sullivan's*[94] actual malice defense is required by article 10 of the Convention. However, the Court's judgment was sympathetic to the principles that explain *Sullivan.* It stated that:

> Freedom of the press . . . affords the public one of the best means of discovering and forming an opinion of the ideas and attitudes of political leaders. More generally, freedom of political debate is at the very core of the concept of a democratic society which prevails throughout the Convention.
>
> The limits of acceptable criticism are accordingly wider as regards a politician as such than as regards a private individual. Unlike the latter, the former inevitably and knowingly lays himself open to close scrutiny of his every word and deed by both journalists and the public at large. . . .[95]

First amendment case law has had powerful persuasive authority in other jurisdictions—for example, in the Supreme Court of India's decision about the compatibility of a tax on newsprint with the constitutional guarantee of free expression.[96] It has been invoked in the context of "commercial speech,"[97] including the regulation of commercial advertising and television licensing, though the European Court has thus far failed to address the issues of principle in this area.[98] It remains to be seen whether first amendment doctrine, reflected in article 10 of the European Convention, will be the key that unlocks a common market in broadcasting in Europe.[99]

There are other important areas in which first amendment doctrine has not been followed overseas. In 1978, a planned march by a group of neo-Nazis through the streets of Skokie, Illinois, "raised in a most painful form the question of whether the First Amendment's protection is truly universal."[100] The town passed various ordinances designed to bar the proposed march, with its display of swastikas and military uniforms. In its view, the march would have inflicted direct psychic trauma on those residents who were survivors of the Holocaust. The Court of Appeals for the Seventh Circuit rejected Skokie's justification for the ordinances, holding that speech which inflicts such "psychic trauma" is "indistinguishable in principle from speech that 'invite[s] dispute . . . induces a condition of unrest . . . or even stirs people to anger.' "[101]

By contrast, during the following year, the European Commission of Human Rights decided that the dissemination of ideas encouraging racial discrimination in violation of the rights and freedoms of others was not protected at all by the right to free expression guaranteed by article 10 of the Convention.[102]

Although the Skokie case was not referred to in the European Commission's decision, several recent British cases rejecting free speech claims have at least acknowledged relevant first amendment doctrine. In *Home Office v. Harman,*[103] the House of Lords decided, by three votes to two, that a solicitor had been guilty of contempt of court in passing documents to a journalist that had been obtained from her client's adversary in the course of discovery, even though the documents had been read out in open court at the hearing of the action.[104] Lord Diplock, who was in the majority, stated that the case was "*not* about freedom of speech, freedom of the press, openness of justice or documents coming into 'the public domain.' "[105] A vigorous dissenting judgment by Lord Scarman and Lord Simon of Glaisdale, relied upon first amendment, as well as European Convention doctrine.[106] Even though the doctrine relied upon was subsequently modified by the Supreme Court in the *Seattle Times Case,*[107] it is inconceivable that the Supreme Court would hold that documents obtained by the discovery process and subject to protective order, but read out in open court, were outside the scope of the first amendment. A complaint by Ms. Harman to the European Commission of Human Rights that the House of Lords' decision was in breach of article 10 of the Convention was settled upon the basis that the Government would pay the applicant's legal costs and make necessary amendments to English law.[108]

The most striking difference between first amendment doctrine and English law and practice has arisen in the context of restrictions on the public right of access to governmental information.[109] This was involved to some extent in *Harman,* for the relevant documents revealed the workings of the Prison Department of the Home Office. It is linked with a difference of judicial attitude toward the vices and virtues of the prior restraint upon freedom of speech. For example, in the *Schering Chemicals Case,*[110] Lord Denning MR's dissenting judgment cited Blackstone and *Near v. Minnesota*[111] on the evils of prior restraint and the virtues of press freedom,[112] whereas Templeman, L. J. (as he then was), who was in the majority in the Court of Appeal, observed that "[t]he press is not above the law. Blackstone was concerned to prevent government interference with the press. The times of Blackstone are not relevant to the times of Mr. Murdoch."[113]

The issues have reached near boiling point in the complex web of litigation surrounding the recent publication in the United States of *Spycatcher,*[114] the memoirs of Mr. Peter Wright, a former member of the British Security Services. Law suits have not been concluded in England, Australia, Hong Kong, New Zealand, or Strasbourg. The central issue in the English proceedings is whether British newspapers should be prevented by injunction from publishing government information contained in *Spycatcher,* even though the book is a bestseller in North America and can be freely brought into the United Kingdom. The United Kingdom Government relies upon Mr. Wright's fiduciary duty to the Crown to keep confidential all information obtained by him in the course of his service for the Crown. It also relies upon the need to protect national security.

By three votes to two, the House of Lords has decided that the newspapers should be restrained from publishing, pending the trial of the action.[115] By virtue of a recent decision of the English Court of Appeal extending the law of contempt,[116] the effect of these injunctions is to prevent all other newspapers and broadcasting organizations within the jurisdiction of England and Wales from publishing pending trial. A brief passage from one of the majority judgments of the House of Lords will serve to illustrate the vast difference of judicial approach across the Atlantic. Lord Ackner said this:

> If the publication of this book in America is to have, for all practical purposes, the effect of nullifying the jurisdiction of the English courts to enforce compliance with the duty of confidence both by interlo-

> cutory and by permanent injunction, then . . . English law would have surrendered to the American Constitution. There the courts, by virtue of the First Amendment, are, I understand, powerless to control the press. Fortunately, the press in this country is, as yet, not above the law, although like some other powerful organisations, they would like that to be so, that is, until they require the law's protection.[117]

It would be an example of English understatement to say that the "Pentagon Papers" case,[118] even as modified by *Snepp v. United States,*[119] does not commend itself to the majority of the present members of the English judiciary. However, it remains to be seen how the House of Lords will ultimately balance the competing public interests of free speech and government secrecy when they decide the merits of the *Spycatcher* case.

THE RIGHT OF PRIVACY: IS AMERICA LISTENING?

Sometimes the extraordinary incandescence and persuasive force of the American Bill of Rights are regarded as a serious threat to some compelling national interest. In Ireland, a few years ago, the right-to-life lobby raised widespread alarm that the Irish Supreme Court might follow the American Supreme Court's decision in *Roe v. Wade*[120] holding that the right of privacy was broad enough to encompass a woman's decision to terminate her pregnancy. No doubt such fears were greatly exaggerated and exploited for Irish electoral purposes. But it was hostility to the perceived implications of the decision in *Roe v. Wade* that caused Ireland to undergo a painfully divisive referendum campaign in 1983 and to amend the Irish Constitution so as to protect fetal life against the libertarian values of the American Supreme Court.[121]

It is ironic that the right to personal privacy, developed by the American Supreme Court in *Griswold v. Connecticut*[122] and *Roe v. Wade,* was regarded as too libertarian for importation into Ireland. More recently, after all, the American Supreme Court has become markedly more restrictive in recognizing privacy rights where sexual behavior is involved. And this is in striking contrast to the stronger protection given by the European Court of Human Rights, whose judgments are binding upon Ireland, even when the Irish Constitution itself conflicts with the European Convention.

Last year, in *Bowers v. Hardwick,*[123] the American Supreme Court, by five votes to four, upheld Georgia's sodomy statute, saying the U.S. Constitution does not guarantee a fundamental right to respect for the private life of adult male homosexuals. Only five years earlier, the European Court had decided, by fifteen votes to four, in *Dudgeon v. United Kingdom,*[124] that an adult male homosexual living in Northern Ireland had suffered an unjustified interference with his right to respect for his private life, expressly guaranteed by article 8 of the European Convention, by reason of the existence in Northern Ireland of laws making some homosexual acts between consenting adult males criminal offenses. Mr. Dudgeon and others had been conducting a campaign aimed at bringing the law in Northern Ireland into line with that in force in England and Wales. He had been questioned by the police about his sexual life, and a police investigation file had been sent to the Director of Public Prosecutions, who had decided not to prosecute him for the offence of gross indecency between males.

The European Court, adopting a liberal approach to Mr. Dudgeon's standing to complain, held that the maintenance in force of the impugned legislation constituted a continuing interference with Mr. Dudgeon's right to respect for his private life (which includes his sexual life). According to the Court, the very existence of the legislation continuously and directly affected his private life:

> either he respects the law and refrains from engaging—even in private with consenting male partners—in prohibited sexual acts to which he is disposed by reason of his homosexual tendencies, or he commits such acts and thereby becomes liable to criminal prosecution.[125]

The central issue was therefore whether the maintenance in force of the legislation was, in the language of article 8 of the Convention, "necessary in a democratic society" for "the protection of the rights and freedoms of others" or for "the protection of morals."[126] According to the Court's well-established case law, "a restriction on a Convention right cannot be regarded as 'necessary in a democratic society'—two hallmarks of which are tolerance and broadmindedness—unless . . . it is proportionate to the legitimate aim pursued."[127] The Court considered the United Kingdom Government's justifications and concluded that such justifications as there were "for retaining the law in force unamended are outweighed by the detrimental effects which the very existence of the legislative provisions in question can have on the life of a person of homosexual orientation"[128] like Mr. Dudgeon.

> Although members of the public who regard homosexuality as immoral may be shocked, offended or disturbed by the commission by others of private homosexual acts, this cannot on its own warrant the application of penal sanctions when it is consenting adults alone who are involved.[129]

The *Dudgeon Case* was not cited in any of the principal briefs for the Supreme Court in *Bowers v. Hardwick. Dudgeon* was mentioned only cursorily and inaccurately in the amicus curiae brief filed by Lambda Legal Defense and Education Fund.[130] No one drew the Supreme Court's attention to the importance of *Dudgeon* as a recent decision by the strongest international court of human rights, dealing with a closely analogous problem and having potential persuasive value.

If *Dudgeon* had been relied upon in this way, Chief Justice Burger would surely have narrowed the observation in his concurring opinion that, "[t]o hold that the act of homosexual sodomy is somehow protected as a fundamental right would be to cast aside millennia of moral teaching."[131] In Chief Justice Burger's words, that teaching had been "cast aside" by the European Court in October 1981 for the several hundred million citizens of the diverse twenty-one member states of the Council of Europe. If *Dudgeon* had been relied upon, Justice White might not have characterized Mr. Bowers' claim that his right was "implicit in the concept of ordered liberty" as being "at best, facetious."[132] Indeed, it is possible that one of the negative majority might have been persuaded by the cogency of the reasoning in *Dudgeon* to uphold the claim.

Bowers illustrates, among other things, the continuing isolation of American constitutional law from international human rights law. Granted that the European Convention (unlike the American Bill of Rights) expressly guarantees the right to privacy, until *Bowers* I had believed that the European Convention merely contained more specific guarantees of fundamental rights whose existence was derived from the general guarantee of liberty in the American Bill of Rights. From an overseas perspective, it seems extraordinary that there is any doubt that the right to privacy can properly be inferred from the structure, history, genesis, language, and nature of that great instrument. If that were not the case, the American Bill of Rights would surely be found wanting as a charter of ordered liberty, suitable to the needs and values of the citizens of the United States in the twenty-first century.

CONCLUSION: STRENGTHENING THE TWO-WAY TRADE IN RIGHTS

These various examples of the overseas trade in the American Bill of Rights, and of the limits of that trade, will doubtless add to your reasons for celebrating the bicentennial of the United States Constitution. But if that is the main effect of this account, then it will have failed in its central purpose. Professor Louis Henkin has observed that:

> For the United States, human rights have been a kind of "white man's burden," and international human rights have been "for export only."

> An abiding isolationism (or unilateralism) . . . continues to appeal to many Americans, even some who readily judge others and are eager to intervene on behalf of democracy and human rights in other countries. There is some reluctance to accept, and have our courts apply, standards perceived to have been created by others, even if they were borrowed from us and reflect our own values. There is some reluctance to have the United States subject to scrutiny by others, even though Americans pride themselves on an open society.[133]

The overseas trade in the American Bill of Rights is an important means of strengthening international human rights. It is a misfortune that the precious commodity continues to be regarded as only for export. The failure of the United States to ratify the United Nations Covenants is oft noted, but equally troubling is the apparent reluctance of the U.S. Supreme Court to consider overseas interpretations of its own cases, especially when, as in *Bowers v. Hardwick,* the Justices' opinions so clearly could have profited from such attention. Indeed, with honorable exceptions (most notably in this great law school) the United States judiciary, legal profession, and law schools are as isolated from international human rights law as are the legislative and executive branches of the United States. That isolation is a matter of regret for those of us who trade overseas in the American Bill of Rights. I respectfully submit that it is also a misfortune for the United States itself, not only in diminishing American influence overseas, but also in separating American constitutional law from the ideas and values of other advanced democratic nations and their courts.

I hope that, during the third century of the Constitution, the United States will accept that the obligation to protect human rights is an international obligation to be accepted by the United States themselves. I also hope that the United States judiciary will not retreat from the strong interpretation of the Bill of Rights into literalism, positivism, and historicism. If American human rights are diminished, so are the rights of the rest of humanity.

ENDNOTES

1. H. L. A. Hart, *Essays on Bentham* (1982), 79.
2. Sorabjee, Fundamental Rights in the Indian Constitution, in *Public Law in India* (1979), 30.
3. L. Goodrich, E. Hambru, and A. Simons, *Charter of the United Nations* (1969), 1.
4. U.N. Dep't of Pub. Info. Universal Declaration of Human Rights, U.N. Sales No. 58.I.4 (1948).
5. International Covenant on Economic, Social and Cultural Rights, Dec. 19, 1966, 993

U.N.T.S. 3; International Covenant on Civil and Political Rights, Dec. 19, 1966, 993 U.N.T.S. 171.

6. Center for Human Rights, Status of International Instruments at 1, 25, U.N. Doc. ST/HR/5, U.N. Sales No. E.87.XIV.2 (1987) [hereinafter Center for Human Rights].

7. Id.

8. Id. at 1–3, 25–27.

9. See generally Henkin, The United States and International Human Rights, in *Justice for a Generation,* Papers presented in London, England, July 15–19, 1985, at the plenary sessions of a meeting between the American Bar Association, the Senate of the Inns of Court and the Bar, and the Law Society of England and Wales, at 373–80 (international human rights standards have influenced U.S. foreign and domestic policies, but the U.S. has failed to adhere to international agreements creating these standards).

10. Center for Human Rights, supra note 6, at 1–3, 25–27. For a list of member states of the Council of Europe, see Council of Europe, European Convention on Human Rights: Collected Texts 68 (1987) [hereinafter Council of Europe].

11. Center for Human Rights, supra note 6, at 52–58 (listing nations that have accepted the competence of the Human Rights Committee).

12. Statute of the Council of Europe, May 5, 1949, ch. 1, art. 1(b), 87 U.N.T.S. 103, 106.

13. Convention for the Protection of Human Rights and Fundamental Freedoms, Nov. 4, 1950, 213 U.N.T.S. 221–22 and n.1 [hereinafter European Convention].

14. Council of Europe, supra note 10, at 68.

15. Id. at 73. Turkey has since accepted such jurisdiction after publication of this source.

16. Id. at 74.

17. See, e.g., case of *Silver and Others,* 51 *Eur. Ct. H.R.* (ser. B) (1983) (convicts' letters censored by prison authorities).

18. See, e.g., *Dudgeon v. United Kingdom,* 45 *Eur. Ct. H.R.* (ser. A) (1981) (Northern Ireland law making homosexual acts illegal).

19. See, e.g., *Sunday Times v. United Kingdom,* 30 *Eur. Ct. H.R.* (ser. A) (1979) (House of Lords contempt order against newspaper); *Lingens v. Austria,* 103 *Eur. Ct. H.R.* (ser. A) 11 (1986) (Vienna Court of Appeal libel ruling).

20. Treaty Establishing the European Economic Community, March 25, 1957, art. 119, 298 U.N.T.S. 11, 62.

21. Id., art. 48(1), 298 U.N.T.S. at 36.

22. Id., art. 48(2), 298 U.N.T.S. at 36.

23. See generally Ontario Economic Council, *The U.S. Bill of Rights and the Canadian Charter of Rights and Freedoms* (W. McKercher ed. 1983).

24. See infra notes 26–30 and accompanying text.

25. J. Campbell, *Lives of the Lord Chancellors* (3d ser. 1847), 6:104. For a description of the entire episode, see id. at 104–12.

26. *Ong Ah Chuan v. Public Prosecutor,* App. Cas. (1981), 648, 669 (P.C. 1980) (Singapore). See generally D. Pannick, *Judicial Review of the Death Penalty* (1982) (status of capital punishment in countries otherwise recognizing constitutional human rights).

27. Brennan, Landmarks of Legal Liberty, in B. Schwartz ed., *The Fourteenth Amendment* (1970) 11 (cited in *Maneka Gandhi v. Union of India* [1978], 65 A.I.R. (S.C.) (India 1978), 597, 616 (Chandrachud, J.). Thus do legal ideas cross frontiers.

28. W. B. Yeats, Cathleen Ni Houlihan, in *Collected Plays of W. B. Yeats* (1953), 57 (concluding words of the play).

29. 438 U.S. 568 (1978); see also *Sumner v. Shuman,* 107 S. Ct. 2716 (1987).

30. *Ong Ah Chuan,* 1981 App. Cas. at 670.

31. *Minister of Home Affairs v. Fisher,* 1980 App. Cas. (P.C. 1979), 319, 328 (Bermuda).

32. B. Shiva Rao, *The Framing of India's Constitution: A Study* (1968), 235.

33. India Const., art. 21.

34. Kenpō (Constitution), art. 31 (Japan).

35. B. Shiva Rao, supra note 32, at 236–49.

36. 37 A.I.R. (S.C.) (India 1950), 27.

37. III India Code 673 (1955).

38. *Gopalan, A.I.R.* (S.C.) 37:101 (Mukherjea, J.).

39. Id.

40. III India Code 779 (1978). In 1978, this act was repealed. *India A.I.R. Manual* (1984), 25:97.

41. A. D. M. Jabalpur v. Shivakant Shukla, S.C.C. (1976), 2:521.

42. H. M. Seervai, *Constitutional Law of India* (3d ed. 1983), 1:1016.

43. *Maneka Gandhi v. Union,* 2 S.C.R. 621, 621 (1978).

44. Id. at 621–22.

45. Id. at 622.

46. Bhagwati, Human Rights as Evolved by the Jurisprudence of the Supreme Court of India, *Commonwealth Law Bulletin* (1987), 13:236, 238–41.

47. *Winterwerp* case, *Eur. Ct. H.R.* (ser. A) (1979), 33:17.

48. *Ong Ah Chuan v. Public Prosecutor,* 1981 App. Cas. (P.C. 1980), 648, 669 (Singapore).

49. The United Kingdom member, Professor Rosalyn Higgins, has been seeking to persuade the Human Rights Committee to adopt a normative interpretation of the references to "law" in the Covenant. See, e.g., Human Rights Committee, Thirtieth Session (749th mtg.), U.N. Doc. CCPR/C/SR.749 (1987); (752d mtg.) U.N. Doc. CCPR/C/SR.752 (1987).

50. Joint Declaration of the Government of the United Kingdom of Great Britain and Northern Ireland and the Government of the People's Republic of China on the Future of Hong Kong, Sept. 26, 1984, Annex I, section XIII, *I.L.M.* (1984), 23:1371, 1377.

51. See Xianfa (Constitution), ch. 2 ("The Fundamental Rights and Duties of Citizens") (PRC).

52. See *Miranda v. Arizona,* 384 U.S. 436 (1966).

53. A confession obtained by oppression is inadmissible at common law. *Rennie W.L.R.* (1982), 1:64. The subject is now governed by the Police and Criminal Evidence Act, 1984, ch. 60, § 76.

54. See *Mapp v. Ohio,* 367 U.S. 643 (1961).

55. At English common law, except in respect of confessions or analogous matters, the method by which evidence has been obtained is strictly irrelevant. *Regina v. Sang,* [1980] App. Cas. (1979), 402. Therefore evidence is admissible that has been stolen, *Kuruma v. The Queen* [1955], App. Cas. 197, 203 (P.C.), or obtained by an illegal search, *Jeffrey v. Black* [1978], *All E.R.* (1977), 1:555, 559. The power to exclude unfair evidence is now contained in the Police and Criminal Evidence Act, 1984, ch. 60, § 78(1).

56. See, e.g., *Gujarat v. Shri Ambica Mills, A.I.R.* (S.C.) (1974), 61:1300, 1312–16 (step-by-step approach to regulation held reasonable, citing *West Coast Hotel v. Parrish,* 300 U.S. 379 (1936)); *West Bengal v. Ansar Ali, A.I.R.* (S.C.) (1952), 39:75, 88 (criminal procedure statute held unreasonable classification, citing *Southern Pacific Ry. Co. v. Greene,* 216 U.S. 400 (1910) and others).

In *Uttar Pradesh v. Deoman Puadhyaya, A.I.R.* (S.C.) (1960), 47:1125, the Indian court was particularly explicit in acknowledging the influence of American equal protection doctrine on parallel Indian constitutional guarantees: "Article 14 of the Constitution of India is adopted from the last clause of s. 1 of the 14th Amendment of the Constitution of the United States of America, and it may reasonably be assumed that our Constituent Assembly when it enshrined the guarantee of equal protection of the laws in our Constitution, was aware of its content delimited by judicial interpretation in the United States of America. In considering the authorities of the superior courts in the United States, we would not therefore be incorporating principles foreign to our Constitution. . . ." Id. at 1131–32. See generally P. Polyviou, *The Equal Protection of the Laws* (1983), 88–122.

57. *East African Asians* case, *Eur. H.R. Rep.* (Eur. Law Ctr.) (Eur. Comm'n on Hum. Rts. 1973), 3:76, 83.

58. Id. at 85.

59. Id.

60. Id.

61. Id. at ¶ 31 (this portion of the report has not been released to the public).

62. Commonwealth Immigrants Act, 1968, ch. 9.

63. Article 14 provides: 'The enjoyment of the rights and freedoms set forth in this Convention shall be secured without discrimination on any ground such as sex, race, colour, language, religion, political or other opinion, national or social origin, association with a national minority, property, birth or other status." European Convention, supra note 13, at 232.

64. Exceptions are those rights and freedoms guaranteed by the Fourth Protocol to the Convention to which the United Kingdom was not and is not a contracting party. Council of Europe, supra note 10, at 4, 37.

65. European Convention, supra note 13, at 224.

66. 100 U.S. 303 (1880).

67. 163 U.S. 537, 552 (1896) (Harlan, J., dissenting).

68. 356 U.S. 86 (1958).

69. *East African Asians* case, *Eur. H.R. Rep.* (Eur. Law Ctr.) (Eur. Comm'n on Hum. Rts. 1973), 3:76, 86.

70. Id.

71. For Judge Pollak's participation in Thurgood Marshall's team in arguing *Brown v. Board of Educ.*, 347 U.S. 483 (1954), see R. Kluger, *Simple Justice* (1976), 531, 553–55.

72. I. Pollak, *Discrimination in Employment: The American Response* (1974), 15–19 (on file at *Columbia Law Review*).

73. 401 U.S. 424 (1971).

74. Id. at 431.

75. Sex Discrimination Act, 1975, ch. 65, § (1)(b); Race Relations Act, 1976, ch. 74, § (1)(b).

76. 426 U.S. 229 (1976).

77. Id. at 240.

78. The International Convention on the Elimination of All Forms of Racial Discrimination, art. 1, ¶ 1, March 7, 1966, 660 U.N.T.S. 195, defines the term "racial discrimination" to mean "any distinction, exclusion, restriction or preference based on race, colour, descent, or national or ethnic origin which has the purpose or effect of nullifying or impairing the recognition, enjoyment, or exercise, on an equal footing, of human rights and fundamental freedoms in the political, economic, social, cultural or any other field of public life." Id. at 216. The International Convention on the Elimination of All Forms of Discrimination Against Women, art. 1, G.A. Res. 180, 34 U.N. GAOR Supp. (No. 46), at 193, 194, U.N. Doc. A/34/46 (1980), is phrased in similarly broad terms. The case law of the Permanent Court of International Justice reflected a generous and realistic

approach toward the concept of discrimination. See Certain Questions Relating to Settlers of German Origin in the Territory Ceded by Germany to Poland (*Ger. v. Pol.*). 1923 P.C.I.J. (ser. B) No. 6, at 23–25 (Sept. 10) (Polish expulsion of German settlers violated treaty banning discrimination against minorities); Treatment of Polish Nationals and Other Persons of Polish Origin or Speech in the Danzig Territory (*Pol. v. Danzig*) 1932 P.C.I.J. (ser. A/B) No. 44 at 28 (Feb. 4) (applying antidiscrimination provision of Versailles Treaty); Minority Schools in Albania (*Greece v. Alb.*) 1935 P.C.I.J. (ser. A/B) No. 64, at 19 (Apr. 6) (Albanian Constitution's provision forbidding private schools an infringement on minority rights).

79. *Jenkins v. Kingsgate (Clothing Productions) Ltd., E. Comm. Ct. J. Rep.* (1981), 911, 936–37, *Comm. Mkt. L.R.* (1981–2), 24, 35–36 (Mr. Advocate General Warner's opinion, as distinct from the Court's ambiguous judgment, expressly applied *Griggs* in the context of community law).

80. See *Bilka-Kaufhaus G.m.b.H. v. Weber von Hartz* [1985–1986 Transfer Binder] *Common Mkt. Rep (CCH)* (1986), ¶ 14, 301.

81. *Rainey v. Greater Glasgow Health Bd.* [1987], App. Cas. (1986), 5:224, 240.

82. *Attorney-General v. Times Newspapers Ltd.* [1974] App. Cas. (1973), 273, 300 (Lord Reid).

83. *Sunday Times v. United Kingdom,* 30 *Eur. Ct. H.R.* (ser. A) (1978).

84. Contempt of Court Act, 1981, ch. 49. In particular, see § 5.

85. See European Convention, supra note 13, at 230.

86. *Sunday Times, Eur. Ct. H.R.* (ser. B) 28:193–95, 241–42.

87. Id., *Eur. Ct. H.R.* (ser. A) 30:40.

88. Id. at 41.

89. Id.

90. Id. at 41–42.

91. 427 U.S. 539, 559 (1976) ("prior restraints on speech and publication are the . . . least tolerable infringement on First Amendment rights").

92. *Lingens v. Austria, Eur. Ct. H.R.* (ser. A) (1986), 103:11.

93. Id. at 22.

94. 376 U.S. 254, 279–80 (1964).

95. *Lingens, Eur. Ct. H.R.* (ser. A) 103:26.

96. See *Indian Express Newspapers v. Union,* S.C.R. (1985), 2:287, 330–36, 362 (citing *Murdock v. Pennsylvania,* 319 U.S. 105 (1943), and *Grosjean v. American Press Co.,* 297 U.S. 233 (1936).

97. See, e.g., A. Lester and D. Pannick, *Advertising and Freedom of Expression in Europe* (1984), 15–20.

98. See *Barthold v. Germany, Eur. Ct. H.R.* (ser. A) (1985) 90:31–32 (Pettiti, J., concurring).

99. See generally Europe-Wide Television, Green Paper on the Establishment of a Common Market in Broadcasting, Especially Broadcasting by Satellite and Cable, Commission of the European Communities, COM (83) 800, Dec. 14, 1983.

100. L. Tribe, *Constitutional Choices* (1985), 219.

101. *National Socialist Party v. Skokie,* 578 F.2d 1197, 1206 (7th Cir.), cert. denied, 439 U.S. 916 (1978) (quoting *Terminiello v. Chicago,* 337 U.S. 1, 4 (1949)).

102. *Glimmerveen and Hagenbeek v. The Netherlands, Eur. Comm'n H.R.* (1979), 18:187, 196.

103. [1983] 4 App. Cas. (1982), 280.

104. Id. at 306 (Lord Diplock).

105. Id. at 299 (Lord Diplock).

106. Id. at 316–18 (Lord Scarman and Lord Simon, dissenting).
107. *Seattle Times Co. v. Rhinehart,* 467 U.S. 20, 33–34 (1984).
108. See, e.g., Rules of the Supreme Court, Order 24, Rule 14a, S.I. 1987, No. 1423 (amended by R.S.C., effective Oct. 1, 1987).
109. See generally Goldman, Combatting the Opposition: English and United States Restrictions on the Public Right of Access to Governmental Information, *Hastings Int'l* and *Comp. L. Rev.* (1985), 8:250.
110. *Schering Chemicals Ltd. v. Falkman Ltd.* [1982], 1 Q.B. (C.A. 1981).
111. 283 U.S. 697 (1931) (state statute permitting injunction against publication of allegedly defamatory material unconstitutional).
112. *Schering Chemicals* [1982], I Q.B. at 17.
113. Id. at 39 (Templeman, L. J.).
114. P. Wright, *Spycatcher: The Candid Autobiography of a Secret Intelligence Officer* (1987).
115. *Attorney-General v. Guardian Newspapers Ltd. W.L.R.* (1987), 1:1248, 1291 (Lord Brandon of Oakbrook).
116. See *Attorney-General v. Newspaper Publishing Plc W.L.R.* (1987), 3:942.
117. *Guardian Newspapers, W.L.R.* 1:1306.
118. *New York Times Co. v. United States,* 403 U.S. 713 (1971) (lifting prior restraint on publication of information relating to U.S. policy in Vietnam).
119. 444 U.S. 507 (1980) (upholding CIA prepublication screening of book by ex-CIA employee).
120. 410 U.S. 113 (1973).
121. Ir. Const. art. 40.3.3.
122. 381 U.S. 479 (1965).
123. 106 S. Ct. 2841 (1986).
124. 45-II *Eur. Ct. H.R.* (ser. A) (1981).
125. Id. at 18.
126. Article 8, ¶ 1 provides that "[e]veryone has the right to respect for his private and family life, his home and his correspondence." Article 8, ¶ 2 provides: "There shall be no interference by a public authority with the exercise of this right except such as in accordance with the law and is necessary in a democratic society in the interests of national security, public safety or the economic well-being of the country, for the prevention of disorder of crime, for the protection of health or morals, or for the protection of the rights and freedoms of others." European Convention, supra note 13, at 230.
127. *Eur. Ct. H.R.* (ser. A) 45:21–22.
128. Id. at 24.
129. Id.
130. Amicus Curiae Brief for Lambda Legal Defense and Education Fund, at 15 nn.10, 24, *Bowers v. Hardwick,* 106 S. Ct. 2841 (1986) (No. 85–140). The brief referred to the Commission's report and the pleadings rather than to the Court's judgment.
131. 106 S. Ct. at 2847.
132. Id. at 2846.
133. See Henkin, supra note 9, at 377.

THE SAMUEL RUBIN LECTURES

The Hon. J. Skelly Wright	January 27, 1982 Money and the Pollution of Politics: Is the First Amendment an Obstacle to Political Equality?
Anthony Lewis	October 21, 1982 *New York Times v. Sullivan* Reconsidered: Time to Return to "The Central Meaning of the First Amendment"
Vincent Blasi	February 16, 1983 The First Amendment in the Worst of Times
Vernon E. Jordon	March 2, 1983 Civil Rights: Revolution and Counterrevolution
Vilma Martinez	April 14, 1983 Immigration: Entering Through the Back Door
Jerome J. Shestack	October 31, 1983 International Human Rights: Present Denigration and Future Hope
Hon. Wade McCree, Jr.	February 28, 1984 Partners in a Process: The Academy and the Courts

Justice P.N. Bhagwati	October 3, 1984 Judicial Activism and Public Law Litigation
Rt. Rev. Desmond Tutu	November 1, 1984 South Africa: A Land of Beauty, Love, and Injustice
Marian Wright Edelman	November 27, 1984 Children and Social Justice in the 1980s
Abram Chayes	March 27, 1985 Nicaragua, The World Court, and Judicial Review
Henry G. Cisneros	February 24, 1986 Equality in America: The New Challenge
Charles L. Black, Jr.	March 20, 1986 Further Reflections on the Constitutional Justice of Livelihood
Sanford H. Kadish	April 9, 1986 Excusing Crime
Cass R. Sunstein	October 9, 1986 *Lochner's* Legacy
Anthony Lester, Q.C.	September 22, 1987 The Overseas Trade in the American Bill of Rights
Roberto Mangabeira Unger	March 30, 1988 Alternative Futures of Legal Analysis
Lee Bollinger	February 27, 1989 The Tolerant Society: A Response to Critics
Elizabeth Drew	January 23, 1990 Washington: Reading Between the Lines

GPSR Authorized Representative: Easy Access System Europe, Mustamäe tee 50, 10621 Tallinn, Estonia, gpsr.requests@easproject.com

www.ingramcontent.com/pod-product-compliance
Lightning Source LLC
LaVergne TN
LVHW101440200926
848483LV00004B/413

9780231071987